Where to Stay in

$\mathcal{F}$LORIDA

2nd Edition

Phil Philcox

HUNTER
PUBLISHING INC

Hunter Publishing, Inc.
300 Raritan Center Parkway
Edison NJ 08818
(908) 225 1900

ISBN 1-55650-682-1

© 1995 Phil Philcox

Cover Photograph: Sunset with palms
Superstock

Florida - All New Edition!

All of the property listings, information on facilities and rates were current as of press time. To keep future editions up to date, we request you submit any new listing, changes in information and current rates to The Where-To-Stay Book, 131B North Bay Drive, Lynn Haven FL 32444. Please include all telephone numbers (including fax and toll-free) along with number of rooms, facilities, rates and other information of interest to travelers.

Contents

Introduction

If you're Florida bound for business or pleasure, this is the ultimate guide to finding a place to bed down for the night. Need a convenient downtown hotel within walking distance of the Convention Center or full-service resort along the beach with lighted tennis courts and in-room computer hookups? Prefer a high-rise apartment or home rental for an extended stay? How about a private cabin far away from the maddening crowds or a county inn that includes a free breakfast and a chance to relax in a century-old former mansion? If your choices range from out-of-the-way motels to hotel suites in the center of the business district, you'll find something to your liking – and budget – in this guide.

Included are the names and telephone numbers of regional rental sources that handle an assortment of accommodation options – from private homes to condos and apartments. These agencies are excellent sources of information on what's available in each area in different price ranges and most have toll-free numbers.

The toll-free and fax numbers can be contacted to request literature, rate cards and reservations. Many properties will fax their literature directly to your machine.

Rates are constantly changing and vary considerably with location and season, so use the prices listed here to determine the price range of the property and always call prior to making your reservations. Use the toll-free number when available. Most toll-free numbers listed are valid from all states, but some properties have outside-their-state numbers or in-state numbers. If you reach an invalid number, check with the toll-free operator at 800-555-1212.

Also included is a list of chain hotels and motels you can contact for free accommodations directories, their locations and descriptions of their special clubs and offerings.

Abbreviations Used In This Guide

SGL: single room - rate for one person.
DBL: double room - rate for two people sharing one room.
EFF: efficiency - usually one room with kitchen or kitchenette.
STS: suites
1BR/2BR/3BR: one- , two- , or three-bedroom condo, apartment, villa or townhouse, usually with full kitchen facilities, washer-dryer, etc.
NS ROOMS: rooms available for non-smokers.
NS: smoking not permitted on the property.
AIRPORT COURTESY CAR: free transportation to and from local airports.
AIRPORT TRANSPORTATION: transportation is available to and from local airports for a fee.
LOCAL TRANSPORTATION: free transportation is available to local attractions.
RESTAURANT: indicates there is a restaurant either on the property, adjacent to it, or across the street.
CC: accepts major credit cards.
LS/HS: low season/high season.
$00-$000: daily rate span.
$W-$W: weekly rate span.
$00-$W: daily rate followed by weekly rate.
AP: charge for an additional person in the room.
Modified American Plan: some meals included in room rate, usually breakfast and dinner.
American Plan: all meals included in room rate.

Chain Hotels

Locations & Special Deals

($) indicates there is a cost for membership

Adam's Mark Hotels
11330 Olive Street Road
St. Louis MO 63141
Reservations: 800-444-ADAM

Locations: *Clearwater Beach.*

Adam's Mark Hotels offer a variety of packages and mini-holiday weekend rates. When you stay seven nights at an Adam's Mark Hotel over a period of 12 months, you qualify for membership in the Gold Mark Club. The club offers corporate room rates, automatic upgrades when available, complimentary coffee and newspaper, gift shop discounts, free weekend stays and other benefits.

For each stay you earn a 10% discount on an overnight stay at any Adam's Mark Hotel, valid only on Friday, Saturday and Sunday. Discounts can be accumulated, redeem two coupons for a 20% discount, three coupons for a 30% discount, 10 coupons for a free overnight mini-vacation.

Best Inns of America
Box 1719
Marion IL 62959
Reservations: 800-237-8466

Locations: *Jacksonville; Tallahassee.*

Best Inns offers a free cereal breakfast, free local telephone calls, free evening coffee, fax service and children stay free with parents in the same room. The B.I.P Club – Best Inns Preferred Guest Program – provides instant reservations, immediate check-in, check cashing privileges and room reservations held until 9 p.m. Points are awarded for each night's stay and the 13th night is free. Seniors First Club offers members $5 off any room on any night of the week, $10 off any room on Sundays and select holidays and 1 p.m. check-out. Members must be 50 years of age or older.

Best Western
Box 10203
Phoenix AZ 85064
Reservations: 800-528-1234

Locations: *Arcadia; Baldwin; Boca Raton; Bonifay; Bushnell; Chiefland; Clearwater; Clearwater Beach; Cocoa Beach; Crystal River; Cypress Gardens; Daytona Beach; Defuniak Springs; Deltona; Dunedin; Ellenton; Fort Lauderdale; Fort Myers; Jacksonville; Key Largo; Key West; Kissimmee; Lake Buena Vista; Lake City; Lake Hamilton; Lake Placid; Lakeland; Live Oak; Marianna; Miami; Naples; Orange Park; Orlando; Ormond Beach; Palm Beach Shores; Panama City; Pensacola; Pompano Beach; Port St. Lucie; St. Augustine; St. Augustine Beach; St. Petersburg;*

Sanibel Island; Sarasota; Starke; Tallahassee; Tarpon Springs; Titusville; Venice; Zephyrhills; West Palm Beach; Winter Garden.

The Gold Crown Club International Card earns points redeemable for room nights and other awards. Many locations offer a 10% discount to senior travelers on a space-available basis with advanced reservations. The Government-Military Travel Program provides discounts to federal employees and military personnel.

Budget Host Inns
2601 Jackboro Highway
Fort Worth TX 76114
Reservations: 800-BUD-HOST

Locations: *Leesburg; Ocala; Tampa; Winter Haven.*

Budget Host-Bottom Line Bonus Coupons provide discounts worth $1 to $5 a night at participating properties. Some motels provide a 10% discount to seniors upon request.

Budgetel Inns
212 West Wisconsin Avenue
Milwaukee WI 53203
Reservations: 800-428-3438

Locations: *Fort Lauderdale; Fort Myers; Jacksonville; Miami; Ocala; Orlando; Tampa.*

Budgetel Inns offers a free room-delivered continental breakfast, extra long beds, free satellite movies 24-hours-a-day, in-room VCRs, free local telephone calls, executive conference center with speaker phones, in-room computer and fax hookups and children stay free with parents. The RoadRunners Club offers a free night's stay after 12 paid nights.

Clarion-Choice Hotels
10750 Columbia Pike
Silver Spring MD 20901
Reservations: 800-221-2222

Locations: *Alachua; Atlantic Beach; Avon Park; Bonita Springs; Bradenton; Callahan; Cape Coral; Captiva; Clearwater; Clearwater Beach; Cocoa Beach; Crestview; Crystal River; Cypress Gardens; Dayton Beach; Daytona Beach Shores; Deerfield Beach; DeFuniak Springs;*

Destin; Fern Park; Florida City; Fort Lauderdale; Fort Myers; Fort Pierce; Gainesville; Haines City; Hollywood; Jacksonville; Jacksonville Beach; Jasper; Jennings; Jupiter; Key West; Kissimmee; Lake Buena Vista; Lake City; Lakeland; Leesburg; Live Oak; Longwood; Macclenny; Marianna; Melbourne; Miami; Miami Beach; Mount Dora; Naples; Navarre; New Port Richey; Niceville; North Palm Beach; Ocala; Orange Park; Orlando; Ormond Beach; Palm Harbor; Panama City; Panama City Beach; Pensacola; Perdido Key; Pompano Beach; Port Charlotte; Port Richey; Sarasota; St. Augustine; St. Petersburg; Silver Springs; Sun City Center; Tallahassee; Tampa; Tarpon Springs; Titusville; Treasure Island; Vero Beach; Wildwood; Winter Haven; Weeki Wachee; West Palm Beach.

Clarion and Choice Hotels consist of Sleep Inn, Comfort Inns, Friendship Inn, Econo Lodges, Rodeway Inns, Quality Inns and Clarion Hotels and Resorts.

Special discounts of 10%-20% are available at participating locations for members of AAA. The Small Organizations Savings (SOS) Program is available to companies with over 10 employees and offers a 10% discount off the first 15 rooms used by company employees. The Weekender Rate Program offers special room rates of $20, $30 or $35 per night with an advanced reservation. All local, state and federal government employees and military personnel receive special per diem rates and upgrades when available at participating hotels. The Family Plan allows children to stay free when sharing a parents room. Prime Time and PrimeTime Senior Saver for people over age 60 offers a 10% discount at all hotels year-round and a 30% discount at limited locations when you call 800-221-2222 and ask for this rate.

Crown Sterling Suites
1900 South Norfolk
San Mateo CA 94403
Reservations: 800-433-4600

Locations: *Boca Raton; Deerfield Beach; Miami; Tampa.*

Days Inn
2751 Buford Highway
Atlanta GA 30324
Reservations: 800-325-2525

Locations: *Bradenton; Clearwater; Cocoa Beach; Destin; Fort Lauderdale; Fort Myers; Fort Pierce; Gainesville; Jacksonville; Lake City; Mac-*

clenny; Madison; Miami; Miami Beach; Naples; Orlando; Palm Bay; Panama City Beach; Perry; Port Charlotte; St. Augustine; St. Augustine Beach; Sarasota; Siesta Key; Venice; Vero Beach; West Palm Beach.

The September Days Club ($) offers travelers over the age of 50 up to 40% discount on rooms, 10% discount on food and gifts, a quarterly club magazine, seasonal room discounts and special trips. The Inn Credible Card is designed for business travelers and provides up to 30% savings on room rates, free stays for spouses and other benefits. The Days GemClub is a travel club for military personnel and government employees that offers up to 30% savings on room rates. SchoolDays Club for academic staff and educators offers a minimum of 10% savings on room rates, special group rates and additional benefits. The Sport Plus Club is designed for coaches and team managers who organize team travel. It offers 10% discounts on rates, special team rates and late check-outs.

Doral Hotels and Resorts
600 Madison Ave.
New York, NY 10022
Reservations: 800-327-6334

Locations: *Miami; Miami Beach.*

Doubletree-Compri Hotels
410 North 44th Street
Phoenix AZ 85008
Reservations: 800-528-0444

Locations: *Miami; Lake Buena Vista.*

Doubletree operates 38 hotels in the United States, including Doubletree Club Hotels that provide oversized rooms, complimentary, cooked-to-order breakfasts, club rooms and hosted evening receptions. Family Plans allow up to two children under the age of 18 to stay free when they share a room with their parents. Most hotels offer secretarial services, photocopying, fax machines and computer hook-ups. A special discount rate is available to seniors. A Corporate Plus Program is available at all business center locations.

Business Class offers quick check-in and check-out, complimentary breakfast in a private lounge, free newspaper and additional benefits. The Entree Gold floor provides concierge services, an exclusive lounge for use by guests, complimentary breakfast and cocktail hour and use of a private boardroom.

Economy Inns of America
755 Raintree Drive
Carlsbad CA 92009
Reservations: 800-826-0778

Most properties offer senior citizen rates.

Locations: *Jacksonville; Kissimmee; Orlando; Tampa; Palm Beach.*

Most properties offer a senior citizen rates.

Embassy Suites
222 Las Colinas Boulevard
Irving TX 75039
Reservations: 800-528-1100

Locations: *Boca Raton; Jacksonville; Lake Buena Vista; Orlando; Palm Beach; Tampa.*

Embassy Suites offer two-room suites with living room, bedroom and kitchenettes. Complimentary breakfasts are served daily and a two-hour complimentary beverage program is offered nightly.

Guest Quarters Suite Hotels
30 Rowes Wharf
Boston MA 02110
Reservations: 800-424-2900

Locations: *Ft. Lauderdale; Lake Buena Vista; Orlando; Tampa; Vero Beach.*

Family and Romance Packages is a special program that varies with each location. Some packages include discounted room rates, complimentary meals, discounts at local attractions and other services. The Family Plan offers free accommodations to children under the age of 18 when sharing a room with their parents or accompanying adult. Some locations offer senior citizen discounts.

Hampton Inns
6800 Poplar
Memphis TN 38138
Reservations: 800-426-7866

Locations: *Clearwater; Daytona Beach; Fort Lauderdale; Fort Myers; Jacksonville; Key West; Miami; Naples; Orlando; Pensacola; Sarasota; Tampa; Vero Beach; West Palm Beach.*

Hampton Inns offer free continental breakfast and free local telephone calls. Children under 18 stay free in same room with parents. Most Hampton Inns offer a Hospitality Suite that can be used as a small meeting facility. The LifeStyle 50 Club provides discounts for guests over age 50 with no charge for a third person staying in the room.

Hilton Hotels and Resorts
9336 Civic Center Drive
Beverly Hills CA 90209
Reservations: 800-HILTON

Locations: *Altamonte Springs; Clearwater Beach; Cocoa Beach; Deerfield Beach; Daytona Beach; Deland; Fort Lauderdale; Gainesville; Jupiter Beach; Kissimmee; Longboat Key; Marco Island; Melbourne; Miami; Miami Beach; North Redington Beach; Ocala; Orlando; Palm Beach; Pensacola; St. Petersburg, Sanibel Island, Tampa.*

Zip-Out-Quick Check-Out is available to travelers using major credit cards. An itemized statement of charges is provided the night before departure. Many Hilton locations have hotels-within-hotels, Tower and Executive accommodations offering room upgrades, use of a private lounge, access to business services, complimentary cocktails and continental breakfast and use of telex, fax machines and photocopying equipment.

The HHonors Guest Reward Program is a free program that earns points toward free or discounted stays at participating properties and members-only privileges that include rapid check-ins, free daily newspaper, free stay with spouse and complimentary use of health club facilities when available.

The Corporate Rate Program offers business travelers guaranteed rates annually, speed reservations, Tower and Executive accommodations and Quick Check-Out facilities.

Hilton's Senior HHonors offers special amenities to travelers over the age of 60. Included are room discounts up to 50%, a 20% dinner discount and money-back guarantee, a private toll-free reservation number and automatic enrollment in Hilton's Guest Reward Programs. BounceBack Weekend offers a free daily continental breakfast, children free in parents' rooms and special rates for Thursday to Sunday with a Saturday stay. During the summer, these discounted rates apply Monday to Wednesday.

Hilton Leisure Breaks includes packages for honeymooners and special occasions with special rates. Hilton Meeting 2000 is a network of business meeting facilities available at some locations and includes special meeting room, audiovisual systems, refreshments and assistance in providing meeting rooms and programs.

Holiday Inn
1100 Ashwood Parkway
Atlanta GA 30338
Reservations: 800-HOLIDAY

Locations: *Altamonte Springs; Boca Raton; Boynton Beach; Bradenton; Brooksville; Clearwater Beach; Clermont; Cocoa Beach; Coral Gables; Coral Springs; Crestview; Daytona Beach; Deland; Delray Beach; Destin; Dundee; Fern Park; Fort Lauderdale; Fort Myers Beach; Fort Pierce; Fort Walton Beach; Gainesville; Gulf Breeze; Haines City; Hallandale; Hialeah; Highland Beach; Hollywood; Homestead; Indialantic; Jacksonville; Jennings; Jensen Beach; Juno Beach; Key Largo; Key West; Kissimmee; Lake Buena Vista; Lake City; Lake Worth; Lakeland; Longboat Key; Maderia Beach; Marathon; Marianna; Melbourne; Merritt Island; Miami; Miami Beach; Miami Springs; Naples; New Port Richey; New Smyrna Beach; Ocala; Ocoee; Orange Park; Orlando; Ormond Beach; Palatka; Palm Beach Gardens; Panama City; Panama City Beach; Pensacola; Pensacola Beach; Plant City; Plantation; Pompano Beach; Port St. Lucie; Punta Gorda; Sanford; Sarasota; Sebring; Silver Springs; Singer Island; Spring Hill; St. Augustine; St. Augustine Beach; St. Petersburg; Stuart; Surfside; Tallahassee; Tampa; Titusville; Treasure Island; Vero Beach; West Palm Beach; Winter Haven.*

Holiday Inn Preferred Senior Traveler program offers a 20% savings on the single-person rate and a 10% discount at participating restaurants. Members of the American Association of Retired Persons receive a 10% discount at participating hotels.

Best Break Bed and Breakfast packages are offered at participating hotels and includes a guest room and a breakfast coupon good for $12.

Great Rates are offered with advance reservations and include discounts of at least 10%. Most Holiday Inns offer Government-Military rates based on the per diem rate offered to government employees and contractors. Many hotels participate in the Government-Military Amenities program which offers coupons redeemable for free local phone calls with a $5 limit, 10% dinner discounts and a free continental breakfast.

The Priority Club is designed for frequent travelers and provides points that can be exchanged for travel and merchandise awards.

Homewood Suites
3742 Lamar Avenue
Memphis TN 38195
Reservations: 800-225-5466

Locations: *Jacksonville; Kissimmee.*

Homewood Suites offers complimentary breakfast and evening social hour, on-site convenience store, free newspaper and use of computers, copiers, telephone and fax machines in the Executive Center. Members of AARP are entitled to a 15% discount on the standard room rates.

Hospitality International Inns
1726 Montreal Circle
Tucker GA 30084
Reservations: 800-251-1962

Hospitality International consists of Red Carpet Inns; Scottish Inns; Master Host Inns; Passport Inns and Downtowner Motor Inns.

Locations: *Davenport; Daytona Beach; Fort Lauderdale; Fort Myers; Gainesville; Jacksonville; Jasper; Kissimmee; Lake City; Lakeland; Leesburg; Live Oak; Micanopy; Ocala; Orlando; Ormond Beach; Panama City; Panama City Beach; Pensacola; Sarasota; Silver Springs; St. Augustine; Tallahassee; Tampa; Tarpon Springs; White Springs; Wildwood; Winter Haven.*

The Identicard Program provides room discounts at participating inns and resorts.

Howard Johnson
3838 East Van Buren
Phoenix AZ 85038
Reservations: 800-654-2000

Locations: *Apopka; Boca Raton; Bradenton; Clearwater; Clearwater Beach; Clermont; Cocoa Beach; Coral Gables; Cypress Gardens; Davenport; Daytona Beach; Deerfield Beach; Fort Lauderdale; Fort Pierce; Fort Walton Beach; Gainesville; Grand Ridge; Hollywood; Hollywood Beach; Homestead; Islamorada; Jacksonville; Juno Beach; Kendall; Key Largo; Key West; Kissimmee; Lake Buena Vista; Lake City; Lauderdale-by-the-Sea; Marathon; Miami; Naples; New Port Richey; Ocala; Orlando; Ormond Beach; Palm Bay; Palm Beach; Panama City; Pensacola; Pompano Beach; Punta Gorda; St. Augustine; St. Petersburg; Sarasota; Sebring; Silver Springs; Stuart; Tallahassee; Tampa; Tavares; Titusville; Treasure Island; Vero Beach; West Palm Beach; Winter Haven; Yulee.*

The Howard Johnson Road Rally Program offers discounts to senior travelers over the age of 60 and members of AARP and other national senior's organizations. With advanced reservations, a 30% discount is available at some locations. The Family Plan lets children under the age of 12 stay free at all locations with some properties extending the age limit to 18.

Government Rate Programs offer special rates to federal employees, military personnel and government contractors. The Corporate Rate Program offers special rates to companies and business travelers. Howard Johnson Executive Section offers guests special rooms, complimentary wake-up coffee and newspapers, and snacks. Kids Go Hojo provides children with free FunPacks that include toys, puzzles, coloring books and games.

Hyatt Hotels International
Madison Plaza,
200 West Madison
Chicago IL 60606
Reservations 800-228-9000

Locations: *Key West; Miami; Orlando; Sarasota; Tampa.*

Hyatt Gold Passport earns credits for free stays, and offers a private toll-free reservation number, express check-in, special members-only rooms, free newspaper daily, complimentary morning coffee and use of fitness centers where available. Hyatt Reserved

Upgrade coupon booklets are available for confirmed room upgrades. Hyatt Gold Passport At Leisure is available at over 155 locations worldwide and includes invitations to private receptions, room amenities, priority room and dining reservations and a quarterly newsletter with member-only offers.

The Regency Club is a hotel within a hotel offering VIP accommodations. Located on the topmost floors of participating hotels, the rooms are reached by special elevators requiring a passkey. Also included is a free morning paper, complimentary breakfast, afternoon hors d'oeuvres, wine and cocktails.

Camp Hyatt is for children and their parents. Upon arrival at any Hyatt hotel or resort, children receive a free cap, frequent travel passport and a registration card. The program offers special childrens' menus in the dinning room, room discounts, kitchen tours and other pastimes.

Knights Inns and Courts
26650 Emery Parkway
Cleveland OH 44128
Reservations: 800-843-5644

Locations: *Florida City; Kissimmee; Lake Wales; Lantana; Orlando; Palm Bay; Palm Harbor; Pensacola; Port Charlotte; Punta Gorda; Sanford; Tallahassee; West Palm Beach.*

LaQuinta Inns
10010 San Pedro
San Antonio TX 78279
Reservations: 800-531-5900

Locations: *Altamonte Springs; Clearwater; Daytona Beach; Deerfield Beach; Fort Myers; Gainesville; Jacksonville; Miami; Orlando; Pensacola; St. Petersburg; Tallahassee; Tampa.*

Special rates are available to business travelers, government and military employees, seniors over the age of 55 and families.

La Quinta Returns Club credit for a free night stay, guaranteed reservations and check cashing privileges.

La Quinta Senior Class ($) is available to travelers over the age of 60 and offers a 20% discount on room rates, credit for free night stays and guaranteed reservations.

La Quint Per Diem Preferred offers credits and discounts to military personnel, U.S. government workers and cost-reimbursable contractors. La Quinta Returns earns credits for free nights, special room rates, guaranteed reservation for late arrivals, account summaries and $50 check cashing privileges.

Lexington Hotels and Suite Connections
2120 Walnut Hill Lane
Irving TX 75038
Reservations: 800-537-8483

Locations: *Orlando.*

Some properties offer senior citizen rates.

Marriott
Marriott Drive
Washington DC 20058
Reservations: *Marriott Hotels* 800-228-9290, *Courtyard by Marriott* 800-321-2211, *Fairfield Inn* 800-228-2800, *Residence Inn* 800-331-3131

Marriott consists of Marriott Hotels and Resorts, Marriott Suites, Courtyard by Marriott, Residence Inns and Fairfield Inns

Fairfield Inn locations: *Delray Beach; Gainesville; Key West; Miami; Orlando.*

Marriott Hotel, Resort, and Suite locations: *Boca Raton; Daytona Beach; Fort Lauderdale; Jacksonville; Key West; Marco Island; Miami; Orlando; Palm Beach Gardens; Panama City Beach; Ponte Vedra Beach; Tampa.*

Courtyard by Marriott Hotel locations: *Boca Raton; Fort Lauderdale; Fort Myers; Jacksonville; Jensen Beach; Melbourne.*

Residence Inn locations: *Boca Raton; Gainesville; Jacksonville; Miami; Orlando; Pensacola; St. Petersburg; Tampa.*

Super Saver rates offer discounts on weekday and weekend stays at participating hotels. Discounts start at 10%. The TFB program

(Two For Breakfast) offers discounts for weekend stays for two adults that includes complimentary breakfasts. Advance Purchase Rates are discounts of up to 50% for prepaid, non-refundable reservations 7, 14, 21 and 30 days in advance. Senior Citizen discounts for members of senior groups are available at participating hotels.

The Marriott Honored Guest Award offers special upgrades to members at participating hotels. After a 15-night stay during a 12-month period, members receive express check-out services, free newspaper, check cashing privileges, free luggage tags and discounts.

Master Economy Inns
7080 Abercorn Street
Savannah GA 42416
Reservations: 800-633-3434

Locations: *Tampa.*

Some properties offer corporate, government and senior rates.

Motel 6
14651 Dallas Parkway
Dallas TX 75240
Reservations: 800-437-7486

Locations: *Bradenton; Cocoa Beach; Dania Beach; Davenport; Fort Lauderdale; Fort Myers; Fort Pierce; Gainesville; Jacksonville; Lake City; Lakeland; Lantana; Orlando; Pensacola; Pompano Beach; Punta Gorda; Riviera Beach; Sarasota; Tallahassee; Tampa; Venice; Winter Park.*

Children under 17 stay free in the same room as their parent(s). If you call and explain where you're going and how far you want to travel each day, rooms at Motel 6s along the route will be reserved in advance and information on local points of interest will be provided. Most locations offer senior citizen discounts.

National 9 Inns
2285 South Main
Salt Lake City UT 84115
Reservations: 800-524-9999

Locations: *Clearwater Beach; Daytona Beach.*

Some locations offer corporate rates and senior citizen discounts.

Omni Hotels
515 Madison Avenue
New York NY 10022
Reservations: 800-THE-OMNI

Locations: *Jacksonville; Miami; Orlando; West Palm Beach.*

The Omni Club Program is available at selected hotels and offers concierge service, private lounge facilities, complimentary breakfast, evening cocktails and hors d'oeuvres and specially-appointed rooms.

The Omni Hotel Select Guest Program provides special services, priority room availability, accommodations upgrade, complimentary coffee and morning newspaper and a newsletter announcing additional programs. The Omni Hotel Executive Service Plan is available to corporate members and includes a variety of special benefits. For planning and scheduling meetings, the Omni Hotels Gavel Service and Omni-Express Programs provide assistance by experienced meeting planners. City'scapes is a special weekend package that offers discounts and special amenities.

Park Inn International Hotels
4425 West Airport Freeway
Irving TX 75062
Reservations: 800-437-PARK

Locations: *Bradenton; Daytona Beach; Dunedin; Kissimmee; Miami; Orlando; Pensacola.*

The Silver Citizens Club offers a 20% room discount and 10% food discount at participating hotels, free morning paper and coffee, special directory, all-night emergency pharmacy telephone number and personal check cashing.

Preferred Hotels
1901 South Meyers Road
Oakbrook Terrace IL 60181
Reservations: 800-323-7500

Locations: *Coconut Grove; Coral Gables; Fort Lauderdale; Jacksonville; Miami; Orlando; Palm Beach; Ponte Vedra; Vero Beach.*

Radisson Hotels International
Carlson Parkway
Minneapolis MN 55459
Reservations: 800-333-3333

Locations: *Clearwater Beach; Fort Myers; Kissimmee; Marco Island; Melbourne; Miami Beach; Orlando; Palm Beach Gardens.*

Radisson operates 270 hotels and affiliates worldwide. Plaza Hotels are usually located in the city center or suburban locations. Suite Hotels offer oversized rooms with living room, mini-bar and kitchenettes. Resort Hotels usually include locations near beaches, golf course and recreational facilities.

Ramada Inn
1850 Parkway Place
Marietta GA 30067
Reservations: 800-2-RAMADA

Locations: *Alachua; Boca Raton; Bradenton; Clearwater; Clearwater Beach; Cocoa; Daytona Beach; Deerfield Beach; Fort Lauderdale; Fort Myers; Fort Myers Beach; Fort Walton Beach; Hallandale; Hialeah; Jacksonville; Jacksonville Beach; Key West; Kissimmee; Lake City; Lakeland; Melbourne; Miami; Miami Beach; Ocala; Palm Beach; Panama City; Pensacola; Pompano Beach; St. Augustine; St. Augustine Beach; St. Petersburg; Sanibel Island; Sarasota; Stuart; Tallahassee; Tampa; Titusville; Treasure Island; West Palm Beach.*

Membership in the Ramada Business Card Program earns points for trips and merchandise based on dollars spent at Ramada properties. The card is available free. Membership includes favorable rates, automatic room upgrade when available, express check-in and check-out, free newspaper on business days, free same-room accommodations for your spouse when you travel together, extended check-out times, newsletter and points redeemable for hotel stays, air travel, car rentals and over 10,000 Service Merchandise catalog items.

Participating Ramada Inn properties offer Super Save Weekend discounts. These rates apply on Friday, Saturday and Sunday for one-, two-, and three-night stays. Extra person rates may apply for a third or fourth person in the room. Because some hotels limit availability on certain dates, reservations are recommended.

When traveling with family or friends, the Ramada 4-for-1 Program permits up to four people to share the same room and pay the single rate. At participating properties, the Best Years Seniors Program provides travelers over the age of 60 who are members of AARP, the Global Horizons Club, Catholic Golden Age, The Golden Buckeye Club, Humana Seniors Association, The Retired Enlisted Association, The Retired Officers Association and United Airlines Silver Wings Plus with a 25% discount off regular room rates.

The Ramada Per Diem Value Program is available at more than 350 locations. Properties honor the maximum lodging per diem rates set by the U.S. General Services Administration. Federal employees, military personnel and employees of cost-reimbursable contractors traveling on official government business are eligible. In addition to the per diem limits for lodging, the single person room rate at participating locations includes full American breakfast and all applicable taxes. All Ramada properties provide corporate customers favorable rates. Companies need a minimum of 10 travelers with a combined total of 100 room nights per year.

Red Carpet Inns
1726 Montreal Circle
Tucker GA 30084
Reservations: 800-251-1962

Locations: *Davenport; Daytona Beach; Fort Lauderdale; Fort Myers; Gainesville; Jacksonville; Jasper; Kissimmee; Lake City; Lakeland; Leesburg; Live Oak; Micanopy; Ocala; Orlando; Ormond Beach; Panama City; Pensacola; Sarasota; Silver Springs; St. Augustine; Tallahassee; Tampa; Tarpon Springs; White Springs; Wildwood; Winter Haven.*

Red Roof Inns
4355 Davidson Road
Hilliard OH 43026
Reservations: 800-843-7663

Locations: *Jacksonville; Kissimmee; Orlando; Pensacola; Tallahassee; Tampa.*

Redi Card membership offers 8 p.m. holds on reservations, complimentary USA Today newspaper, member-only newsletters, first priority advance room requests, check cashing privileges up to $50 per stay, express check-in and check-out and complimentary late stays upon request.

Ritz Carlton Hotels
3414 Peachtree Road NE
Atlanta GA 30326
Reservations: 800-241-3333

Locations: *Amelia Island; Naples; Palm Beach.*

The Desk Recognition program keeps guest profiles on file that list personal likes and dislikes and offers automatic upgrades when available. All hotels offer corporate rates and some hotels offer senior citizen discounts.

Sheraton Hotels, Inns and Resorts
60 State Street
Boston MA 02109
Reservations: 800-325-3535

Locations: *Boca Raton; Clearwater Beach; Fort Lauderdale; Fort Walton Beach; Key Biscayne; Key Largo; Lakeland; Maitland; Miami; Miami Beach; New Port Richey; Orlando; Palm Beach; Palm Coast; Plantation; Tallahassee; Tampa; West Palm Beach.*

ITT Sheraton Club International ($) benefit include automatic room upgrade whenever available, double club point and free night stays in selected hotels. Express pass check-in and check-out service is also available.

Shoney's Inns
217 West Main Street
Gallatin TN 37066
Reservations 800-222-2222

Locations: *Fernandina Beach; Fort Walton Beach; Kissimmee; Melbourne; Tallahassee; Tampa.*

Shoney Inns offer free local telephone calls and complimentary newspaper. Shoney Inn's Merit Club offers discounts to senior citizens.

Sonesta Hotels
200 Clarendon Street
Boston MA 02116
Reservations: 800-766-3782

Locations: *Key Biscayne; Orlando; Sanibel Island.*

Some properties offer senior citizen rates.

Stouffer Hotels
29800 Bainbridge Road
Cleveland OH 44139
Reservations: 800-HOTELS-1

Locations: *Orlando; St. Petersburg.*

Weekend Breakouts offers one- and two-day special rates at select locations. All hotels offer corporate rates. Most senior citizen discounts.

Club Express is for the corporate business traveler and offers automatic room upgrades, express check-in and check-out, credits for free stays, plus American Express Gift Cheques and Savings Bonds.

Summerfield Suites
8100 East 22nd Street North
Wichita KS 67226
Reservations: 800-833-4353

Locations: *Orlando.*

Summerfield Suites offers a variety of discounts, a free night's stay with six paid nights, 30% off during certain times of the year, $50 off after a two-night paid stay. All Summerfield Suites hotels offer a complimentary breakfast buffet and social hour.

Sundowner International
622 Wade Circle
Goodlettesville TN 37072
Reservations: 800-322-8029

Locations: *Boca Raton; Daytona Beach; Fort Walton Beach; Marianna.*

Some properties offer senior citizen rates and corporate discounts.

Super 8 Motels
1910 8th Avenue NE
Aberdeen SD 57402
Reservations: 800-800-8000

Locations: *Clearwater; Crestview; Daytona Beach; Florida City; Fort Walton Beach; Gainesvile; Homestead; Jacksonville; Lake City; Lake Wales; Leesburg; Naples; Orlando; Panama City; Pensacola; Riviera Beach; St. Petersburg; Tallahassee; West Palm Beach.*

Super 8's VIP Card offers a 10% discount at all Super 8 motels, guaranteed reservations, express check-out, car rental discounts and authorization to pay by personal check. Most locations offer senior citizen discounts to travelers 55 and over.

TraveLodge
1973 Friendship Drive
El Cajon CA 92020
Reservations: 800-255-3050

Locations: *Clearwater; Daytona Beach; Fort Lauderdale; Fort Myers; Gainesville; Jacksonville; Lake City; Marianna; Miami Beach; Miami Springs; Ocala; Orlando; Sarasota; St. Augustine; Tampa.*

The Business Break Club Program offers a 10% discount off the lowest published room rate, express check-in and check-out, free local telephone calls and morning coffee and a special 800 number for fast reservations. The Corporate Business Break Club provides a 10% room discount off the lowest published rate, free morning coffee, newsletters and car rental discounts.

The Classic Travel Club is available to travelers over the age of 50. It offers room discounts of 15%, a quarterly newsletter, check cashing privileges, free morning coffee, car rental discounts and express check-in and check-out services.

Coaches, Athletic Directors and Educators are eligible for Team TraveLodge which offers a free stay with groups of 10 or more, a minimum 10% discount, upgrades for group leaders, late check-out, free morning coffee, newsletter and car rental discounts.

All federal, state and local government employees and members of the armed forces and their families traveling on official government business or pleasure receive special rates equal to or less than the prevailing per diem rates. Information on these rates is available from 800-GOVT-RES.

Under the Family Plan, there is no charge for children under the age of 17 when sharing a room with their parents. The Government Traveler-Value America Plan offers rates equal to or less than the prevailing per diem rates paid and is available to federal employees, military personnel and contractors on government business.

Wellesly Inns
700 Route 46 East
Fairfield NJ 07007
Reservations: 800-444-8888

Locations: *Amelia Island; Coral Springs; Deerfield Beach; Fort Lauderdale; Fort Myers; Fort Walton Beach; Jupiter; Kissimmee; Melbourne; Miami; Miami Lakes; Naples; Orlando; Plantation; Sarasota; Tallahassee; Tampa; West Palm Beach.*

Some properties offer senior citizen rates.

Wyndham Hotels and Resort
2001 Bryan Street, Suite 2300Dallas TX 75210
Reservations: 800-822-4200

Locations: *Orlando, Tampa.*

Accommodations Directory

Alachua
Area Code 904

Comfort Inn (Hwy. I-75 and Hwy. 441, 32615; 462-2414, Fax 462-2220, 800-221-2222) 50 rooms, outdoor pool, whirlpools, a/c, TV, children free with parents, NS rooms, wheelchair access, in-room refrigerators and microwaves, senior rates, CC. 11 miles from Itchetucknee Springs Park, 15 miles from Florida Stadium. LS SGL/DBL$38-$55; HS SGL/DBL$38-$58.

Days Inn (Alachua 32615; 462-3251, 800-325-2525) 57 rooms, free breakfast, outdoor pool, a/c, TV, wheelchair access, NS rooms, no pets, laundry facilities, senior rates, children free with parents, meeting facilities, CC. SGL/DBL$36-$100.

Ramada Inn (Route 1, 32615; 462-4200, 800-2-RAMADA) 44 rooms and suites, restaurant, lounge, outdoor pool, wheelchair access, NS rooms, free parking, a/c, TV, children free with parents, pets OK, local transportation, room service, laundry facilities, meeting facilities, senior rates, CC. 15 miles from the downtown area and the University of Florida, 17 miles from Itchetucknee Springs State Park. SGL/DBL$47-$95.

Altamonte Springs
Area Code 407

Days Inn (450 Douglas Ave., 32714; 862-7111, 800-329-7466) 331 rooms and 1-bedroom suites, restaurant, free breakfast, heated pool, kitchenettes, a/c, TV, wheelchair access, NS rooms, no pets, local transportation, laundry facilities, senior rates, meeting facilities, CC. LS SGL/DBL$30-$40; HS SGL/DBL$50-$55.

Days Inn (235 South Wymore Rd., 32714; 862-2800, Fax 862-2804, 800-325-2525) 178 rooms, free breakfast, outdoor pool, children free with parents, a/c, TV, wheelchair access, NS rooms, no pets, laundry facilities, senior rates, CC. 7 miles from the Orlando Sports Arena, 5 miles from the AAA Office Center. SGL/DBL$35-$65.

Embassy Suites Orlando North (225 East Altamonte Dr., 32701; 834-2400, Fax 834-2117, 800-EMBASSY) 210 1-bedroom suites, restaurant, lounge, free breakfast, lounge, indoor heated pool, whirlpool, exercise center, sauna, room service, gift shop, a/c, TV, laundry service, wheelchair access, complimentary newspaper, free local calls, NS rooms, gift shop, local transportation, 6 meeting rooms, senior rates, CC. 6 miles from the Orlando Sports Arena, 12 miles from the Citrus Bowl. 1BR$130-$145.

Hilton Hotel North (350 South North Lake Blvd., 32715; 830-1985, Fax 331-2911, 800-HILTONS) 325 rooms and suites, restaurant, lounge, entertainment, outdoor pool, exercise center, whirlpools, sauna, game room, children free with parents, gift shop, NS rooms, wheelchair access, car rental desk, no pets, room service, laundry facilities, a/c, TV, 15 meeting rooms, meeting facilities for 1,800, senior rates, CC. 5 miles from the downtown Orlando, 28 miles from Walt Disney World, 18 miles from the Orlando airport. SGL/DBL$80-$135.

Holiday Inn (230 West Hwy. 436, 32714; 862-4455, Fax 682-5982, 800-HOLIDAY, 800-242-6862) 202 rooms and suites, restaurant, outdoor pool, exercise center, airport transportation, in-room refrigerators, laundry facilities, a/c, TV, game room, in-room computer hookups, children free with parents, NS rooms, wheelchair access, no pets, senior rates, meeting facilities for 150, CC. 20 miles from the regional airport, 3 miles from the Jai Alai fronton, 1 mile from Maitland Center. SGL/DBL$75-$85.

La Quinta Inn (150 South Westmonte Dr., 32714; 788-1411, Fax 788-6472, 800-531-5900) 115 rooms, free breakfast, outdoor heated pool, complimentary newspaper, free local calls, fax service, laundry service, NS rooms, wheelchair access, local transportation, TV, a/c, in-room computer hookups, pets OK, meeting facilities, senior rates, CC. 18 miles from Sea World, 19 miles from the Orlando airport. SGL/DBL$56-$68.

Marriott Residence Inn (270 Douglas Ave., 32714; 788-7991, Fax 869-5468, 800-228-9290, 800-331-3131) 128 rooms and suites, free breakfast, outdoor heated pool, whirlpools, in-room refrigerators, coffee makers and microwaves, laundry facilities, TV, a/c, VCRs, pets OK, complimentary newspaper, fireplaces, children free with parents, NS rooms, wheelchair access, meeting facilities, CC. 20 miles from the Orlando airport, 10 miles from downtown Orlando. SGL/DBL$110-$155.

Sundance Inn (I-4 and Hwy. 436, 32714; 862-8200, 800-327-5560, 800-432-4428 in Florida) 150 rooms, restaurant, free breakfast, outdoor pool, a/c, TV, wheelchair access, NS rooms, children free with parents, pets OK, CC. 27 miles from Walt Disney World, 14 miles downtown Orlando. LS SGL/DBL$42-$48; HS SGL/DBL$56-$62.

Amelia Island

Area Code 904

Rental & Reservation Services

Amelia Island Lodging Systems (584 South Fletcher, 32034; 261-4148, 800-872-8531) rental condominiums.

□□□

Amelia By The Sea (3240 South Fletcher, 32034; 32034) 2-bedroom suites, ocean view, beach, outdoor pool, tennis courts, a/c, TV, wheelchair access, children free with parents, in-room refrigerators and coffee makers, CC. 2BR$150-$900W.

Amelia Island Plantation (Hwy. A1A South, 32034; 261-6161, Fax 277-5159, 800-874-6878) 550 rooms and 1-, 2-, 3-, and 4-bedroom condominiums and villas, restaurant, lounge, indoor and outdoor heated pools, whirlpools, lighted tennis courts, beach, exercise center, laundry facilities, in-room refrigerators, microwaves and coffee makers, a/c, TV, children free with parents, no pets, wheelchair access, NS rooms, airport transportation, 22,000 square feet of meeting and exhibition space, meeting facilities for 700, senior rates, CC. 6 miles from the Fernandina Municipal airport, 25 miles from the Jacksonville airport. LS SGL/DBL$110-$179; HS SGL/DBL$165-$275.

Amelia Surf and Racquet Club (800 Amelia Pkwy. South, 32034; 261-0511, 800-323-2001) 56 rooms and 1-, 2-, and 3-bedroom villas, outdoor pool, exercise center, lighted tennis courts, beach, a/c, TV, NS rooms, wheelchair access, children free with parents, laundry facilities, no pets, senior rates, CC. 18 miles from the Jacksonville airport. SGL/DBL$120-$210.

The Bailey House (28 South 7th St., 32034; 261-5390) 4 rooms, free breakfast, TV, a/c, NS rooms, private baths, no pets, CC. SGL/DBL$65-$95.

Elizabeth Pointe Lodge (82 South Fletcher Ave., 32034; 277-4851, Fax 261-2653, 800-772-3359) 20 rooms, restaurant, whirlpools, children free with parents, no pets, beach, TV, a/c, senior rates, CC. SGL/DBL$80-$230.

Florida House Inn (22 South 3rd St., 32034; 261-3300, Fax 277-3831, 800-258-3301) 11 rooms, free breakfast, whirlpools, local transportation, NS, Modified American Plan available, no pets, a/c, TV, laundry facilities, private baths, CC. 30 miles from the Jacksonville airport. SGL/DBL$65-$125.

The Lighthouse (736 South Fletcher Ave., 32034) 6 rooms and 2-bedroom suites, free breakfast, a/c, TV, beach, no pets, CC. $125-$875W.

Ritz Carlton (4750 Amelia Island Pkwy., 32034; 277-1100, Fax 261-9063, 800-241-3333) 449 rooms and suites, restaurant, lounge, entertainment, indoor and outdoor heated pools, exercise center, whirlpools, sauna, 24-hour room service, in-room refrigerators, a/c, TV, in-room computer hookups, beach, NS rooms, wheelchair access, children free with parents, 13 meeting rooms, senior rates, CC. 22 miles from the Jacksonville airport. LS SGL/DBL$145-$225; HS SGL/DBL$235-$320.

Seaside Inn (1998 Fletcher Ave., 32034; 261-0954) 10 rooms and suites, restaurant, free breakfast, a/c, TV, NS rooms, laundry facilities, no pets, CC. SGL/DBL$65-$75.

1735 House (584 South Fletcher Ave., 32034; 261-5878, 800-872-8531) 5 rooms, free breakfast, in-room refrigerators and coffee makers, beach, no pets, TV, a/c, CC. 6 miles from the Fernandina Municipal airport. SGL/DBL$75-$150.

Summer Beach Resort (5000 Amelia Pkwy., 32034; 277-2525, Fax 277-8339, 800-432-3047) 55 2- and 3-bedroom condominiums, restaurant, outdoor pool, tennis courts, airport transportation, in-room refrigerators and microwaves, laundry facilities, a/c, TV, children free with parents, wheelchair access, no pets, CC. 22 miles from the Jacksonville airport. 2BR$175, 3BR$200.

Anna Maria
Area Code 813

Rental & Reservation Services

Century 21 Rentals-A-Paradise, Inc. (3018 Ave. C, 34217; 778-4800, 800-237-2252) rental condominiums and apartments.

ㅁㅁㅁ

Anna Maria Motel and Apartments (806 Bay Blvd., 34216; 778-1269) 8 rooms and efficiencies, outdoor pool, kitchenettes, a/c, TV, children free with parents, laundry facilities, wheelchair access, senior rates, CC. SGL/DBL$30-$53.

Rod & Reel Motel (877 North Shore Dr., 34216; 778-2780) 10 rooms, a/c, TV, children free with parents, no pets, CC. SGL/DBL$38-$69.

Sea Isle Motel (601 Bay Blvd., 34216; 778-2919) 6 rooms and efficiencies, outdoor pool, a/c, TV, NS rooms, no pets, senior rates, CC. SGL/DBL$35-$50.

Apalachicola
Area Code 904

The Gibson Inn (100 Market St., 32320; 653-2191) 30 rooms, restaurant, lounge, antique furnishings, TV, a/c, pets OK, meeting facilities, CC. SGL/DBL$60-$110.

The Pink Camellia (145 East Ave. E, 32320; 653-2107) 3 rooms and suites, free breakfast, a/c, no pets, CC. SGL$60-$70, DBL$65-$75.

Rancho Inn (240 Hwy. 98, 32320; 653-9435) 32 rooms, a/c, TV, children free with parents, pets OK, CC. SGL/DBL$32-$38.

Apopka
Area Code 407

Crosby's Motor Inn (1440 West Orange Blossom Trail, 32703; 886-3220, 800-821-6685) 61 rooms and efficiencies, outdoor pool, a/c, TV, kitchenettes, game room, in-room refrigerators, children free with parents, laundry facilities, pets OK, senior rates, CC. 30 miles from the Orlando airport. LS SGL/DBL$40-$60; HS SGL/DBL$50-$70, STS$125-$175.

HoJo Inn (1317 South Orange Blossom Trail, 32703; 886-1010, 800-I-GO-HOJO) 28 rooms, children free with parents, wheelchair access, NS rooms, TV, a/c, laundry facilities, senior rates, no pets, in-room refrigerators and microwaves, meeting facilities, CC. 25 miles from the Orlando airport. SGL/DBL$40-$75.

Apollo Beach
Area Code 813

Holiday Inn (6414 Surfside, 33572; 645-3271, Fax 645-9294, 800-HOLIDAY) 103 rooms, restaurant, lounge, outdoor pool, exercise center, children free with parents, wheelchair access, a/c, TV, NS rooms, fax service, room service, pets OK, laundry service, meeting facilities, senior rates, CC. LS SGL/DBL$55-$85; HS SGL/DBL$65-$100.

Arcadia
Area Code 813

Best Western (504 South Brevard, 33821; 494-4884, 800-528-1234) 36 rooms, free breakfast, outdoor pool, NS rooms, a/c, NS rooms, TV, laundry facilities, wheelchair access, no pets, in-room refrigerators, gift shop, children free with parents, meeting facilities, senior rates, CC. LS SGL/DBL$38-$51; HS SGL/DBL$42-$70.

Atlantic Beach
Area Code 904

Comfort Inn Mayport (2401 Mayport Rd., 32233; 249-0313, Fax 241-2155, 800-437-5892, 800-221-2222) 110 rooms, restaurant, lounge, free breakfast, outdoor pool, a/c, TV, children free with parents, NS rooms, wheelchair access, no pets, in-room refrigerators and microwaves, kitchenettes, laundry facilities, senior rates, CC. 12 miles from the Gator Bowl, 8 miles from the Mayo Clinic and the University of North Florida. SGL/DBL$35-$60.

Aventura

Area Code 305

Best Western Inn (18001 Collins Ave., 33160; 932-1800, Fax 935-5575, 800-528-1234) 118 rooms, restaurant, lounge, outdoor pool, children free with parents, a/c, NS rooms, TV, laundry facilities, wheelchair access, no pets, meeting facilities, senior rates, CC. SGL/DBL$90-$125.

Chateau-by-the-Sea (19115 Collins Ave., 33160; 931-8800, 800-327-0691) 167 efficiencies, lounge, entertainment, outdoor heated pool, a/c, TV, NS rooms, wheelchair access, children free with parents, no pets, beauty shop, in-room refrigerators, CC. 15 miles from downtown Miami. SGL/DBL$60-$88.

Holiday Inn (16701 Collins Ave., 33160; 949-1300, Fax 947-5873, 800-HOLIDAY) 345 rooms, restaurant, lounge, entertainment, outdoor pool, exercise center, children under 19 free with parents, wheelchair access, a/c, TV, NS rooms, boutiques, fax service, room service, laundry service, meeting facilities for 450, senior rates, CC. 3 miles from Bal Harbour Shops and shopping mall. SGL/DBL$89-$129.

Quality Inn (18555 Collins Ave., 33160; 932-1445, 800-221-2222) 119 rooms and suites, restaurant, lounge, entertainment, beach, outdoor pool, exercise center, children free with parents, a/c, TV, wheelchair access, room service, laundry service, NS rooms, meeting facilities, senior rates, CC. 15 miles from the Miami airport. SGL/DBL$70-$145.

Turnberry Isle Resort and Club (19999 West Country Club Dr., 33160; 932-6200, Fax 937-0528, 800-327-7028, 800-223-1588 in Florida) 382 rooms and suites, restaurant, lounge, indoor and outdoor heated pools, exercise center, lighted tennis courts, whirlpools, marina, exercise center, in-room computer hookups, beauty salon, laundry facilities, in-room refrigerators, VCRs, a/c, TV, 24-hour room service, children free with parents, no pets, 12,000 square feet of meeting and exhibition space, senior rates, CC. 10 miles from downtown Miami, 15 miles from the Convention Center. SGL/DBL$175-$380, STS$450-$1,800.

Avon Park

Area Code 813

Econo Lodge (2511 Hwy. 27 South, 33825; 453-2000, Fax 453-0820, 800-4-CHOICE) 58 rooms, outdoor pool, children free with parents, no pets, NS rooms, wheelchair access, a/c, TV, VCRs, laundry facilities, in-room refrigerators and microwaves, senior rates, CC. SGL/DBL$36-$110.

Hotel Jacaranda (19 East Main St., 33825; 453-2211) 60 rooms and suites, restaurant, outdoor pool, no pets, a/c, TV, children free with parents, in-room refrigerators, wheelchair access, CC. SGL$40, DBL$45, STS$35-$50.

Lake Brentwood Motel (2060 Hwy. 27 North, 33825; 453-4358) 14 rooms, a/c, TV, children free with parents, NS rooms, CC. LS SGL/DBL$34-$48; HS SGL/DBL$38-$58.

Babson Park

Area Code 813

Hillcrest Lodge (Babson Park 33827: 638-1712) 22 rooms and villas, restaurant, beach, no pets, a/c, TV, children free with parents, wheelchair access, senior rates, CC. SGL/DBL$35-$44, 1BR$44-$225W.

Baldwin

Area Code 904

Best Western Inn (1088 Hwy. 301, 32234; 266-9759, 800-528-1234) 44 rooms, restaurant, outdoor pool, children free with parents, a/c, NS rooms, TV, laundry facilities, wheelchair access, pets OK, meeting facilities, senior rates, CC. 12 miles from Cecil Field Navy Base, 20 miles from the Gator Bowl. SGL/DBL$35-$55.

Bal Harbour

Area Code 305

Sea View Hotel (9909 Collins Ave., 33154; 866-4441, Fax 866-1898, 800-447-1010) 200 rooms, restaurant, lounge, outdoor heated pool, a/c, TV, room service, laundry facilities, kitchenettes, in-room refrigerators, no pets, beach, CC. 1 block from the Bal Harbour Shops. SGL/DBL$175-$210.

Sheraton Bal Harbour Resort (9701 Collins Ave., 33154; 865-7511, Fax 864-2601, 800-325-3535) 652 rooms and suites, restaurant, lounge, indoor and outdoor heated pools, exercise center, whirlpools, sauna, tennis courts, in-room refrigerators and coffee makers, game room, children free with parents, gift shop, fax service, pets OK, laundry service, 24-hour room service, beach, senior rates, meeting facilities for 2,500, 70,000 square feet of meeting and exhibition space, CC. 17 miles from the Miami airport, 1 block from Bal Harbour Shops. LS SGL/DBL$165-$235; HS SGL/DBL$240-$255.

Singapore Resort Hotel (9601 Collins Ave., 33154; 865-9931, Fax 866-2313) 109 suites, restaurant, lounge, entertainment, outdoor heated pool, Modified American Plan available, no pets, in-room refrigerators, laundry facilities, children free with parents, beach, CC. LS SGL/DBL$57-$77; HS SGL/DBL$100-$115.

Bartow

Area Code 813

Davis Brothers Motor Lodge (1035 North Broadway, 33830; 533-0711) 102 rooms, restaurant, lounge, outdoor pool, pets OK, a/c, TV, children free with parents, laundry facilities, NS rooms, wheelchair access, senior rates, meeting facilities, CC. SGL/DBL$40-$50.

El Jon Motel and Apartments (1460 East Main St., 33830; 533-8191) 46 rooms and 2-bedroom apartments, outdoor heated pool, in-room refrigerators, no pets, a/c, TV, CC. LS SGL/DBL$36-$40; HS SGL/DBL$53-$59.

Bay Harbor Island
Area Code 305

Bay Harbor Inn (9660 East Bay Harbor Dr., 33154; 868-4141, Fax 868-4141 ext 602) 36 rooms and suites, restaurant, lounge, free breakfast, heated pool, a/c, TV, children free with parents, no pets, airport transportation, in-room refrigerators, NS rooms, complimentary newspaper, senior rates, CC. LS SGL/DBL$60-$80; HS SGL/DBL$80-$125.

Belleair Beach
Area Code 813

Belleair Beach Motel (2040 Gulf Blvd., 34635; 595-1696, 800-780-1696) 40 rooms, efficiencies and 1-bedroom apartments, outdoor heated pool, beach, a/c, TV, children free with parents, senior rates, NS rooms, no pets, CC. SGL/DBL$285W, 1BR$366W, 2BR$510W.

The Chateau (2700 Gulf Blvd., 34635; 397-1753) 15 condominiums, outdoor pool, beach, kitchenettes, wheelchair access, a/c, TV, senior rates, CC. LS SGL/DBL$30-$40; HS SGL/DBL$55-$65.

Nautical Watch Resort (3420 Gulf Blvd., 34635; 595-4747) 47 efficiencies, outdoor pool, beach, in-room refrigerators and coffee makers, laundry facilities, children free with parents, a/c, TV, senior rates, CC. LS SGL/DBL$40; HS SGL/DBL$60.

Belle Glade
Area Code 407

Days Inn (1075 South Main St., 33430; 992-8600, 800-325-2525) 52 rooms, free breakfast, a/c, TV, wheelchair access, NS rooms, laundry facilities, children free with parents, senior rates, CC. 15 miles from Lion Country Safari, 30 miles from the Palm Beach airport, 1 mile from Lake Okeechobee. SGL/DBL$35-$85.

Travelers Motor Inn (1300 South Main St., 33430; 996-6761) 26 rooms, a/c, TV, no pets, children free with parents, CC. LS SGL/DBL$38; HS SGL/DBL$44.

Big Pine Key
Area Code 305

Rental & Reservation Services

Land and Sea Vacations (6805 Overseas Hwy., Marathon, 33050; 743-6494, 800-327-4836) private rental homes, condominiums and villas.

Reed Rentals (9499 Overseas Hwy., Marathon, 33050; 743-5181, 800-366-5181) rental condominiums and private homes.

□□□

Big Pine Motel (Route 5, 33043, 872-9090) 30 rooms, restaurant, outdoor pool, no pets, room service, a/c, TV, children free with parents, laundry facilities, CC. LS SGL/DBL$45-$60; HS SGL/DBL$60-$80.

Halcyon Beach Motel (Ave. B and Watson Blvd., 33043; 872-2201) 6 rooms, a/c, TV, beach, children free with parents, CC. SGL/DBL$35-$45.

Blue Mountain
Area Code 904

Sea Bluff (Route 2, 32459; 800-336-GULF) 2-bedroom condominiums, outdoor heated pool, laundry facilities, beach, in-room refrigerators, microwaves and coffee makers, a/c, TV, children free with parents, no pets, CC. 2BR$70-$126.

Blue Mountain Villas (Route 2, 32459; 800-336-GULF) 1- and 2-bedroom condominiums, beach, laundry facilities, in-room refrigerators, microwaves and coffee makers, a/c, TV, children free with parents, no pets, CC. 1BR/2BR$55-$145.

The Beacons (Route 2, 32459; 800-336-GULF) 3-bedroom condominiums, beach, laundry facilities, in-room refrigerators, microwaves and coffee makers, a/c, TV, children free with parents, no pets, wheelchair access, CC. 3BR$79-$157.

Boca Grande
Area Code 813

Rental & Reservation Services

Boca Grande Real Estate (430 West 4th St., 33921; 964-0338, 800-881-2622) rental condominiums, apartments and private homes.

□□□

Gasparilla Inn and Cottages (5th St. and Palm Ave., 33921; 964-2201) 140 rooms and 1-bedroom cottages, restaurant, outdoor pool, exercise center, tennis courts, a/c, TV, laundry facilities, wheelchair access, children free with parents, pets OK, CC. SGL/DBL$145-$200, 1BR$248.

Uncle Henry's Marina Resort (5800 Gasparilla Rd., 33921; 964-2300, Fax 964-2098) 18 rooms and 2-bedroom suites, restaurant, outdoor heated pool, a/c, TV, wheelchair access, NS rooms, laundry facilities, no pets, kitchenettes, senior rates, CC. LS SGL/DBL$85-$155; HS SGL/DBL$125-$235.

Boca Raton
Area Code 407

Rental & Reservation Services

H.D.S. Enterprises (148 South Federal Hwy., 33432; 347-8754) rental condominiums, apartments and private homes.

□□□

Best Western University Inn (2700 North Federal Hwy., 33432; 395-5225, Fax 338-9180, 800-528-1234) 90 rooms, restaurant, lounge, free breakfast, outdoor heated pool, sauna, exercise center, fax service, children free with parents, a/c, NS rooms, TV, in-room refrigerators and microwaves, no pets, local transportation, in-room computer hookups, laundry facilities, wheelchair access, meeting facilities for 125, senior rates, CC. LS SGL/DBL$42-$50; HS SGL/DBL$70-$99.

Boca Raton Marriott Crocker Center (5150 Town Center Circle, 33432; 392-4600, Fax 395-8258, 800-962-9786, 800-228-2800) 256 rooms and suites, restaurant, lounge, entertainment, outdoor heated pool, whirlpools, sauna, in-room refrigerators, children free with parents, a/c, TV, wheelchair access, gift shop, NS rooms, no pets, 7,000 square feet of meeting and exhibition space, meeting facilities for 800, senior rates, CC. LS SGL/DBL$130-$140; HS SGL/DBL$70-$185.

Boca Raton Resort and Club (501 East Camino Real, 33421; 395-3000, Fax 391-3183, 800-327-0101) 963 rooms and 1- and 2-bedroom suites, restaurant, lounge, entertainment, indoor and outdoor heated pools, whirlpools, lighted tennis courts, exercise center, Modified American Plan available, children free with parents, no pets, in-room refrigerators and coffee makers, laundry facilities, local transportation, 24-hour room service, senior rates, 29 meeting rooms, 65,000 square feet of meeting and exhibition space, meeting facilities for 1,500, CC. 45 miles from the Miami airport, 20 miles from the Ft. Lauderdale-Hollywood airport. LS SGL/DBL$110-$260; HS SGL/DBL$250-$445.

Courtyard by Marriott (2000 Northwest Executive Center, 33431; 241-7070, Fax 241-7080, 800-331-3131) 152 rooms and suites, restaurant, lounge, free breakfast, outdoor pool, in-room refrigerators, microwaves and coffee makers, VCRs, no pets, complimentary newspaper, children free with parents, kitchenettes, a/c, TV, NS rooms, wheelchair access, meeting facilities, senior rates, CC. SGL/DBL$70-$80; HS SGL/DBL$110-$120.

Days Inn Downtown (2899 North Federal Hwy., 33431; 395-7172, 800-329-7466) 48 rooms, free breakfast, outdoor pool, laundry facilities, children free with parents, no pets, in-room refrigerators, a/c, TV, wheelchair access, NS rooms, senior rates, CC. 20 miles from the Ft. Lauderdale-Hollywood airport, 1 mile from Atlantic beaches, 19 miles from the Palm Beach airport. LS SGL/DBL$42-$55; HS SGL/DBL$70-$100.

Holiday Inn (1950 Glades Rd., 33431; 368-5200, Fax 395-4783, 800-HOLIDAY) 184 rooms, restaurant, lounge, entertainment, outdoor heated pool, exercise center, whirlpools, children free with parents, wheelchair access, a/c, TV, NS rooms, fax service, room service, no pets, laundry service, limousine service, fax service, in-room refrigerators, microwaves and coffee makers, 2,400 square feet of meeting and exhibition space, meeting facilities for 300, senior rates, CC. 2 miles from the regional airport, a 1/2-mile from the shopping mall, 3 miles to Atlantic beaches. LS SGL/DBL$70-$120; HS SGL/DBL$100-$150.

Holiday Inn (8144 Glades Rd., 33431; 482-7070, Fax 482-6076, 800-HOLIDAY) 97 rooms, restaurant, lounge, outdoor pool, exercise center, boutiques, children free with parents, wheelchair access, a/c, TV, NS rooms, fax service, boutiques, room service, no pets, laundry service, meeting facilities for 50, senior rates, CC. 3 miles from the shopping mall, 20 miles from the West Palm Beach and Ft. Lauderdale airports. LS SGL/DBL$60-$70; HS SGL/DBL$100-$105.

Howard Johnson Motor Lodge (80 East Camino Real, 33432; 395-4545, Fax 338-5491, 800-I-GO-HOJO) 53 rooms, restaurant, outdoor pool, children free with parents, wheelchair access, NS rooms, TV, a/c, in-room refrigerators, pets OK, laundry facilities, senior rates, meeting facilities, CC. 23 miles from the Palm Beach airport, 1 mile from the downtown area, 4 blocks from the Town Center Mall and Mizner Park. LS SGL/DBL$46-$68; HS SGL/DBL$110.

Inn at Boca Teeca Country Club (5800 Northwest 2nd Ave., 33487; 994-0400, 800-344-6995) 46 rooms and efficiencies, restaurant, free breakfast, outdoor heated pool, tennis courts, whirlpools, sauna, exercise center, kitchenettes, laundry facilities, no pets, children free with parents, a/c, TV, wheelchair access, NS rooms, senior rates, meeting facilities, CC. LS SGL/DBL$50-$60; HS SGL/DBL$95-$105.

Radisson Bridge Hotel (999 East Camino Real, 33432; 368-9500, Fax 362-0492, 800-327-0130, 800-333-3333) 121 rooms and suites, restaurant, lounge, entertainment, pool, exercise center, in-room refrigerators, microwaves and coffee makers, VCRs, wheelchair access, free parking, NS rooms, TV, a/c, children free with parents, senior rates, CC. SGL/DBL$75-$100, STS$100-$115.

Radisson Suite Hotel (7920 Glades Rd., 33432; 483-3600, Fax 479-2280, 800-333-3333) 201 rooms and 1-bedroom suites, restaurant, free breakfast, lounge, outdoor heated pool, exercise center, whirlpools, in-room refrigerators, microwaves and coffee makers, a/c, TV, wheelchair access, laundry facilities, local transportation, gift shop, pets OK, kitchenettes, NS rooms, senior rates, 3 meeting rooms, CC. LS SGL/DBL$90-$140; HS SGL/DBL$130-$170.

Ramada Inn Hotel (2901 North Federal Hwy., 33431; 395-6850, Fax 368-7964, 800-2-RAMADA) 100 rooms and suites, restaurant, lounge, outdoor pool, wheelchair access, NS rooms, free parking, a/c, TV, children free with parents, room service, kitchenettes, laundry facilities, meeting facilities, senior rates, CC. SGL/DBL$55-$112.

Residence Inn by Marriott (525 Northwest 77th St., 33487; 994-3222, Fax 994-3339, 800-331-3131) 120 rooms and suites, free breakfast, in-room refrigerators, coffee makers and microwaves, laundry facilities, TV, a/c, VCRs, complimentary newspaper, fireplaces, children free with parents, pets OK, NS rooms, wheelchair access, meeting facilities for 40, CC. 18 miles from the Palm Beach airport, 2 miles from Atlantic beaches, 4 miles from Town Center Mall and Mizner Park. SGL/DBL$74-$125.

Sheraton Boca Raton (2000 Northwest 19th St., 33431; 368-5252, 800-325-3535) 193 rooms and suites, restaurant, lounge, entertainment, outdoor heated pool, exercise center, whirlpools, lighted tennis courts, laundry facilities, in-room refrigerators, NS rooms, a/c, room service, room service, TV, children free with parents, wheelchair access, 13 meeting rooms, 4,000 square feet of meeting and exhibitions space, meeting facilities for 600, senior rates, CC. 25 miles from the Palm Beach airport. LS SGL/DBL$50-$89; HS SGL/DBL$80-$130.

Bokeelia

Area Code 813

Beach House Motel (7702 Bocilla Lane, 33922; 283-4303, 800-348-6306) 4 rooms and 1-bedroom apartments, no pets, beach, laundry facilities, a/c, TV, children free with parents, CC. SGL/DBL$50, 1BR$60-$70.

Bonifay

Area Code 904

Best Western Tivoli Inn (2004 South Waukesha St., 32425; 547-4251, 800-528-1234) 56 rooms, free breakfast, outdoor pool, children free with parents, a/c, NS rooms, TV, VCRs, laundry facilities, wheelchair access, pets OK, meeting facilities, senior rates, CC. 1 mile to tennis courts, 9 miles to golf course. SGL/DBL$35-$60.

Econo Lodge (2210 South Waukesha St., 32425; 547-9345, 800-55-ECONO) 64 rooms, children free with parents, no pets, NS rooms, wheelchair access, a/c, TV, senior rates, CC. SGL/DBL$45-$55.

Bonita Springs

Area Code 813

Bonita Beach Resort Motel (26395 Hickory Blvd., 33923; 992-2137, Fax 454-0333) 19 rooms and 2-bedroom condominiums, outdoor pool, tennis courts, kitchenettes, wheelchair access, a/c, TV, laundry facilities, senior rates, CC. SGL/DBL$32-$44, 2BR$59-$89.

Comfort Inn (9800 Bonita Beach Rd., 33923; 992-5001, Fax 992-9283, 800-221-2222) 69 rooms, restaurant, outdoor heated pool, whirlpools, in-room refrigerators, laundry facilities, no pets, a/c, TV, VCRs, children free with parents, NS rooms, wheelchair access, senior rates, CC. 20 miles from the regional airport, 2 miles from Gulf beaches, 10 miles from Safari Jungle and Olde Naples. LS SGL/DBL$45-$55; HS SGL/DBL$85-$95.

Econo Lodge (28090 Quail's Nest Lane, 33932; 948-3366, Fax 947-6789, 800-4-CHOICE) 100 rooms and efficiencies, restaurant, outdoor heated pool, laundry facilities, children free with parents, pets OK, a/c, TV, complimentary newspaper, meeting facilities, senior rates, CC. 25 miles from the regional airport, 5 miles from the Greyhound Race Track. LS SGL/DBL$38-$52; HS SGL/DBL$65-$85.

Mangold's Apartment Motel (27684 Southwest Imperial River Rd., 33932; 992-5230) 10 rooms and 1-bedroom apartments, outdoor heated pool, water view, a/c, TV, wheelchair access, NS rooms, laundry facilities, no pets, senior rates, CC. SGL/DBL$280W-$490W.

Shangri La Natural Hygiene Institute (27850 Old Hwy. 41, 33959; 992-3811) 53 rooms, restaurant, pool, room service, a/c, TV, laundry facilities, no pets, NS rooms, CC. LS SGL/DBL$65-$150; HS SGL/DBL$75-$170.

Boynton Beach

Area Code 407

Ann Marie Motel (911 South Federal Hwy., 33435; 732-9283, Fax 732-9441) 14 rooms, restaurant, outdoor heated pool, kitchenettes, no pets, in-room refrigerators, a/c, TV, senior rates, CC. LS SGL/DBL$35-$45; HS SGL/DBL$56-$68.

Golden Sands Inn (520 South East 21st Ave., 33435; 732-6075) 24 rooms and efficiencies, room service, a/c, TV, in-room refrigerators and microwaves, no pets, children free with parents, laundry facilities, CC. LS SGL/DBL$35-$55; HS SGL/DBL$45-$65.

Holiday Inn Catalina (1601 North Congress Ave., 33436; 737-4600, Fax 734-6523, 800-HOLIDAY) 150 rooms and suites, restaurant, lounge, entertainment, outdoor heated pool, exercise center, whirlpools, children free with parents, wheelchair access, a/c, TV, NS rooms, fax service, no pets, room service, laundry service, 7 meeting rooms, meeting facilities for 400, senior rates, CC. 3 miles from Atlantic beaches, 1/4 mile from the shopping mall, 1.5 miles from the golf course. SGL/DBL$50-$120.

Holiday Inn (480 West Boynton Beach Blvd., 33435; 734-9100, 800-HOLIDAY) 100 rooms and suites, free breakfast, outdoor pool, exercise center, children free with parents, wheelchair access, a/c, in-room computer hookups, free local calls, TV, car rental desk, NS rooms, fax service, room service, in-room refrigerators, no pets, laundry service, meeting facilities for 175, senior rates, CC. 10 miles from the West Palm Beach airport, 1 mile from the shopping mall, 10 miles from the dog track. LS SGL/DBL$46-$56; HS SGL/DBL$70-$80.

Ramada Inn (1935 South Federal Hwy., 33435; 736-5805, Fax 736-5805, 800-2-RAMADA) 150 rooms and suites, restaurant, lounge, outdoor heated pool, lighted tennis courts, exercise center, kitchenettes, wheelchair access, NS rooms, pets OK, a/c, TV, children free with parents, in-room refrigerators and microwaves, room service, laundry facilities, meeting facilities, senior rates, CC. LS SGL/DBL$60-$79; HS SGL/DBL$85-$125.

Shane's Motor Lodge (2607 South Federal Hwy., 33435; 732-4446, Fax 731-0325, 800-782-4446) 21 rooms and efficiencies, restaurant, outdoor pool, a/c, TV, NS rooms, no pets, children free with parents, senior rates, CC. LS SGL/DBL$34-$40; HS SGL/DBL$55-$60.

Bradenton

Area Code 813

Rental & Reservation Services

Century 21 Rentals-A-Paradise, Inc. (3018 Ave. C, 34217; 778-4800, 800-237-2252) rental condominiums and apartments.

□□□

Aqua Resort (4315 Aquatel Rd., 34202; 746-6884) 9 rooms and efficiencies, a/c, TV, no pets, CC. SGL/DBL$17-$26.

Bahia Court (1905 Cortez Road West, 34207; 755-2188) 10 rooms and efficiencies, outdoor pool, children free with parents, a/c, TV, CC. SGL/DBL$35-$41.

Baxter's Motel (3225 14th St. West, 34205; 746-6448) 17 rooms and efficiencies, outdoor pool, a/c, TV, children free with parents, CC. SGL/DBL$22-$40.

Beacon Motel (1800 13th St. West, 34205; 746-8982) 12 rooms and efficiencies, a/c, TV, children stay free with parents, CC. SGL/DBL$75-$110.

Bradenton Inn (2303 1st St. East, 34208; 747-6465, Fax 746-4758) 203 rooms, outdoor heated pool, no pets, children free with parents, in-room computer hookups, laundry facilities, in-room refrigerators, a/c, TV, wheelchair access, NS rooms, senior rates, CC. LS SGL/DBL$35; HS SGL/DBL$45-$60.

Comfort Inn (707 East Manatee Palm Dr., 34208; 800-221-2222) 70 rooms, outdoor pool, whirlpools, no pets, a/c, TV, children free with parents, NS rooms, wheelchair access, senior rates, CC. 7 miles from the downtown area and Gulf beaches, 9 miles from the DeSoto Speedway, 10 miles from the Manatee Civic Center. SGL/DBL$40-$80.

Cortez West Motel (8620 Cortez Road West, 34210; 792-8995) 12 rooms and efficiencies, pets OK, children free with parents, a/c, TV, CC. SGL/DBL$35-$40.

Days Inn (644 67th St. Circle East, 34208; 746-2505) 60 rooms, restaurant, outdoor pool, children free with parents, in-room refrigerators, laundry facilities, a/c, TV, wheelchair access, NS rooms, senior rates, CC. 12 miles from Gulf beaches, 15 miles from the Sun Dome, 25 miles from Busch Gardens. SGL/DBL$28-$65.

Days Inn (3506 1st St. West, 34208; 746-1141, 800-325-2525) 134 rooms, restaurant, outdoor pool, American Plan available, a/c, TV, wheelchair access, children free with parents, NS rooms, no pets, laundry facilities, senior rates, meeting facilities for 100, CC. 7 miles from Gulf beaches and the Ringling Museum, 3 miles from the Manatee Civic Center, 15 miles from the DeSoto Speedway. SGL/DBL$42-$72.

Econo Lodge Airport (6727 14th St. West, 34207; 758-7199, 800-55-ECONO) 79 rooms, outdoor pool, children free with parents, no pets, in-room refrigerators and microwaves, NS rooms, wheelchair access, a/c, TV, meeting facilities, senior rates, CC. 2 miles from the Ringling Museum, 3 miles from the Sarasota airport, 15 miles from Gulf beaches. LS SGL/DBL$33-$48; HS SGL/DBL$60-$75.

Econo Lodge East (607 67th St., 34208; 745-1988, 800-4-CHOICE) 53 rooms, outdoor pool, children free with parents, no pets, NS rooms, wheelchair access, a/c, TV, senior rates, CC. 10 miles from the Civic Center, 9 miles from the DeSota Speedway, 8 miles from downtown. LS SGL/DBL$29-$44; HS SGL/DBL$55-$85.

Florida Bound (2003 West 14th St., 34205; 746-7569) 15 rooms and efficiencies, outdoor pool, children free with parents, a/c, TV, wheelchair access, NS rooms, CC. SGL/DBL$22-$29.

Holiday Inn Riverfront (100 Riverfront Drive West, 34205; 747-3727, 800-HOLIDAY) 153 rooms, restaurant, lounge, entertainment, outdoor heated pool, exercise center, whirlpools, children free with parents, wheelchair access, a/c, TV, NS rooms, fax service, room service, in-room refrigerators and coffee makers, complimentary newspaper, gift shop, no pets, laundry service, meeting facilities, senior rates, CC. 7 miles from the regional airport and Gulf beaches, 1 mile from Tropicana. LS SGL/DBL$59-$89; HS SGL/DBL$90-$110.

Kentucky Colonel Motel (1431 14th St. West, 34205; 747-2122) 31 rooms and efficiencies, outdoor pool, a/c, TV, children free with parents, NS rooms, laundry service, senior rates, CC. SGL/DBL$28.

Motel 6 (660 67th St. Circle East, 34208; 505-891-6161) 121 rooms, outdoor pool, a/c, TV, children free with parents, NS rooms, wheelchair access, pets OK, senior rates, CC. 8 miles from the DeSoto Race Track, 10 miles from the Ringling Museum, 16 miles from Gulf beaches. SGL/DBL$20-$33.

Parkway Motel and Apartments (713 17th St. West, 34207; 722-2712) 12 rooms and apartments, outdoor pool, a/c, TV, no pets, laundry facilities, in-room refrigerators and microwaves, CC. SGL/DBL$25-$45.

Park Inn International (668 67th St. Circle East, 34208; 745-1876, Fax 747-9244, 800-437-PARK) 105 rooms and suites, outdoor pool, a/c, TV, complimentary newspaper, wheelchair access, NS rooms, VCRs, senior rates, CC. 15 miles from Gulf beaches and DeSoto Speedway, 15 miles from the Sarasota airport. SGL/DBL$40-$65.

Park Inn Club and Breakfast (4450 47th St., 34210; 795-4633, Fax 795-0808) 100 rooms and 2-bedroom suites, restaurant, free breakfast, outdoor heated pool, whirlpools, a/c, TV, complimentary newspaper, wheelchair access, in-room refrigerators, NS rooms, senior rates, CC. 7 miles from the Sarasota airport, 4 miles from Gulf beaches and the Civic Center, 9 miles from the Ringling Museum. LS SGL/DBL$52-$63; HS SGL/DBL$80-$97.

Pointe Pleasant (1717 1st Ave. West, 34205; 747-3511) 2 rooms, free breakfast, no pets, a/c, NS, CC. SGL/DBL$35-$45.

Shorewalk Vacation Villas (4601 46th Ct., 34210; 794-9800, Fax 795-9800) 255, 2-bedroom condominiums and villas, outdoor heated pool, lighted tennis courts, whirlpools, children free with parents, a/c, TV, wheelchair access, NS rooms, laundry facilities, senior rates, CC. 2BR$500W-$785W.

Thrifty Lodge Motel (6516 14th St. West, 34207; 756-6656) 49 rooms, outdoor pool, kitchenettes, children free with parents, pets OK, in-room refrigerators and microwaves, a/c, TV, NS rooms, laundry facilities, senior rates, CC. LS SGL/DBL$30-$59; HS SGL/DBL$33-$66.

Bradenton Beach
Area Code 813

Anna Maria Island Club (2600 Gulf Drive North, 34217; 792-8933, 800-237-2252) 21 2-bedroom condominiums, outdoor pool, beach, a/c, TV, children free with parents, laundry facilities, wheelchair access, pets OK. 2BR$650W-$850W.

Bayview Condominiums (109 9th St. South, 34217; 778-4800, 800-237-2252) 8 2-bedroom condominiums, outdoor pool, a/c, TV, wheelchair access, children free with parents, no pets, laundry service, CC. 2BR$550W-$750W.

Baywatch Condominiums (1301 Bay Dr., 34217; 778-4800, 800-237-2252) 16, 1- and 2-bedroom condominiums, outdoor pool, a/c, TV, laundry facilities, wheelchair access, children free with parents, no pets, CC. 2BR$475W-$675W.

Beach House Resort (1000 Gulf Drive North, 34217; 778-1000) 9 rooms and efficiencies, a/c, TV, wheelchair access, children free with parents, no pets, laundry facilities, CC. SGL/DBL$35-$75.

Bridgeport Condominiums (501 Gulf Drive North, 34217; 778-4800, 800-237-2252) 5 1- and 2-bedroom condominiums, outdoor pool, laundry facilities, children free with parents, no pets, a/c, TV, wheelchair access, CC. 1BR$475W, 2BR$535W.

Catalina Beach Resort (1325 Gulf Drive North, 34217; 778-6611, Fax 778-6748) 34 rooms and 2-bedroom suites, restaurant, outdoor heated pool, kitchenettes, no pets, children free with parents, laundry facilities, beach, a/c, TV, water view, CC. LS SGL/DBL$315W-$490W; HS SGL/DBL$430W-$680W.

Coquina Beach Club (1906 Gulf Dr., 34217; 778-4800, 800-237-2252) 6 2-bedroom condominiums, outdoor pool, a/c, TV, laundry facilities, wheelchair access, kitchenettes, children free with parents, no pets, CC. 2BR$395W.

Gulf Pride (2201 Gulf Dr., 34217; 778-7900) 14 rooms and efficiencies, outdoor pool, a/c, TV, wheelchair access, no pets, children free with parents, senior rates, CC. SGL/DBL$30-$60.

Gulf Watch Condominiums (601 Gulf Drive North, 34217; 778-4800, 800-237-2252) 18 condominiums, outdoor pool, a/c, TV, wheelchair access, children free with parents, no pets, senior rates, CC. SGL/DBL$525W.

La Costa (1800 Gulf Dr., 34217; 778-4800, 800-237-2252) 40 1- and 2-bedroom condominiums, outdoor pool, beach, tennis courts, laundry facilities, children free with parents, in-room refrigerators and microwaves, a/c, TV, wheelchair access, no pets, CC. 2BR$625W-$825W.

Pelican Cove Resort (901 Gulf Drive South, 34217; 778-4800, 800-237-2252) 16 2-bedroom condominiums, outdoor pool, a/c, in-room refrigerators and microwaves, laundry facilities, children free with parents, TV, wheelchair access, no pets, CC. 2BR$550W.

Runaway Bay Condominiums (1801 Gulf Drive North, 34217; 778-0000, 800-346-7340) 186 1-, 2-, and 3-bedroom condominiums, outdoor pool, sauna, tennis courts, wheelchair access, a/c, TV, no pets, children free with parents, CC. 1BR/2BR/3BR$455W-$765W.

Silver Surf Motel (1301 Gulf Dr., 34217; 778-6626, Fax 778-4308, 800-441-SURF) 50 rooms and efficiencies, restaurant, outdoor heated pool, a/c, TV, no pets, NS rooms, wheelchair access, beach, in-room refrigerators, CC. SGL/DBL$65-$95.

Sunset Terrace Condominiums (2316 Gulf Dive, 34217; 778-4800, 800-237-2252) 14 1- and 2-bedroom condominiums, outdoor pool, pets OK, a/c, TV, wheelchair access, laundry facilities, children free with parents, CC. 1BR/2BR$95-$450W.

Sunset Villas Condominiums (1001 Gulf Dr., 34217; 778-4800, 800-237-2252) 15 2-bedroom condominiums, outdoor pool, laundry facilities, kitchenettes, a/c, TV, no pets, children free with parents, CC. 2BR$625W.

Thrifty Lodge Motel (1509 60th Ave. West, 34217; 756-6656) 49 rooms and efficiencies, outdoor pool, a/c, TV, children free with parents, in-room refrigerators and microwaves, senior rates, CC. SGL/DBL$35-$54.

Tropic Isle Motel (2103 Gulf Drive North, 34217; 778-1237) 10 rooms and efficiencies, outdoor pool, a/c, TV, children free with parents, CC. SGL/DBL$29-$60.

Via Roma Beach Resort (2408 Gulf Drive North, 34217; 778-6691) 28 efficiencies and condominiums, outdoor pool, a/c, TV, CC. SGL/DBL$45-$130.

Brandon

Area Code 813

Brandon Motor Lodge (906 East Brandon Blvd., 33511; 689-1261, Fax 685-0975) 35 rooms, lounge, outdoor pool, laundry facilities, a/c, TV, pets OK, children free with parents, in-room refrigerators and microwaves, wheelchair access, NS rooms, senior rates, CC. SGL/DBL$30-$48.

Brooksville

Area Code 904

Days Inn (31015 Cortez Blvd., 34602; 796-9486, Fax 796-1615, 800-325-2525) 120 rooms, restaurant, lounge, free breakfast, outdoor pool, no pets, a/c, TV, wheelchair access, NS rooms, laundry facilities, children free with parents, senior rates, CC. 24 miles from Weeki Wachee. SGL/DBL$30-$55.

Holiday Inn (30307 Cortez Blvd., 34602; 796-9481, Fax 799-7595, 800-HOLIDAY) 122 rooms, restaurant, lounge, outdoor pool, lighted tennis courts, in-room refrigerators and microwaves, children free with parents, gift shop, wheelchair access, a/c, TV, NS rooms, fax service, room service, pets OK, laundry facilities, meeting facilities for 100, senior rates, CC. 1 block from the Croom Motorcross Park, 18 miles from the golf course, 10 miles from the Christmas House. SGL/DBL$65-$70.

Bushnell

Area Code 904

Best Western Guest House (Bushnell 33513; 793-5010, Fax 793-1310, 800-528-1234) 48 rooms, outdoor pool, children free with parents, a/c, NS rooms, TV, laundry facilities, in-room refrigerators, wheelchair access, gift shop, pets OK, meeting facilities, senior rates, CC. LS SGL/DBL$36-$48; HS SGL/DBL$36-$55.

Cypress House Bed and Breakfast (Bushnell 33513; 568-0909) 2 rooms, free breakfast, TV, a/c, VCRs, children free with parents, NS rooms, no pets, CC. SGL/DBL$40-$50.

Callahan
Area Code 904

Friendship Inn (Route 23, 32011; 879-3451, 800-424-4777) 31 rooms, restaurant, outdoor pool, exercise center, a/c, TV, NS rooms, no pets, children free with parents, wheelchair access, senior rates, CC. 18 miles from the Osborne Convention Center, 12 miles from FAA Center, 25 miles from Fernandina Beach. SGL/DBL$33-$36.

Cape Canaveral
Area Code 407

Cape Winds Resort (7400 Ridgewood Ave., 32920; 799-2676, 800-248-1030) 70 1- and 2-bedroom efficiencies, outdoor pool, a/c, TV, in-room refrigerators, microwaves and coffee makers, no pets, children free with parents, laundry facilities. CC 1BR$115, 2BR$140.

Radisson Resort Hotel (8701 Astronaut Blvd., 32920; 784-0000, Fax 783-3070, 800-333-3333) 200 rooms and suites, restaurant, lounge, entertainment, outdoor heated pool, exercise center, whirlpools, lighted tennis courts, in-room refrigerators, microwaves and coffee makers, children free with parents, VCRs, wheelchair access, NS rooms, TV, a/c, no pets, laundry facilities, room service, senior rates, CC. LS SGL/DBL$60-$75; HS SGL/DBL$60-$125.

Royal Mansion Resort (8600 Ridgewood Ave., 32920; 784-8484, Fax 799-2907, 800-346-7222) 106, 1- and 2-bedroom condos and villas, outdoor pool, beach, pets OK, children free with parents, a/c, TV, laundry facilities, wheelchair access, in-room refrigerators, microwaves and coffee makers, CC. 1BR$100-$130, 2BR$160-$205.

Cape Coral
Area Code 813

Cape Coral Golf and Tennis Resort (4003 Palm Tree Blvd., 33904; 542-3191, Fax 542-4694, 800-648-1475) 100 rooms and suites, restaurant, lounge, entertainment, outdoor pool, tennis courts, golf, NS rooms, a/c, TV, children free with parents, in-room refrigerators, Modified American Plan available, CC. LS SGL/DBL$60-$70; HS SGL/DBL$105-$120.

Casa Loma Motel (3608 Del Prado Blvd., 33904; 549-6000) 47 efficiencies, outdoor pool, laundry facilities, a/c, TV, children free with parents, CC. LS SGL/DBL$33-$38; HS SGL/DBL$65-$75.

Del Prado Inn (1502 Miramar, 33904; 542-3151, 800-231-6818) 125 rooms, restaurant, lounge, entertainment, outdoor pool, in-room refrigerators, NS rooms, pets OK, a/c, TV, children free with parents, wheelchair access, senior rates, CC. SGL/DBL$60-$75.

Quality Inn Nautilus (1538 Cape Coral Pkwy., 33904; 542-2121, 800-221-2222) 146 rooms and suites, restaurant, free breakfast, lounge, entertainment, pool, exercise center, children free with parents, a/c, TV, wheelchair access, room service, laundry service, pets OK, NS rooms, meeting facilities, senior rates, CC. 15 miles from the regional airport, 7 miles from the Thomas Edison home, 10 miles from Captiva Island. LS SGL/DBL$44-$61; HS SGL/DBL$45-$68.

Rose Wind Motel (4628 Santa Barbara Blvd., 33904; 542-0465) 17 rooms and 1- and 2-bedroom apartments, outdoor pool, kitchenettes, in-room refrigerators, a/c, TV, no pets, CC. SGL/DBL$40-$80.

Cape Haze

Area Code 813

Palm Island Resort (7092 Placida Rd., 33946; 697-4800, Fax 697-0696) 180 rooms and 1- , 2- , and 3-bedroom suites, restaurant, lounge, heated pool, whirlpools, tennis courts, NS rooms, gift shop, a/c, TV, VCRs, no pets, kitchenettes, meeting facilities, CC. LS SGL/DBL$560W-$1,355W; HS SGL/DBL$825W-$2,395W.

Captiva
Area Code 813

Rental & Reservation Services

The Vacation Shoppe (11595 Kelly Rd., Fort Myers 33908; 454-1400) rental condominiums, apartments and townhouses.

□□□

South Seas Plantation (South Seas Plantation Rd., 33924; 472-5111, Fax 472-7541, 800-237-3102, 800-282-3402 in Florida) 620 rooms and suites, restaurant, lounge, entertainment, indoor and outdoor heated pools, whirlpools, golf, lighted tennis courts, kitchenettes, in-room refrigerators, children free with parents, local transportation, boutiques, gift shop, barber and beauty shop, a/c, TV, wheelchair access, NS rooms, no pets, laundry facilities, airport transportation, meeting facilities for 650, senior rates, CC. 30 miles from the Ft. Myers airport. LS SGL/DBL$60-$145.

Tween Waters Inn (Sanibel Captiva Rd., 33924; 472-5161, Fax 472-0249, 800-223-5865, 800-282-7560) 126 rooms and efficiencies, restaurant, lounge, entertainment, outdoor pool, tennis courts, beach, pets OK, a/c, TV, NS rooms, children free with parents, laundry facilities, wheelchair access, CC. LS SGL/DBL$85-$220.

Carrabelle & Carrabelle Beach
Area Code 904

The Moorings (1000 Hwy. 98, 32322; 697-2800) 21 rooms, outdoor pool, laundry facilities, a/c, TV, kitchenettes, children free with parents, pets OK, CC. SGL/DBL$50-$55.

Cassadaga
Area Code 904

Cassadaga Hotel (355 Cassadaga Rd., 32706; 228-2323) 30 rooms and suites, restaurant, children free with parents, a/c, TV, wheelchair access, CC. SGL/DBL$50-$55, STS$85.

Cedar Key
Area Code 904

Rental & Reservation Services

Proctor and Associates Rentals (543-5500, 800-729-0297) rental condominiums and private homes.

Old Fenmore Mill Rentals (543-6163, 800-545-8810) rental rooms and condominiums.

□□□

Cedar Cove Inn (Cedar Key 32625; 543-5332, 800-366-5312) 1- and 2-bedroom efficiencies, a/c, TV, children free with parents, no pets, NS rooms, laundry facilities, kitchenettes, CC. 1BR/2BR$75-$96.

Dockside Motel (11 Dock St., 32625; 543-5432) 10 rooms, children free with parents, water view, pets OK, a/c, TV, CC. SGL/DBL$45-$55.

The Island Hotel (2nd and B Sts., 32625; 543-5111) 10 rooms, restaurant, free breakfast, lounge, a/c, TV, NS, no pets, CC. SGL/DBL$65-$75.

The Island Place (1st and C Sts., 32625; 543-5307) 30 1- and 2-bedroom condominiums, outdoor pool, sauna, hot tubs, a/c, TV, laundry facilities, in-room refrigerators, children free with parents, no pets, CC. 1BR/2BR$75-$130.

Mermaid's Landing Waterfront Cottages (Cedar Key 32625; 543-6163) 1-bedroom cottages, TV, a/c, kitchenettes, laundry facilities, CC. 1BR$45-$60.

Park Place Motel (Cedar Key 32625; 543-5737) 34 rooms and efficiencies, a/c, children free with parents, TV, pets OK, senior rates, CC. SGL/DBL$65-$80.

Chattahoochee
Area Code 904

Chattahoochee Inn (516 West Washington St., 32324; 663-4026) 23 rooms, a/c, TV, children free with parents, no pets, CC. SGL/DBL$22-$30.

Morgan Motel (East Hwy. 90, 32324; 663-4336) 22 rooms, outdoor pool, a/c, TV, children free with parents, CC. SGL$25, DBL$30.

Chiefland
Area Code 904

Best Western Inn (1125 North Young Blvd., 32626; 493-0663, 800-528-1234) 48 rooms, outdoor pool, children free with parents, a/c, NS rooms, TV, laundry facilities, wheelchair access, no pets, meeting facilities, senior rates, CC. A 1/2-hour from mall, 5 miles from golf course, SGL/DBL$40-$60.

Chipley
Area Code 813

Days Inn (Chipley 32428; 638-7335, Fax 638-2285, 800-325-2525) 32 rooms, a/c, TV, wheelchair access, NS rooms, no pets, laundry facilities, children free with parents, senior rates, CC. 15 miles from the factory outlet mall, 2 miles from Falling Water Park, 20 miles from Florida Caverns State Park. SGL/DBL$40-$48.

Clearwater
Area Code 813

American Inns (16405 Hwy. 19 North, 34624; 535-0505, 800-727-4545) 50 rooms and efficiencies, outdoor heated pool, a/c, no pets, TV, senior rates, CC. SGL/DBL$28-$58.

Bay Queen Motel (1925 Edgewater Dr., 34615; 441-3295) 18 rooms, restaurant, outdoor pool, children free with parents, in-room refrigerators, kitchenettes, no pets, a/c, TV, CC. SGL/DBL$35-$70.

The Belleview Mido (25 Belleview Blvd., 34616; 442-6171, Fax 441-4173, 800-237-8947, 800-282-8072 in Florida) 292 rooms and suites, restaurant, lounge, entertainment, heated pool, sauna, tennis courts, exercise center, whirlpools, a/c, TV, children free with parents, in-room refrigerators, VCRs, Modified American and American Plans available, 11 meeting rooms, senior rates, no pets, CC. LS SGL/DBL$100-$240; HS SGL/DBL$125-$345.

Best Western Clearwater Central (21338 Hwy. 19 North, 34625; 799-1565, Fax 797-6801, 800-528-1234) 150 rooms, outdoor heated pool, whirlpools, spa, tennis courts, local transportation, children free with parents, a/c, NS rooms, TV, laundry facilities, wheelchair access, no pets, in-room refrigerators, meeting facilities, senior rates, CC. 2 blocks from shopping mall. SGL/DBL$45-$70.

Best Western Le Parc Inn (11333 Hwy. 19 North, 34624; 572-4929, 800-528-1234) 64 rooms, outdoor pool, whirlpools, sauna, children free with parents, a/c, NS rooms, TV, laundry facilities, wheelchair access, no pets, kitchenettes, meeting facilities, senior rates, CC. 5 miles from the St. Petersburg-Clearwater airport, 20 miles from Tampa, 2 miles from shopping mall, 8 miles from Gulf beaches. SGL/DBL$35-$70.

Budget Inn (1471 Court St., 34616; 446-8586) 26 rooms, outdoor pool, a/c, TV, NS rooms, no pets, children free with parents, CC. LS SGL/DBL$20-$32; HS SGL/DBL$35-$55.

Butterfly Motel (12500 Hwy. 19 North, 34624; 536-1500) 20 rooms and efficiencies, outdoor pool, a/c, TV, CC. SGL/DBL$20-$29.

Clearwater Bay Motel (1824 North Fort Harrison Ave., 34616; 446-0681) 20 rooms and efficiencies, outdoor pool, a/c, TV, children free with parents, CC. SGL/DBL$25-$50.

Comfort Inn (3580 Ulmerton Rd., 34622; 573-1171, Fax 573-1171, 800-221-2222) 120 rooms, outdoor heated pool, whirlpools, exercise center, local transportation, a/c, TV, children free with parents, NS rooms, no pets, wheelchair access, senior rates, CC. 3 miles from Gulf beaches, 6 miles from Tampa. LS SGL/DBL$50-$56; HS SGL/DBL$65-$80.

Comfort Inn (27988 Hwy. 19, 34621; 796-0135, Fax 796-7597, 800-221-2222) 72 rooms, outdoor heated pool, whirlpools, kitchenettes, children free with parents, no pets, fax service, a/c, in-room refrigerators, TV, meeting facilities, senior rates, CC. 16 miles from the St. Petersburg-Clearwater airport, 3 miles from Gulf beaches. SGL/DBL$35-$75.

Courtyard by Marriott (3131 Ulmerton Rd., 34622; 321-2211, Fax 572-6991, 800-331-3131) 149 rooms and suites, free breakfast, restaurant, lounge, outdoor heated pool, whirlpools, exercise center, in-room refrigerators, microwaves and coffee makers, a/c, VCRs, no pets, complimentary newspaper, children free with parents, kitchenettes, TV, NS rooms, wheelchair access, meeting facilities, senior rates, CC. SGL/DBL$75-$95.

Days Inn (2940 Gulf To Bay Blvd., 34619; 799-0100, Fax 726-6569, 800-329-7466) 91 rooms and 2-bedroom suites, free breakfast, outdoor heated pool, whirlpools, sauna, a/c, TV, wheelchair access, NS rooms, no pets, laundry facilities, children free with parents, kitchenettes, in-room computer hookups, senior rates, CC. 5 miles from the St. Petersburg-Clearwater airport, 7 miles from the Tampa airport, 4 miles to Gulf beaches. LS SGL/DBL$40-$57; HS SGL/DBL$63-$80.

Days Inn (3910 Ulmerton Rd., 34622; 573-3334, Fax 573-3334, 800-325-2525) 118 rooms, free breakfast, outdoor heated pool, a/c, airport transportation, children free with parents, TV, in-room refrigerators, microwaves and coffee makers, wheelchair access, NS rooms, airport transportation, no pets, laundry facilities, senior rates, CC. 17 miles from Busch Gardens, a 1/2-mile from the St. Petersburg-Clearwater airport, 1 mile from the shopping center. SGL/DBL$32-$62; HS SGL/DBL$79-$84.

Econo Lodge Central (21252 Hwy. 19 North, 34625; 799-1569, 800-4-CHOICE) 121 rooms, outdoor pool, children free with parents, no pets, NS rooms, wheelchair access, a/c, TV, meeting facilities, senior rates, CC. 5 miles from Gulf beaches and the St. Petersburg-Clearwater airport, SGL/DBL$44-$65.

Edgewater Inn (1919 Edgewater Dr., 34615; 446-7858) 22 rooms and efficiencies, restaurant, outdoor pool, in-room refrigerators, a/c, TV, children free with parents, no pets, NS rooms, CC. SGL/DBL$40-$65.

Hampton Inn (3655 Hospitality Lane, 34622; 577-9200, Fax 572-8931, 800-HAMPTON) 116 rooms, free breakfast, outdoor pool, exercise center, whirlpools, sauna, in-room refrigerators and microwaves, children free with parents, NS rooms, wheelchair access, in-room computer hookups, fax service, TV, a/c, free local calls, no pets, meeting facilities, senior rates, CC. 12 miles from the Tampa airport, 3 miles from the dog track, 9 miles from Gulf beaches. SGL/DBL$50-$75.

Holiday Inn Clearwater Airport (3535 Ulmerton Rd., 34622; 577-9100, Fax 573-5022, 800-HOLIDAY) 174 rooms, restaurant, lounge, outdoor pool, exercise center, lighted tennis courts, in-room refrigerators, microwaves and coffee makers, gift shop, children free with parents, wheelchair access, a/c, TV, car rental desk, NS rooms, fax service, room service, no pets, laundry service, 5 meeting rooms, meeting facilities for 300, senior rates, CC. 9 miles from Gulf beaches, 2 miles from the dog track, 8 miles from the Suncoast Dome. SGL/DBL$65-$115.

Holiday Inn (21030 Hwy. 19 North, 34625; 797-8173, Fax 791-7759, 800-HOLIDAY) 193 rooms, restaurant, lounge, outdoor heated pool, exercise center, children free with parents, wheelchair access, a/c, TV, NS rooms, fax service, room service, laundry service, 5 meeting rooms, meeting facilities for 200, no pets, senior rates, CC. A 1/2-mile from Ruth Eckerd Hall, 1 block from the shopping mall, 5 miles from the St. Petersburg-Clearwater airport. SGL/DBL$55-$73.

Holiday Inn (13625 Icot Blvd., 34620; 836-7275, Fax 530-3053, 800-HOLIDAY) 128 rooms, restaurant, lounge, outdoor heated pool, exercise center, whirlpools, in-room computer hookups, pets OK, children free with parents, wheelchair access, a/c, TV, NS rooms, fax service, room service, laundry service, meeting facilities for 25, senior rates, CC. 15 miles from Gulf beaches, 12 miles from the Salvador Dali museum. LS SGL/DBL$53-$58; HS SGL/DBL$70-$79.

Howard Johnson (20788 Hwy. 19 South, 34625; 797-5021, 800-I-GO-HOJO) 86 rooms, outdoor pool, children free with parents, wheelchair access, NS rooms, TV, a/c, no pets, laundry facilities, senior rates, meeting facilities, CC. SGL/DBL$45-$95.

Howard Johnson (20967 Hwy. 19, 34625; 799-1181, 800-I-GO-HOJO) 114 rooms, outdoor heated pool, restaurant, lounge, entertainment, wheelchair access, NS rooms, children free with parents, a/c, VCRs, pets OK, laundry facilities, TV, in-room refrigerators, senior rates, meeting facilities for 400, CC. 5 miles from the Toronto Blue Jays Training Camp, 20 miles from Busch Gardens, 1 block from the Clearwater Mall, 12 miles from the Tampa airport. SGL/DBL$45-$75.

La Quinta Inn Airport (3301 Ulmerton Rd., 34622; 572-7222, Fax 572-0076, 800-531-5900) 118 rooms, free breakfast, outdoor heated pool, sauna, whirlpools, exercise center, airport transportation, in-room refrigerators, pets OK, complimentary newspaper, free local calls, fax service, laundry service, NS rooms, wheelchair access, TV, a/c, meeting facilities, senior rates, CC. 1 mile from the

St. Petersburg-Clearwater airport, 15 miles from the Tampa airport. LS SGL/DBL$45-$55; HS SGL/DBL$60-$70.

Motel Ann (1630 Gulf to Bay Blvd., 34615; 442-4392) 26 rooms and efficiencies, outdoor pool, a/c, TV, children free with parents, laundry facilities, CC. LS SGL/DBL$25-$40; HS SGL/DBL$40-$55.

New Ranch Motel (2275 Gulf to Bay Blvd., 34625; 799-0512, 800-441-6707) 32 rooms, outdoor pool, a/c, TV, NS rooms, wheelchair access, children free with parents, CC. LS SGL/DBL$22-$41; HS SGL/DBL$25-$50.

Ramada Inn Countryside (26508 Hwy. 19 North, 34621; 796-1234, Fax 796-0452, 800-228-2828) 129 rooms and suites, restaurant, lounge, outdoor pool, whirlpools, lighted tennis courts, jacuzzi, no pets, wheelchair access, local transportation, NS rooms, kitchenettes, a/c, TV, children free with parents, room service, laundry facilities, meeting facilities, senior rates, CC. 1 block from the shopping mall, 20 miles from the Tampa airport, 10 miles from the Gulf beaches, 10 miles from the Toronto Blue Jays Training Camp. SGL/DBL$56-$100.

Royal Palm Motel (1250 Cleveland St., 34615; 446-9575) 19 rooms and efficiencies, restaurant, outdoor pool, a/c, TV, children free with parents, NS rooms, wheelchair access, CC. LS SGL/DBL$22-$48.

Suncoast Inn (20162 Hwy. 19 North, 34615; 799-6133) 51 rooms and efficiencies, restaurant, outdoor pool, children free with parents, NS rooms, a/c, TV, CC. LS SGL/DBL$38; HS SGL/DBL$48-$58.

Super 8 Motel (13260 34th St., 34622; 572-8881, 800-800-8000) 81 rooms, restaurant, entertainment, outdoor heated pool, pets OK, children free with parents, free local calls, a/c, TV, NS rooms, wheelchair access, meeting facilities, senior rates, CC. 10 miles from Gulf beaches, 2 miles from the St. Petersburg-Clearwater airport, 20 miles from Busch Gardens. LS SGL/DBL$36-$55; HS SGL/DBL$56-$73.

TraveLodge (22950 Hwy. 19 North, 34615; 799-2678, Fax 726-7263, 800-578-7878) 120 rooms, wheelchair access, free newspaper, laundry service, TV, a/c, free local calls, fax service, NS rooms, in-room refrigerators and microwaves, children free with parents, no pets, meeting facilities, senior rates, CC. SGL/DBL$35-$55.

TraveLodge Downtown (711 Cleveland St., 34619; 446-9183, Fax 446-9185, 800-578-7878) 48 rooms, restaurant, lounge, free breakfast, outdoor heated pool, wheelchair access, complimentary newspaper, laundry service, TV, a/c, free local calls, fax service, NS rooms, local transportation, children free with parents, no pets, meeting facilities, senior rates, CC. 5 miles from Gulf beaches, 16 miles from the Tarpon Springs sponge docks, 40 miles from Busch Gardens. LS SGL/DBL$40-$50; HS SGL/DBL$55-$70.

Clearwater Beach

Area Code 813

Adam's Mark Caribbean Gulf Resort (430 South Gulfview Blvd., 34630; 443-5714, Fax 442-8389, 800-444-ADAM) 207 rooms and suites, restaurant, lounge, entertainment, outdoor heated pool, whirlpools, children free with parents, airport transportation, laundry facilities, beach, a/c, TV, gift shop, game room, NS rooms, in-room refrigerators, senior rates, 10 meeting rooms, 4,000 square feet of meeting and exhibition space, 6 meeting rooms, CC. 26 miles from the Tampa airport. LS SGL/DBL$100-$155; HS SGL/DBL$120-$200.

Aegean Sands Resort Motel (421 South Gulfview Blvd., 34630; 447-3464, 800-94-AEGEAN) 80 rooms, efficiencies and suites, outdoor heated pool, a/c, TV, NS rooms, beach, in-room refrigerators, pets OK, laundry facilities, senior rates, CC. 25 miles from the Tampa airport. SGL/DBL$55-$130.

Albatros Motel and Efficiency Apartments (346 Hamden Dr., 34630; 442-9420) 12 rooms and efficiencies, outdoor pool, a/c, TV, no pets, children free with parents, CC. SGL/DBL$35-$85.

Americana Gulf Resort (325 South Gulfview Blvd., 34630; 461-7695, Fax 442-9983, 800-462-1213) 60 rooms and efficiencies, outdoor heated pool, no pets, a/c, TV, wheelchair access, NS rooms, senior rates, CC. SGL/DBL$45-$125.

Ann's Edgewater Apartment Motel (441 East Shore Dr., 34630; 446-3387) 16 apartments, outdoor pool, kitchenettes, children free with parents, a/c, TV, no pets, in-room refrigerators and coffee makers, laundry facilities, CC. SGL/DBL$155W-$280W.

Bel Crest Beach Resort (706 Bayview Blvd., 34630; 442-4923, Fax 442-7455, 800-521-0045) 18 rooms and 2-bedroom suites, outdoor heated pool, no pets, laundry facilities, a/c, TV, water view, kitchenettes, CC. 11 miles from the St. Petersburg airport. LS SGL/DBL$45-$90; HS SGL/DBL$80-$140.

Best Western Sea Stone Resort (445 Hamden Dr., 34630; 441-1722, Fax 449-1580, 800-528-1234, 800-444-1919) 108 rooms and 1-bedroom suites, restaurant, lounge, entertainment, outdoor heated pool, children free with parents, a/c, NS rooms, VCRs, TV, laundry facilities, beach, in-room refrigerators, airport transportation, kitchenettes, wheelchair access, pets OK, meeting facilities, senior rates, CC. LS SGL/DBL$60-$115; HS SGL/DBL$100-$188.

Best Western Sea Wake Inn (691 South Gulfview Blvd., 34630; 443-7652, Fax 449-1580, 800-528-1234, 800-444-1919) 110 rooms, restaurant, lounge, entertainment, outdoor pool, children free with parents, a/c, NS rooms, TV, laundry facilities, beach, airport transportation, in-room refrigerators, wheelchair access, gift shop, no pets, meeting facilities, senior rates, CC. SGL/DBL$70-$115.

Blue Jay Apartment Motel (150 Brightwater Dr., 34630; 446-0356) 18 rooms, outdoor heated pool, a/c, TV, laundry facilities, kitchenettes, NS rooms, no pets, children free with parents, CC. LS SGL/DBL$230W-$260W; HS SGL/DBL$265W-$290W.

Casa Rosa Motel (200 Brightwater Dr., 34630; 446- 9775, 800-537-6235) 12 efficiencies and 1-bedroom apartments, outdoor pool, a/c, TV, in-room refrigerators and coffee makers, no pets, children free with parents, CC. EFF$220-$240, 1BR$295.

Clearwater Beach Hotel (500 Mandalay Ave., 34630; 441-2425, Fax 449-2083, 800-292-2295, 800-282-3566 in Florida) 210 rooms, efficiencies and 1-bedroom suites, restaurant, outdoor heated pool, whirlpools, lighted tennis courts, gift shop, a/c, TV, NS rooms, senior rates, CC. SGL/DBL$100-$150.

Coral Resort Condo Motel (483 East Shore Dr., 34630; 446-3711) 12 1-bedroom apartments, outdoor pool, a/c, TV, laundry facilities, in-room refrigerators, no pets, children free with parents, CC. 1BR$200W-$350W.

Days Inn (60 West Clearwater Beach, 34630; 447-8444, Fax 446-2370, 800-325-2525) 70 rooms, restaurant, lounge, free breakfast, outdoor pool, a/c, TV, wheelchair access, NS rooms, laundry facilities, children free with parents, senior rates, CC. 20 miles from the Tampa airport and Busch Gardens. SGL/DBL$75-$135.

Dolphin Watch Motel (607 Bay Esplanade, 34630; 449-9039) 6 rooms and efficiencies, outdoor pool, a/c, TV, children free with parents, NS rooms, no pets, senior rates, CC. SGL/DBL$279W-$400W.

Dunes Motel (514 South Gulfview Blvd., 34630; 441-4939, 800-829-0490) 36 efficiencies, 1- , 2- , and 3-bedroom apartments, outdoor pool, children free with parents, in-room refrigerators, no pets, a/c, TV, NS rooms, wheelchair access, laundry facilities, senior rates, CC. EFF$56, 1BR$59, 2BR$69, 3BR$79.

Ebb Tide Apartments (621 Bay Esplanade, 34630; 441-4421) 18 rooms and apartments, outdoor heated pool, no pets, a/c, TV, NS rooms, kitchenettes, children free with parents, senior rates, CC. SGL/DBL$55-$88.

Econo Lodge Beachfront Resort (625 South Gulfview Blvd., 34630; 446-3400, Fax 446-4615, 800-4-CHOICE) 64 rooms, outdoor heated pool, exercise center, whirlpools, local transportation, children free with parents, no pets, NS rooms, wheelchair access, game room, a/c, VCRs, TV, beach, senior rates, CC. SGL/DBL$50-$115.

Flamingo Beachfront Suite (450 North Gulfview Blvd., 34630; 441-8019, Fax 446-6599, 800-821-8019) 35 suites, outdoor pool, a/c, TV, in-room refrigerators and microwaves, children free with parents, no pets, laundry facilities, senior rates, CC. LS SGL/DBL$30-$85; HS SGL/DBL$55-$85.

Four Hundred Resort Apartments (401 South Gulfview Blvd., 34630; 446-8305, Fax 442-9983, USA 800-462-1213) 54 rooms and suites, outdoor heated pool, children free with parents, airport transportation, a/c, TV, kitchenettes, no pets, laundry facilities, in-room refrigerators and microwaves, senior rates, CC. LS SGL/DBL$45-$60; HS SGL/DBL$85-$108.

Glass House Apartment Motel (229 South Gulfview Blvd., 34630; 446-9998) 47 rooms and efficiencies, outdoor pool, a/c, TV, no pets, laundry facilities, CC. SGL/DBL$25-$75.

Gulf Beach Motel (419 Coronado Dr., 34630; 447-3236) 47 rooms, outdoor pool, a/c, TV, no pets, CC. LS SGL/DBL$29-$47; HS SGL/DBL$45-$63.

The Haddon House Inn (14 Idlewild St., 34630; 461-2914) 1-bedroom apartments, a/c, TV, laundry facilities, no pets, children free with parents. 1BR$420W-$490W.

Hilton Hotel (715 South Gulfview Blvd., 34630; 447-9566, Fax 449-2083, 800-HILTONS, 800-248-1831, 800-282-3566 in Florida) 207 rooms and suites, restaurant, lounge, entertainment, outdoor heated pool, exercise center, gift shop, in-room refrigerators and coffee makers, beach, car rental desk, children free with parents, NS rooms, wheelchair access, room service, laundry facilities, a/c, TV, 8 meeting rooms, senior rates, CC. 23 miles from the Tampa airport, 10 miles from the St. Petersburg-Clearwater airport. SGL/DBL$110-$170, STS$310-$425.

HiSeas Motel (455 South Gulfview Blvd., 34630; 446-6003) 33 rooms, outdoor pool, a/c, TV, children free with parents, NS rooms, CC. LS SGL/DBL$38-$57; HS SGL/DBL$75-$95.

Holiday House Resort Motels (495 North Gulfview Blvd., 34630; 447-1577, 800-338-2896) 30 2- and 3-bedroom apartments, outdoor pool, beach, a/c, TV, NS rooms, pets OK, children free with parents, senior rates, CC. 20 miles from the Tampa airport, 25 miles from the Salvador Dali Museum. SGL/DBL$49-$65.

Holiday Inn Surfside North (400 Mandalay Ave., 34630; 461-3222, Fax 461-0610, 800-HOLIDAY) 428 rooms and suites, restaurant, lounge, outdoor heated pool, exercise center, children free with parents, wheelchair access, beach, boutiques, gift shop, in-room refrigerators, a/c, TV, NS rooms, fax service, room service, laundry service, water view, no pets, 8 meeting rooms, meeting facilities for 1,200, senior rates, CC. 20 miles from the Tampa airport, 1 block from the shopping mall, 24 miles from the greyhound race track. SGL/DBL$135-$210, STS$375-$525.

Holiday Inn (521 South Gulfview Blvd., 34630; 447-6461, Fax 443-5888, 800-HOLIDAY) 288 rooms and suites, restaurant, lounge, entertainment, heated pool, exercise center, children free with parents, wheelchair access, a/c, TV, NS rooms, gift shop, car rental desk, game room, in-room refrigerators, no pets, local transportation, fax service, room service, laundry service, meeting facilities for 140, senior rates, CC. 15 miles from the St. Petersburg-Clearwater airport, 5 miles from Jack Russell Stadium. SGL/DBL$105-$145.

Island Bay Apartments (580 Bay Esplanade, 34630; 447-6808) 5 apartments, outdoor pool, tennis courts, a/c, TV, children free with parents, in-room refrigerators and coffee makers, laundry facilities, CC. SGL/DBL$40-$50.

Island Queen Resort Motel (158 Brightwater Dr., 34630; 442-8068, Fax 442-2412) 14 rooms and efficiencies, outdoor heated pool, a/c, TV, kitchenettes, no pets, wheelchair access, NS rooms, senior rates, CC. LS SGL/DBL$39-$44; HS SGL/DBL$60-$80.

King Cole Motel (401 East Shore Dr., 34630; 446-8411, 800-553-1977) 15 rooms and efficiencies, outdoor pool, in-room refrigerators, no pets, children free with parents, laundry facilities, CC. SGL/DBL$30-$55.

Lagoon Resort Motel (619 Gulfview Blvd., 34630; 442-5107, Fax 446-4238, 800-237-8477) 66 rooms and efficiencies, restaurant, outdoor pool, in-room refrigerators, a/c, TV, children free with parents, room service, no pets, senior rates, CC. LS SGL/DBL$42-$76; HS SGL/DBL$60-$100.

Mannings On The Bay (530 South Gulfview Blvd., 34630; 447-6407) 25 rooms and efficiencies, outdoor heated pool, children free with parents, in-room refrigerators, a/c, TV, CC. LS SGL/DBL$38-$50; HS SGL/DBL$75-$88.

New Yorker Motel and Apartments (332 Hamden Dr., 34630; 446-2437) 16 rooms and apartments, outdoor heated pool, a/c, TV, beach, NS rooms, kitchenettes, senior rates, CC. SGL/DBL$65-$85.

Orleans Apartment Motel (181 Brightwater Dr., 34630; 442-1726) 6 apartments, outdoor pool, whirlpools, a/c, TV, no pets, children free with parents, CC. SGL/DBL$50-$60.

Palm Pavilion Inn (18 Bay Esplanade, 34630; 446-6777) 28 rooms, outdoor pool, no pets, a/c, TV, wheelchair access, NS rooms, children free with parents, laundry facilities, senior rates, CC. LS SGL/DBL$49-$74; HS SGL/DBL$70-$110.

Quality Inn Gulf Sands Beach Resort (655 South Gulfview Blvd., 34630; 442-7171, 800-221-2222) 91 rooms and suites, restaurant, outdoor pool, exercise center, children free with parents, a/c, TV, wheelchair access, room service, laundry service, in-room refrigerators, beach, NS rooms, meeting facilities, senior rates, CC. 19 miles from the St. Petersburg-Clearwater airport. SGL/DBL$62-$150.

Radisson Suite Resort On Sand Key (1201 Gulf Blvd., 34630; 596-1100, Fax 595-4292, 800-333-3333) 220 rooms and suites, restaurant, lounge, entertainment, outdoor heated pool, exercise center, in-room refrigerators, microwaves and coffee makers, children free with parents, airport transportation, VCRs, wheelchair access, laundry facilities, NS rooms, TV, a/c, children free with parents, boutiques, barber and beauty shop, pets OK, senior rates, 11 meeting rooms, CC. SGL/DBL$165-$235.

Ramada Inn (674 Bayway Blvd., 34630; 446-2688, Fax 446-7177, 800-2-RAMADA) 22 rooms and suites, restaurant, free breakfast, lounge, outdoor pool, wheelchair access, NS rooms, free parking, a/c, TV, children free with parents, kitchenettes, local transportation, room service, laundry facilities, meeting facilities, senior rates, CC. SGL/DBL$65-$115.

Residence Inn (5050 Ulmerton Rd., 34630; 573-4444, 800-331-3131) 88, 2-bedroom suites, free breakfast, in-room refrigerators, coffee makers and microwaves, laundry facilities, TV, a/c, VCRs, pets OK, complimentary newspaper, fireplaces, children free with parents, NS rooms, wheelchair access, meeting facilities for 40, senior rates, CC. 2 miles from the St. Petersburg-Clearwater airport, 10 miles from Gulf beaches, 12 miles from the Florida Suncoast Dome. SGL/DBL$125-$175.

Riviera Apartment Motel (217 Coronado Dr., 34630; 441-2625) 22 rooms and apartments, restaurant, outdoor pool, a/c, TV, in-room refrigerators, no pets, children free with parents, laundry facilities, CC. LS SGL/DBL$37-$47.

Sandman Motel (300 Hamden Dr., 34630; 442-4374) 20 rooms, efficiencies and apartments, outdoor pool, laundry facilities, a/c, TV, in-room refrigerators, children free with parents, no pets, CC. LS SGL/DBL$25-$42; HS SGL/DBL$55-$72.

Sea Captain Resort Motel (40 Devon Dr., 34630; 441-2125) 27 rooms and efficiencies, outdoor heated pool, NS, a/c, TV, wheelchair access, kitchenettes, senior rates, CC. SGL/DBL$65-$75; STS$90-$115.

Sheraton Sand Key Resort (1160 Gulf Blvd., 34630; 596-8488, Fax 596-8488, 800-325-3535) 390 rooms and suites, restaurant, outdoor heated pool, exercise center, lighted tennis courts, beach, NS rooms, game room, a/c, room service, TV, children free with parents, wheelchair access, laundry facilities, gift shop, 24,600 square feet of meeting and exhibition space, meeting facilities for 1,200, senior rates, CC. 21 miles from the Tampa airport, 30 miles from Busch Gardens. SGL/DBL$120-$168, STS$235-$435.

Silver Sands Motel (415 Hamden Dr., 34630; 442-9550) 9 rooms and 2-bedroom efficiencies, outdoor pool, laundry facilities, a/c, TV, wheelchair access, no pets, CC. SGL/DBL$40-$70.

Spy Glass Motel (215 Gulfview Blvd., 34630; 447-3464) 75 efficiencies and apartments, outdoor pool, beach, a/c, TV, pets OK, children free with parents, NS rooms, CC. SGL/DBL$28-$70.

Tropical Breeze Resort (333 Hamden Dr., 34630; 442-6865) 20 rooms and efficiencies, outdoor heated pool, children free with parents, laundry facilities, a/c, TV, in-room refrigerators and microwaves, no pets, senior rates, CC. LS SGL/DBL$45-$55; HS SGL/DBL$70-$85.

Watergate Resort Apartments (445 South Gulfview Blvd., 34630; 441-4902) 60 rooms, efficiencies and suites, outdoor heated pool, a/c, TV, NS rooms, no pets, in-room refrigerators and microwaves, wheelchair access, children free with parents, CC. SGL/DBL$45-$105.

Clermont

Area Code 813

HoJo Inn (9240 West Hwy. 192, 34711; 424-6099, Fax 424-5779, 800-I-GO-HOJO) 54 rooms, free breakfast, outdoor pool, children free with parents, wheelchair access, NS rooms, TV, a/c, laundry facilities, in-room refrigerators and microwaves, senior rates, meeting facilities, CC. 5 miles from Walt Disney World, 18 miles from Sea World, 22 miles from Universal Studios, 28 miles from the Orlando airport. SGL/DBL$45-$98.

Holiday Inn (20329 North Hwy. 27, 34711; 429-9033, Fax 420-9556, 800-HOLIDAY) 154 rooms, restaurant, free breakfast, lounge, outdoor pool, exercise center, whirlpools, car rental desk, children free with parents, free local calls, wheelchair access, a/c, TV, NS rooms, fax service, room service, laundry service, meeting facilities for 75, senior rates, CC. 5 miles from the Atlantic beaches. SGL/DBL$60-$70.

Vacation Village Motel (Clermont 34712; 394-4091, 800-962-9969) 90 efficiencies, outdoor pool, lighted tennis courts, a/c, TV, NS rooms, children free with parents, no pets, senior rates, CC. SGL/DBL$65-$85.

Clewiston
Area Code 813

Clewiston Inn Hotel (Hwy. 27 and Royal Palm Dr., 33440; 983-8151, Fax 983-4602, 800-749-4466) 60 rooms, restaurant, lounge, a/c, TV, children free with parents, no pets, laundry facilities, CC. LS SGL/DBL$45-$80; HS SGL/DBL$55-$90.

Cocoa
Area Code 407

Best Western Cocoa Inn (4225 West King St., 32926; 632-1065, Fax 631-3302, 800-528-1234) 120 rooms, restaurant, lounge, outdoor pool, children free with parents, in-room refrigerators and microwaves, a/c, NS rooms, TV, game room, gift shop, laundry facilities, wheelchair access, pets OK, meeting facilities, senior rates, CC. 5 miles from tennis courts and golf course. LS SGL/DBL$34-$44; HS SGL/DBL$46-$55.

Brevard Hotel (112 Riverside Dr., 32922; 636-1411) 56 rooms, restaurant, a/c, TV, NS rooms, no pets, children free with parents, CC. SGL$30, DBL$40.

Days Inn (5600 Hwy. 524, 32926; 636-6500, 800-325-2525) 180 rooms, free breakfast, outdoor pool, a/c, TV, wheelchair access, NS rooms, no pets, laundry facilities, in-room refrigerators and microwaves, children free with parents, beach, in-room computer hookups, senior rates, CC. 3 miles from the cruise terminal, 18 miles from the Kennedy Space Center. SGL/DBL$53-$80.

Econo Lodge (3220 North Cocoa Blvd., 32926; 632-4561, Fax 632-3756, 800-4-CHOICE) 137 rooms, restaurant, lounge, outdoor pool, children free with parents, no pets, NS rooms, wheelchair access, a/c, VCRs, TV, senior rates, meeting facilities, laundry facilities,

CC. 8 miles from the Kennedy Space Center and cruise ship terminal. SGL/DBL$35-$65.

Ramada Inn Kennedy Space Center (900 Friday Rd., 32922; 631-1210, Fax 636-8661, 800-2-RAMADA) 149 rooms and suites, restaurant, lounge, outdoor pool, wheelchair access, NS rooms, free parking, a/c, TV, VCRs, children free with parents, in-room refrigerators and microwaves, room service, laundry facilities, meeting facilities, CC. 12 miles from the Kennedy Space Center, 10 miles from Atlantic beaches, 5 miles from the golf course, 20 miles from Canaveral National Seashore. SGL/DBL$50-$70.

Cocoa Beach
Area Code 407

Beach Inn International (4001 North Atlantic Ave., 32931; 784-1260, Fax 784-2866) 40 rooms, restaurant, outdoor pool, a/c, TV, wheelchair access, NS rooms, children free with parents, CC. LS SGL/DBL$26-$46; HS SGL/DBL$39-$64.

Cape Colony Resort (1275 North Atlantic Ave., 32931; 783-2252) 128 rooms, restaurant, outdoor pool, lounge, laundry facilities, pets OK, a/c, TV, NS rooms, senior rates, CC. SGL/DBL$55-$77.

Cape Winds Resort (7400 Ridgewood Ave., 32931; 783-6226, 800-248-1030) 67 1- and 2-bedroom suites, outdoor heated pool, whirlpools, sauna, in-room microwaves and coffee makers, no pets, children free with parents, laundry facilities, a/c, TV, CC. 1BR$75-$95, 2BR$95-$105.

Comfort Inn and Suite Resort (3901 North Atlantic Ave., 32931; 783-2221, Fax 783-0461, 800-221-2222) 144 rooms, restaurant, lounge, entertainment, outdoor pool, whirlpools, a/c, TV, children free with parents, NS rooms, wheelchair access, in-room refrigerators and microwaves, game room, laundry facilities, no pets, senior rates, 4,600 square feet of meeting and exhibitions space, meeting facilities for 475, CC. LS SGL/DBL$50-$100; HS SGL/DBL$58-$110.

Discovery Beach Resort (300 Barlow Ave., 32931; 783-8000, Fax 868-0086) 1- , 2- , and 3-bedroom villas, outdoor heated pool, whirlpools, sauna, lighted tennis courts, exercise center, laundry facilities, a/c, beach, children free with parents, TV, VCRs, no pets, in-room microwaves and coffee makers, senior rates, CC. LS SGL/DBL$100-$115; HS SGL/DBL$170-$240.

Econo Lodge Beachside (5500 North Atlantic Ave., 32931; 784-2550, Fax 868-7124, 800-55-ECONO, 800-446-6900) 102 rooms, restaurant, outdoor pool, children free with parents, no pets, NS rooms, wheelchair access, free local calls, kitchenettes, a/c, TV, senior rates, CC. 13 miles from the Kennedy Space Center, 5 miles from the shopping mall, 1 block from the city fishing pier. SGL/DBL$40-$80.

Hilton Hotel (1550 North Atlantic Ave., 32931; 799-0003, Fax 799-0344, 800-HILTONS) 297 rooms and suites, restaurant, lounge, entertainment, outdoor pool, exercise center, whirlpools, children free with parents, NS rooms, wheelchair access, room service, beach, in-room computer hookups, laundry facilities, no pets, a/c, gift shop, TV, 5,000 square feet of meeting and exhibition space, meeting facilities for 750, CC. 40 miles from the Orlando airport, 22 miles from the Melbourne airport. SGL/DBL$70-$135.

Holiday Inn (1300 North Atlantic Ave., 32931; 783-2271, Fax 784-8878, 800-HOLIDAY) 500 rooms and suites, restaurant, lounge, entertainment, outdoor heated pool, exercise center, whirlpools, lighted tennis courts, in-room refrigerators and microwaves, children free with parents, wheelchair access, kitchenettes, a/c, TV, NS rooms, gift shop, beauty shop, no pets, beach, fax service, room service, laundry service, meeting facilities for 500, senior rates, CC. 12 miles from the Kennedy Space Center, 3 miles from the Port Canaveral Cruise Terminal. SGL/DBL$85-$125.

Howard Johnson Plaza (2080 North Atlantic Ave., 32931, 793-9222, Fax 799-3234, 800-I-GO-HOJO) 210 rooms and suites, restaurant, lounge, entertainment, indoor and outdoor heated pools, exercise center, beach, children free with parents, game room, wheelchair access, NS rooms, TV, a/c, no pets, laundry facilities, senior rates, 11 meeting rooms, meeting facilities for 800, CC. SGL/DBL$75-$145, STS$145-$175.

The Inn At Cocoa Beach (4300 Ocean Beach Blvd., 32931; 799-3460, Fax 784-8632, 800-343-5307) 50 rooms, free breakfast, outdoor pool, a/c, TV, NS rooms, children free with parents, beach, no pets, CC. 8 miles from the downtown area, 12 miles from the Atlantic beach. SGL/DBL$89-$175.

Motel 6 (3701 North Atlantic Ave., 32931; 783-3103, 505-891-6161) 150 rooms, outdoor pool, free local calls, children free with parents, NS rooms, beach, wheelchair access, a/c, TV, CC. 11 miles from the Kennedy Space Center, 12 miles from Gulf beaches and Patrick Air Force Base. SGL/DBL$35-$40.

Ocean Landings Resort and Racquet Club (900 North Atlantic Ave., 32931; 783-9430, Fax 783-1339, 800-323-8413) 228 rooms and 1- and 2-bedroom apartments, outdoor pool, tennis, children free with parents, in-room refrigerators and microwaves, no pets, laundry facilities, senior rates, CC. 1BR$106, 2BR$154-$202.

Ocean Suite Hotel (5500 Ocean Beach Blvd., 32931; 784-4343, Fax 783-6514, 800-367-1223, 800-843-9680 in Florida) 50 rooms and 2-bedroom suites, restaurant, outdoor heated pool, children free with parents, TV, VCRs, a/c, laundry facilities, in-room refrigerators and microwaves, meeting facilities, CC. LS SGL/DBL$69-$105; HS SGL/DBL$80-$135.

Satellite Motel On The Ocean (1600 North Atlantic Ave., 32931; 783-7714) 56 rooms, outdoor pool, beach, children free with parents, NS rooms, no pets, CC. SGL/DBL$45-$55.

Sea Esta Luxury Apartment Suites (686 South Atlantic Ave., 32931; 783-1739, Fax 783-8572, 800-872-9444) 10 rooms and 1- and 2-bedroom apartments, outdoor pool, beach, laundry facilities, in-room microwaves and coffee makers, a/c, TV, VCRs, no pets, CC. SGL/DBL$115-$175.

Sunrise Motel (3185 North Atlantic Ave., 32931; 783-0500, 800-348-0348) 44 rooms and efficiencies, outdoor pool, a/c, TV, children free with parents, no pets, NS rooms, senior rates, CC. SGL$36-$52, DBL$42-$62.

Surf Studio Beach Resort (1801 South Atlantic Ave., 32931; 783-7100, Fax 783-2695) 11 rooms and efficiencies, heated pool, in-room refrigerators and microwaves, kitchenettes, children free with parents, pets OK, beach, laundry facilities, a/c, TV, NS rooms, CC. SGL/DBL$40-$110.

Wakulla Motel (3550 North Atlantic Ave., 32931; 783-2230, 783-0980, 800-992-5852) 116 rooms and 2-bedroom suites, heated outdoor pool, in-room refrigerators and microwaves, laundry facilities, a/c, TV, NS rooms, children free with parents, no pets, CC. SGL/DBL$72-$89.

Coconut Grove
Area Code 305

Doubletree Hotel at Coconut Grove (2649 South Bayshore Dr., 33133; 858-2500, Fax 858-5766, 800-528-0444, 800-828-7447) 172 rooms and suites, restaurant, lounge, entertainment, outdoor heated pool, lighted tennis courts, a/c, laundry facilities, NS rooms, gift shop, room service, 6 meeting rooms, meeting facilities for 250. 4 miles from the downtown area, 13 miles from Miami airport. SGL/DBL$100-$190.

Grand Bay Hotel (2669 South Bayshore Dr., 33133; 858-9600, Fax 858-1532, 800-323-7500) 165 rooms and suites, restaurant, lounge, entertainment, outdoor pool, sauna, whirlpools, exercise center, 24-hour room service, a/c, TV, beauty shop, meeting facilities for 350, 4,000 square feet of meeting and exhibition space, senior rates, CC. 12 miles from the downtown area, 16 miles from the Miami airport. SGL$205-$295, DBL$200-$270, STS$325-$1,100.

Mayfair House (3000 Florida Ave., 33133; 441-0000, 800-433-4555, 800-341-0809 in Florida) 182 2-bedroom suites, restaurant, lounge, outdoor pool, sauna, whirlpools, exercise center, boutiques, kitchenettes, no pets, a/c, TV, NS rooms, airport courtesy car, 24-hour room service, gift shop, complimentary newspaper, in-room refrigerators, microwaves and coffee makers, meeting facilities, CC. SGL/DBL$230-$550.

Coral Gables
Area Code 305

Biltmore Hotel (1200 Anastasia Ave., 33134; 445-1926, Fax 448-9976) 280 rooms and suites, restaurant, lounge, entertainment, outdoor heated pool, lighted tennis courts, sauna, children free with parents, no pets, in-room refrigerators, airport transportation, in-room computer hookups, NS rooms, senior rates, meeting facilities. LS SGL/DBL$130-$190; HS SGL/DBL$190-$250.

The Colonnade Hotel (180 Aragon Ave., 33134; 441-2600, Fax 445-3929) 157 rooms and suites, restaurant, lounge, outdoor heated pool, exercise center, sauna, whirlpools, in-room computer hook-ups, American Plan available, complimentary newspaper, gift shop, beauty shop, no pets, a/c, TV, wheelchair access, NS rooms, room service, 9,000 square feet of meeting and exhibition space, meeting facilities for 450, senior rates, CC. 5 miles from the Miami airport, 1 block from the Miracle Mile shopping area. LS SGL/DBL$180-$210; HS SGL/DBL$255-$290.

David William Apartment Hotel (700 Biltmore Way, 33134; 445-7821, 800-327-8770) 130 rooms and suites, restaurant, lounge, entertainment, heated pool, a/c, TV, kitchenettes, in-room refrigerators and microwaves, airport transportation, laundry facilities, children free with parents, no pets, room service, NS rooms, CC. SGL/DBL$125-$150.

Holiday Inn Downtown (2051 LeJeune Rd., 33134; 443-2301, Fax 446-6827, 800-HOLIDAY) 168 rooms and suites, restaurant, lounge, entertainment, outdoor pool, saunas, no pets, children free with parents, wheelchair access, airport transportation, a/c, TV, NS rooms, fax service, room service, laundry service, meeting facilities for 250, CC. 3 miles from the Miami airport and the Orange Bowl, 6 miles from the Port of Miami. SGL/DBL$80-$85.

Holiday Inn (1350 South Dixie Hwy., 33146; 667-5611, Fax 669-3153, 800-HOLIDAY) 155 rooms, restaurant, lounge, outdoor pool, exercise center, children free with parents, wheelchair access, in-room refrigerators and microwaves, beauty shop, kitchenettes, game room, a/c, TV, NS rooms, fax service, room service, laundry service, 4 meeting rooms, senior rates, CC. 1 block from the University of Miami, 8 miles from the Port of Miami, 5 miles from the Orange Bowl. SGL/DBL$70-$95.

Hotel Place Saint Michel (162 Alcazar, 33134; 444-1666, 800-247-8526) 30 rooms and suites, restaurant, lounge, entertainment, children free with parents, no pets, antique furnishings, laundry service, a/c, TV, NS rooms, meeting facilities, senior rates, CC. SGL/DBL$100-$115.

Hotel Ponce De Leon (1721 Ponce De Leon Blvd., 33134; 444-9934) 27 rooms, a/c, TV, no pets, CC. LS SGL/DBL$36; HS SGL/DBL$48.

Howard Johnson (1430 South Dixie Hwy., 33146; 665-7501, Fax 662-2903, 800-I-GO-HOJO, 800-635-4656) 80 rooms, restaurant, lounge, outdoor pool, children free with parents, wheelchair access, NS rooms, pets OK, airport transportation, TV, a/c, laundry facilities, meeting facilities, CC. 8 miles from the Miami airport. SGL/DBL$58-$100.

Hyatt Regency Coral Gables (50 Alhambra Place, 33134; 441-1234, Fax 443-7702, 800-228-9000, 800-233-1234) 242 rooms and suites, restaurant, lounge, entertainment, heated pool, whirlpools, laundry service, exercise center, gift shop, in-room computer hookups, room service, TV, a/c, NS rooms, wheelchair access, 57,000 square feet of meeting and exhibition space, senior rates, CC. LS SGL/DBL$120-$185; HS SGL/DBL$150-$260.

Riviera Court Motel (5100 Riviera Dr., 33134; 665-3538) 31 rooms and efficiencies, outdoor heated pool, no pets, kitchenettes, a/c, TV, NS rooms, children free with parents, senior rates, CC. LS SGL/DBL$55-$75; HS SGL/DBL$68-$78, EFF$78-$85.

Villa Cortez Motel (4700 Southwest 8th St., 33134; 445-5453, Fax 445-5041, 800-833-6028) 31 rooms, restaurant, outdoor pool, a/c, TV, no pets, children free with parents, CC. SGL/DBL$45-$65.

Coral Springs

Area Code 305

Holiday Inn (3701 University Dr., 33065; 753-900, Fax 755-4012, 800-HOLIDAY) 120 rooms and 2-room suites, restaurant, lounge, entertainment, outdoor heated pool, exercise center, in-room refrigerators and microwaves, children free with parents, wheelchair access, a/c, car rental desk, no pets, TV, NS rooms, fax service, room service, laundry service, 6 meeting rooms, meeting facilities for 300, senior rates, CC. 2 miles from the shopping mall, 3.5 miles from Aquatic Center, 1.5 miles from the City Centre Theater, 23 miles from the Ft. Lauderdale-Hollywood airport, 18 miles from the Broward Convention Center. LS SGL/DBL$45-$80; HS SGL/DBL$70-$95.

Wellesley Inns (3100 North University Dr., 33065; 344-2200, Fax 344-7885, 800-444-8888) 106 rooms and suites, free breakfast, outdoor pool, wheelchair access, no pets, a/c, TV, children free with parents, laundry service, fax service, meeting facilities for 35, senior rates, CC. 20 miles from the Ft. Lauderdale-Hollywood airport, 22 miles from the Broward Convention Center. SGL/DBL$40-$95.

Crescent Beach
Area Code 904

Beacher's Lodge (6970 Hwy. A1A South, 32086; 471-8849, Fax 471-3002) 120 rooms and 1-bedroom efficiencies, outdoor pool, in-room refrigerators, beach, a/c, TV, wheelchair access, NS rooms, no pets, laundry facilities, senior rates, CC. SGL/DBL$50-$100.

Crescent City
Area Code 904

Sprague House Inn (125 Central Ave., 32012; 698-2430) 4 rooms and suites, restaurant, free breakfast, outdoor pool, children free with parents, a/c, TV, no pets, CC. SGL/DBL$55-$75.

Crestview
Area Code 904

Days Inn (I-10 and Hwy. 85, 32536; 682-8842, Fax 682-5878, 800-325-2525) 64 rooms and suites, restaurant, outdoor pool, children free with parents, pets OK, a/c, TV, wheelchair access, NS rooms, laundry facilities, senior rates, CC. 6 miles from the Pensacola airport, 1 mile from the downtown area. SGL/DBL$35-$45.

Econo Lodge (3107 South Ferdon Blvd., 32536; 682-6255, 800-55-ECONO) 84 rooms, restaurant, children free with parents, free local calls, no pets, NS rooms, wheelchair access, a/c, TV, senior rates, CC. SGL/DBL$44-$53.

Holiday Inn (Hwy. 85 South, 32536; 682-6111, Fax 689-1189, 800-HOLIDAY) 120 rooms, restaurant, free breakfast, lounge, outdoor pool, children free with parents, wheelchair access, a/c, TV, VCRs, NS rooms, pets OK, fax service, room service, laundry service, meeting facilities for 150, senior rates, CC. 2 miles from the golf course, 13 miles from the regional airport, 1 mile from the shopping center. SGL/DBL$50-$58.

Super 8 Motel (3925 South Ferdon Blvd., 32536; 682-9649, 800-800-8000) 63 rooms, children free with parents, free local calls, a/c, TV, in- room refrigerators and microwaves, fax service, NS rooms, pets

OK, wheelchair access, meeting facilities, senior rates, CC. 22 miles from the Okaloosa airport, 5 miles from the Okaloosa Correctional Institute. SGL/DBL$29-$39.

Cross City
Area Code 904

Carriage Inn (North Hwy. 19, 32628; 498-3910, Fax 498-5054) 25 rooms, restaurant, outdoor pool, a/c, TV, pets OK, children free with parents, NS rooms. CC. SGL/DBL$34-$39.

Crystal River
Area Code 904

Best Western Crystal River Resort (614 Northwest Hwy. 19, 34428; 796-3171, Fax 795-3179, 800-528-1234, 800-435-4409) 96 rooms, restaurant, lounge, outdoor heated pool, whirlpools, children free with parents, a/c, NS rooms, gift shop, dive center, TV, laundry facilities, wheelchair access, pets OK, meeting facilities, senior rates, CC. A 1/2-mile from the shopping mall. SGL/DBL$48-$75.

Comfort Inn (4486 North Suncoast Blvd., 34428; 563-1500, 800-CLARION) 60 rooms, restaurant, outdoor pool, whirlpools, lighted tennis courts, a/c, TV, children free with parents, NS rooms, in-room refrigerators and microwaves, laundry facilities, pets OK, wheelchair access, senior rates, CC. 10 miles from Homosassa Springs Nature World, 3 miles from the Fort Island Gulf Beach and the regional airport. LS SGL/DBL$40-$54; HS SGL/DBL$43-$65.

Days Inn (2380 Hwy. 19 Northwest, 34428; 795-2111, Fax 795-4126, 800-325-2525) 108 rooms, restaurant, lounge, entertainment, outdoor pool, a/c, TV, wheelchair access, NS rooms, in-room refrigerators and microwaves, pets OK, local attractions, children free with parents, laundry facilities, kitchenettes, meeting facilities, senior rates, CC. A 1/2-mile from the shopping center, 1 mile from the Arch Site, 10 miles from Homosassa Springs. SGL/DBL$40-$55.

Plantation Inn and Golf Resort (9301 West Fort Island Trail, 34429; 795-4211, Fax 795-1368, 800-632-6262) 136 rooms, restaurant, lounge, outdoor heated pool, sauna, lighted tennis courts, whirlpools, in-room refrigerators, a/c, TV, wheelchair access, children free with parents, Modified American Plan available, pets OK, NS rooms, senior rates, 8 meeting rooms, CC. SGL/DBL$79-$110.

Cypress Gardens
Area Code 813

Best Western Inn (5665 Cypress Gardens Blvd., 33884; 324-5950, Fax 324-2376, 800-528-1234) 156 rooms, restaurant, lounge, outdoor heated pool, children free with parents, a/c, NS rooms, TV, laundry facilities, wheelchair access, pets OK, meeting facilities for 600, senior rates, CC. 1 mile from golf course. SGL/DBL$39-$69.

Dade City
Area Code 904

Rainbow Fountain Motel (2102 Hwy. 301 North, 33525; 567-3427) 21 rooms, outdoor pool, no pets, in-room refrigerators and microwaves, a/c, TV, laundry facilities, CC. SGL/DBL$26-$46.

Dania
Area Code 305

Becky Studio Apartments (211 Southeast Park St., 33004; 927-7168) 11 apartments, outdoor pool, kitchenettes, laundry facilities, a/c, TV, CC. SGL/DBL$150W-$250W.

Hilton Hotel Airport (1870 Griffin Rd., 33004; 920-3300, Fax 920-3348, 800-HILTONS, 800-426-8578, 800-654-8266 in Florida) 388 rooms and suites, restaurant, lounge, entertainment, outdoor pool, exercise center, lighted tennis courts, sauna, children free with parents, NS rooms, wheelchair access, room service, laundry facilities, airport courtesy car, gift shop, a/c, TV, in-room refrigerators, no pets, 14 meeting rooms, 18,000 square feet of meeting and exhibition space, meeting facilities for 1,200, senior rates, CC. 10 miles from Port Everglades, 15 miles from Atlantic beaches, 1 mile from the Ft. Lauderdale-Hollywood airport, 8 miles from the downtown area, 3 miles from Port Everglades. LS SGL/DBL$80-$130; HS SGL/DBL$125-$175.

Motel 6 (825 East Dania Beach Blvd., 33004; 922-0988, 505-891-6161) 163 rooms, outdoor pool, free local calls, children free with parents, NS rooms, wheelchair access, a/c, TV, CC. 3/4-mile from the Jai Alai fronton, 1 mile from Atlantic beaches. SGL/DBL$32-$44.

Sheraton Design Center Hotel (1825 Griffin Rd., 33004; 920-3500, Fax 920-3535, 800-325-3535) 251 rooms and suites, restaurant, lounge, entertainment, outdoor heated pool, exercise center, sauna, whirlpools, lighted tennis courts, laundry service, airport transportation, in-room refrigerators and coffee makers, NS rooms, a/c, room service, TV, children free with parents, wheelchair access, 10 meeting rooms, meeting facilities for 400, 13,000 square feet of meeting and exhibition space, 14 meeting rooms, senior rates, CC. 1.5 miles from the Ft. Lauderdale-Hollywood airport, 4 miles from the Convention Center. LS SGL/DBL$125-$185; HS SGL/DBL$135-$200.

Davenport
Area Code 813

Budget Inn (3800 Hwy. 27 North, 33837; 424-2401, 800-275-2311, 800-527-0700) 99 rooms and efficiencies, restaurant, outdoor pool, NS rooms, children free with parents, no pets, a/c, TV, senior rates, CC. SGL/DBL$30-$44.

Comfort Inn (5510 Hwy. 27 North, 33837; 424-2811, 800-221-2222, 800-255-4386) 150 rooms, restaurant, free breakfast, outdoor pool, whirlpools, no pets, in-room refrigerators and microwaves, airport transportation, laundry facilities, a/c, TV, children free with parents, NS rooms, wheelchair access, meeting facilities, senior rates, CC. 20 miles from the Orlando airport and Sea World, 9 miles from Walt Disney World. SGL/DBL$35-$90.

Howard Johnson Motor Lodge (I-4 and Hwy. 27, 33837; 424-2120, Fax 424-5317, 800-654-6920, 800-I-GO-HOJO) 102 rooms, restaurant, lounge, outdoor pool, exercise center, children free with parents, wheelchair access, NS rooms, TV, a/c, laundry facilities, senior rates, meeting facilities, CC. 25 miles from the Orlando airport, 25 miles from downtown Orlando. SGL/DBL$35-$70.

Motel 6 (5620 Hwy. 27 North, 33837; 424-2521, 505-891-6161) 159 rooms, outdoor pool, free local calls, children free with parents, NS rooms, wheelchair access, a/c, TV, CC. 15 miles from Universal Studios, 12 miles from Walt Disney World, 22 miles from Cypress Gardens. SGL/DBL$38-$44.

Red Carpet Inn (10736 Hwy. 27 North, 33837; 424-2450, 800-251-1962) 119 rooms, outdoor pool, children free with parents, TV, a/c, NS rooms, meeting facilities, senior rates, CC. 20 miles from Cypress Gardens, 8 miles from Walt Disney World, 30 miles from the Orlando airport, 6 miles from Old Town. SGL/DBL$25-$30.

Ted Williams Inn (Davenport 33837; 424-2511, Fax 424-3889) 159 rooms, lounge, outdoor pool, a/c, TV, wheelchair access, NS rooms, kitchenettes, laundry facilities, children free with parents, no pets, meeting facilities, senior rates, CC. SGL/DBL$35-$70.

Daytona Beach

Area Code 904

Rental & Reservation Services

Check-In Reservation Services (7282 55th Ave. East, Bradenton 34205; 867-7760, 800-237-1033) rental condos and apartments.

Condo Rentals of Daytona (2410 South Atlantic Ave., 32118; 255-2233, 800-447-3685) rental condominiums.

Daytona Beach Ocean Home Rentals (541 South Atlantic Ave., 32176; 0720, 800-666-0720) private rental homes.

Erdman Realty (3162 South Atlantic Ave., 32118; 788-2250, Fax 767-1272) rental condominiums.

Ocean Properties (4168 South Atlantic Ave, New Smyrna Beach 32169; 428-0513, 800-521-9657) rental condominiums.

□□□

Acapulco Inn (2505 South Atlantic Ave., 32118; 761-2210, Fax 253-9935, 800-874-7420) 133 rooms, restaurant, lounge, outdoor heated pool, whirlpools, beach, a/c, TV, wheelchair access, NS rooms, game room, in-room refrigerators, laundry facilities, no pets, senior rates, CC. SGL/DBL$80-$155.

The Aladdin Inn (2323 South Atlantic Ave., 32118; 255-0476, Fax 255-3376, 800-874-7517) 120 rooms, restaurant, outdoor heated pool, beach, a/c, TV, wheelchair access, in-room refrigerators, children free with parents, game room, gift shop, kitchenettes, no pets, laundry facilities, NS rooms, senior rates, CC. LS SGL/DBL$40-$75; HS SGL/DBL$75-$135.

Americana Beach Lodge (1260 North Atlantic Ave., 32118; 255-7431, Fax 253-9513, 800-874-1824) 198 rooms and suites, restaurant, outdoor pool, beach, in-room refrigerators, a/c, TV, no pets. CC. SGL/DBL$58, STS$68.

Aruba Inn (1254 North Atlantic Ave., 32118; 253-5643, Fax 677-0625) 33 rooms, outdoor pool, kitchenettes, children free with parents, beach, laundry facilities, a/c, TV, in-room refrigerators, pets OK, CC. LS SGL/DBL$30-$45; HS SGL/DBL$50-$65.

Bahama House Apartments (2001 South Atlantic Ave., 32118; 248-2001, Fax 253-9935) 87 rooms and apartments, outdoor heated pool, laundry facilities, children free with parents, kitchenettes, a/c, TV, in-room computer hookups, beach, CC. SGL/DBL$64-$105.

Beach Haven Inn (2115 South Atlantic Ave., 32118; 252-6651) 29 rooms, outdoor heated pool, beach, in-room refrigerators, children free with parents, a/c, TV, wheelchair access, NS rooms, no pets, kitchenettes, airport transportation, laundry facilities, senior rates, CC. SGL/DBL$35-$125.

Beach Hut Motel (3247 South Atlantic Ave., 32118; 761-8450) 50 rooms and 2-bedroom efficiencies, outdoor heated pool, beach, laundry facilities, children free with parents, NS rooms, no pets, a/c, TV, senior rates, CC. LS SGL/DBL$30-$70; HS SGL/DBL$65-$125.

Beachcomber Oceanfront Inn (2000 North Atlantic Ave., 32119; 252-8513, Fax 253-9935, 800-874-7420) 184 rooms, restaurant, lounge, outdoor heated pool, whirlpools, no pets, a/c, TV, children free with parents, game room, gift shop, kitchenettes, beach, laundry facilities, in-room refrigerators, senior rates, CC. LS SGL/DBL$60-$90; HS SGL/DBL$95-$160.

Best Western Aku Tiki Inn (2225 South Atlantic Ave., 32118; 252-9631, Fax 252-1198, 800-AUK-TIKI, 800-528-1234) 132 rooms, restaurant, lounge, entertainment, outdoor heated pool, children free with parents, beach, a/c, NS rooms, TV, laundry facilities, in-room refrigerators, wheelchair access, local transportation, pets OK, meeting facilities, senior rates, CC. 5 miles from Daytona International Speedway. LS SGL/DBL$55-$65; HS SGL/DBL$110-$118.

Best Western La Playa Resort (2500 North Atlantic Ave., 32118; 672-0990, Fax 677-0982, 800-528-1234, 800-874-6996) 239 rooms, restaurant, lounge, entertainment, indoor and outdoor heated pools, whirlpools, sauna, no pets, children free with parents, a/c, NS rooms, TV, laundry facilities, wheelchair access, game room, beach, in-room refrigerators and microwaves, meeting facilities, senior rates, CC. LS SGL/DBL$60-$97; HS SGL/DBL$85-$135.

Breakers Beach Motel (27 South Ocean Ave., 32118; 252-0863, Fax 238-1247, 800-441-8459) 21 rooms and efficiencies, outdoor pool, kitchenettes, a/c, TV, laundry facilities, wheelchair access, children free with parents, senior rates, CC. SGL/DBL$45-$55.

Cabana Motel Oceanfront (8166 North Atlantic Ave., 32118- 255-1481, 800-327-1481) 70 rooms, outdoor pool, a/c, TV, children free with parents, in-room refrigerators, NS rooms, laundry facilities, CC. SGL/DBL$55-$65.

Capri Motel (832 North Atlantic Ave., 32118; 252-2555, 800-874-1820) 24 rooms and 1-bedroom efficiencies, outdoor pool, kitchenettes, game room, laundry facilities, a/c, TV, children free with parents, no pets, senior rates, CC. SGL/DBL$35-$55, 1BR$40-$70.

Comfort Inn Oceanfront (3135 South Atlantic Ave., 32118; 767-8533, 800-221-2222) 115 rooms, restaurant, lounge, outdoor heated pool, a/c, TV, children free with parents, a/c, TV, laundry facilities, NS rooms, wheelchair access, senior rates, CC. 10 miles from the Daytona Beach airport, 5 miles from Daytona International Speedway and Jai Alai fronton, 2 miles from the Convention Center. LS SGL/DBL$33-$65; HS SGL/DBL$52-$110.

The Coquina Inn (544 South Palmetto Ave., 32114; 254-4969) 4 rooms, free breakfast, a/c, no pets, NS, antique furnishings, CC. SGL/DBL$75-$150.

Cypress Cove Inn (3245 South Atlantic Ave., 32118; 761-1660) 40 rooms and apartments, outdoor heated pool, kitchenettes, a/c, TV, laundry facilities, beach, children free with parents, in-room refrigerators, no pets, CC. LS SGL/DBL$30-$40; HS SGL/DBL$60-$80.

Days Inn Oceanside (800 North Atlantic Ave., 32118; 252-6491, Fax 258-1458, 800-325-2525) 117 rooms and efficiencies, restaurant, outdoor heated pool, beach, children free with parents, a/c, TV, wheelchair access, NS rooms, no pets, laundry facilities, senior rates, CC. 7.5 miles from the Daytona International Speedway, 1.5 miles from the shopping mall, 7 miles from the Daytona airport. SGL/DBL$95-$150.

Days Inn (1909 South Atlantic Ave., 32118; 255-4492, 800-325-2525) 196 rooms, restaurant, lounge, outdoor pool, a/c, TV, wheelchair access, NS rooms, no pets, laundry facilities, children free with parents, senior rates, meeting facilities, CC. SGL/DBL$45-$95.

Days Inn (3209 South Atlantic Ave., 32118; 761-2050, Fax 761-3922, 800-325-2525) 196 rooms and efficiencies, restaurant, lounge, free breakfast, outdoor pool, beach, game room, kitchenettes, a/c, TV, wheelchair access, NS rooms, no pets, laundry facilities, senior rates, CC. SGL/DBL$40-$150.

Days Inn (2900 International Speedway Blvd., 32124; 255-0541, Fax 253-1468, 800-325-2525) 180 rooms, restaurant, outdoor pool, a/c, TV, wheelchair access, NS rooms, pets OK, gift shop, laundry facilities, children free with parents, senior rates, CC. 1 mile from the Jai Alai fronton and Daytona International Speedway, 2 miles from Daytona airport. SGL/DBL$30-$110.

Daytona Inn At Broadway (219 South Atlantic Ave., 32118; 252-3626, Fax 255-3680, 800-HILTONS, 800-874-1822) 150 rooms and efficiencies, restaurant, outdoor heated pool, children free with parents, no pets, laundry facilities, a/c, TV, NS rooms, beach, 2 meeting rooms, CC. LS SGL/DBL$45-$60; HS SGL/DBL$105-$115.

Daytona Inn At Seabreeze (730 North Atlantic Ave., 32118; 255-5491, Fax 255-3680, 800-HILTONS, 800-874-1822) 98 rooms, restaurant, outdoor heated pool, children free with parents, a/c, TV, no pets, beach, laundry facilities, CC. LS SGL/DBL$35-$40; HS SGL/DBL$75-$110.

Del Aire Motel (744 North Atlantic Ave., 32118; 252-2563) 20 rooms and efficiencies, outdoor heated pool, a/c, TV, beach, kitchenettes, children free with parents, no pets, CC. SGL/DBL$35-$75.

Desert Inn (900 North Atlantic Ave., 32118; 258-6555, Fax 673-1991, 800-826-1711) 217 rooms and suites, outdoor pool, exercise center, a/c, TV, NS rooms, in-room refrigerators and microwaves, no pets, wheelchair access, children free with parents, 10 meeting rooms, CC. SGL/DBL$50-$59, STS$72.

Econo Lodge (2250 Volusia Ave., 32114; 255-3661, 800-4-CHOICE) 48 rooms, children free with parents, no pets, NS rooms, wheelchair access, a/c, TV, laundry facilities, senior rates, CC. 1 mile from the Daytona airport, 1 block from the Daytona International Speedway. SGL/DBL$26-$125.

Econo Lodge Beachfront (301 South Atlantic Ave., 32118; 255-6421, 800-55-ECONO) 100 rooms, restaurant, lounge, entertainment, outdoor pool, laundry facilities, children free with parents, no pets, NS rooms, wheelchair access, a/c, TV, senior rates, CC. 6 miles from the Jai Alai fronton, dog track, and Daytona airport. LS SGL/DBL$40-$100; HS SGL/DBL$50-$150.

El Caribe Motel (2125 South Atlantic Ave., 32119; 252-1558, 800-445-9889) 125 rooms, efficiencies and suites, outdoor pool, beach, a/c, TV, NS rooms, no pets, children free with parents, in-room refrigerators and microwaves, laundry facilities, CC. SGL/DBL$60-$90, 1BR$200, 2BR$280.

Esquire Beach Motel (422 North Atlanta Ave., 32118; 255-3601) 68 rooms, outdoor pool, in-room refrigerators, a/c, TV, wheelchair access, NS rooms, no pets, kitchenettes, senior rates, CC. SGL/DBL$45-$55.

Flamingo Inn (2011 South Atlantic Ave., 32118; 252-1412, Fax 252-1412) 27 rooms and efficiencies, outdoor pool, beach, a/c, TV, wheelchair access, NS rooms, no pets, children free with parents, in-room refrigerators and microwaves, senior rates, CC. SGL/DBL$30-$150.

Hampton Inn (1715 Volusia Ave., 32114; 257-4030, Fax 257-5721, 800-426-7866, 800-HAMPTON) 121 rooms, outdoor pool, exercise center, whirlpools, airport transportation, children free with parents, NS rooms, wheelchair access, in-room computer hookups, fax service, no pets, in-room refrigerators, TV, a/c, local transportation, free local calls, meeting facilities, senior rates, CC. 6 miles from Atlantic beaches, 1 mile from Embry-Riddle University. LS SGL/DBL$55-$60; HS SGL/DBL$60-$70.

Hawaiian Inn (2310 South Atlantic Ave., 32118; 255-5411, Fax 253-1209, 800-922-3023) 211 rooms and suites, restaurant, lounge, outdoor heated pool, no pets, children free with parents, in-room refrigerators, laundry facilities, a/c, TV, wheelchair access, NS rooms, meeting facilities, senior rates, CC. LS SGL/DBL$45-$50; HS SGL/DBL$85-$115.

Hilton Resort (2637 South Atlantic Ave., 32118; 767-7350, Fax 760-3651, 800-HILTONS, 800-525-7350) 213 rooms and suites, restaurant, lounge, entertainment, outdoor heated pool, exercise center, whirlpools, lighted tennis courts, children free with parents, NS rooms, in-room refrigerators and microwaves, no pets, beauty shop, airport courtesy car, gift shop, beach, wheelchair access, room service, laundry facilities, a/c, TV, meeting facilities, senior rates, CC. 7 miles from the Daytona airport. SGL/DBL$80-$175.

HoJo Inn (2015 South Atlantic Ave., 32118; 255-2446, 800-I-GO-HOJO) 41 rooms, restaurant, lounge, outdoor heated pool, beach, children free with parents, wheelchair access, NS rooms, TV, a/c, laundry facilities, kitchenettes, no pets, senior rates, meeting facilities, CC. 5 miles from the Daytona airport and Daytona International Speedway, 4 miles from the Museum of Art. SGL/DBL$35-$80.

Holiday Inn (400 North Atlantic Ave., 32118; 255-0251, Fax 238-0907, 800-HOLIDAY) 143 rooms, restaurant, lounge, outdoor pool, exercise center, children free with parents, wheelchair access, kitchenettes, no pets, gift shop, game room, a/c, TV, beach, water view, NS rooms, fax service, room service, laundry service, meeting facilities for 125, senior rates, CC. 6 miles from the regional airport, 1 block from the shopping mall. SGL/DBL$55-$120.

Holiday Inn Indigo Lakes (2620 International Speedway Blvd., 32115; 258-6333, Fax 254-3698, 800-HOLIDAY) 151 rooms, restaurant, lounge, outdoor pool, exercise center, lighted tennis courts, children free with parents, wheelchair access, a/c, TV, NS rooms, gift shop, fax service, room service, in-room refrigerators and microwaves, no pets, in-room computer hookups, laundry service, kitchenettes, airport courtesy car, meeting facilities for 300, senior rates, CC. 2 miles from the International Speedway, SGL/DBL$65-$75.

Holiday Inn Oceanfront (905 South Atlantic Ave., 32118; 255-5432, Fax 254-0885, 800-HOLIDAY) 107 rooms, restaurant, lounge, outdoor pool, exercise center, children free with parents, wheelchair access, in-room refrigerators and microwaves, no pets, beach, a/c, TV, NS rooms, fax service, room service, laundry service, meeting facilities, senior rates, CC. 1 mile from the Convention Center, 6 miles from the regional airport and International Speedway. LS SGL/DBL$45-$68; HS SGL/DBL$75-$200.

Holiday Inn Oceanfront I (2560 North Atlantic Ave., 32118; 672-1440, Fax 677-8811, 800-HOLIDAY) 143 rooms and suites, restaurant, lounge, outdoor heated pool, exercise center, whirlpools, children free with parents, beach, wheelchair access, a/c, TV, NS rooms, fax service, room service, laundry service, in-room refrigerators and microwaves, no pets, meeting facilities for 50, senior rates, CC. 1 block from the shopping mall, 7 miles from the regional airport and race track. LS SGL/DBL$55-$95; HS SGL/DBL$75-$133.

Holiday Inn Speedway (1798 Volusia Ave., 32114; 255-2422, Fax 253-1749, 800-HOLIDAY) 127 rooms, restaurant, lounge, outdoor pool, exercise center, children free with parents, wheelchair access, a/c, TV, NS rooms, local transportation, free local calls, in-room refrigerators, pets OK, fax service, room service, laundry service, meeting facilities, senior rates, CC. At the airport, 5 miles from Atlantic beaches, a 1/4-mile from the Daytona Beach Industrial Park. SGL/DBL$55-$160.

Howard Johnson (3501 South Atlantic Ave., 32127; 767-8740, Fax 788-8609, 800-I-GO-HOJO) 173 rooms, restaurant, lounge, entertainment, outdoor pool, beach, children free with parents, wheelchair access, NS rooms, gift shop, game room, TV, a/c, laundry facilities, no pets, senior rates, meeting facilities, CC. 8 miles from the Daytona International Speedway and Daytona airport, 5 miles from the Boardwalk. LS SGL/DBL$45-$75; HS SGL/DBL$199-$255.

Howard Johnson Hotel (600 North Atlantic Ave., 32118; 255-4471, Fax 253-7543, 800-I-GO-HOJO, 800-767-4471) 323 rooms and suites, restaurant, lounge, entertainment, outdoor heated pool, beach, gift shop, game room, in-room refrigerators, children free with parents, wheelchair access, NS rooms, TV, a/c, laundry facilities, senior rates, 10 meeting rooms, 25,000 square feet of meeting and exhibition space, meeting facilities for 1,000, CC. 6 miles from the Daytona airport, 4 miles from the Daytona International Speedway, 1 mile from the downtown area. SGL/DBL$75-$125, STS$120-$225.

La Quinta Inn (2725 Volusia Ave., 32114; 255-7412, Fax 255-5350, 800-531-5900) 143 rooms, free breakfast, outdoor pool, complimentary newspaper, free local calls, fax service, laundry service, NS rooms, in-room refrigerators and microwaves, children free with parents, pets OK, wheelchair access, TV, a/c, meeting facilities, senior rates, CC. 5 miles from the Jai Alai fronton and Atlantic beaches, 2 miles from the regional airport. LS SGL/DBL$55-$65; HS SGL/DBL$60-$70.

Live Oak Inn and Bed and Breakfast (444 South Beach St., 32114, 252-4667, 800-253-INNS) 4 rooms, restaurant, free breakfast, whirlpools, TV, a/c, VCRs, American Plan available, no pets, NS, airport transportation, CC. SGL/DBL$55-$150.

Lynn Scott Lee Motel (3707 South Atlantic Ave., 32127; 767-0691) 15 rooms and efficiencies, outdoor heated pool, beach, kitchenettes, a/c, TV, children free with parents, in-room refrigerators, NS rooms, no pets, laundry facilities, CC. SGL/DBL$35-$70.

Magic Carpet Motel (2601 South Atlantic Ave., 32119; 767-7312, Fax 253-8351) 44 rooms and efficiencies, outdoor pool, kitchenettes, a/c, TV, laundry facilities, no pets, CC. SGL/DBL$32-$50, EFF$50-$56.

Marriott Hotel (100 North Atlantic Ave., 32118; 254-8200, Fax 254-8841, 800-228-9290) 402 rooms and suites, restaurant, lounge, indoor and outdoor pools, whirlpools, sauna, laundry facilities, no pets, in-room refrigerators, gift shop, game room, boutiques, beauty shop, airport transportation, VCRs, children free with parents, a/c, TV, NS rooms, wheelchair access, 15 meeting rooms, 13,000 square feet of meeting and exhibition space, senior rates, CC. 10 miles from the Daytona airport, 1 block from the Convention Center. SGL/DBL$95-$113.

Morgan's Bed and Breakfast (3711 South Atlantic Ave., 32127; 767-3119) free breakfast, NS, no pets, a/c, TV, CC. SGL$71, DBL$82.

National 9 Tropical Seas Motel (3357 South Atlantic Ave., 32127; 767-8737, 800-524-9999) 75 rooms and 2-bedroom efficiencies, outdoor pool, NS rooms, wheelchair access, a/c, TV, children free with parents, senior rates, CC. SGL/DBL$50-$80, 2BR$80-$110.

Nautilus Inn (1525 South Atlantic Ave., 32118; 254-8600, Fax 253-9935, 800-874-7420) 90 rooms, free breakfast, outdoor pool, beach, whirlpools, kitchenettes, children free with parents, in-room refrigerators and microwaves, no pets, laundry facilities, NS rooms, a/c, TV, senior rates, CC. SGL/DBL$50-$125.

Nomad Motel (3101 South Atlantic Ave., 32119; 767-7272) 24 rooms, outdoor pool, kitchenettes, in-room refrigerators, a/c, TV, children free with parents, beach, senior rates, CC. SGL/DBL$28-$60.

Ocean Court (2315 South Atlantic Ave., 32118; 253-8185) 33 rooms, outdoor pool, beach, kitchenettes, beach, a/c, TV, senior rates, CC. SGL/DBL$28-$100.

Ocean Inn (101 South Ocean Ave., 32118; 238-6440, 800-338-6440) 55 efficiencies and suites, outdoor pool, beach, children free with parents, no pets, wheelchair access, CC. SGL/DBL$35, STS$60-$80.

Ocean Sands Hotel (1024 North Atlantic Ave., 32118; 225-1131, 800-543-2923) 94 rooms and apartments, restaurant, lounge, indoor and outdoor pools, a/c, TV, wheelchair access, children free with parents, kitchenettes, laundry facilities, no pets, water view, NS rooms, senior rates, CC. LS SGL/DBL$55-$75; HS SGL/DBL$125-$145.

Ocean Villa Motel (828 North Atlantic Ave., 32118; 252-4644, 800-225-3691) 37 rooms and suites, outdoor heated pool, beach, kitchenettes, in-room refrigerators, game room, laundry facilities, no pets, children free with parents, CC. LS SGL/DBL$38-$66; HS SGL/DBL$75-$130.

Old Salty's Inn (1921 South Atlantic Ave., 32119; 252-8090) 19 rooms and 1- and 2-bedroom apartments, outdoor pool, beach, a/c, TV, wheelchair access, kitchenettes, in-room refrigerators, laundry facilities, children free with parents, NS rooms, no pets, senior rates, CC. LS SGL/DBL$30-$40; HS SGL/DBL$50-$58.

Palm Circle Villas (2327 South Atlantic Ave., 32118; 255-4004, 800-217-3947) 18 1- and 2-bedroom cottages, outdoor pool, beach, pets OK, a/c, TV, in-room refrigerators and microwaves, complimentary newspaper, children free with parents, NS rooms, wheelchair access, CC. SGL/DBL$30-$100.

Palm Plaza Motel (3301 South Atlantic Ave., 32118; 767-1711, Fax 756-8394, 800-448-2286) 153 rooms and 1- and 2-bedroom room apartments, restaurant, outdoor heated pool, beach, whirlpools, a/c, TV, wheelchair access, kitchenettes, no pets, laundry facilities, in-room refrigerators and microwaves, NS rooms, senior rates, CC. LS SGL/DBL$65-$125; HS SGL/DBL$135-$265.

Park Inn International (930 North Atlantic Ave., 32118; 255-6591, 800-437-PARK) 118 rooms and suites, restaurant, lounge, outdoor pool, gift shop, airport courtesy car, kitchenettes, a/c, TV, complimentary newspaper, wheelchair access, NS rooms, senior rates, CC. SGL/DBL$50-$95.

Perry Ocean Edge (2209 South Atlantic Ave., 32119; 255-0581, Fax 258-7315, 800-447-0002, 800-342-0102 in Florida) 204 rooms and suites, restaurant, free breakfast, indoor and outdoor heated pools, whirlpools, no pets, a/c, TV, wheelchair access, laundry facilities, gift shop, game room, beach, in-room refrigerators, microwaves and coffee makers, NS rooms, senior rates, 2 meeting rooms, CC. SGL/DBL$45-$120.

Pier Side Inn (3703 South Atlantic Ave., 32127; 767-4650, 800-728-4650) 35 rooms and efficiencies, heated pool, beach, a/c, TV, in-room refrigerators, children free with parents, no pets, laundry facilities, wheelchair access, NS rooms, senior rates, CC. LS SGL/DBL$35-$60; HS SGL/DBL$85-$110.

Quality Inn On The Beach (1615 South Atlantic Ave., 32118; 255-0921, Fax 255-3849, 800-CLARION, 800-874-0975, 800-221-2222) 195 rooms and suites, restaurant, lounge, outdoor pool, exercise center, children free with parents, a/c, TV, wheelchair access, water view, room service, laundry service, no pets, gift shop, beach, NS rooms, meeting facilities, senior rates, CC. 10 miles from the Daytona International Speedway. SGL/DBL$55-$135.

Ramada Inn Surfside (3125 South Atlantic Ave., 32118; 788-1000, Fax 788-1000, 800-2-RAMADA, 800-255-3838) 110 rooms and 2-bedroom suites, restaurant, lounge, entertainment, outdoor heated pool, beach, wheelchair access, NS rooms, a/c, TV, children free with parents, room service, laundry facilities, in-room refrigerators, no pets, meeting facilities for 500, senior rates, CC. 10 miles from the Jai Alai fronton. SGL/DBL$60-$150.

Ramada Inn (1000 North Atlantic Ave., 32118; 239-9795, Fax 238-7900, 800-2-RAMADA) 110 rooms and suites, restaurant, lounge, outdoor heated pool, wheelchair access, NS rooms, free parking, a/c, TV, children free with parents, beach, kitchenettes, room service, laundry facilities, meeting facilities, senior rates, CC. 1 mile from the Convention Center. SGL/DBL$55-$155.

Ramada Beach Resort (2700 North Atlantic Ave., 32118; 672-3700, Fax 673-7262, 800-2-RAMADA) 383 rooms and suites, restaurant, lounge, outdoor pool, wheelchair access, NS rooms, free parking, a/c, TV, children free with parents, pets OK, room service, game room, kitchenettes, laundry facilities, 12 meeting rooms, meeting facilities for 1,000, 17,000 square feet of meeting and exhibition space, senior rates, CC. SGL/DBL$70-$110.

The Reef (935 South Atlantic Ave., 32118; 252-2581, Fax 257-3608, 800-874-0136) 235 rooms and efficiencies, outdoor pool, beach, in-room refrigerators, a/c, TV, children free with parents, no pets, senior rates, CC. SGL/DBL$30-$40, 1BR$40-$50.

Rodeway Inn (1299 South Atlantic Ave., 32118; 225-4545, 800-424-4777) 100 rooms, restaurant, outdoor heated pool, wheelchair access, beach, kitchenettes, NS rooms, children free with parents, no pets, laundry facilities, a/c, TV, senior rates, CC. 4 miles from the regional airport and Daytona International Speedway. SGL/DBL$30-$135.

Royal Holiday Beach Motel (3717 South Atlantic Ave., 32127; 761-5984) 30 rooms, outdoor heated pool, beach, no pets, a/c, TV, wheelchair access, children free with parents, in-room refrigerators, laundry facilities, NS rooms, senior rates, CC. SGL/DBL$35-$75.

Sand Castle Motel (3619 South Atlantic Ave., 32127; 767-3182) 31 rooms, efficiencies and 1-bedroom apartments, outdoor pool, beach, in-room refrigerators, laundry facilities, pets OK, children free with parents, CC. LS SGL/DBL$30-$42; HS SGL/DBL$45-$65.

Scottish Inn (1855 South Ridgewood Ave., 32119; 767-6681, 800-251-1962) 30 rooms, outdoor pool, a/c, TV, wheelchair access, NS rooms, children free with parents, free local calls, in-room refrigerators, kitchenettes, pets allowed, senior rates, CC. 3 miles from the Daytona airport, 10 miles from the Daytona International Speedway. SGL/DBL$18-$28.

Scottish Inn (133 South Ocean Ave., 32118; 253-0666, 800-251-1962) 79 rooms, outdoor pool, no pets, laundry facilities, a/c, TV, wheelchair access, NS rooms, children free with parents, free local calls, kitchenettes, senior rates, CC. 7 miles from the Daytona International Speedway and Daytona airport. SGL/DBL$25-$50.

Scottish Inns (1515 South Ridgewood Ave., 32114; 258-5742, 800-251-1962) 20 rooms and efficiencies, outdoor pool, free local calls, laundry facilities, pets OK, a/c, TV, wheelchair access, NS rooms, in-room refrigerators, children free with parents, free local calls, senior rates, CC. 1 mile from the golf course. SGL/DBL$18-$32.

Sea Oats Beach Motel (2539 South Atlantic Ave., 32118; 767-5684, 800-SEA-OATS) 44 rooms, heated pool, beach, a/c, TV, children free with parents, laundry facilities, pets OK, in-room refrigerators and microwaves, senior rates, CC. SGL/DBL$40-$120.

Seagarden Inn (3161 South Atlantic Ave., 32118; 761-2335, 800-245-7420) 144 rooms and condominiums, restaurant, lounge, outdoor heated pool, beach, whirlpools, laundry facilities. a/c, TV, no pets, children free with parents, kitchenettes, gift shop, room service, wheelchair access, NS rooms, senior rates, CC. SGL/DBL$100-$110.

Speedway Inn (2992 West International Speedway Blvd., 32124; 253-0643, 800-553-6499) 114 rooms, restaurant, outdoor pool, laundry facilities, pets OK, NS rooms, wheelchair access, a/c, TV, children free with parents, senior rates, CC. SGL/DBL$45-$100.

Sun Viking Lodge (2411 South Atlantic Ave., 32119; 252-6252, Fax 252-5463, 800-874-4469) 91 rooms, restaurant, Modified American Plan available, indoor and outdoor heated pools, whirlpools, sauna, exercise center, no pets, a/c, TV, wheelchair access, children free with parents, game room, VCRs, in-room refrigerators, NS rooms, senior rates, CC. LS SGL/DBL$48-$80; HS SGL/DBL$90-$144.

Sunny Shore Motel (2037 South Atlantic Ave., 32118; 252-4569) 34 rooms, outdoor pool, beach, laundry facilities, children free with parents, a/c, TV, wheelchair access, NS rooms, no pets, in-room refrigerators, senior rates, CC. LS SGL/DBL$36-$50; HS SGL/DBL$55-$70.

Thunderbird Beach Motel (500 North Atlantic Ave., 32118; 253-2562, Fax 238-3676, 800-243-6543) 97 rooms and efficiencies, outdoor pool, beach, no pets, laundry facilities, kitchenettes, a/c, TV, senior rates, CC. LS SGL/DBL$27-$37; HS SGL/DBL$30-$65.

Treasure Island Inn (2025 South Atlantic Ave., 32119; 255-8371, Fax 253-9935, 800-543-5070) 232 rooms and suites, restaurant, lounge, entertainment, heated pool, whirlpools, a/c, children free with parents, game room, beach, no pets, in-room refrigerators, microwaves and coffee makers, laundry facilities, beach, TV, wheelchair access, NS rooms, 6 meeting rooms, senior rates, CC. SGL/DBL$75-$175.

Tropical Manor Motel (2237 South Atlantic Ave., 32118; 252-4920, 800-253-4920) 36 rooms, efficiencies and 1- and 2-bedroom apartments, outdoor heated pool, a/c, TV, wheelchair access, beach, no pets, in-room refrigerators, NS rooms, senior rates, CC. LS SGL/DBL$25-$65; HS SGL/DBL$40-$80.

Tropical Winds Motel (1398 North Atlantic Ave., 32118; 258-1016, 800-245-6099) 94 rooms and efficiencies, indoor and outdoor heated pools, beach, kitchenettes, laundry facilities, in-room refrigerators, a/c, TV, VCRs, children free with parents, no pets, senior rates, CC. LS SGL/DBL$45-$60; HS SGL/DBL$105-$140.

Whitehall Inn (640 North Atlantic Ave., 32118; 258-5435, Fax 253-0735, 800-874-7016) 204 rooms and efficiencies, restaurant, lounge, outdoor pool, beach, game room, NS rooms, wheelchair access, a/c, TV, children free with parents, no pets, senior rates, CC. SGL/DBL$70-$150.

Deerfield Beach

Area Code 305

Rental & Reservation Services

H.D.S. Enterprises (148 South Federal Hwy., Boca Raton, 33432; 347-8754, 800-242-0437) condos, apartments and private homes.

□□□

Beachside Gardens (2019 Northeast 4th Ct., 33441; 427-0523, Fax 428-1148) 11 rooms, outdoor pool, a/c, TV, local transportation, no pets, children free with parents, NS rooms, CC. SGL/DBL$55-$85.

Berkshire Beach Club (500 North Hwy. A1A, 33441; 428-1000) 13 1- and 2-bedroom apartments, outdoor pool, a/c, TV, wheelchair access, in-room refrigerators, microwaves and coffee makers, no pets, children free with parents, laundry facilities, senior rates, CC. SGL/DBL$65-$85.

Carriage House Resort Motel (250 South Ocean Blvd., 33441; 427-7670) 30 rooms, efficiencies and apartments, outdoor heated pool, a/c, TV, wheelchair access, laundry facilities, in-room refrigerators and coffee makers, NS rooms, no pets, airport courtesy car, senior rates, CC. LS SGL/DBL$45-$65; HS SGL/DBL$65-$108.

Comfort Suites (1040 East Newport Center, 33442; 570-8887, 800-221-2222) 100 suites, restaurant, lounge, free breakfast, outdoor pool, whirlpools, lighted tennis courts, no pets, gift shops, a/c, TV, children free with parents, NS rooms, wheelchair access, senior rates, CC. 15 miles from the regional airport, 4 miles to Atlantic beaches, 5 miles from the Boca Raton Town Center Mall. SGL/DBL$80-$125.

Days Inn Oceanside (50 Southeast 20th Ave., 33441; 428-0650, Fax 427-2666, 800-325-2525) 69 rooms, restaurant, lounge, outdoor pool, a/c, TV, wheelchair access, NS rooms, pets OK, children free with parents, beach, laundry facilities, in-room refrigerators and microwaves, senior rates, CC. 15 miles from the Ft. Lauderdale and Palm Beach airports, 1 block to Atlantic beaches. LS SGL/DBL$39-$59; HS SGL/DBL$79-$109.

Days Inn (1250 West Hillsboro Blvd., 33441; 427-2200, Fax 421-1618, 800-325-2525) 225 rooms, restaurant, outdoor pool, pets OK, a/c, TV, wheelchair access, NS rooms, laundry facilities, children free with parents, senior rates, CC. 2 miles from the shopping center, 1 mile from Century Village. SGL/DBL$45-$110.

Deerfield Beach Motel (641 South Hwy. A1A, 33441; 427-5958, 800-433-4600) 14 rooms, outdoor heated pool, a/c, TV, no pets, kitchenettes, CC. SGL/DBL$30-$65.

Deerfield Beach Resort Crown Sterling Suites (950 Southeast 20th Ave., 33441; 426-0478, Fax 360-0539, 800-433-4600, 800-545-

SAND in Florida) 244 suites, restaurant, free breakfast, lounge, entertainment, outdoor heated pool, beach, whirlpools, children free with parents, no pets, a/c, TV, NS rooms, in-room refrigerators, microwaves and coffee makers, wheelchair access, 6 meeting rooms, meeting facilities for 300, senior rates, CC. 30 miles from the Ft. Lauderdale-Hollywood airport and Broward Convention Center. LS SGL/DBL$100-$160; HS SGL/DBL$185-$275.

Frantony Resort Apartment Motel (665 South Hwy. A1A, 33441; 427-3509) 16 rooms, efficiencies and 1-bedroom apartments, outdoor pool, a/c, TV, in-room refrigerators and microwaves, no pets, children free with parents, CC. SGL/DBL$30-$60, EFF$35-$70, 1BR$50-$80.

Hansel and Gretel's Tropical Guesthouse (97 South Hwy. A1A, 33441; 427-4381, Fax 427-5979) 34 rooms, efficiencies and 1- and 2-bedroom apartments, outdoor pool, a/c, TV, no pets, children free with parents, CC. SGL/DBL$30-$80, EFF$49-$89, 1BR$50-$100, 2BR$60-$110.

Hilton Hotel (100 Fairway Dr., 33441; 427-7700, Fax 427-2308, 800-HILTONS, 800-624-3606 in Florida) 220 rooms and suites, restaurant, lounge, entertainment, outdoor heated pool, exercise center, whirlpools, complimentary newspaper, children free with parents, NS rooms, in-room computer hookups, wheelchair access, car rental desk, room service, laundry facilities, a/c, TV, no pets, in-room refrigerators, 9 meeting rooms, meeting facilities for 700, senior rates, CC. 2 miles from the Town Center Mall and Atlantic beaches, 26 miles from the Ft. Lauderdale-Hollywood airport and Broward Convention Center. LS SGL/DBL$50-$89; HS SGL/DBL$99-$129.

Howard Johnson Ocean Resort and Cone Center (2096 Northeast 2nd St., 33441; 428-2850, Fax 480-9639, 800-426-0084, 800-I-GO-HOJO) 177 rooms, restaurant, lounge, entertainment, outdoor heated pool, in-room refrigerators, no pets, children free with parents, game room, Modified American Plan available, gift shop, wheelchair access, room service, NS rooms, TV, a/c, laundry facilities, senior rates, 8 meeting rooms, meeting facilities for 400, CC. 23 miles from the Ft. Lauderdale-Hollywood airport, 18 miles from the Broward Convention Center. SGL/DBL$45-$75.

La Quinta Inn (351 West Hillsboro Blvd., 33441; 421-1004, Fax 427-8069, 800-531-5900) 130 rooms, restaurant, free breakfast, outdoor pool, complimentary newspaper, free local calls, fax service, laundry service, NS rooms, pets OK, children free with parents, wheelchair access, TV, a/c, meeting facilities, senior rates, CC. 5 miles from Atlantic beaches and Town Center Mall, 10 miles from Ft. Lauderdale. SGL/DBL$45-$75.

Ocean Terrace Motel (2080 Hillsboro Blvd., 33441; 427-8400, 800-728-1594) 27 rooms and 1-, 2-, and 3-bedroom apartments, outdoor heated pool, kitchenettes, a/c, TV, in-room refrigerators and microwaves, wheelchair access, laundry facilities, no pets, NS rooms, senior rates, CC. LS SGL/DBL$65-$89; HS SGL/DBL$114-$154.

Panther Motel and Apartments (715 Southeast Hwy. A1A, 33441; 427-0700) 20 rooms, efficiencies and 1-bedroom apartments, outdoor pool, a/c, TV, in-room refrigerators, microwaves and coffee makers, laundry facilities, wheelchair access, NS rooms, senior rates, CC. LS SGL/DBL$245W-$345W; HS SGL/DBL$320W-$485W.

Quality Suites Hotel (1050 East Newport Center Dr., 33442; 570-8888, Fax 570-5346) 107 rooms and suites, restaurant, lounge, outdoor heated pool, whirlpools, lighted tennis courts, gift shop, in-room refrigerators, microwaves and coffee makers, children free with parents, VCRs, wheelchair access, laundry facilities, NS rooms, TV, a/c, children free with parents, 3 meeting rooms, meeting facilities for 200, senior rates, CC. 15 miles from the Ft. Lauderdale-Hollywood airport and Broward Convention Center. SGL/DBL$100-$150.

Ramada Inn (1401 South Federal Hwy., 33441; 421-5000, Fax 436-2811, 800-2-RAMADA) 107 rooms and suites, restaurant, lounge, outdoor heated pool, wheelchair access, NS rooms, free parking, a/c, TV, in-room refrigerators, children free with parents, beauty shop, local transportation, room service, laundry facilities, meeting facilities, senior rates, CC. 5 miles from Atlantic beaches, 1 block from the shopping mall, 3 miles from the golf course. SGL/DBL$40-$100.

Shore Road Inn (460 South Hwy. A1A, 33441; 427-8820) 18 rooms, efficiencies and 1-bedroom apartments, outdoor pool, kitchenettes, in-room refrigerators, no pets, laundry facilities, CC. SGL/DBL$35-$100.

Tropic Isle Apartments and Motel (370 South Hwy. A1A, 33441; 427-1000, Fax 429-9745) 15 rooms and 1-bedroom apartments, outdoor heated pool, laundry facilities, a/c, TV, no pets, children free with parents, CC. SGL/DBL$215W-$565W.

Wellesley Inn (100 Southwest 12th Ave., 33442; 428-0661, Fax 427-6701, 800-444-8888) 79 rooms, outdoor heated pool, laundry facilities, a/c, TV, in-room refrigerators and microwaves, children free with parents, pets OK, senior rates, CC. SGL/DBL$40-$100.

De Funiak Springs
Area Code 904

Best Western Crossroads Inn (Hwy. 331, 32433; 892-5111, 800-528-1234) 100 rooms, restaurant, lounge, outdoor pool, children free with parents, a/c, NS rooms, TV, laundry facilities, wheelchair access, room service, pets OK, meeting facilities, senior rates, CC. SGL/DBL$40-$50.

Comfort Inn (1326 South Freeport Rd., 32433; 892-1333, 800-221-2222) 62 rooms, free breakfast, outdoor pool, pets OK, laundry facilities, a/c, TV, VCRs, children free with parents, NS rooms, wheelchair access, meeting facilities, senior rates, CC. 3 miles from the regional airport and golf course. SGL/DBL$42-$47.

Econo Lodge (1325 South Freeport Rd., 32433; 892-6115, 800-4-CHOICE) 60 rooms, outdoor pool, children free with parents, no pets, NS rooms, wheelchair access, a/c, TV, senior rates, CC. SGL/DBL$40-$100.

Deland
Area Code 904

Chimney Corner Motel (1941 South Woodland Blvd., 32720; 734-3146) 32 rooms, outdoor pool, kitchenettes, a/c, TV, wheelchair access, children free with parents, no pets, NS rooms, senior rates, CC. SGL/DBL$35-$55.

Holiday Inn (350 International Speedway Blvd., 32724; 738-5200, Fax 734-7552, 800-HOLIDAY) 149 rooms, restaurant, lounge, outdoor pool, whirlpools, jacuzzi, children free with parents, wheelchair access, a/c, TV, NS rooms, in-room computer hookups, fax service, room service, laundry service, 5 meeting rooms, meeting facilities for 600, senior rates, CC. 2 miles from Stetson University, 15 miles from Blue Springs State Park. SGL/DBL$60-$135.

Hontoon Landing Marina and Riverview Motel (2317 River Ridge Rd., 32720; 734-2474, 800-248-2474) 18 rooms, efficiencies and suites, children free with patents, in-room refrigerators, a/c, TV, VCRs, airport transportation, no pets, kitchenettes, senior rates, CC. SGL/DBL$40-$150.

Quality Inn (2801 East New York Ave., 32724; 736-3440, 800-221-2222) 112 rooms and suites, restaurant, free breakfast, lounge, entertainment, outdoor pool, exercise center, VCRs, in-room refrigerators and microwaves, children free with parents, a/c, TV, wheelchair access, room service, laundry service, NS rooms, no pets, meeting facilities, senior rates, CC. 15 miles from the Daytona International Speedway, a 1/2-mile from the Volusia City Fairgrounds, 5 miles from Stetson University. LS SGL/DBL$35-$45; HS SGL/DBL$45-$150.

Delray Beach

Area Code 407

Rental & Reservation Services

H.D.S. Enterprises (148 South Federal Hwy., Boca Raton, 33432; 347-8754, 800-242-0437) rental condominiums, apartments and private homes.

□□□

The Breakers on the Ocean (1875 South Ocean Blvd., 33483; 278-4501) 22 rooms and 2-bedroom suites, free breakfast, outdoor heated pool, in-room coffee makers, a/c, TV, NS rooms, beach, senior rates, CC. SGL/DBL$60-$185.

Colony Hotel (Atlantic Ave. and Route 1, 33483; 276-4123, Fax 274-0035, 800-552-2363) 70 rooms and suites, restaurant, lounge, entertainment, a/c, TV, pets OK, CC. SGL/DBL$75-$190.

Dover House (110 South Ocean Blvd., 33483; 276-0309, Fax 276-7364) 32 rooms, beach, a/c, TV, wheelchair access, laundry facilities, no pets, CC. SGL/DBL$45-$55.

Holiday Inn (1229 East Atlantic Ave., 33483; 278-0882, Fax 278-1845, 800-HOLIDAY) 150 rooms and suites, restaurant, lounge, entertainment, outdoor heated pool, whirlpools, beach, in-room refrigerators and coffee makers, gift shop, beach, a/c, TV, children free with parents, pets OK, senior rates, meeting facilities for 300, CC. 20 miles from the Palm Beach airport, 1 block from the shopping mall. SGL/DBL$70-$160.

Sea Aire Villas (1715 South Ocean Blvd., 33483; 276-7491) 16 rooms and apartments, a/c, TV, no pets, kitchenettes, laundry facilities, senior rates, CC. SGL/DBL$450W-$1,190W.

Seagate Hotel and Beach Club (400 South Ocean Blvd., 33483; 276-2421, Fax 243-4714, 800-233-3581) 70 1- and 2-bedroom apartments, restaurant, lounge, entertainment, outdoor heated pool, kitchenettes, a/c, TV, wheelchair access, no pets, room service, beach, senior rates, CC. LS 1BR$69-$79, 2BR$109; HS 1BR$219-$241, 2BR$285.

Spanish River Resort (1111 East Atlantic Ave., 33483; 243-7946, 800-543-SWIM) 72 rooms and 1-, 2-, and 3-bedroom suites, outdoor pool, sauna, tennis courts, in-room refrigerators and microwaves, no pets, children free with parents, wheelchair access, senior rates, CC. SGL/DBL$75, 1BR$110, 2BR$158-$175.

Wright by the Sea (1901 South Ocean Blvd., 33483; 278-3355, Fax 278-2871) 28 rooms and suites, outdoor heated pool, beach, kitchenettes, a/c, TV, VCRs, laundry facilities, wheelchair access, NS rooms, senior rates, CC. LS SGL/DBL$65-$130; HS SGL/DBL$140-$295.

Deltona

Area Code 407

Best Western Inn Deltona (481 Deltona Blvd., 32725; 6693, Fax 860-2687, 800-528-1234) 130 rooms, restaurant, lounge, outdoor pool, children free with parents, a/c, NS rooms, TV, laundry facilities, wheelchair access, no pets, meeting facilities, senior rates, CC. 5 miles from zoo. SGL/DBL$40-$125.

Destin

Area Code 904

Rental & Reservation Services

Abbott Realty Services (3500 Emerald Coast Pkwy., 837-4853, 800-336-4853) rental condos, apartments and private homes.

Resort Access (1114 Santa Rosa Blvd., Fort Walton Beach 32548; 837-7990, 800-282-9880) rental condominiums and apartments.

Sandi Nichols Associates (4987 East Hwy. 30A, Santa Rosa Beach, 32459; 231-1522, 800-648-5833) rental condominiums, townhouses and private homes.

□□□

Admiral Benbow Inn (713 Hwy. 98 East, 32541; 837-5455, 800-451-1986) 81 rooms and efficiencies, outdoor pool, a/c, TV, VCRs, in-room refrigerators, pets OK, children free with parents, NS rooms, wheelchair access, senior rates, CC. SGL/DBL$40-$70.

Beach House Condominiums (Hwy. 98 East, 32541; 837-4853, 800-336-4853) 106 1- ,2- , and 3-bedroom condominiums, outdoor pool, lighted tennis courts, a/c, TV, children free with parents, no pets, in-room refrigerators, laundry facilities, senior rates, CC. 1BR$181, 2BR$215, 3BR$264.

Best Rest Inn (402 Hwy. 98 East, 32540; 837-7326, 800-874-0470) 70 rooms, outdoor pool, a/c, TV, laundry facilities, children free with parents, CC. SGL/DBL$55-$65.

Breakers East Condominium (1010 Hwy. 98 East, 32541; 837-1010, 800-338-4418) 2- and 3-bedroom condominiums, beach, outdoor pool, a/c, kitchenettes, TV, no pets, children free with parents, laundry facilities, senior rates, CC. 2BR$169-$123, 3BR$185-$232.

Canal Townhouses (20 Durango Rd., 32541; 800-336-Gulf) 3-bedroom townhouses, in-room refrigerators, microwaves and coffee makers, a/c, TV, children free with parents, no pets, wheelchair access, CC. 3BR$75-$150.

Comfort Inn (405 Hwy. 98 East, 32541; 837-0007, 800-221-2222) 131 rooms, outdoor pool, a/c, TV, kitchenettes, children free with parents, laundry facilities, NS rooms, wheelchair access, in-room refrigerators, no pets, senior rates, CC. 3 miles from the Destin airport, 15 miles from the Pensacola airport, 1 mile to Gulf beaches. SGL/DBL$40-$70.

Days Inn (1029 Hwy. 98 East, 32541; 837-2599, Fax 837-2490, 800-325-2525) 60 rooms, free breakfast, outdoor pool, whirlpools, a/c, TV, children free with parents, wheelchair access, in-room refrigerators, pets OK, NS rooms, beach, laundry facilities, senior rates, CC. 14 miles from the Pensacola airport and Eglin Air Force Base. SGL/DBL$35-$75.

Destin Towers (1008 Hwy. 98 East, 32541; 837-7212, 800-338-4418) 2-bedroom condos, outdoor pool, beach, lighted tennis courts, a/c, TV, wheelchair access, children free with parents, in-room refrigerators, microwaves and coffee makers, laundry facilities, senior rates, CC. 2BR$1,325.

East Pass Towers (100 Gulfshore Dr., 32541; 837-4191, 800-541-4191) 2-bedroom apartments, outdoor pool, a/c, TV, wheelchair access, kitchenettes, no pets, children free with parents, VCRs, laundry facilities, in-room refrigerators, microwaves, and coffee makers, beach, senior rates, CC. 2BR$100-$160.

Frangista Beach Inn (4150 Hwy. 98 East, 32541; 654-5501, Fax 654-5876, 800-382-2612) 21 rooms and 1- and 2-bedroom suites, children free with parents, kitchenettes, no pets, beach, laundry facilities, a/c, TV, wheelchair access, NS rooms, senior rates, CC. SGL/DBL$80-$185.

Green Reef (3650 Hwy. 98 East, 32541; 837-0002, 800-869-7590) 20 2-bedroom townhouses, outdoor pool, beach, children free with parents, kitchenettes, no pets, laundry facilities, senior rates, CC. 2BR$1,340W-$1,400W.

Gulf Winds East (3855 Hwy. 98 East, 32541; 837-6195, 800-426-6196) 165 2-bedroom townhouses, outdoor pool, jacuzzi, a/c, TV, children free with parents, VCRs, no pets, laundry facilities, beach, CC. 2BR$675W.

Henderson Park Inn (2700 Hwy. 98 East, 32541; 654-0400, Fax 837-5390, 800-336-4853) 37 rooms and villas, restaurant, free breakfast, outdoor heated pool, beach, a/c, TV, NS rooms, in-room coffee makers, children free with parents, no pets, kitchenettes, senior rates, meeting facilities for 60, CC. SGL/DBL$90-$260.

Hidden Dunes (5394 Hwy. 98, 32541; 837-3521, 800-824-6335) 2- and 3-bedroom condominiums and beach cottages, outdoor pool, tennis, exercise center, beach, in-room refrigerators, microwaves and coffee makers, a/c, TV, children free with parents, laundry facilities, CC. 2BR$1,395, 3BR$1,975.

Holiday Inn (1020 Hwy. 98 East, 32541; 837-6181, 800-HOLIDAY) 230 rooms and suites, restaurant, lounge, outdoor pool, beach, exercise center, gift shop, no pets, a/c, TV, beach, water view, children free with parents, laundry service, gift shop, 7 meeting rooms, meeting facilities for 200, senior rates, CC. 8 miles from the Gulfarium and the outlet malls, 1 mile from the regional airport. SGL/DBL$60-$250.

Holiday Surf and Racquet Club (510 Gulfshore Dr., 32541; 800-336-Gulf) 1- , 2- , and 3-bedroom condominiums, outdoor heated pool, exercise center, tennis courts, sauna, laundry facilities, in-room refrigerators, microwaves and coffee makers, a/c, TV, children free with parents, no pets, wheelchair access, CC. 1BR/3BR$80-$175.

Jetty East (500 Gulfshore Dr., 32541; 837-2141) 85 1- to 4-bedroom townhouses and suites, outdoor pool, beach, lighted tennis courts, a/c, TV, kitchenettes, wheelchair access, laundry facilities, children free with parents, senior rates, CC. 1BR/4BR$100-$365.

Sandestin (5500 Hwy. 98 East, 32541; 267-8160, Fax 267-8197, 800-277-0803) 535 rooms, suites and villas, restaurant, lounge, heated pool, whirlpools, sauna, exercise center, a/c, TV, kitchenettes, wheelchair access, children free with parents, beach, NS rooms, in-room refrigerators, room service, 16 meeting rooms, senior rates, CC. LS SGL/DBL$55-$135; HS SGL/DBL$225-$325.

Sandestin Beach Hilton (5540 Hwy. 98 East, 32541; 267-9500, Fax 267-3076, 800-HILTONS, 800-367-1271) 400 suites, restaurant, lounge, entertainment, heated pool, exercise center, whirlpools, sauna, tennis courts, children free with parents, NS rooms, wheelchair access, room service, laundry facilities, in-room refrigerators, airport transportation, no pets, a/c, TV, 14 meeting rooms, 22,000 square feet of meeting and exhibition space, senior rates, CC. 25

miles from the Fort Walton airport, 62 miles from the Pensacola airport. SGL/DBL$190-$260.

Seascape Resort and Conference Center (100 Seascape Dr., 32541; 837-9181, Fax 837-4769, 800-874-9106, 800-342-2710 in Florida) 115 cottages, restaurant, lounge, outdoor pool, exercise center, beach, lighted tennis courts, a/c, TV, NS rooms, wheelchair access, children free with patents, no pets, senior rates, CC. SGL/DBL$105-$220.

Sleep Inn (50000 Emerald Coast Pkwy., 32541; 654-7022, 800-221-2222) 77 rooms, restaurant, free breakfast, outdoor pool, in-room computer hookups, wheelchair access, NS rooms, children free with parents, in-room refrigerators and microwaves, no pets, senior rates, a/c, TV, meeting facilities, CC. 3 blocks from Gulf beaches, 11 miles from Pensacola airport, 3 miles from Destin airport. SGL/DBL$55-$85.

Sun Destin Beach and Meeting Resort (1040 Hwy. 98 East, 32541; 800-336-Gulf) 268 1-, 2-, and 3-bedroom condominiums, lounge, indoor and outdoor heated pools, exercise center, sauna, whirlpools, game room, beach, laundry facilities, in-room refrigerators, microwaves and coffee makers, a/c, TV, children free with parents, no pets, wheelchair access, CC. 1BR$70-$160, 2BR$95-$229, 3BR$129-$275.

Tops'L Beach Manor (5554 Hwy. 98 East, 32541; 267-9222, Fax 267-2955, 800-476-9222) 57 rooms and 1-, 2-, and 3-bedroom apartments, restaurant, lounge, entertainment, indoor and outdoor pools, whirlpools, lighted tennis courts, sauna, kitchenettes, children free with parents, in-room refrigerators, fireplaces, no pets, a/c, TV, wheelchair access, NS rooms, 11 meeting rooms, senior rates, CC. SGL/DBL$120-$250.

Waterview Towers Condominiums (150 Gulfshore Dr., 32541; 800-336-Gulf) 2- and 3-bedroom condominiums, outdoor pool, lighted tennis courts, jacuzzi, beach, laundry facilities, in-room refrigerators, microwaves and coffee makers, a/c, TV, children free with parents, no pets, wheelchair access, CC. 2BR$89-$286.

Dundee

Area Code 813

Rental & Reservation Services

G.K. Properties (Dundee 33838; 439-3688) rental apartments.

□□□

Holiday Inn (Hwy. 27, 33838; 439-1591, Fax 439-5297, 800-HOLI-DAY) 100 rooms, restaurant, lounge, entertainment, outdoor heated pool, children free with parents, wheelchair access, a/c, TV, NS rooms, fax service, room service, in-room refrigerators, pets OK, laundry service, meeting facilities for 100, senior rates, CC. 10 miles from Bok Tower and Passion Play Theater, 6 miles from the Cleveland Indians training park. SGL/DBL$40-$98.

Dunedin

Area Code 813

Amberlee Motel (1035 Broadway, 34698; 733-3228) 22 rooms, outdoor pool, a/c, TV, wheelchair access, no pets, children free with parents, laundry facilities, CC. LS SGL/DBL$24-$34; HS SGL/DBL$44-$58.

Best Western Jamaica Inn (150 Marina Plaza, 34698; 733-4121, Fax 736-4365, 800-528-1234, 800-447-4728) 55 rooms, restaurant, lounge, outdoor heated pool, kitchenettes, children free with parents, a/c, NS rooms, TV, laundry facilities, wheelchair access, water view, no pets, meeting facilities, senior rates, CC. LS SGL/DBL$59-$69; HS SGL/DBL$85-$95.

Econo Lodge (1414 Bayshore Blvd., 34698; 734-8851, 800-4-CHOICE) 38 1- to 4-room suites, outdoor pool, children free with parents, no pets, NS rooms, wheelchair access, in-room refrigerators and coffee makers, a/c, TV, senior rates, CC. 15 miles from the regional airport. SGL/DBL$50-$155.

Inn on the Bay (1420 Bayshore Blvd., 34698; 734-7689, 800-759-5045) 41 efficiencies, free breakfast, outdoor heated pool, a/c, TV, NS rooms, CC. SGL/DBL$60-$90.

Eastpoint
Area Code 904

The Sportsman's Lodge (119 North Bayshore Dr., 32328; 670-8423) 30 rooms and efficiencies, children free with parents, kitchenettes, a/c, TV, CC. SGL/DBL$35-$45.

Edgewater
Area Code 904

The Colonial House (110 Yelca Terrace, 32032; 427-4570) 2 rooms and suites, outdoor pool, kitchenettes, no pets, children free with parents, a/c, TV, CC. SGL/DBL$45-$55.

Ellenton
Area Code 813

Rental & Reservation Services

Check-In Reservation Services (7282 55th Ave. East, Bradenton 34205; 867-7760, 800-237-1033) rental condos and apartments.

□□□

Best Western Inns (5218 East 17th St., 34222; 729-8505, Fax 729-1110, 800-528-1234) 73 rooms and efficiencies, free breakfast, outdoor heated pool, whirlpools, spa, children free with parents, a/c, NS rooms, TV, laundry facilities, wheelchair access, pets OK, meeting facilities, senior rates, CC. SGL/DBL$80-$115.

Elliston
Area Code 904

Red Carpet Inn (I-75 and Hwy. 441, 32055, 752-7582, 800-251-1962) 50 rooms, children free with parents, TV, a/c, NS rooms, meeting facilities, pets OK, senior rates, CC. 7 miles from the Itchetucknee Springs State Park, 30 miles from the Gainesville airport and University of Florida, 15 miles from the Florida Sports Hall of Fame. SGL/DBL$35-$40.

Englewood

Area Code 813

Rental & Reservation Services

Check-In Reservation Services (7282 55th Ave. East, Bradenton 34205; 867-7760, 800-237-1033) rental condos and apartments.

□□□

Colony Don Pedro (7050 Placida Rd., 34224; 697-2192) 29 rooms and 2-bedroom villas, outdoor heated pool, whirlpools, lighted tennis courts, VCRs, a/c, TV, wheelchair access, water view, NS rooms, senior rates, CC. SGL/DBL$600W-$950W.

Days Inn (2540 South McCall Rd., 34224; 474-5544, Fax 475-2124, 800-325-2525) 84 rooms, restaurant, free breakfast, outdoor heated pool, free local calls, children free with parents, a/c, TV, wheelchair access, NS rooms, no pets, laundry facilities, senior rates, CC. 2.5 miles from Gulf beaches, 25 miles from the Ringling Museums, 7 miles from Boca Grande. SGL/DBL$45-$53.

Manasota Beach Club (7660 Manasota Key, 34223; 474-2614) 29 rooms and 18 cottages, restaurant, outdoor pool, tennis, wheelchair access, kitchenettes, NS rooms, children free with parents, laundry facilities, no pets. SGL/DBL$280-$300.

Palm Manor Condominiums (1531 Placida Rd., 34223; 475-0900, Fax 475-5366, 800-848-8141) 50 2-bedroom apartments, outdoor heated pool, tennis courts, children free with parents, kitchenettes, wheelchair access, no pets, a/c, TV, CC. SGL/DBL$375W-$650W.

Seafarer Beach Motel (8520 Manasota Key Rd., 34223; 474-4388) 8 rooms, outdoor heated pool, laundry facilities, kitchenettes, no pets, a/c, TV, beach, CC. SGL/DBL$310W-$610W.

Veranda Inn of Englewood (2073 South McCall Rd., 34224; 475-6533, 800-633-8115) 38 rooms and 1-bedroom apartments, restaurant, outdoor pool, in-room refrigerators and microwaves, pets OK, children free with parents, laundry facilities, CC. SGL/DBL$45-$57, 1BR$60-$67.

Weston Resort (985 Gulf Blvd., 34223; 874-9883) 80 apartments, outdoor pool, a/c, TV, in-room refrigerators and microwaves, no pets, children free with parents, laundry facilities, CC. LS 1BR$41-$65, 2BR$55-$78, 3BR$70-$95; HS 1BR$55-$95, 2BR$85-$125, 3BR$115-$125.

Everglades City
Area Code 813

The Ivey House (107 Camellia St., 33929; 695-3299) 10 rooms, free breakfast, NS, no pets, a/c, TV, CC. SGL/DBL$40-$100.

The Rod and Gun Club (200 Riverside Dr., 33929; 695-2101) 25 rooms and cottages, restaurant, outdoor pool, tennis courts, pets OK, a/c, TV, CC. SGL/DBL$75.

Fern Park
Area Code 407

Comfort Inn (8245 Hwy. 17, 32730; 339-3333, 800-221-2222) 75 rooms and suites, outdoor pool, whirlpools, no pets, a/c, TV, VCRs, children free with parents, NS rooms, wheelchair access, senior rates, CC. 18 miles from the Orlando airport, 1 mile from the Jai Alai fronton, 23 miles from Walt Disney World. SGL/DBL$45-$99.

Holiday Inn (7400 South Hwy. 17, 32730; Fax 831-3951, 800-HOLI-DAY) 54 rooms and suites, free breakfast, outdoor pool, whirlpools, children free with parents, wheelchair access, a/c, TV, free local calls, NS rooms, fax service, room service, no pets, laundry service, meeting facilities for 20, senior rates, CC. 10 miles from Church Street Station. SGL/DBL$45-$55.

Fernandina Beach
Area Code 904

Rental & Reservation Services

Amelia Rental and Management Service (5225 South 1st Coast Hwy., 32034; 261-9129, Fax 261-2121, 800-874-8679) rental condos.

Atlantis on Amelia Condominium Association (3420 South Fletcher, 32034; 261-4400) rental rooms and condominiums.

Pelicans Condo Association (3460 South Fletcher, 32034; 261-4059) rental condominiums and apartments.

□□□

Bailey House (Fernandina Beach 32034; 824-2116) 4 rooms, free breakfast, NS, a/c, TV, antique furnishings, children over 10 welcome, CC. SGL/DBL$75-$95.

Balogh and Bride Bed and Breakfast (20 South 6th St., 32034; 261-3345) 4 rooms, free breakfast, no pets, no children, a/c, TV, CC. SGL$30, DBL$35-$45.

Beachside Motel (3172 Fletcher Ave., 32034; 261-4236) 20 rooms and efficiencies, restaurants, free breakfast, outdoor pool, beach, a/c, TV, children free with parents, no pets, NS rooms, senior rates. LS SGL/DBL$34-$68; HS SGL/DBL$40-$98.

Ocean View Motel (2801 Atlantic Ave., 32034; 261-0193, 800-942-WAVE) 26 rooms and efficiencies, outdoor pool, pets OK, a/c, TV, kitchenettes, laundry facilities, children free with parents, CC. LS SGL/DBL$33-$40; HS SGL/DBL$50-$75.

Oceans of Amelia (382 South Fletcher Ave., 32034; 261-4013, 800-331-7428) 25 2-bedroom villas, outdoor pool, beach, in-room refrigerators, microwaves and coffee makers, laundry facilities, children free with parents, a/c, TV, wheelchair access, CC. 2BR$140.

The Phoenix's Nest (619 South Fletcher Ave., 32034; 277-2129) 5 suites, free breakfast, outdoor pool, antique furnishings, a/c, TV, in-room coffee makers, NS, beach, senior rates, CC. SGL/DBL$60-$85.

Shoney's Inn (2707 Sadler Rd., 32034; 277-2300, Fax 277-2300, 800-222-2222) 135 rooms, restaurant, lounge, entertainment, outdoor pool, whirlpools, lighted tennis courts, beauty shop, a/c, TV, NS rooms, children free with parents, complimentary newspaper, wheelchair access, fax service, senior rates, CC. SGL/DBL$60-$75.

Williams House (103 South 9th St., 32034; 277-2328) 4 rooms, free breakfast, no children, no pets, a/c, TV, CC. SGL/DBL$50.

Fisher Island

Area Code 305

Fisher Island Club (1 Fisher Island Dr., 33109; 535-6000, Fax 535-6003, 800-537-3708) 60 rooms and suites, restaurant, lounge, outdoor pool, whirlpools, jacuzzi, room service, a/c, TV, no pets, children free with parents, laundry facilities, in-room coffee makers, complimentary newspaper, local transportation, wheelchair access, senior rates, CC. LS SGL/DBL$250-$800; HS SGL/DBL$300-$975.

Flagler Beach

Area Code 904

Topaz Hotel and Motel (1224 South Oceanshore Blvd., 32036; 439-3301) 55 rooms and efficiencies, outdoor pool, whirlpools, a/c, TV, children free with parents, pets OK, wheelchair access, NS rooms, senior rates, CC. SGL/DBL$45-$90.

Flamingo

Area Code 305

Flamingo Lodge Marina and Outpost Resort (Flamingo 33030; 695-3101, 800-600-3813) 120 rooms, restaurant, lounge, outdoor pool, gift shop, children free with parents, a/c, TV, NS rooms, laundry facilities, CC. SGL/DBL$97-$114.

Florida City

Area Code 305

A-1 Motel (814 North Krome Ave., 33034; 248-2741, 800-833-1884) 45 rooms, outdoor pool, laundry facilities, a/c, TV, in-room refrigerators, children free with parents, no pets, senior rates, CC. SGL/DBL$36-$70.

Comfort Inn (333 Southeast 1st Ave., 33034; 248-4009, 800-221-2222) 65 rooms, outdoor pool, a/c, TV, no pets, children free with parents, laundry facilities, in-room refrigerators, NS rooms, wheelchair access, senior rates, CC. 2.5 miles from Coral Castle, 8 miles from Parrot Jungle, 26 miles from Everglades National Park. SGL/DBL$40-$80.

Grandma Newton's Bed and Breakfast (40 Northwest 5th Ave., 33034; 247-4413) 4 rooms, free breakfast, a/c, TV, pets OK, CC. LS SGL$30, DBL$45; HS SGL$40, DBL$60.

Hampton Inn (124 East Palm Dr., 33034; 247-8833, 800-HAMP-TON) 122 rooms, free breakfast, outdoor pool, children free with parents, NS rooms, wheelchair access, fax service, in-room refrigerators, pets OK, TV, a/c, free local calls, meeting facilities, senior rates, CC. SGL/DBL$47-$77.

Rodeway Inn (815 North Krome Ave., 33034; 268-2741, 800-424-4777) 45 rooms, outdoor pool, wheelchair access, laundry facilities, NS rooms, children free with parents, a/c, TV, senior rates, CC. 27 miles from the regional airport, 9 miles from Everglades National Park, 5 miles from Coral Castle. SGL/DBL$40-$80.

Sea Glades Motel (1223 Northeast 1st Ave., 33034; 247-6621) 49 rooms and efficiencies, outdoor pool, a/c, TV, kitchenettes, no pets, children free with parents, wheelchair access, NS rooms, senior rates, CC. SGL/DBL$40-$70.

Super 8 Motel (1202 North Krome Ave., 33034; 245-0311, Fax 247-9136, 800-800-8000) 52 rooms and suites, children free with parents, free local calls, a/c, TV, in-room refrigerators and microwaves, no pets, laundry facilities, fax service, NS rooms, wheelchair access, senior rates, CC. 9 miles from the Everglades National Park, 8 miles from Bayfront Park, 3 miles from Coral Castle. SGL/DBL$45-$80.

Ft. Lauderdale

Area Code 305

Rental & Reservation Services

Great Miami Reservation Systems (12555 Biscayne Blvd., 33180; 800-821-2183) hotel and condominium reservations.

Admiral's Court (21 Hendrick's Isle, 33301; 462-5072, Fax 763-8863, 800-248-6669) 37 rooms and 2-bedroom suites, outdoor pool, pets OK, a/c, TV, laundry facilities, in-room refrigerators, CC. SGL/DBL$50-$65, 2BR$85.

Bahia Cabana Beach Resort (3001 Harbor Dr., 33316; 524-1555, Fax 764-5961, 800-BEACHES) 116 rooms and 1- and 2-bedroom suites, restaurant, lounge, entertainment, indoor and outdoor heated pools, whirlpools, exercise facilities, wheelchair access, in-room refrigerators, microwaves and coffee makers, no pets, children free with parents, CC. 1BR$100, 2BR$120.

Bahia Mar Resort and Yachting Center (801 Seabreeze Blvd., 33316; 764-2233, Fax 524-6912, 800-327-8154) 298 rooms, restaurant, lounge, entertainment, outdoor pool, beach, no pets, tennis, exercise center, a/c, TV, children free with parents, boutiques, gift shop, car rental desk, wheelchair access, laundry facilities, 6 meeting rooms, meeting facilities for 2,200, CC. 5 miles from the Ft. Lauderdale-Hollywood airport, 1 mile from the Convention Center. SGL/DBL$99-$119.

Beach Breeze Resort Motel (550 Breakers Ave., 33304; 564-2345, Fax 565-7217, 800-443-0590) 10 rooms and 1-bedroom apartments, outdoor pool, a/c, TV, no pets, in-room refrigerators, laundry facilities, children free with parents, CC. SGL/DBL$30-$150W, 1BR$50-$220W.

Beach Plaza Hotel (625 North Atlantic Blvd., 33304; 566-7631, Fax 537-9358, 800-452-4711) 43 rooms, efficiencies and suites, outdoor heated pool, tennis courts, children free with parents, laundry facilities, in-room refrigerators and microwaves, a/c, TV, wheelchair access, NS rooms, senior rates, CC. SGL/DBL$45-$100.

Best Western Cypress Creek (999 West Cypress Creek Rd., 33309; 491-7666, Fax 491-4927, 800-528-1234) 145 rooms, free breakfast, outdoor pool, whirlpools, exercise center, hot tubs, children free with parents, a/c, NS rooms, TV, laundry facilities, wheelchair access, no pets, 4 meeting rooms, meeting facilities for 250, senior rates, CC. 4 miles from beach, 14 miles from the Convention Center, 1 mile from harness race track. SGL/DBL$47-$98.

Best Western Marina Inn and Yacht Harbor (2150 Southeast 17th St., 33316; 525-3184, Fax 764-2915, 800-528-1234, 800-327-1390) 157 rooms, restaurant, lounge, free breakfast, entertainment, outdoor heated pool, whirlpools, children free with parents, a/c, NS rooms, TV, laundry facilities, wheelchair access, in-room refrigerators, room service, no pets, airport transportation, pets OK, meeting facilities for 140, senior rates, CC. 2 blocks from the Convention Center, 1 block from shopping mall, 3 miles from the Ft. Lauderdale-Hollywood airport. SGL/DBL$60-$120.

Best Western Oceanside Inn (1180 Seabreeze Blvd., 33316; 525-8115, Fax 525-8115, 800-528-1234, 800-367-1007) 100 rooms, restaurant, lounge, outdoor heated pool, children free with parents, a/c, NS rooms, TV, laundry facilities, wheelchair access, in-room refrigerators, no pets, meeting facilities for 120, senior rates, CC. 1 mile from the Convention Center and Ocean World, 3 miles from the downtown area, 5 miles from the Ft. Lauderdale-Hollywood airport. SGL/DBL$75-$115.

Bon Aventure Resort (250 Racquet Club, 33326; 389-3300, Fax 389-3300, 800-327-8090) 504 rooms and suites, restaurant, lounge, entertainment, indoor and outdoor heated pools, lighted tennis courts, whirlpools, sauna, a/c, TV, in-room refrigerators and coffee makers, airport transportation, wheelchair access, children free with parents, no pets, NS rooms, 25 meeting rooms, 83,000 square feet of meeting and exhibition space, meeting facilities for 3,000, senior rates, CC. 20 miles from the Convention Center. SGL/DBL$80-$200.

Budgetel Inn (3800 West Commercial Blvd., 33309; 485-7900, Fax 735-5469, 800-428-3438) 102 rooms and suites, free breakfast, children free with parents, laundry facilities, a/c, wheelchair access, NS rooms, free local calls, in-room computer hookups, fax service, VCRs, TV, meeting facilities, CC. 3 miles from Lockhart Stadium, 6 miles from the Sunrise Musical Theater, 12 miles from the Ft. Lauderdale-Hollywood airport. SGL/DBL$45-$55.

By-Eddy Motel Apartments (1021 Northeast 13th Ave., 33304; 764-7555) 20 rooms, efficiencies and 1-bedroom apartments, outdoor heated pool, a/c, TV, kitchenettes, children free with parents, no pets, CC. SGL/DBL$45-$65.

Cadillac Motel (3101 Bay Shore Dr., 33304; 564-0523, Fax 564-1313) 31 efficiencies and apartments, outdoor pool, tennis courts, children free with parents, no pets, a/c, TV, CC. EFF$39-$80, 1BR$55-$115.

Casa Ciento Motel and Apartments (700 Orton Ave., 33304; 561-2468, 800-544-8932) 21 efficiencies and 1-bedroom apartments, outdoor pool, in-room refrigerators, a/c, TV, pets OK, children free with parents, CC. EFF$35, 1BR$40.

Casa Granada Apartments (3003 Granada St., 33304; 467-2037) 10 rooms, efficiencies and 1-bedroom apartments, outdoor pool, airport courtesy car, a/c, TV, kitchenettes, children free with parents, laundry facilities, senior rates, CC. SGL/DBL$30-$55, EFF$45-$65, 1BR$50-$78.

Comfort Suites Convention Center (1800 South Federal Hwy., 33316; 767-8700, 800-221-2222) 110 rooms, outdoor pool, a/c, TV, VCRs, in-room refrigerators, coffee makers and microwaves, local transportation, children free with parents, NS rooms, in-room computer hookup, wheelchair access, airport courtesy car, no pets, meeting facilities, senior rates, CC. 2 miles from the Ft. Lauderdale airport, 1 mile from the Broward Convention Center and Port Everglades. LS SGL/DBL$60-$110; HS SGL/DBL$90-$140.

Crossroads Motor Lodge Airport (2460 Hwy. 84, 33312; 792-4700, Fax 792-4744, 800-327-8484, 800-233-9954 in Florida) 285 rooms and suites, a/c, TV, wheelchair access, airport courtesy car, laundry facilities, children free with parents, pets OK, meeting facilities for 40. SGL/DBL$25-$30.

Crown Sterling Suites (555 Northwest 62nd St., 33309; 772-5400, Fax 772-5490, 800-433-4600) 254 suites, restaurant, free breakfast, lounge, entertainment, outdoor heated pool, whirlpools, sauna, a/c, TV, NS rooms, in-room refrigerators and microwaves, wheelchair access, local transportation, no pets, in-room computer hookups, 10 meeting rooms, meeting facilities for 1,000, senior rates, CC. 12 miles from the Ft. Lauderdale-Hollywood airport, 14 miles from the Broward Convention Center. SGL/DBL$100-$155.

Crown Sterling Suites (1100 Southeast 17th St., 33316; 527-2700, Fax 760-7202, 800-433-4600) 363 suites, restaurant, free breakfast, lounge, outdoor heated pool, sauna, whirlpools, a/c, TV, NS rooms, in-room refrigerators, microwaves and coffee makers, wheelchair access, laundry service, airport transportation, 19 meeting rooms, 14,000 square feet of meeting and exhibition space, senior rates, CC. 3 miles from Atlantic beaches, 1 mile from the Ft. Lauderdale-Hollywood airport, 3/4 mile from Port Everglades, 2 blocks from the Broward Convention Center. SGL/DBL$120-$180.

Days Inn (4240 Galt Ocean Dr., 33308; 566-8631, Fax 566-8505, 800-325-2525) 94 rooms, restaurant, lounge, entertainment, outdoor pool, a/c, TV, gift shop, wheelchair access, NS rooms, no pets, laundry facilities, beach, meeting facilities for 75, senior rates, CC. 5 miles from the Broward Convention Center. SGL/DBL$50-$150.

Days Inn (3355 North Federal Hwy., 33306; 566-4301, Fax 566-1472, 800-325-2525) 140 rooms and suites, restaurant, lounge, outdoor pool, exercise center, in-room refrigerators and microwaves, free breakfast, a/c, TV, wheelchair access, NS rooms, no pets, laundry facilities, senior rates, CC. 1 block from the Coral Ridge Shopping Mall, 8 miles from the Ft. Lauderdale-Hollywood airport and Port Everglades. SGL/DBL$40-$110.

Days Inn (1595 West Oakland Park Blvd., 33311; 484-9290, 800-325-2525, 800-533-3297) 145 rooms, restaurant, outdoor pool, children free with parents, a/c, TV, wheelchair access, NS rooms, no pets, laundry facilities, senior rates, CC. 4 miles from the downtown area, 2 miles from the New York Yankees Training Camp, 7 miles from the Ft. Lauderdale-Hollywood airport. SGL/DBL$40-$100.

Days Inn (435 North Atlantic Blvd., 33304; 462-0444, Fax 462-1575, 800-325-2525) 80 rooms, restaurant, lounge, outdoor a/c, TV, wheelchair access, children free with parents, kitchenettes, beach, NS rooms, no pets, laundry facilities, senior rates, CC. 5 miles from the Ft. Lauderdale-Hollywood airport, 3 miles from the Broward County Convention Center. SGL/DBL$45-$125.

Days Inn Downtown-Airport (1700 West Broward Blvd., 33312; 463-2500, Fax 763-6504, 800-325-2525) 144 rooms, restaurant, outdoor pool, a/c, TV, wheelchair access, NS rooms, no pets, laundry facilities, 2 meeting rooms, meeting facilities for 210, senior rates, CC. 5 miles from the Ft. Lauderdale-Hollywood airport and Convention Center, 1 mile from the Performing Arts Center, 5 miles from Ocean World and the Plantation Mall. SGL/DBL$50-$110.

East Wind Apartment Motel (2922 Poinsettia St., 33316; 463-3122) 20 2- and 3-bedroom apartments, outdoor pool, a/c, TV, laundry facilities, wheelchair access, children free with parents, in-room refrigerators, senior rates, CC. 2BR$33-$73, 3BR$38-$80.

Estoril Apartments (2648 Northeast 32nd St., 33306; 563-3840, Fax 568-0286, 800-548-9398) 12 1- and 2-bedroom suites, a/c, TV, children free with parents, in-room refrigerators and coffee makers, laundry facilities, senior rates, CC. 1BR$390W, 2BR450W.

Flamingo Resort Inn (2727 Terramar St., 33304; 503-561-4658, Fax 568-2688, 800-283-4786) 12 1-bedroom apartments, a/c, TV, children free with parents, NS rooms, kitchenettes, laundry facilities, CC. 1BR$85.

Flying Cloud Motel (533 Orton Ave., 33304; 563-7067, Fax 561-2767) 10 rooms, outdoor heated pool, laundry facilities, no pets, a/c, TV, in-room refrigerators and coffee makers, children free with parents, CC. SGL/DBL$33-$90.

Fort Lauderdale Beach Resort (909 Breakers Ave., 33304; 566-8800, Fax 566-8802) 210 rooms and suites, restaurant, lounge, entertainment, outdoor heated pool, sauna, whirlpools, NS rooms, game room, a/c, TV, children free with parents, no pets, 3 meeting rooms, meeting facilities for 400, senior rates, CC. 8 miles from the Convention Center. SGL/DBL$130-$345.

Fort Lauderdale Motel (501 Southeast 17th St., 33316; 525-5194, Fax 522-5194, 800-222-5194) 90 1-bedroom efficiencies, restaurant, outdoor pool, a/c, TV, in-room refrigerators, children free with parents, laundry facilities, airport courtesy car, meeting facilities for 130, senior rates, CC. 2 miles from the Ft. Lauderdale-Hollywood airport, 1/2 mile from the Broward Convention Center. EFF$245W.

Guest Quarters Suite Hotel (2670 East Sunrise Blvd., 33304; 565-3800, Fax 561-0387, 800-424-2900) 230 1- and 2-room suites, restaurant, lounge, outdoor pool, exercise center, sauna, whirlpools, TV, a/c, local transportation, 24-hour room service, airport transportation, pets OK, in-room refrigerators and coffee makers, laundry service, fax service, NS rooms, gift shop, wheelchair access, 7 meeting rooms, meeting facilities for 700, senior rates, CC. 7 miles from the Ft. Lauderdale-Hollywood airport, 4 miles from the Broward Convention Center. LS SGL/DBL$90-$140; HS SGL/DBL$130-$190.

Gold Coast Apartment Hotel (545 North Atlantic Blvd., 33304; 564-4361, Fax 565-7217, 800-228-4701) 34 rooms and efficiencies, restaurant, heated pool, in-room refrigerators and microwaves, no pets, children free with parents, a/c, TV, wheelchair access, 24-hour room service, CC. LS SGL/DBL$60-$80; HS SGL/DBL$90-$110.

Hampton Inn (720 East Cypress Creek, 33334; 776-7677, Fax 776-0805, 800-426-7866) 122 rooms, free breakfast, outdoor pool, exercise center, whirlpools, no pets, children free with parents, NS rooms, wheelchair access, in-room computer hookups, fax service, TV, a/c, free local calls, meeting facilities, senior rates, CC. 6 miles from Atlantic beaches, 10 miles from the Broward Convention Center, 12 miles from the Ft. Lauderdale-Hollywood airport, 12 miles from Port Everglades. SGL/DBL$55-$100.

Holiday Inn (4900 Powerline Rd., 33309; 776-4880, Fax 776-1261, 800-HOLIDAY) 240 rooms, restaurant, lounge, outdoor pool, exercise center, children free with parents, wheelchair access, a/c, TV, NS rooms, fax service, room service, laundry service, 6 meeting rooms, meeting facilities for 400, senior rates, CC. 7 miles from the Ft. Lauderdale-Hollywood airport and the Broward Convention Center, 1 block from Lockhart Stadium, 2 miles from the race track. SGL/DBL$55-$90.

Holiday Inn Airport (2275 Hwy. 84, 33312; 584-4000, Fax 791-7680, 800-HOLIDAY) 261 rooms and suites, restaurant, lounge, outdoor pool, exercise center, children free with parents, wheelchair access, gift shop, airport courtesy car, a/c, TV, in-room coffee makers, no pets, NS rooms, fax service, room service, laundry service, meeting facilities for 200, senior rates, CC. 12 miles from the Ft. Lauderdale-Hollywood airport, 3 miles from the Sunrise Music Theater. SGL/DBL$55-$95.

Holiday Inn (999 North Atlantic Blvd., 33304; 563-5961, Fax 564-5261, 800-HOLIDAY) 240 rooms and suites, restaurant, lounge, outdoor heated pool, children free with parents, wheelchair access, a/c, TV, NS rooms, fax service, in-room refrigerators and microwaves, no pets, room service, laundry service, gift shop, 6 meeting facilities for 125, senior rates, CC. 1.5 miles from the International Swimming Hall of Fame, 2 miles from Port Everglades, 7 miles from the Ft. Lauderdale-Hollywood airport, 3 miles from the Broward Convention Center. SGL/DBL$70-$135.

Holiday Inn Northbeach (4116 North Ocean Dr., 33308; 776-1212, 800-HOLIDAY) 187 rooms, restaurant, lounge, outdoor heated pool, exercise center, tennis courts, children under 19 free with parents, wheelchair access, a/c, TV, NS rooms, fax service, room service, laundry service, beach, kitchenettes, gift shop, 3 meeting rooms, meeting facilities for 375, senior rates, CC. 4 miles from Port Everglades and the Broward Convention Center, 3 miles from the

International Swimming Hall of Fame, 6 miles from the Ft. Lauderdale-Hollywood airport. SGL/DBL$55-$78.

Holiday Inn Pier 66 Resort and Marina (2301 Southeast 17th St., 33316; 525-6666, Fax 728-33541, 800-HOLIDAY, 800-432-1956 in Florida) 384 rooms and suites, restaurant, lounge, entertainment, heated pool, laundry facilities, in-room refrigerators, 24-hour room service, a/c, TV, wheelchair access, NS rooms, meeting facilities for 1,100, 7,500 square feet of meeting and exhibition space, senior rates, CC. 2 blocks from the Broward Convention Center and Ocean World, 5 miles from the golf course, 3 blocks from the beach, 3.5 miles from the Ft. Lauderdale-Hollywood airport. SGL/DBL$105-$165; HS SGL/DBL$180-$270.

Holiday Inn West (5100 North Hwy. 441, 33319; 739-4000, 800-HOLIDAY) 259 rooms, restaurant, lounge, outdoor pool, exercise center, lighted tennis courts, game room, kitchenettes, children under 19 free with parents, wheelchair access, a/c, TV, NS rooms, fax service, room service, laundry service, 26 meeting rooms, meeting facilities for 900, senior rates, CC. 12 miles from the Ft. Lauderdale-Hollywood airport, 15 miles from the Broward Convention Center, 6 miles from the Sunrise Musical Theater, 9 miles to Atlantic beaches. SGL/DBL$65-$85.

Horizon Hotel (607 North Atlantic Blvd., 33304; 564-5211, Fax 565-1503) 59 rooms, efficiencies and 2-bedroom apartments, outdoor pool, children free with parents, kitchenettes, laundry facilities, no pets, CC. SGL/DBL$39-$75, EFF$55-$95, 2BR$63-$109.

Hostel International (3811 North Ocean Blvd., 33308; 568-1615, Fax 568-1595) 96 beds, pool, color TV, laundry facilities, a/c, CC. SGL/DBL$12-$15.

Howard Johnson Oceans Edge Resort (700 North Atlantic Blvd., 33304; 563-2451, Fax 564-8153, 800-343-9213 in Florida) 144 rooms, restaurant, lounge, entertainment, outdoor heated pool, children free with parents, in-room refrigerators, room service, beach, no pets, wheelchair access, NS rooms, TV, a/c, laundry facilities, senior rates, meeting facilities, CC. 5 miles from the Ft. Lauderdale-Hollywood airport, 2 miles from the downtown area. LS SGL/DBL$50-$75; HS SGL/DBL$95-$115.

Marriott Marina Hotel (1881 Southeast 17th St., 33316; 463-4000, Fax 527-6705, 800-228-9290) 580 rooms and suites, restaurant, lounge, entertainment, outdoor heated pool, whirlpools, exercise center, tennis courts, sauna, whirlpools, local transportation, gift shop, room service, TV, a/c, NS rooms, water view, wheelchair access, 17 meeting rooms, meeting facilities for 2,600, CC. 1 mile to Atlantic beaches, 3 miles from the Ft. Lauderdale-Hollywood airport, 1 block from Port Everglades, a 1/4-mile from the Broward Convention Center. SGL/DBL$65-$195.

Imperial Apartment Motel (3054 Harbor Dr., 33316; 525-1533) 11 2-bedroom apartments, outdoor pool, no pets, kitchenettes, a/c, TV, wheelchair access, CC. SGL/DBL$40-$85.

Ireland's Inn Resort Hotel (2220 North Atlantic Blvd., 33305; 565-6661, Fax 565-8893, 800-327-4460, 800-423-4359 in Florida) 76 rooms, restaurant, lounge, entertainment, gift shop, in-room refrigerators, NS rooms, a/c, TV, children free with parents, no pets, wheelchair access, laundry facilities, meeting facilities for 220, senior rates, CC. 4 miles from the Broward Convention Center, 7 miles from the Ft. Lauderdale-Hollywood airport. SGL/DBL$125-$185.

King Henry Arms (543 Breakers Ave., 33304; 561-0039) 12 rooms and 1-bedroom apartments, outdoor pool, kitchenettes, a/c, TV, laundry facilities, no pets, CC. SGL/DBL$38-$61, 1BR$51-$83.

Lamplighter Resort Motel (2401 North Ocean Blvd., 33305; 565-1531, Fax 565-7217, 800-443-0590) 20 1-bedroom efficiencies, outdoor pool, a/c, TV, no pets, children free with parents, in-room refrigerators and coffee makers, laundry facilities, CC. SGL/DBL$49.

Lago Mar Resort and Club (1700 South Ocean Lane, 33316; 523-6511, Fax: 523-6511, 800-255-5246) 4 rooms and 1- and 2-bedroom suites, restaurant, lounge, outdoor pool, whirlpools, tennis courts, in-room refrigerators, microwaves and coffee makers, room service, a/c, TV, no pets, children free with parents, 4 meeting rooms, meeting facilities for 700, CC. 5 miles from the Ft. Lauderdale-Hollywood airport, 1 mile from the Broward Convention Center. SGL/DBL$85-$90, 1BR$120-$140, 2BR$195.

Lauderdale Beach Hotel (101 South Atlantic Blvd., 33316; 764-0088, Fax 463-9154, 800-327-7600) 185 rooms and efficiencies, restaurant, outdoor pool, a/c, TV, kitchenettes, laundry facilities, in-room refrigerators and coffee makers, children free with parents, CC. SGL/DBL$50-$60.

Lauderdale Colonial Motel (3049 Harbor Dr., 33315; 525-3676) 12 rooms and 1- and 2-bedroom apartments, outdoor heated pool, kitchenettes, laundry facilities, a/c, TV, in-room refrigerators, microwaves and coffee makers, no pets, senior rates. LS SGL/DBL$55-$230; HS SGL/DBL$90-$295.

Mark IV Apartments (715 Northeast 6th St., 33304; 763-8016) 16 1- and 2-bedroom apartments, outdoor pool, airport courtesy car, children free with parents, a/c, TV, laundry facilities, CC. 1BR$165W-$185W, 2BR$195W-$215W.

Mark 2100 Resort Hotel (2100 North Atlantic Blvd., 33305; 566-8383, Fax 566-4325, 800-334-6275) 125 rooms and efficiencies, restaurant, outdoor pool, exercise facility, tennis, children free with parents, kitchenettes, pets OK, in-room refrigerators and microwaves, meeting facilities for 175, senior rates, CC. 7 miles from the Ft. Lauderdale-Hollywood airport, 3 miles from the Broward Convention Center. SGL/DBL$52-$64, EFF$60-$72.

Marriott's Harbor Beach Resort (3030 Holiday Dr., 33316; 525-4000, Fax 766-6165, 800-228-9290) 625 rooms and suites, restaurant, lounge, indoor and outdoor heated pools, exercise center, tennis courts, whirlpools, sauna, beach, in-room refrigerators and coffee makers, laundry facilities, 24-hour room service, no pets, a/c, VCRs, children free with parents, a/c, TV, NS rooms, local transportation, wheelchair access, 27 meeting rooms, meeting facilities for 4,000, senior rates, CC. 8 miles from the Ft. Lauderdale-Hollywood airport, 3 miles from the Broward Convention Center. LS SGL/DBL$135-$185; HS SGL/DBL$235-$350.

Marriott North (6650 North Andrews Ave., 33309; 771-0440, Fax 771-7519, 800-331-3131) 321 rooms and suites, restaurant, lounge, free breakfast, outdoor pool, whirlpools, exercise center, sauna, complimentary newspaper, in-room refrigerators, VCRs, children free with parents, a/c, TV, NS rooms, wheelchair access, gift shop, no pets, 11 meeting rooms, meeting facilities for 1,500, senior rates, CC. 10 miles from Atlantic beaches, 20 miles from Joe Robbie Stadium and Sawgrass Mills, 12 miles from the Ft. Lauderdale-Hollywood airport, 14 miles from the Broward Convention Center. SGL/DBL$125-$170, STS$250.

Martindale Apartment Motel (3006 Bayshore Dr., 33304; 467-1841, Fax 763-8109, 800-666-1841) 19 rooms, efficiencies and 1- and 2-bedroom apartments, outdoor pool, a/c, TV, children free with parents, in-room refrigerators and coffee makers, no pets, laundry facilities, senior rates, CC. 1BR$50, 2BR$90, 3BR$125.

Merrimac Beach Resort Hotel (551 North Atlantic Blvd., 33304; 564-2345, Fax 565-7217, 800-443-0590) 37 rooms and efficiencies, outdoor pool, in-room refrigerators, children free with parents, a/c, TV, laundry facilities, CC. SGL/DBL$40, EFF$45.

Moby Dick Motel (3100 Windamar St., 33304; 565-0306, Fax 565-1747, 800-548-5960) 20 rooms and 1-bedroom apartments, outdoor pool, a/c, TV, kitchenettes, children free with parents, no pets, CC. SGL/DBL$30-$40, 1BR$50.

Motel 6 (1801 Hwy. 84, 33315; 525-1363, 505-891-6161) 107 rooms, outdoor pool, free local calls, children free with parents, NS rooms, wheelchair access, a/c, TV, CC. 3 miles from the International Swimming Hall of Fame, the Ft. Lauderdale-Hollywood airport and Port Everglades, 6 miles from Atlantic beaches. SGL/DBL$30-$40.

Nina Lee Apartment Hotel (3048 Harbor Dr., 33316; 524-1568) 14 rooms and efficiencies, outdoor heated pool, a/c, TV, in-room refrigerators and coffee makers, no pets, children free with parents, CC. SGL/DBL$40-$92.

Oakland East Motor Lodge (3001 North Federal Hwy., 33306; 565-4601, Fax 565-0384, 800-633-6279) 108 rooms and apartments, outdoor heated pool, beach, VCRs, TV, a/c, children free with parents, no pets, CC. SGL/DBL$35-$145.

One Ten Tower Hotel (110 Southeast 6th St., 33301; 779-3700, Fax 779-3700) 38 1-bedroom suites, restaurant, free breakfast, outdoor pool, exercise center, wheelchair access, no pets, children free with parents, laundry facilities, a/c, TV, 3 meeting rooms, meeting facilities for 620, senior rates, CC. 3 miles from the Ft. Lauderdale-Hollywood airport, 1.5 miles from the Broward Convention Center. 1BR$100-$175.

Orton Terrace Apartment Motel (606 Orton Ave., 33304; 566-5068, Fax 564-8646) 16 rooms and 1- and 2-bedroom apartments, outdoor pool, a/c, TV, children free with parents, laundry facilities, kitchenettes, wheelchair access, NS rooms, senior rates, CC. SGL/DBL$29-$60, 1BR$41-$86, 2BR$70-$147.

Palace Bleu At The Beach (520 North Birch Rd., 33304; 566-7950, Fax 566-2342) 16 rooms and 1-bedroom apartments, outdoor pool, a/c, TV, children free with parents, no pets, in-room refrigerators and coffee makers, CC. SGL/DBL$150W, 1BR$175W.

Panorama Apartments Hotel (539 North Birch Rd., 33304; 564-3251, Fax 568-5043) 35 rooms and 1- and 2-bedroom apartments, outdoor pool, a/c, TV, children free with parents, in-room refrigerators and coffee makers, wheelchair access, laundry facilities, CC. SGL/DBL$30-$58, 1BR$45-$67, 2BR$55-$78.

Pillars Waterfront Motel (111 North Birch Rd., 33304; 467-9639, Fax 763-2845) 22 rooms, efficiencies and 1-bedroom apartments, outdoor pool, a/c, TV, children free with parents, laundry facilities, CC. SGL/DBL$30-$125.

Red Carpet Inn (4011 North Ocean Blvd., 33308; 563-0660, 800-251-1962) 45 rooms and efficiencies, restaurant, outdoor pool, children free with parents, TV, a/c, pets OK, NS rooms, meeting facilities, senior rates, CC. 5 miles from the Ft. Lauderdale-Hollywood airport and the golf course, 2 miles from the shopping mall. SGL/DBL$35-$45.

Riverside Hotel (620 East Las Olas Blvd., 33301; 467-0671, Fax 462-2148, 800-325-3280) 117 rooms, restaurant, lounge, in-room computer hookups, a/c, TV, wheelchair access, NS rooms, no pets, children free with parents, airport courtesy car, in-room refrigerators, 7 meeting rooms, meeting facilities for 800, senior rates, CC. 4 miles from the Broward Convention Center, 5 miles from the Ft. Lauderdale-Hollywood airport. SGL/DBL$70-$145.

Riviera Hotel Resort (505 North Atlantic Blvd., 33304; 565-4433) 60 rooms, efficiencies and 1-bedroom apartments, restaurant, outdoor pool, tennis courts, beach, a/c, TV, kitchenettes, laundry facilities, CC. SGL/DBL$55-$80, EFF$60-$90, 1BR$70-$100.

Rolling Hills Golf Resort (3501 West Rolling Hills Circle, 33328; 475-0400, 800-327-7735) 300 rooms and suites, restaurant, lounge, outdoor pool, exercise center, tennis courts, a/c, TV, VCRs, wheelchair access, NS rooms, kitchenettes, no pets, children free with parents, 24 meeting rooms, meeting facilities for 1,200, senior rates, CC. 10 miles from the Ft. Lauderdale-Hollywood airport, 12 miles from the Broward Convention Center. SGL/DBL$60-$65.

Sandi Shores Motel (3008 Bayshore Dr., 33304; 728-8649, Fax 767-9063, 800-637-9604) 12 rooms and 1-bedroom apartments, outdoor pool, a/c, TV, in-room refrigerators, NS rooms, no pets, children free with parents, CC. SGL/DBL$30, 1BR$40.

Sandpiper Island Resort (91 Isle of Venice, 33301; 527-0026, Fax 527-1732, 800-543-2006) 20 1- and 2-bedroom apartments, outdoor pool, whirlpools, a/c, TV, wheelchair access, children free with parents, in-room refrigerators, laundry facilities, CC. 1BR$75-$475W, 2BR$105-$595W.

Sea Isle Apartments (3003 Viramar St., 33304; 564-8556, Fax 566-5159) 19 rooms and 1-bedroom apartments, kitchenettes, children free with parents, laundry facilities, a/c, TV, in-room refrigerators, no pets, senior rates. LS SGL/DBL$30-$47; HS SGL/DBL$55-$80.

Sea View Apartments (550 North Birch Rd., 33304; 564-3151, Fax 561-9147, 800-356-2326) 22 rooms, efficiencies and 1- and 2-bedroom apartments, outdoor heated pool, in-room refrigerators, microwaves and coffee makers, no pets, children free with parents, a/c, TV, CC. SGL/DBL$40-$130.

Shamrock Apartment Motel (555 Antioch Ave., 33304; 566-1432, Fax 563-2298) 18 rooms, efficiencies and 1- and 2-bedroom apartments, outdoor pool, children free with parents, a/c, TV, wheelchair access, no pets, CC. SGL/DBL$30-$60, EFF$35-$70, 1BR$40-$75, 2BR$70-$140.

Sheraton Execuport Hotel (2440 West Cypress Creek Rd., 33309; 772-7770, Fax 772-4780, 800-325-3535) 139 rooms and suites, restaurant, lounge, outdoor heated pool, NS rooms, a/c, room service, TV, children free with parents, wheelchair access, no pets, 5 meeting rooms, meeting facilities for 450, 5,200 square feet of meeting and exhibition space, senior rates, CC. 10 miles from Ft. Lauderdale-Hollywood airport, 7 miles from the Broward Convention Center. SGL/DBL$65-$130.

Sheraton Yankee Clipper Hotel (1140 Seabreeze Rd., 33316; 524-5551, Fax 523-5376, 800-325-3535) 245 rooms and suites, restaurant, lounge, entertainment, indoor and outdoor heated pools, exercise center, spa, laundry facilities, beach, in-room computer hookups, no pets, NS rooms, a/c, room service, TV, children free with parents, wheelchair access, meeting facilities for 80, senior rates, CC. 5 miles from the Ft. Lauderdale-Hollywood airport, 10 miles from the Jai Alai fronton, 1 mile from the Broward Convention Center. SGL/DBL$70-$150.

Sheraton Yankee Trader Beach Resort (321 North Atlantic Blvd., 33304; 467-1111, Fax 462-2342, 800-325-3535) 465 rooms and suites, restaurant, lounge, entertainment, outdoor heated pool, exercise center, whirlpools, tennis courts, in-room refrigerators, beach, children free with parents, no pets, a/c, TV, wheelchair access, boutiques, gift shop, NS rooms, 8 meeting rooms, 9,750 square feet of meeting and exhibition space, senior rates, CC. 6 miles from the Ft. Lauderdale-Hollywood airport, 20 miles from Joe Robbie Stadium, 2 miles from the Broward Convention Center. LS SGL/DBL$65-$85; HS SGL/DBL$110-$150.

Surf and Sun Motel (512 North Atlantic Blvd., 33304; 564-4341, 800-248-0463) 40 1- and 2-bedroom efficiencies, outdoor pool, beach, a/c, TV, in-room refrigerators and coffee makers, children free with parents, pets OK, 1BR$53-$310W, 2BR$86-$500W.

TraveLodge Airport (1500 West Commercial Blvd., 33309; 776-4222, Fax 771-5026, 800-578-7878) 118 rooms, free breakfast, outdoor pool, exercise center, in-room computer hookups, wheelchair access, complimentary newspaper, laundry service, TV, a/c, VCRs, free local calls, fax service, NS rooms, in-room refrigerators and microwaves, children free with parents, 4 meeting rooms, meeting facilities for 150, senior rates, CC. 8 miles from the Ft. Lauderdale-Hollywood airport, 12 miles from the Broward Convention Center, 4 miles from Atlantic beaches. SGL/DBL$41-$55.

Trevers At The Beach (552 North Birch Rd., 33304; 564-9601, Fax 564-5618, 800-533-4744) 14 rooms, efficiencies and 1- and 2-bedroom apartments, outdoor heated pool, laundry facilities, pets OK, senior rates, CC. SGL/DBL$36-$90.

Tropic Cay Resort Motel (529 North Atlantic Blvd., 33304; 564-5900, Fax 568-1396) 48 rooms, efficiencies and 2-bedroom apartments, outdoor pool, a/c, TV, children free with parents, NS rooms, senior rates, CC. SGL/DBL$43-$79, EFF$55-$109, 2BR$63-$109.

Wellesley Inn (4800 Northwest 9th Ave., 33309; 776-6333, Fax 776-3648, 800-444-8888) 106 rooms, outdoor pool, kitchenettes, a/c, TV, wheelchair access, children free with parents, pets OK, NS rooms, senior rates, CC. SGL/DBL$40-$100.

Wellesley Inn (5070 North Hwy. 7, 33319; 484-6909, Fax 731-2374, 800-444-8888) 100 rooms and suites, free breakfast, outdoor heated pool, in-room refrigerators and microwaves, a/c, TV, wheelchair access, NS rooms, laundry facilities, meeting facilities, pets OK, senior rates, CC. SGL/DBL$40-$100.

Westin Hotel Cypress Creek (400 Corporate Dr., 33334; 772-1331, Fax 491-9087, 800-228-3000) 292 rooms and suites, restaurant, lounge, entertainment, outdoor heated pool, whirlpools, exercise center, sauna, kitchenettes, children free with parents, local transportation, room service, pets OK, a/c, TV, wheelchair access, NS rooms, 20,000 square feet of meeting and exhibition space, senior rates, CC. 12 miles from the Ft. Lauderdale-Hollywood airport, 14 miles from the Broward Convention Center. LS SGL/DBL$90-$145; HS SGL/DBL$170-$185.

Windsor Manor-Marabelle (2835 Terramar St., 33304; 565-0304, Fax 564-0386) 18 rooms, efficiencies and 1-bedroom apartments, outdoor pool, a/c, TV, NS rooms, wheelchair access, children free with parents, CC. SGL/DBL$27-$50, EFF$35-$64, 1BR$45-$80.

Worthington (543 North Birch Rd., 33304; 563-6819, 800-445-7036) 14 rooms, efficiencies and 1-bedroom apartments, outdoor pool, a/c, TV, laundry facilities, in-room refrigerators, microwaves and coffee makers, no pets, children free with parents. SGL/DBL$35, EFF$40, 1BR$45.

Fort Myers

Area Code 813

Rental & Reservation Services

Vacations in Paradise Rentals (800-237-8906) rental condominiums and apartments.

ooo

Best Western Robert E. Lee Motor Inn (13021 North Cleveland Ave., 33903; 997-551, Fax 656-6962, 800-528-1234, 800-274-5511) 108 rooms, restaurant, lounge, entertainment, outdoor heated pool, whirlpools, children free with parents, water view, a/c, NS rooms, TV, no pets, beach, laundry facilities, wheelchair access, meeting facilities, senior rates, CC. 1 mile from Thomas Edison home, 3 miles from Shell Factory. SGL/DBL$45-$135.

Budgetel Inn (2717 Colonial Blvd., 33907; 275-3500, Fax 275-3500 ext 436, 800-4-BUDGET) 122 rooms and suites, free breakfast, children free with parents, a/c, wheelchair access, NS rooms, free local calls, pets OK, in-room coffee makers, in-room computer hookups, fax service, VCRs, TV, meeting facilities, CC. 10 miles from the regional airport, 3 miles from the Thomas Edison home. SGL/DBL$45-$86.

Comfort Inn (11501 Cleveland Ave., 33907; 936-3993, Fax 936-7234, 800-228-5150, 800-221-2222) 80 rooms, outdoor pool, a/c, in-room computer hookups, TV, VCRs, children free with parents, NS rooms, laundry facilities, no pets, in-room coffee makers, wheelchair access, senior rates, CC. 3 miles from the Thomas Edison home, 10 miles from Sanibel Island and the Ft. Myers airport, 2 miles from the shopping mall. SGL/DBL$55-$80.

Comfort Inn Airport (13651A Indian Paint Lane, 33912; 768-0005, 800-221-2222) 65 suites, restaurant, lounge, free breakfast, outdoor heated pool, exercise center, whirlpools, a/c, TV, in-room refrigerators, microwaves, coffee makers, laundry facilities, airport transportation, pets OK, children free with parents, NS rooms, wheelchair access, senior rates, CC. 18 miles from Thomas Edison home, 3 miles from the Ft. Myers airport, 4 miles from the Minnesota Twins Training Camp. LS SGL/DBL$65-$85; HS SGL/DBL$85-$105.

Courtyard by Marriott (4455 Metro Pkwy., 33901; 275-8600, 800-331-3131) 149 rooms and suites, free breakfast, outdoor heated pool, whirlpools, exercise center, laundry facilities, in-room refrigerators, microwaves and coffee makers, a/c, VCRs, no pets, complimentary newspaper, children free with parents, kitchenettes, a/c, TV, NS rooms, wheelchair access, meeting facilities, senior rates, CC. SGL/DBL$75-$110.

Days Inn North (13353 North Cleveland Ave., 33903; 995-0535, Fax 656-2769, 800-325-2525) 127 rooms, restaurant, outdoor pool, a/c, TV, wheelchair access, children free with parents, kitchenettes, pets OK, NS rooms, laundry facilities, senior rates, CC. 18 miles from Sanibel Island, 12 miles from Fort Myers Beach. SGL/DBL$35-$80.

Days Inn (11435 Cleveland Ave., 33907; 936-1311, 800-325-2525) 122 rooms, restaurant, lounge, outdoor pool, a/c, TV, laundry facilities, children free with parents, pets OK, senior rates, CC. 10 miles from the regional airport, 4 miles from the Thomas Edison home, 10 miles from Gulf beaches. SGL/DBL$35-$75.

Econo Lodge North (13301 North Cleveland Ave., 33903; 995-0571, 800-55-ECONO) 48 rooms, restaurant, outdoor pool, children free with parents, laundry facilities, no pets, NS rooms, wheelchair access, a/c, TV, VCRs, senior rates, CC. 3 miles from the Thomas Edison home and Shell Factory, 15 miles from the regional airport. LS SGL/DBL$35-$49; HS SGL/DBL$45-$75.

Hampton Inn (13000 North Cleveland Ave., 33903; 656-4000, 800-426-7866) 123 rooms, free breakfast, outdoor pool, children free with parents, NS rooms, wheelchair access, in-room computer hookups, fax service, no pets, TV, a/c, free local calls, meeting facilities, senior rates, CC. 2 miles from the Thomas Edison home, 10 miles from Gulf beaches, 2 miles from the Convention Center, 15 miles from the regional airport. SGL/DBL$45-$85.

Holiday Inn (2431 Cleveland Ave., 33901; 332-3232, Fax 332-0590, 800-HOLIDAY) 126 rooms, restaurant, lounge, outdoor heated pool, exercise center, in-room refrigerators, children free with parents, wheelchair access, a/c, TV, VCRs, airport courtesy car, room service, pets OK, NS rooms, fax service, room service, laundry service, meeting facilities for 75, senior rates, CC. 1/8 mile from the Red Sox Stadium and Convention Center, 18 miles from the regional airport. LS SGL/DBL$60-$70; HS SGL/DBL$110-$120.

Holiday Inn Airport (13051 Bell Tower Dr., 33907; 482-2900, 800-HOLIDAY) 227 rooms, restaurant, lounge, entertainment, outdoor pool, exercise center, in-room refrigerators, children free with parents, wheelchair access, airport courtesy car, a/c, no pets, TV, NS rooms, fax service, room service, laundry service, meeting facilities for 400, senior rates, CC. 6 miles from the Red Sox Training Camp, 1 block from the shopping mall, 8 miles from the regional airport and Convention Center. LS SGL/DBL$60-$90; HS SGL/DBL$100-$150.

La Quinta Inn (4850 South Cleveland Ave., 33907; 275-3300, Fax 275-6661, 800-531-5900) 130 rooms, free breakfast, outdoor heated pool, complimentary newspaper, free local calls, fax service, laundry service, NS rooms, children free with parents, pets OK, wheelchair access, TV, a/c, meeting facilities, senior rates, CC. 1 block from Page Field, 12 miles from the regional airport, 18 miles from Sanibel and Captiva Islands. SGL/DBL$48-$78.

Motel 6 (3350 Marinatown Lane, 33903; 656-5544, 505-891-6161) 110 rooms, outdoor pool, free local calls, children free with parents, NS rooms, wheelchair access, a/c, TV, CC. 3 miles from the Shell Factory, 1 mile from the downtown area, 2 miles from the Thomas Edison home. SGL/DBL$28-$40.

Radisson Inn Sanibel Gateway (20091 Summerlin Rd., 33908; 466-1200, Fax 446-3797, 800-333-3333) 153 rooms and suites, restaurant, lounge, entertainment, outdoor pool, exercise center, in-room refrigerators, microwaves and coffee makers, VCRs, wheelchair access, laundry facilities, game room, NS rooms, pets OK, TV, a/c, children free with parents, senior rates, CC. LS SGL/DBL$60-$80; HS SGL/DBL$120-$125.

Ramada Inn Airport (12635 Cleveland Ave., 33907; 936-4300, 936-2058, 800-2-RAMADA) 222 rooms and suites, restaurant, lounge, entertainment, outdoor pool, lighted tennis courts, gift shop, wheelchair access, NS rooms, free parking, a/c, TV, children free with parents, local transportation, room service, laundry facilities, meeting facilities for 500, senior rates, CC. 10 miles from Sanibel Island, 4 miles from the Thomas Edison home. SGL/DBL$80-$100, STS$130.

Red Carpet Inn (4811 Cleveland Ave., 33907; 936-3229, 800-251-1962) 128 rooms, restaurant, lounge, outdoor pool, children free with parents, TV, a/c, NS rooms, meeting facilities, pets OK, fax service, senior rates, CC. 10 miles from the Fort Myers airport and Gulf beaches, 2 miles from the downtown area and shopping mall. SGL/DBL$40-$44.

Roadway Inn Airport (4760 South Cleveland Ave., 33907; 275-1111, 800-228-2000, 800-424-4777) 140 rooms, restaurant, lounge, entertainment, outdoor pool, whirlpools, free local calls, laundry facilities, wheelchair access, NS rooms, children free with parents, a/c, TV, senior rates, meeting facilities, CC. LS SGL/DBL$40-$45; HS SGL/DBL$70-$145.

Sanibel Harbour Resort (17260 South Harbour Pointe Dr., 33908; 466-4000, Fax 466-2150) 340 rooms and suites, restaurant, lounge, entertainment, indoor and outdoor heated pools, lighted tennis courts, exercise center, whirlpools, beauty shop, a/c, TV, wheelchair access, kitchenettes, beach, in-room refrigerators, local transportation, children free with parents, no pets, in-room computer hookups, NS rooms, senior rates, CC. SGL/DBL$220-$300, STS$270-$850.

Santa Maria (7317 Estero Blvd., 33908; 765-6700, Fax 765-6909, 800-765-6701) 60 1- , 2- , and 3-bedroom suites, outdoor pool, sauna, whirlpools, beach, a/c, TV, wheelchair access, in-room refrigerators and microwaves, children free with parents, laundry facilities, no pets, CC. 1BR$79, 2BR$99-$109, 3BR$139.

Shell Point Village Guest House (15000 Shell Point Blvd., 33908; 466-1111, Fax 454-2220) 39 rooms, restaurant, outdoor heated pool, lighted tennis courts, laundry facilities, no pets, a/c, TV, children stay free with parents, senior rates, CC. SGL/DBL$35-$80.

Sheraton Harbor Place Hotel (2500 Edwards Dr., 33901; 337-0300, Fax 334-6835, 800-325-3535) 417 rooms and suites, restaurant, lounge, entertainment, indoor and outdoor heated pools, exercise center, lighted tennis courts, jacuzzis, sauna, in-room refrigerators and coffee makers, pets OK, airport transportation, NS rooms, a/c, room service, game room, TV, children free with parents, wheelchair access, meeting facilities for 600, 10,000 square feet of meeting and exhibition space, senior rates, CC. In the downtown area, 30 miles from Gulf beaches, 15 miles from the Ft. Myers airport. SGL/DBL$80-$120; HS SGL/DBL$150-$170.

Sleep Inn Airport (13651B Indian Paint Lane, 33912; 768-0005, 800-221-2222) 65 suites, restaurant, lounge, free breakfast, outdoor heated pool, exercise center, whirlpools, a/c, TV, in-room refrigerators, microwaves, coffee makers, laundry facilities, airport transportation, pets OK, children free with parents, NS rooms, wheelchair access, senior rates, CC. 18 miles from Thomas Edison home, 4 miles from the Minnesota Twins Training Camp, 3 miles from the Ft. Myers airport. LS SGL/DBL$65-$85; HS SGL/DBL$85-$105.

Ta Ki-Ki Motel (2631 1st St., 33916; 334-2135) 23 rooms, outdoor heated pool, kitchenettes, pets OK, in-room refrigerators, a/c, TV, CC. SGL/DBL$30-$55.

Toucan Resort (2220 West 1st St., 33901; 332-4888, Fax 334-3844) 170 rooms, restaurant, lounge, entertainment, outdoor heated pool, whirlpools, in-room computer hookups, laundry facilities, no pets, a/c, TV, wheelchair access, NS rooms, meeting facilities, senior rates, CC. SGL/DBL$40-$100.

TraveLodge (2038 West 1st St., 33901; 334-2284, Fax 334-2366, 800-578-7878) 48 rooms, outdoor pool, wheelchair access, complimentary newspaper, laundry service, TV, a/c, free local calls, fax service, no pets, NS rooms, in-room refrigerators and microwaves, children free with parents, meeting facilities, senior rates, CC. 3 blocks from the downtown area, 5 blocks from the Convention Center, a 1/2-mile from the Thomas Edison Home, 16 miles from Sanibel Island. SGL/DBL$35-$75.

Wellesley Inn (4400 Ford St., 33916; 278-3949, Fax 278-3670, 800-444-8888) 106 rooms, free breakfast, outdoor heated pool, in-room refrigerators and microwaves, pets OK, a/c, TV, wheelchair access, fax service, children free with parents, NS rooms, senior rates, CC. LS SGL/DBL$40-$45; HS SGL/DBL$80-$100.

Fort Myers Beach

Area Code 813

Rental & Reservation Services

Vacations in Paradise Rentals (800-237-8906) rental condominiums and apartments.

The Prudential Florida Realty Rental Division (7130 Estero Blvd., 33931; 463-3151, Fax 463-5542, 800-237-6285) rental condominiums, apartments, townhouses and private homes.

Realty World (30 Colorado Rd., 33936; 369-5841) rental condominiums, apartments and private homes.

The Vacation Shoppe (11595 Kelly Rd., Fort Myers 33908; 454-1400, Fax 466-3299) rental condominiums, apartments and townhouses.

□□□

Anchor Inn Cottages (285 Virginia Ave., 33931; 463-2630) 10 rooms and cottages, outdoor heated pool, kitchenettes, a/c, laundry facilities, TV, pets OK, CC. SGL/DBL$375W-$1,000W.

Bay To Beach Resorts (740 Estero Blvd., 33932; 463-5846) 14 rooms and 2-bedroom efficiencies, beach, laundry facilities, kitchenettes, no pets, a/c, TV, CC. LS SGL/DBL$45-$80; HS SGL/DBL$85-$140.

The Beach House of Ft. Myers Beach (4960 Estero Blvd., 33931; 463-4004, 800-226-4005) 12 rooms and 2-bedroom suites, no pets, a/c, TV, beach, laundry facilities, CC. SGL/DBL$45-$140.

Best Western Beach Resort (684 Estero Blvd., 33931; 463-6000, Fax 463-3013, Fax 463-3013, 800-528-1234) 75 rooms, outdoor heated pool, beach, kitchenettes, in-room refrigerators, children free with parents, a/c, NS rooms, water view, game room, TV, kitchenettes, VCRs, laundry facilities, wheelchair access, pets OK, meeting facilities, senior rates, CC. 1 mile to gambling facilities, 4 blocks to shopping mall and golf course. SGL/DBL$90-$180.

Buccaneer Resort Inn (4864 Estero Blvd., 33932; 463-5728, Fax 463-5757) 27 rooms and efficiencies, outdoor heated pool, laundry facilities, children free with parents, NS rooms, a/c, TV, no pets, wheelchair access, CC. SGL/DBL$100-$125.

Days Inn (1130 Estero Blvd., 33931; 463-9759, Fax 765-4240, 800-325-2525) 33 rooms and efficiencies, restaurant, free breakfast, outdoor pool, a/c, TV, wheelchair access, NS rooms, no pets, laundry facilities, beach, VCRs, senior rates, CC. LS SGL/DBL$90-$125; HS SGL/DBL$90-$170.

Days Inn (8701 Estero Blvd., 33931; 765-4422, Fax 765-4422 ext 160, 800-325-2525) 75 rooms, restaurant, free breakfast, outdoor pool, kitchenettes, a/c, TV, wheelchair access, children free with parents, beach, NS rooms, pets OK, laundry facilities, senior rates, CC. SGL/DBL$95-$180.

Estero Island Beach and Tennis Club (1840 Estero Blvd., 33931; 454-1400, Fax 454-0333, 800-237-7370) 70 efficiencies and 1-bedroom apartments, outdoor pool, tennis courts, beach, a/c, TV, children free with parents, in-room refrigerators and coffee makers, laundry facilities, no pets, CC. EFF$475W, 1BR$695W.

Gulfview Manor (6530 Estero Blvd., 33931; 463-4446) 33 rooms and 1-, 2-, and 3-bedroom apartments, outdoor pool, laundry facilities, a/c, TV, wheelchair access, NS rooms, senior rates, CC. LS SGL/DBL$395W-$500W; HS SGL/DBL$870W-$975W.

Holiday Inn (6890 Estero Blvd., 33931; 463-5711, Fax 463-7038, 800-HOLIDAY) 103 rooms and suites, restaurant, lounge, entertainment, outdoor heated pool, exercise center, children free with parents, wheelchair access, kitchenettes, in-room refrigerators, beach, a/c, TV, NS rooms, fax service, room service, laundry service, kitchenettes, meeting facilities for 40, senior rates, CC. 23 miles from the regional airport, 15 miles from the Thomas Edison home. SGL/DBL$67-$155.

LaFontaine Inn (6950 Estero Blvd, 33931; 463-6662) 10 efficiencies, restaurant, outdoor heated pool, a/c, no children, no pets, NS rooms, TV, CC. SGL/DBL$95-$125.

Lani Kai Island Resort Hotel (1400 Estero Blvd., 33931; 463-3111, 800-237-6133) 100 rooms and efficiencies, restaurant, lounge, entertainment, outdoor heated pool, in-room refrigerators and coffee makers, children free with parents, no pets, a/c, TV, wheelchair access, NS rooms, senior rates, CC. LS SGL/DBL$75; HS SGL/DBL$150.

Lighthouse Island Resort (1051 5th St., 33931; 463-93932) 30 rooms and apartments, outdoor heated pool, laundry facilities, a/c, TV, wheelchair access, NS rooms, kitchenettes, children free with parents, no pets, senior rates, CC. SGL/DBL$385W-$735W.

Mariners Lodge (17990 San Carlos Blvd., 33931; 466-9700, Fax 466-6116) 34 rooms, outdoor heated pool, whirlpools, no pets, a/c, TV, laundry facilities, children free with parents, in-room coffee makers, CC. SGL/DBL$45-$105.

Neptune Inn (2310 Estero Blvd., 33931; 463-6141) 63 efficiencies, outdoor pool, a/c, TV, laundry facilities, NS rooms, wheelchair access, children free with parents, no pets, CC. SGL/DBL$95-$120.

The Outrigger Beach Resort (6200 Estero Blvd., 33931; 463-3131, Fax 463-6577, 800-749-3131) 144 rooms and efficiencies, restaurant, lounge, outdoor heated pool, beach, gift shop, a/c, TV, no pets, in-room refrigerators, laundry facilities, CC. SGL/DBL$70-$110.

Pink Shell Beach and Bay Resort (275 Estero Blvd., 33931; 463-6181, Fax 463-1229, 800-237-5786) 173 efficiencies and cottages, restaurant, outdoor pool, lighted tennis courts, game room, in-room refrigerators, a/c, TV, NS rooms, wheelchair access, children free with parents, no pets, senior rates, CC. SGL/DBL$155-$315.

Pointe Estero (6640 Estero Blvd., 33931; 765-1155, Fax 765-0657, 800-237-5141) 60 2-bedroom apartments, outdoor pool, beach, tennis courts, no pets, a/c, TV, children free with parents, kitchenettes, laundry facilities, senior rates, CC. 2BR$120-$140.

Ramada Inn Beachfront (1160 Estero Blvd., 33931; 463-6158, Fax 765-4240, 800-2-RAMADA) 70 rooms and suites, restaurant, lounge, entertainment, outdoor heated pool, wheelchair access, NS rooms, free parking, a/c, TV, children free with parents, beach, kitchenettes, room service, laundry facilities, meeting facilities, senior rates, CC. 15 miles from the Fort Myers airport. SGL/DBL$85-$155.

Sandpiper Gulf Resort (5550 Estero Blvd., 33931; 463-5721) 62 efficiencies, outdoor pool, whirlpools, laundry facilities, children stay free with parents, NS rooms, gift shop, a/c, TV, no pets, beach, CC. SGL/DBL$60-$120.

Tropical Inn Resort Motel (5210 Estero Blvd., 33931; 463-3124) 28 rooms and apartments, outdoor heated pool, beach, in-room refrigerators, a/c, TV, laundry facilities, no pets, CC. SGL/DBL$55-$125.

Fort Pierce
Area Code 407

Comfort Inn (3236 South Hwy. 1, 34982; 461-2323, 800-221-2222) 60 rooms, free breakfast, outdoor pool, whirlpools, no pets, a/c, TV, children free with parents, NS rooms, wheelchair access, kitchenettes, laundry facilities, senior rates, CC. 4 miles from the Jai Alai fronton and Gulf beaches. SGL/DBL$45-$65.

Days Inn (1920 Seaway Dr., 34949; 461-8738, 800-325-2525) 32 rooms, free breakfast, outdoor pool, kitchenettes, a/c, TV, wheelchair access, beach, NS rooms, no pets, laundry facilities, senior rates, meeting facilities for 65, CC. SGL/DBL$90-$120.

Days Inn (3224 Hwy. 1 South, 34982; 465-7000, Fax 467-0160, 800-325-2525) 100 rooms, free breakfast, a/c, TV, wheelchair access, NS rooms, laundry facilities, children free with parents, senior rates, CC. 1 mile from the downtown area, 5 miles from the shopping mall. SGL/DBL$35-$50.

Days Inn (6651 Darter Center, 34945; 466-4066, Fax 468-3260, 800-325-2525) 125 rooms and suites, restaurant, free breakfast, outdoor heated pool, in-room refrigerators and coffee makers, children free with parents, a/c, TV, wheelchair access, NS rooms, no pets, laundry facilities, senior rates, CC. 1 mile from the shopping mall and Jai Alai fronton, 8 miles from Gulf beaches, 7 miles from Met Stadium. SGL/DBL$45-$75.

Dockside Inn (1152 Seaway Dr., 34949; 461-4824, Fax 563-0758) 20 rooms, outdoor pool, no pets, a/c, TV, children free with parents, laundry facilities, senior rates, CC. LS SGL/DBL$36-$60; HS SGL/DBL$48-$78.

Econo Lodge (7050 Okeechobee Rd., 34945; 465-8600, 800-4-CHOICE) 60 rooms, children free with parents, no pets, laundry facilities, NS rooms, wheelchair access, a/c, TV, senior rates, CC. 2 miles from the Orange Mall and Mets Spring Training Stadium, 45 miles from the regional airport. SGL/DBL$35-$65.

Harbor Light Inn Edgewater Motel and Apartments (1160 Seaway Dr., 34949; 468-3555, 800-433-0004 in Florida) 21 rooms and suites, outdoor pool, kitchenettes, no pets, a/c, TV, in-room refrigerators and coffee makers, laundry facilities, children free with parents, senior rates, CC. LS SGL/DBL$32-$94; HS SGL/DBL$41-$120.

Holiday Inn Sunshine Parkway (7151 Okeechobee Rd., 34945; 464-5000, 800-HOLIDAY) 149 rooms, restaurant, lounge, entertainment, outdoor pool, beach, no pets, in-room refrigerators and microwaves, children free with parents, wheelchair access, a/c, TV, NS rooms, fax service, room service, laundry service, meeting facilities, senior rates, CC. 8 miles from Atlantic beaches, 4 miles from the Civic Center, 2 miles from the shopping mall. SGL/DBL$70-$145.

Howard Johnson (7150 Okeechobee Rd., 34945; 464-4500, 800-I-GO-HOJO) 64 rooms, restaurant, lounge, outdoor pool, children free with parents, wheelchair access, NS rooms, TV, a/c, laundry facilities, senior rates, meeting facilities, CC. 5 miles from the St. Lucie airport, 4 miles from the downtown area. SGL/DBL$55-$70.

Motel 6 (2500 Peters Rd., 34945; 461-9937, 505-891-6161) 120 rooms, outdoor pool, free local calls, children free with parents, NS rooms, wheelchair access, a/c, TV, CC. 2 miles from the Jai Alai fronton,

3.5 miles from the Civic Center, 1 block from the factory outlet mall. SGL/DBL$29-$38.

Super 8 Motel (612 South 4th St., 34950; 800-800-8000) 40 rooms, outdoor pool, children free with parents, free local calls, a/c, TV, in-room refrigerators and microwaves, fax service, NS rooms, wheelchair access, no pets, meeting facilities, senior rates, CC. SGL/DBL$60-$74.

Fort Walton Beach
Area Code 904

Rental & Reservation Services

Abbott Realty Rentals (35000 Emerald Coast Pkwy., Fort Walton Beach, 32541; 837-Gulf, 800-336-4853) rental condominiums and private homes.

Resort Access (1114 Santa Rosa Blvd., Fort Walton Beach 32548; 837-7990, 800-282-9880) rental condominiums and apartments.

□□□

Blue Horizon Hotel and Beach Cabanas (1120 Santa Rosa Blvd., 32548; 244-5186, 800-336-3630) 250 rooms and efficiencies, outdoor pool, in-room refrigerators, microwaves and coffee makers, laundry facilities, a/c, TV, NS rooms, children free with parents, CC. SGL/DBL$68-$94.

Conquina Isle Condominiums (856 Scallop Ct., 32548; 800-336-Gulf) 1-bedroom condominiums, outdoor pool, laundry facilities, in-room refrigerators, microwaves and coffee makers, a/c, TV, children free with parents. 1BR$79-$100.

Days Inn (135 Miracle Strip Pkwy., 32548; 244-6184, 800-325-2525) 62 rooms, outdoor pool, a/c, TV, wheelchair access, NS rooms, children free with parents, no pets, laundry facilities, senior rates, CC. 2 miles from Gulf beach, 7 miles from the Pensacola airport, 1 block from the factory outlet mall. SGL/DBL$36-$65.

Econo Lodge (1284 Marler Dr., 32548; 243-7123, 800-4-CHOICE) 60 rooms, children free with parents, no pets, NS rooms, laundry facilities, wheelchair access, a/c, TV, senior rates, CC. 10 miles from the Pensacola airport, 1/4 mile from Gulfarium and Fern Park. SGL/DBL$35-$70.

El Matador Condominium (909 Santa Rosa Blvd., 32548; 800-336-Gulf) 2-bedroom condominiums, outdoor pool, tennis courts, sauna, whirlpools, game room, beach, a/c, TV, children free with parents, in-room refrigerators, microwaves and coffee makers, no pets, CC. 2BR$66-$126.

Greenwood Motel (Hwy. 98 East, 32548; 244-1141) 55 rooms, outdoor pool, a/c, TV, no pets, CC. LS SGL/DBL$30-$35; HS SGL/DBL$50-$55.

Island Echos Condominiums (676 Santa Rosa Blvd., 32548; 800-336-Gulf) 90 1- , 2- , and 3-bedroom condominiums, outdoor heated pool, lighted tennis courts, beach, in-room refrigerators, microwaves and coffee makers, a/c, TV, children free with parents, no pets, wheelchair access, CC. 1BR$63-$132, 2BR$74-$160, 3BR$110-$214.

Holiday Inn (1110 Santa Rosa Blvd., 32548; 243-9181, Fax 664-7652, 800-HOLIDAY) 385 rooms and suites, restaurant, lounge, outdoor heated pool, exercise center, lighted tennis courts, in-room refrigerators and coffee makers, beach, no pets, children free with parents, wheelchair access, a/c, TV, NS rooms, fax service, boutiques, game room, room service, laundry service, 5 meeting rooms, meeting facilities for 750, senior rates, CC. 1/2 mile from Gulfarium, 4 miles from the shopping mall, 8 miles from the Air Force Armament Museum. LS SGL/DBL$60-$80; HS SGL/DBL$95-$125.

Howard Johnson (314 Miracle Strip Pkwy., 32548; 243-6162, Fax 664-2735, 800-I-GO-HOJO) 140 rooms, restaurant, lounge, outdoor pool, children free with parents, wheelchair access, NS rooms, TV, a/c, laundry facilities, senior rates, meeting facilities, CC. 2 miles from the downtown area, 3 miles from the shopping mall and the Air Force Armament Museum. SGL/DBL$45-$64.

Marina Bay Resort (80 Miracle Strip Pkwy., 33548; 244-5132) 121 rooms, outdoor pool, exercise center, sauna, laundry facilities, kitchenettes, TV, VCRs, a/c, no pets, beach, meeting facilities, CC. SGL/DBL$40-$120.

Nautilus Condominiums (660 Nautilus Ct., 32548; 800-336-Gulf) 1- , 2- , and 3-bedroom condominiums, outdoor pool, beach, laundry service, in-room refrigerators, microwaves and coffee makers, a/c, TV, children free with parents, no pets, wheelchair access, CC. 1BR-3BR$60-$125.

Ramada Inn Beach Resort (Hwy. 98, 32548; 243-9161, Fax 243-2391, 800-2-RAMADA) 454 rooms and suites, restaurant, lounge, entertainment, indoor and outdoor heated pools, wheelchair access, NS rooms, free parking, a/c, TV, children free with parents, gift shop, beach, room service, laundry facilities, 5 meeting rooms, senior rates, CC. SGL/DBL$65-$130.

Sea Isle Motel (1214 Hwy. 98 East, 32548; 243-5563) 60 rooms and efficiencies, children free with parents, in-room refrigerators and microwaves, no pets, a/c, TV, CC. LS SGL/DBL$35-$45; HS SGL/DBL$50-$75.

Sea Oats Condominium (1114 Santa Rosa Blvd., 32548; 800-336-Gulf) 2- and 3-bedroom condominiums, outdoor pool, tennis courts, game room, laundry facilities, in-room refrigerators, microwaves and coffee makers, a/c, TV, children free with parents, no pets, wheelchair access, CC. 2BR/3BR$75-$205.

Sheraton Coronado Beach Resort (1325 Miracle Strip Pkwy. East, 32548; 243-8116, Fax 244-3064, 800-325-3535, 800-874-8104) 154 rooms and suites, restaurant, lounge, entertainment, outdoor pool, exercise center, hot tubs, NS rooms, a/c, room service, game room, beach, TV, children free with parents, wheelchair access, meeting facilities for 250, 2,500 square feet of meeting and exhibition space, in-room refrigerators and microwaves, no pets, senior rates, CC. 10 miles from Gulf beaches, 4 miles from Destin Harbor. SGL/DBL$65-$120.

Shoney's Inn (203 Miracle Strip Pkwy., 32548; 244-8663, 800-222-2222) 102 rooms and efficiencies, restaurant, free breakfast, lounge, outdoor pool, a/c, TV, NS rooms, children free with parents, complimentary newspaper, no pets, fax service, in-room coffee makers, NS rooms, wheelchair access, senior rates, CC. SGL/DBL$50-$60.

Super 8 Motel (333 Miracle Strip Pkwy., 32548; 244-4999, 800-848-8888) 34 rooms and efficiencies, outdoor pool, children free with parents, free local calls, a/c, TV, in-room refrigerators and microwaves, no pets, kitchenettes, fax service, NS rooms, wheelchair access, meeting facilities, senior rates, CC. 2 miles from Gulf beaches, 8 miles from Eglin Air Force Base. LS SGL/DBL$35-$50; HS SGL/DBL$45-$70.

Surf Dweller (554 Santa Rosa Blvd., 32548; 244-4242, 800-338-4418) 83 2-bedroom condominiums, outdoor pool, tennis courts, beach, a/c, TV, children free with parents, in-room refrigerators and coffee makers, laundry facilities, a/c, TV, children free with parents, no pets, CC. 2BR$160.

Gainesville

Area Code 904

Apartment Inn Motel (4401 Southwest 13th St., 32608; 371-3811) 35 rooms, a/c, TV, pets OK, children free with parents, laundry facilities, CC. SGL/DBL$28-$65.

Bambi Motel (2119 Southwest 13th St., 32608; 376-2622, 800-34-BAMBI in Florida) 34 rooms and efficiences, outdoor pool, room service, a/c, TV, children free with parents, kitchenettes, laundry facilities, CC. SGL/DBL$22-$36.

Cabot Lodge (3726 Southwest 40th Blvd., 32608; 375-2400, 800-331-8215) 208 rooms, free breakfast, outdoor pool, whirlpools, children free with parents, a/c, TV, NS rooms, kitchenettes, laundry facilities, senior rates, CC. SGL/DBL$49-$56.

Comfort Inn (2435 Southwest 13th St., 32608; 373-6500, 800-221-2222) 59 rooms, outdoor pool, whirlpools, no pets, laundry facilities, kitchenettes, a/c, TV, children free with parents, NS rooms, wheelchair access, senior rates, CC. 1/2 mile from the downtown area, Alachua General Hospital and Shands Medical Center. 6 blocks from the Florida State Museum. SGL/DBL$40-$85.

Days Inn (2820 Northwest 13th St., 32609; 376-1211, 800-325-2525) 78 rooms and suites, free breakfast, outdoor pool, pets OK, a/c, TV, wheelchair access, NS rooms, laundry facilities, senior rates, CC. 15 miles from the University of Florida, 17 miles from Itchetucknee Springs State Park. SGL/DBL$35-$90.

Days Inn (7516 Newberry Rd., 32606; 332-3033, 800-325-2525) 102 rooms, free breakfast, a/c, TV, wheelchair access, NS rooms, no pets, laundry facilities, senior rates, CC. 5 miles from Shands Hospital, 3 blocks from the shopping mall, 3.5 miles from Florida State Museum. SGL/DBL$40-$90.

Econo Lodge (700 Northwest 75th St., 32601; 378-2346, 800-55-ECONO) 48 rooms, lighted tennis courts, children free with parents, no pets, laundry service, NS rooms, wheelchair access, a/c, TV, senior rates, CC. SGL/DBL$24-$75.

Econo Lodge (2649 Southwest 13th St., 32608; 373-7816, 800-55-ECONO) 53 rooms, restaurant, children free with parents, laundry facilities, pets OK, NS rooms, wheelchair access, a/c, TV, VCRs, senior rates, CC. 6 miles from the Gainesville Raceway, 6 blocks from Alachua General Hospital and University of Florida. SGL/DBL$30-$60.

Fairfield Inn by Marriott (6901 Northwest 4th Blvd., 32607; 332-8292, 800-228-2800) 135 rooms, outdoor heated pool, children free with parents, NS rooms, free cable TV, free local calls, in-room computer hookups, no pets, in-room refrigerators, laundry service, a/c, wheelchair access, fax service, meeting facilities, senior rates, CC. 2 miles from the Oaks Mall, 12 miles from the Gainesville airport, 5 miles from the University of Florida, 15 miles from the Gainesville Raceway. SGL/DBL$40-$55.

Herlong Mansion Bed and Breakfast (402 Northeast Cholokka Blvd., 32667; 466-3322) 6 rooms and suites, no pets, a/c, TV, CC. SGL/DBL$75-$115.

Hilton Inn (2900 Southwest 13th St., 32608; 377-4000, Fax 371-1159, 800-HILTONS) 195 rooms and suites, restaurant, lounge, entertainment, outdoor pool, exercise center, children free with parents, NS rooms, wheelchair access, room service, airport transportation, in-room refrigerators, no pets, laundry facilities, a/c, TV, 10 meeting rooms, senior rates, CC. 9 miles from the Gainesville airport, 1 mile from Shands Hospital, 1.5 miles from the University of Florida. SGL/DBL$70-$115.

Ho Jo Inn (1900 Southwest 13th St., 462-2244, Fax 236-5656, 800-I-GO-HOJO) 91 rooms, restaurant, free breakfast, lounge, entertainment, outdoor pool, children free with parents, wheelchair access, NS rooms, TV, a/c, laundry facilities, fax service, local transportation, pets OK, in-room refrigerators and microwaves, senior rates, meeting facilities, CC. 5 miles from the Gainesville airport, 1/4 mile from the University of Florida, 2 miles from Alachua General Hospital.SGL/DBL$30-$40.

Holiday Inn (7417 Northwest 8th Ave., 32605; 221-7500, Fax 332-0487, 800-HOLIDAY, 800-426-4287) 280 rooms and suites, restaurant, lounge, entertainment, outdoor heated pool, exercise center, whirlpools, children free with parents, wheelchair access, a/c, TV, NS rooms, fax service, in-room refrigerators, airport transportation, no pets, room service, laundry service, 10 meeting rooms, meeting facilities for 500, senior rates, CC. 4 miles from the University of Florida, 1/4 mile from the shopping mall, 12 miles from the regional airport. SGL/DBL$50-$90.

Holiday Inn University Center (1250 West University Ave., 32601; 376-1661, Fax 336-8717, 800-HOLIDAY) 167 rooms and suites, restaurant, lounge, outdoor pool, exercise center, children free with parents, wheelchair access, a/c, TV, NS rooms, beauty shop, airport courtesy car, fax service, beauty shop, car rental desk, room service, laundry service, 5 meeting rooms, meeting facilities for 600, senior rates, CC. 6 miles from the regional airport, 1 mile from Shands Hospital, 4 blocks from the Orange Dome. SGL/DBL$70-$90.

Howard Johnson (7400 Northwest 8th Ave., 32605; 332-3200, Fax 332-5500, 800-I-GO-HOJO) 63 rooms, free breakfast, outdoor pool, children free with parents, wheelchair access, NS rooms, TV, a/c, laundry facilities, fax service, senior rates, meeting facilities, CC. 12 miles from the Gainesville airport, 1 mile from the golf course and the University of Florida, 1/4 mile from the Oaks Mall. SGL/DBL$35-$55.

Knights Inn (4021 Southwest 40th Blvd., 32608; 373-0392, 800-843-5644) 115 rooms and efficiencies, outdoor pool, wheelchair access, NS rooms, TV, a/c, in-room refrigerators and microwaves, fax service, children free with parents, pets OK, VCRs, senior rates, CC. SGL/DBL$30-$37.

La Quinta Inn (920 Northwest 69th Terrace, 32601; 332-6466, Fax 332-7074, 800-531-5900) 138 rooms, restaurant, free breakfast, lounge, outdoor heated pool, in-room refrigerators, complimentary newspaper, free local calls, fax service, laundry service, NS rooms, wheelchair access, TV, a/c, meeting facilities, senior rates, CC. 12 miles from the regional airport, 3 miles from the Oaks Mall. SGL/DBL$50-$60.

Motel 6 (4000 Southwest 40th Blvd., 32608; 374-1604) 122 rooms, outdoor pool, free local calls, children free with parents, NS rooms, wheelchair access, a/c, TV, CC. 4 miles from the University of Florida, 1 mile from the Fred Bean Museum. SGL/DBL$44-$60.

Red Carpet Inn (3461 Southwest Williston Rd., 32601; 378-1511, 800-251-1962) 90 rooms, outdoor pool, children free with parents, laundry facilities, pets OK, TV, a/c, NS rooms, meeting facilities, senior rates, CC. 5 miles from the University of Florida, 10 miles from the Oak Mall, 15 miles from Jai Alai fronton. SGL/DBL$23-$33.

Residence Inn by Marriott (4001 Southwest 13th St., 32608; 371-2101, 800-331-3131) 80 suites, free breakfast, outdoor pool, whirlpools, in-room refrigerators, microwaves and coffee makers, pets OK, laundry facilities, TV, a/c, VCRs, complimentary newspaper, fireplaces, airport transportation, children free with parents, NS rooms, wheelchair access, meeting facilities for 25, CC. 7.5 miles from the airport, 4 miles from the University of Florida, 3 miles from Shands Hospital. SGL/DBL$90-$125.

Scottish Inn (4155 Northwest 13th St., 32609; 376-2601, 800-251-1962) 40 rooms, restaurant, lounge, in-room refrigerators, no pets, a/c, TV, wheelchair access, NS rooms, children free with parents, free local calls, senior rates, CC. 1.2 miles from the University of Florida, 1.5 miles from Silver Springs. SGL/DBL$28-$33.

Scottish Inn (4041 Southwest 13th St., 32608; 376-4423, 800-251-1962) 31 rooms, restaurant, outdoor pool, children free with parents, no pets, TV, a/c, NS rooms, meeting facilities, senior rates, CC. SGL/DBL$25-$32.

Super 8 Motel (4202 Southwest 40th Blvd., 32608; 378-3888, 800-848-8888) 62 rooms and suites, restaurant, children free with parents, free local calls, a/c, TV, in-room refrigerators and microwaves, fax service, NS rooms, wheelchair access, meeting facilities, senior rates, CC. 1 mile from Shands Hospital, 3 miles from the Oak Mall, 12 miles from the Gainesville Raceway. SGL/DBL$35-$58.

TraveLodge University (3103 Northwest 13th St., 32609; 372-4316, 800-578-7878) 43 rooms, outdoor pool, wheelchair access, complimentary newspaper, laundry service, TV, a/c, free local calls, no pets, fax service, NS rooms, in-room refrigerators and microwaves, children under 18 free with parents, meeting facilities, senior rates,

CC. 3 miles from Shands Hospital and the downtown area, 5 miles from the Gainesville airport. SGL/DBL$40-$130.

University Centre Hotel (1535 Southwest Archer Rd., 32608; 371-3333, Fax 371-3712, 800-824-5637, 800-251-4069 in Florida) 180 rooms and suites, restaurant, lounge, outdoor pool, a/c, TV, NS rooms, children free with parents, in-room refrigerators, wheelchair access, beauty shop, meeting facilities, senior rates, CC. SGL/DBL$75-$85, STS$155-$350.

Grand Ridge
Area Code 904

Howard Johnson (1376 Hwy. 69, 32442; 592-9113, 800-I-GO-HOJO) 59 rooms, outdoor pool, children free with parents, wheelchair access, NS rooms, TV, a/c, laundry facilities, senior rates, meeting facilities, CC. SGL/DBL$35-$65.

Gulf Breeze
Area Code 904

Rental & Reservation Services

Navaree Agency (1804 Brado St., 32566; 939-2020) rental condominiums, cottages and townhouses.

Navarre Agency (8512 Navarre Pkwy., 32566; 939-2311, 800-821-8790) rental condominiums, homes and townhouses.

□□□

Beachview Condominiums (8425 Gulf Blvd., 32566) 2- and 3-bedroom condominiums, outdoor pool, tennis courts, kitchenettes, TV, a/c, wheelchair access, no pets, children free with parents, laundry facilities, CC. LS 2BR$275W-$340W, 3BR$405W-$525W; HS 2BR$525W-$555W, 3BR$500W-$600W.

Gulf Coast Inn (843 Gulf Breeze Pkwy., 32561; 932-2222) 33 rooms, outdoor pool, a/c, TV, no pets, CC. LS SGL/DBL$28-$46; HS SGL/DBL$32-$56.

Holiday Inn (51 Gulf Breeze Pkwy., 32561; 932-2214, 800-HOLI-DAY) 168 rooms, restaurant, lounge, outdoor pool, in-room refrigerators and coffee makers, children free with parents, wheelchair access, a/c, TV, NS rooms, fax service, room service, no pets, laundry service, meeting facilities, senior rates, CC. 13 miles from the golf course, 7 miles from the Pensacola airport, 2 miles from Gulf beaches, 9 miles from the Naval Air Station. SGL/DBL$45-$86.

Gulfport
Area Code 813

Motel Pine Grove Cottages (5139 South Tangerine Ave., 33707; 321-7263) 10 cottages, kitchenettes, a/c, TV, pets OK, CC. SGL/DBL$115W-$175W.

Park View Motel and Apartments (2808 Beach Blvd., 33707; 321-8582) 15 efficiencies and apartments, outdoor pool, laundry facilities, a/c, TV, kitchenettes, children free with parents, CC. LS SGL/DBL$25; HS SGL/DBL$35-$42.

Haines City
Area Code 813

Best Western Inn (655 Moore Rd., 33844; 421-6929, 800-528-1234) 30 rooms and suites, free breakfast, outdoor heated pool, tennis courts, children free with parents, a/c, NS rooms, TV, laundry facilities, wheelchair access, pets OK, meeting facilities, senior rates, CC. 8 miles from Bok Tower. SGL/DBL$35-$90.

Econo Lodge (1504 Hwy. 27 South, 33844; 800-4-CHOICE) 120 rooms, restaurant, lounge, outdoor pool, children free with parents, no pets, NS rooms, wheelchair access, a/c, TV, laundry facilities, senior rates, CC. 10 miles from Cypress Gardens. SGL/DBL$35-$75.

Grenelefe Resort (3200 Hwy. 546, 33884) 422-7511, Fax 421-1694, 800-237-9549, 800-422-5333 in Florida) 1,100 rooms and suites, restaurant, lounge, entertainment, indoor and outdoor heated pools, whirlpools, sauna, lighted tennis courts, a/c, TV, NS rooms, wheelchair access, Modified American Plan available, children free with parents, car rental desk, beauty and barber shop, no pets, room service, 32 meeting rooms, 70,000 square feet of meeting and exhibition space, senior rates, CC. 1 mile from Walt Disney World, 35 miles from the Orlando airport. 1BR$85-$220, 2BR$180-$385.

Holiday Inn (I-4 and Hwy. 27, 33845; 424-2211, Fax 424-3312, 800-HOLIDAY, 800-422-2414) 250 rooms, restaurant, free breakfast, lounge, outdoor pool, exercise center, children free with parents, wheelchair access, a/c, TV, NS rooms, game room, local transportation, car rental desk, in-room refrigerators, no pets, fax service, room service, laundry service, meeting facilities, senior rates, CC. 1 block from the Baseball City Sports Complex. SGL/DBL$40-$78.

Van-Rook Inn (106 South 1st St., 33844; 421-2242) 5 rooms, free breakfast, a/c, TV, no pets, no children, CC. LS SGL/DBL$55; HS Jan-Apr SGL/DBL$65.

Hallandale

Area Code 305

Holiday Inn (101 Ansin Blvd., 33009; 456-8333, 800-HOLIDAY) 98 rooms, free breakfast, outdoor pool, exercise center, in-room computer hookups, children free with parents, wheelchair access, a/c, TV, NS rooms, free local calls, fax service, in-room refrigerators and microwaves, VCRs, laundry service, meeting facilities, senior rates, CC. 14 miles from the Miami airport, 2 miles from the Calder Race Track, 4 miles from the Ft. Lauderdale-Hollywood airport, 6 miles from the Convention Center. SGL/DBL$55-$85.

Ramada Inn Golf and Racquet Club (26 Diplomat Pkwy., 33009; 454-5881, Fax 456-9641, 800-2-RAMADA) 151 rooms, restaurant, lounge, outdoor heated pool, tennis courts, wheelchair access, NS rooms, a/c, TV, children free with parents, in-room refrigerators, no pets, room service, laundry facilities, meeting facilities, senior rates, CC. 1 mile from the dog track, 7 miles from Joe Robbie Stadium, 7 miles from the Ft. Lauderdale-Hollywood airport. LS SGL/DBL$40-$70; HS SGL/DBL$85-$120.

Regency Health Resort and Spa (2000 South Ocean Dr., 33009; 454-2220, 800-695-9591) 50 rooms and 1- and 2-bedroom suites, restaurant, outdoor pool, exercise center, kitchenettes, American Plan available, no pets, a/c, TV, children free with parents, NS rooms, laundry facilities, senior rates, CC. LS SGL/DBL$600W-

$1200W; HS SGL/DBL$895W-$1600W, 1BR$725W-$1400W, 2BR$950-$1800W.

Riviera Resort Hotel (2080 South Ocean Dr., 33009; 458-6666, Fax 458-7529) 160 rooms and efficiencies, restaurant, outdoor pool, whirlpools, a/c, TV, children free with parents, laundry facilities, wheelchair access, no pets, senior rates, CC. SGL/DBL$55-$120, EFF$90-$130.

Hialeah
Area Code 305

Holiday Inn (6650 West 20th Ave., 33016; 362-7777, Fax 826-8107, 800-HOLIDAY) 144 rooms, restaurant, lounge, outdoor heated pool, jacuzzis, in-room refrigerators, complimentary newspaper, gift shop, children free with parents, wheelchair access, a/c, TV, NS rooms, fax service, room service, laundry service, meeting facilities for 120, senior rates, CC. 6 miles from the Miami airport, 7 miles from Atlantic beaches, 1 mile from the shopping mall. SGL/DBL$60-$105.

Ramada Inn Miami-Hialeah (1950 West 49th St., 33012; 823-2000, Fax 362-4562, 800-2-RAMADA) 255 rooms and suites, restaurant, lounge, entertainment, outdoor pool, wheelchair access, NS rooms, free parking, a/c, TV, children free with parents, room service, gift shop, fax service, car rental desk, complimentary newspaper, airport transportation, laundry facilities, meeting facilities, senior rates, CC. 1 block from the Westland Mall, 10 miles from the Miami airport. SGL/DBL$59-$100.

Highland Beach
Area Code 407

Crown Sterling Suites (701 Northwest 53rd St., 33487; 997-9500, Fax 994-3565, 800-433-4600) 182 suites, restaurant, lounge, free breakfast, lounge, outdoor heated pool, whirlpools, a/c, TV, NS rooms, in-room refrigerators and microwaves, wheelchair access, in-room computer hookups, children free with parents, pets OK, laundry facilities, senior rates, CC. LS SGL/DBL$85-$95; HS SGL/DBL$135-$144.

Embassy Suites (661 Northwest 53rd St., 33487; 994-8200, Fax 994-9518, 800-EMBASSY) 261 2-room suites, restaurant, lounge, free breakfast, outdoor heated pool, whirlpool, exercise center, sauna, room service, laundry service, wheelchair access, complimentary newspaper, free local calls, NS rooms, gift shop, local transportation, in-room refrigerators, microwaves and coffee makers, children free with parents, no pets, in-room computer hookups, 15 meeting rooms, 6,000 square feet of meeting and exhibition space, meeting facilities for 600, senior rates, CC. 20 miles from the Ft. Lauderdale-Hollywood airport. LS SGL/DBL$80-$110; HS SGL/DBL$130-$170.

Holiday Inn (2809 South Ocean Blvd., 33487; 278-6241, 800-HOLIDAY) 114 rooms, restaurant, lounge, entertainment, outdoor heated pool, whirlpools, children free with parents, wheelchair access, a/c, TV, no pets, in-room refrigerators, beach, NS rooms, fax service, room service, laundry service, water view, meeting facilities for 100, senior rates, CC. 20 miles from West Palm Beach airport, 5 miles from the shopping mall. SGL/DBL$70-$170.

Residence Inn by Marriott (525 Northwest 77th St., 33487; 994-3222, 800-331-3131) 120 rooms and 1-bedroom suites, free breakfast, local transportation, in-room refrigerators, coffee makers and microwaves, laundry facilities, TV, in-room computer hookups, local transportation, a/c, VCRs, pets OK, complimentary newspaper, fireplaces, children free with parents, NS rooms, wheelchair access, meeting facilities, CC. LS SGL/DBL$105-$135; HS SGL/DBL$175-$205.

High Springs
Area Code 904

The Great Outdoors Inn (65 North Main St., 32643; 454-2900) 8 rooms, restaurant, free breakfast, outdoor pool, no pets, in-room refrigerators, microwaves and coffee makers, a/c, TV, CC. SGL/DBL$70-$80.

Hillsboro Beach
Area Code 305

Rainbow On The Ocean (1231 Hwy. A1A, 33062; 426-2525) 26 rooms, efficiencies and 1- and 2-bedroom apartments, outdoor pool, kitchenettes, children free with parents, no pets, senior rates, CC. SGL/DBL$76, EFF$83, 1BR$101, 2BR$170.

Royal Flamingo Villas (1225 Hillsboro Mile, 33062; 427-066) 40 1- and 2-bedroom apartments, outdoor heated pool, beach, a/c, TV, in-room refrigerators, microwaves and coffee makers, VCRs, no pets, laundry facilities, CC. SGL/DBL$55-$200.

Seabony Beach Resort (1159 Hillsboro, 33062; 427-2525, Fax 786-5320, 800-777-1961) 63 efficiencies and 1- and 2-bedroom apartments and suites, outdoor pool, beach, a/c, TV, children free, in-room refrigerators, microwaves and coffee makers, laundry facilities, wheelchair access, senior rates, CC. 1BR$89-$129, 2BR$149-$165.

Hobe Sound
Area Code 407

Jonathan Dickinson State Park (16450 Southeast Federal Hwy., 33455; 546-2771) 1-bedroom cabins, kitchenettes, no pets, CC. SGL/DBL$50-$250W.

Holiday
Area Code 813

Best Western Tahitian Resort (2337 Hwy. 19, 34691; 937-4121, Fax 937-3806, 800-528-1234) 140 rooms, restaurant, lounge, outdoor heated pool, children free with parents, a/c, NS rooms, TV, laundry facilities, wheelchair access, pets OK, meeting facilities, senior rates, CC. 5 miles to shopping mall and tennis courts, 24 miles from the Tampa airport. LS SGL/DBL$41-$65; HS SGL/DBL$58-$78.

Holly Hill
Area Code 904

TraveLodge (749 Ridgewood Ave., 32117; 255-6511, Fax 255-5473, 800-578-7878) 38 rooms, outdoor pool, no pets, wheelchair access, complimentary newspaper, laundry service, TV, a/c, free local calls, fax service, NS rooms, in-room refrigerators and microwaves, children under 18 free with parents, meeting facilities, senior rates, CC. SGL/DBL$50-$100.

Hollywood

Area Code 305

Adobe Hacienda Motel (1223 North Federal Hwy., 33020; 929-0389) 27 rooms, efficiencies and 1-bedroom apartments, outdoor pool, pets OK, wheelchair access, children free with parents, a/c, TV, CC. SGL/DBL$30-$65, EFF$35-$70, 1BR$45-$80.

Beach Terrace (321 Wilson St., 33022; 921-5739, Fax 921-6482) 51 1-bedroom apartments, outdoor pool, pets OK, kitchenettes, children free with parents, a/c, TV, senior rates, CC. 1BR$600W-$800W.

Comfort Inn Ft Lauderdale-Hollywood Airport (2520 Stirling Rd., 33020; 922-1600, Fax 922-1600, 800-CLARION, 800-333-1492) 188 rooms, indoor heated pool, a/c, TV, no pets, airport courtesy car, in-room refrigerators and microwave, airport transportation, in-room computer hookups, laundry facilities, children free with parents, NS rooms, wheelchair access, senior rates, CC. 1 mile from the Hollywood airport and Jai Alai fronton, 3 miles from the Convention Center. LS SGL/DBL$45-$65; HS SGL/DBL$80-$95.

Curtis Motel (1501 South Federal Hwy., 33020; 922-5376) 31 rooms, efficiencies and 1-bedroom apartments, outdoor pool, a/c, TV, in-room refrigerators, microwaves and coffee makers, children free with parents, no pets, CC. EFF$45-$70, 1BR$50-$75.

Days Gulfstream Beach Resort (2711 South Ocean Dr., 33022; 922-8200, Fax 925-5117, 800-344-1799) 197 rooms, restaurant, lounge, entertainment, outdoor heated pool, exercise center, laundry facilities, a/c, TV, kitchenettes, in-room refrigerators, no pets, children free with parents, 3 meeting rooms, meeting facilities for 120, senior rates, CC. 3 miles from the Jai Alai fronton and Ft. Lauderdale-Hollywood airport, 10 miles from the Convention Center, 7 miles from Joe Robbie Stadium. LS SGL/DBL$55-$105; HS SGL/DBL$90-$175.

Days Inn Hollywood Airport (2601 North 29th Ave., 33020; 923-7300, Fax 921-6706, 800-325-2525) 114 rooms, restaurant, lounge, free breakfast, outdoor pool, no pets, a/c, TV, wheelchair access, NS rooms, children free with parents, laundry facilities, senior rates, meeting facilities for 85, CC. 4 miles from the Convention Center. SGL/DBL$60-$95.

Diplomat Resort and Country Club (3515 South Ocean Dr., 33022; 457-8111, Fax 458-2077, 800-327-1212) 65 rooms and suites, outdoor pool, exercise facilities, whirlpools, sauna, tennis courts, airport courtesy car, room service, children free with parents, a/c, TV, no pets, laundry facilities, room service, in-room refrigerators and coffee makers, laundry service, CC. 15 miles from the Ft. Lauderdale-Hollywood airport. SGL/DBL$35.

Dolphin Motel (342 Pierce St., 33019; 922-4498, Fax 922-0137) 32 rooms, outdoor pool, a/c, TV, children free with parents, no pets, CC. LS EFF$35, 1BR$45; HS EFF$75, 1BR$70-$85.

Driftwood On The Ocean (2101 Surf Rd., 33022; 923-9528, Fax 922-1062, 800-944-3148) 33 rooms, efficiencies and 1- and 2-bedroom apartments, outdoor pool, a/c, TV, no pets, CC. SGL/DBL$33-$65, EFF$50-$78, 1BR/2BR$100-$175.

HoJo Inn (2900 Polk St., 33020; 923-1216, Fax 929-2579, 800-I-GO-HOJO) 72 rooms, outdoor heated pool, children free with parents, wheelchair access, NS rooms, TV, a/c, laundry facilities, pets OK, senior rates, meeting facilities, CC. 3 miles from Gulf beaches, a 1/4-mile from the Jai Alai fronton, 5 miles from the Ft. Lauderdale-Hollywood airport. LS SGL/DBL$40-$65; HS SGL/DBL$65-$88.

Holiday Inn (1925 Harrison, 33020; 927-3341, Fax 925-1695, 800-HOLIDAY) 95 rooms, restaurant, free breakfast, lounge, outdoor pool, exercise center, children free with parents, wheelchair access, a/c, TV, free local calls, in-room refrigerators, microwaves and coffee makers, no pets, NS rooms, fax service, room service, laundry service, meeting facilities, senior rates, CC. 5 miles from the Ft. Lauderdale-Hollywood airport, 3 miles from the Gulfstream Horse Track, 1 mile to Atlantic beaches. SGL/DBL$56-$80.

Hilton Hotel (4000 South Ocean Dr., 33022; 458-1900, Fax 458-1628, 800-HILTONS) 305 rooms and suites, restaurant, lounge, entertainment, outdoor heated pool, exercise center, sauna, whirlpools, tennis courts, children free with parents, NS rooms, wheelchair access, barber and beauty shop, boutiques, room service, laundry facilities, in-room refrigerators and coffee makers, no pets, a/c, TV, 15 meeting rooms, meeting facilities for 2,000, senior rates, 6,000 square feet of meeting and exhibition space, CC. 8 miles from the Ft. Lauderdale-Hollywood airport, 20 miles from the Miami airport, 12 miles from the Broward Convention Center. LS SGL/DBL$80-$120; HS SGL/DBL$120-$210.

Hollywood Beach Resort Hotel (101 North Ocean Dr., 33022; 921-0990, Fax 920-9480, 800-331-6103) 360 efficiencies and 1-bedroom suites, restaurant, lounge, entertainment, outdoor pool, whirlpools, boutiques, a/c, TV, in-room coffee makers, NS rooms, children free with parents, no pets, game room, beach, meeting facilities for 370, senior rates, CC. 10 miles from the Broward Convention Center. SGL/DBL$95-$155, STS$175-$195.

Howard Johnson Hollywood Beach Resort Inn (2501 North Ocean Dr., 33022; 925-1411, Fax 921-5565, 800-423-8967, 800-643-3970 in Florida) 242 rooms, restaurant, lounge, indoor and outdoor heated pools, in-room computer hookups, no pets, children free with parents, wheelchair access, gift shop, NS rooms, TV, a/c, laundry facilities, in-room refrigerators and coffee makers, beach, senior rates, 2 meeting rooms, meeting facilities for 325, CC. 3 miles from the Ft. Lauderdale-Hollywood airport, 8 miles from the Broward Convention Center. LS SGL/DBL$65-$195; HS SGL/DBL$115-$290.

Inn On The Park Motel (325 North Federal Hwy., 33020; 922-4533) 19 rooms and efficiencies, outdoor pool, airport courtesy car, a/c, TV, children free with parents, NS rooms, senior rates, CC. SGL/DBL$25-$50, EFF$30-$60.

Kent Motel (1120 South Federal Hwy., 33020; 922-6663) 31 rooms, efficiencies and 1-bedroom apartments, outdoor pool, airport courtesy car, a/c, TV, children free with parents, no pets, CC. SGL/DBL$35-$45, EFF$50-$60, 1BR$60-$75.

Ocean Grande Beach Resort (3300 North Surf Rd., 33022; 923-2459, Fax 920-7775) 38 1-bedroom apartments, outdoor pool, a/c, TV, children free with parents, pets OK, laundry facilities, CC. 1BR$65-$135.

Ocean House Resort (4059 South Surf Rd., 33022; 457-955) 22 efficiencies and 1- and 2-bedroom apartments, outdoor pool, a/c, TV, no pets, children free with parents, laundry facilities, senior rates, CC. EFF$60-$80, 1BR$57-$90, 2BR$75-$105.

Ruffy's (2300 North Ocean Dr., 33022; 920-0600, 800-776-8897) 18 rooms and efficiencies, restaurant, outdoor pool, a/c, TV, VCRs, in-room refrigerators, wheelchair access, NS rooms, airport courtesy car, children free with parents, no pets, CC. SGL/DBL$50-$60, EFF$60-$70.

Tide Apartments (2800 North Surf Rd., 33019; 923-3864, Fax 923-8510) 21 apartments, outdoor pool, a/c, TV, in-room refrigerators and coffee makers, laundry facilities, no pets, children free with parents, senior rates, CC. LS SGL/DBL$51-$59; HS SGL/DBL$90-$104.

Tower Motel (1905 Lincoln St., 33020; 922-9743, Fax 922-2408) 18 rooms, efficiencies and 1-bedroom apartments, outdoor pool, children free with parents, in-room refrigerators and coffee makers, wheelchair access, a/c, TV, CC. SGL/DBL$25-$60, EFF$36-$60, 1BR$40-$75.

Holmes Beach

Area Code 813

Rental & Reservation Services

A Paradise Rental Management (5201 Gulf Drive North, 34217; 778-4800, Fax 778-7090, 800-237-2252) rental condominiums.

Century 21 Paradise Rentals (3018 Ave. C, 34217; 778-4800, 800-237-2252) rental condominiums, apartments and private homes.

□□□

Aquarius Motel (105 39th St., 34217; 778-7577) 10 rooms and efficiencies, outdoor pool, a/c, TV, pets OK, in-room refrigerators, CC. SGL/DBL$44-$73.

Beach Inn (101 66th St., 34217; 778-9597) 14 rooms, a/c, TV, laundry service, children free with parents, meeting facilities, CC. LS SGL/DBL$50-$85; HS SGL/DBL$65-$110.

Blue Water Beach Club (6306 Gulf Dr., 34217; 778-6688) 29 rooms and efficiencies, outdoor pool, a/c, TV, children free with parents, no pets, wheelchair access, CC. SGL/DBL$54-$115.

The Coconuts (100 73rd St., 34217; 778-2277, 800-331-2508) 18 rooms, outdoor pool, no pets, a/c, TV, children free with parents, laundry facilities, CC. SGL/DBL$35-$105.

Fountainhead Condominiums (3400 6th Ave., 34217; 778-4800, 800-237-2252) 2 2-bedroom condominiums, outdoor pool, kitchenettes, a/c, TV, no pets, children free with parents, laundry facilities, CC. 2BR$450W-$550W.

Gray Dolphin Apartments (3302 6th Ave., 34217; 778-4400, 800-237-2252) 4 2-bedroom condominiums, outdoor pool, pets OK, laundry facilities, children free with parents, a/c, TV, CC. 2BR$400W-$900W.

Haley's Motel and Resort Complex (8102 Gulf Drive North, 34217; 778-5405, 800-367-7824) 16 rooms and efficiencies, outdoor pool, tennis courts, pets OK, a/c, TV, laundry facilities, CC. SGL/DBL$32-$95.

Resort Sixty-Six (6600 Gulf Drive North, 34217; 778-2238) 41 rooms and efficiencies, restaurant, outdoor pool, children free with parents, room service, a/c, TV, NS rooms, wheelchair access, laundry facilities, CC. SGL/DBL$35-$150.

Sunbow Bay (3705 East Bay Dr., 34217; 778-4800, 800-237-2252) 100 rooms and efficiencies, outdoor pool, exercise center, tennis courts, a/c, TV, no pets, children free with parents, wheelchair access, laundry facilities, CC. SGL/DBL$350W-$550W.

Waters Edge Condominiums (5806 Gulf Dr., 34217; 778-4800, 800-237-2252) 6 1- and 2-bedroom condominiums, outdoor pool, a/c, TV, children free with parents, no pets, laundry facilities, CC. 1BR/2BR$900W-$1200W.

Homestead

Area Code 305

Days Inn (51 South Homestead Blvd., 33030; 245-1260, Fax 247-0939, 800-325-2525) 109 rooms, lounge, entertainment, free breakfast, restaurant, outdoor heated pool, a/c, TV, wheelchair access, NS rooms, no pets, in-room refrigerators, laundry facilities, senior rates, CC. 5 miles from the Coral Castle and Homestead Air Force Base, 10 miles from Everglades National Park, 1/2 mile from the downtown area. SGL/DBL$55-$90.

Everglades Motel (605 South Krome Ave., 33030; 247-4117) 14 rooms, outdoor pool, in-room refrigerators, no pets, laundry facilities, children free with parents, a/c, TV, NS rooms, senior rates, CC. SGL/DBL$35-$54.

Holiday Inn (990 North Homestead Blvd., 33030; 247-7020, 800-HOLIDAY) 145 rooms, restaurant, free breakfast, lounge, outdoor pool, exercise center, children free with parents, wheelchair access, free local calls, in-room refrigerators, fax service, a/c, TV, NS rooms, fax service, room service, laundry service, meeting facilities, senior rates, CC. 4 miles from the Sports Complex, 2 miles from the downtown area. SGL/DBL$56-$86.

Howard Johnson (1020 North Homestead Blvd., 33030; 248-2121, Fax 248-9772, 800-I-GO-HOJO, 800-248-4656) 50 rooms, outdoor pool, children free with parents, wheelchair access, NS rooms, TV, a/c, laundry facilities, pets OK, senior rates, meeting facilities, CC. 15 miles from the Miami airport, 1 mile from the downtown area. SGL/DBL$45-$68.

Homosassa
Area Code 904

Wards Resort (Homosassa 32467; 628-2551) 1-bedroom cottages and 2-bedroom apartments, pets OK, a/c, TV, children free with parents, CC. SGL/DBL$55-$63.

Howey-In-The-Hills
Area Code 904

Mission Inn Golf and Tennis Resort (10400 Country Road 48, 34737; 324-3101, Fax 324-3101, 800-874-9053) 189 rooms and 2-bedroom suites, restaurant, lounge, entertainment, heated pool, exercise center, whirlpools, lighted tennis courts, gift shop, airport courtesy car, fireplaces, complimentary newspaper, Modified American Plan and American Plan available, children free with parents, a/c, TV, NS rooms, in-room refrigerators, microwaves and coffee makers, room service, local transportation, laundry facilities, senior rates, 14 meeting rooms, CC. LS SGL/DBL$100-$115; HS SGL/DBL$185-$210.

Indialantic
Area Code 407

Beach House Motel (405 Hwy. A1A, 32903; 723-7733) 20 rooms and 2-bedroom efficiencies, beach, a/c, TV, in-room refrigerators, no pets, children free with parents, CC. LS SGL/DBL$35-$55; HS SGL/DBL$40-$70.

Hilton Oceanfront Hotel (3003 Hwy. A1A, 32903; 777-5000, Fax 777-3713) 118 rooms and suites, restaurant, lounge, entertainment, outdoor heated pool, children free with parents, NS rooms, wheelchair access, local transportation, room service, laundry facilities, a/c, TV, in-room refrigerators, microwaves and coffee makers, free local calls, complimentary newspaper, no pets, beach, meeting facilities, senior rates, CC. 7 miles from the Melbourne airport, 20 miles from Cape Canaveral. SGL/DBL$80-$140.

Holiday Inn (2605 North Hwy. A1A, 32903; 777-4100, Fax 773-6132, 800-HOLIDAY) 299 rooms, restaurant, lounge, entertainment, indoor and outdoor pools, exercise center, whirlpools, children free with parents, wheelchair access, in-room refrigerators and coffee makers, a/c, TV, gift shop, pets OK, NS rooms, fax service, room service, laundry service, meeting facilities, senior rates, CC. 6 miles from the regional airport, 5 miles from Patrick Air Force Base, 18 miles from Sebastian Inlet State Park. SGL/DBL$90-$160.

Quality Suites (1665 North Hwy. A1A, 32903, 723-4222, Fax 768-2438, 800-221-2222, 800-876-4222) 208 suites, restaurant, free breakfast, lounge, entertainment, outdoor heated pool, whirlpools, gift shop, beach, game room, children free with parents, a/c, TV, wheelchair access, room service, laundry service, NS rooms, meeting facilities, senior rates, CC. 6 miles from the Orlando airport. SGL/DBL$45-$58.

Radisson Suite Hotel Oceanfront (3101 Hwy. 1A, 32903; 773-9260, 800-333-3333) 167 1- and 2-bedroom suites, restaurant, lounge, entertainment, outdoor pool, exercise center, in-room refrigerators, microwaves and coffee makers, gift shop, beach, VCRs, wheelchair access, free parking, NS rooms, TV, a/c, children free with parents, senior rates, CC. STS$110-$160.

Shamrock Shores Resort (1441 South Miramar, 32903; 723-3355) 31 rooms and efficiencies, outdoor pool, beach, exercise center, a/c, TV, laundry facilities, no pets, CC. SGL/DBL$55-$95.

Indian Harbour Beach

Area Code 407

Pines Resort and Tennis Club (1894 South Patrick Dr., 32937; 773-2000) 50 rooms, restaurant, lounge, outdoor pool whirlpools, sauna, tennis courts, a/c, TV, children free with parents, no pets, in-room refrigerators, meeting facilities, senior rates, CC. LS SGL/DBL$30-$40; HS SGL/DBL$40-$50.

Indian Rocks Beach

Area Code 813

Rental & Reservation Services

Best Beach Rentals and Sale (20045 Gulf Blvd., 34635; 595-5700, Fax 593-1095, 800-523-2882) rental condominiums, villas and private homes.

Capalbo Realty Rentals (4700 34th St. South, St. Petersburg, 33711; 866-2494, 800-237-5960, 800-225-3772 in Florida) rental condos.

Plumlee Gulf Realty (417 1st St., 34635; 595-7586, 800-521-7586) rental condominiums.

□□□

Anchor Court Apartments and Motel (940 Gulf Blvd., 34635; 595-4449) 21 rooms and apartments, outdoor pool, a/c, TV, beach, children free with parents, no pets, CC. LS SGL/DBL$50; HS SGL/DBL$90.

Casa Chica Cottages (19000 Gulf Blvd., 34635; 596-1602) 5 1-bedroom cottages, outdoor pool, beach, a/c, TV, children free with parents, no pets, CC. LS SGL/DBL$365W; HS SGL/DBL$435W.

Florida Resort Condominiums (20001 Gulf Blvd., 34635; 595-2001, 800-237-9831) 350 condominiums, outdoor pool, beach, a/c, TV, children free with parents, in-room refrigerators and coffee makers, no pets, laundry facilities, senior rates, CC. LS SGL/DBL$500W; HS SGL/DBL$700W.

Gulf Towers Resort Motel (404 Gulf Blvd., 34635; 595-2563, Fax 595-2553) 45 efficiencies, outdoor pool, a/c, TV, children free with parents, pets OK, in-room refrigerators and microwaves, laundry facilities, CC. SGL/DBL$65-$90.

Hamlin's Landings Resort (401 2nd St. East, 34635; 595-9484, Fax 596-4825) 85 rooms and condominiums, restaurant, outdoor pool, whirlpools, exercise center, a/c, TV, children free with parents, in-room refrigerators, microwaves and coffee makers, no pets, laundry facilities, 5 meeting rooms, CC. LS SGL/DBL$69-$175; HS SGL/DBL$95-$195.

San-Fran Apartments (19644 Gulf Blvd., 34635; 595-7758) 2-bedroom apartments and beach house, outdoor pool, beach, kitchenettes, children free with parents, a/c, TV, no pets, CC. LS SGL/DBL$300W; HS SGL/DBL$425W.

Sea Resort (102 Gulf Blvd., 34635; 595-0461, Fax 595-2092) 14 efficiencies, heated pool, in-room refrigerators, no pets, a/c, TV, laundry facilities, CC. SGL/DBL$60-$95.

Whispering Waters (604 Gulf Blvd., 34635; 593-0737) 40 condominiums, outdoor pool, a/c, TV, no pets, in-room refrigerators and coffee makers, laundry services, children free with parents, wheelchair access, SGL/DBL$400W-$635W.

Indian Shores
Area Code 813

Holiday Villas II (19610 Gulf Blvd., 34635; 596-4852, 800-428-4852) 64 2- and 3-bedroom villas, outdoor pool, a/c, TV, pets OK, in-room refrigerators and coffee makers, CC. 2BR$85-$100, 3BR$95-$115.

Indiantown
Area Code 407

Seminole Country Inn (15885 Southwest Warfield Blvd., 34956; 597-3777) 26 rooms, restaurant, outdoor pool, pets OK, children free with parents, a/c, TV, NS rooms, wheelchair access, laundry facilities, senior rates, CC. SGL$45, DBL$50-$65.

Inlet Beach

Area Code 904

Inlet Dunes Condominiums (Orange St., 32413; 800-366-Gulf) 18 1-bedroom condominiums, outdoor pool, beach, laundry facilities, children free with parents, a/c, TV, kitchenettes, wheelchair access, no pets, wheelchair access, CC. 1BR$50-$89.

Inverness

Area Code 904

Crown Hotel (109 North Seminole Ave., 32650; 344-5555, 800-82-CROWN) 34 rooms, restaurant, lounge, free breakfast, outdoor pool, children free with parents, NS rooms, antique furnishings, room service, no pets, a/c, TV, senior rates, meeting facilities, CC. SGL/DBL$40-$70.

Islamorada

Area Code 305

Rental & Reservation Services

Freewheeler Vacations Realty (Islamorada 33036; 664-2075, Fax 664-2884) rental homes.

Ganim Realty (82205 Overseas Hwy., 33036; 664-4577, 800-741-0541) rental condominiums, private homes and apartments.

□□□

Breezy Palm Resorts (Mile Marker 80, 33036; 664-2361, Fax 664-2572) 39 rooms, outdoor pool, a/c, TV, wheelchair access, NS rooms, no pets, CC. LS SGL/DBL$45-$140; HS SGL/DBL$75-$180.

Cheeca Lodge (Hwy. 1, 33036; 664-4651, Fax 664-2893, 800-327-2888) 203 rooms, restaurant, lounge, entertainment, outdoor heated pool, whirlpools, lighted tennis courts, beach, in-room refrigerators and coffee makers, a/c, TV, VCRs, NS rooms, American Plan available, children free with parents, wheelchair access, no pets, CC. LS SGL/DBL$125-$500; HS SGL/DBL$200-$550.

Chesapeake Motel and Villas (Overseas Hwy., 33036; 664-4662, Fax 664-8595, 800-338-3395) 65 rooms, efficiencies and 1- and 2-bedroom apartments, restaurant, outdoor pool, whirlpools, tennis courts, a/c, TV, NS rooms, no pets, children free with parents, laundry facilities, in-room refrigerators, meeting facilities, senior rates, CC. LS SGL/DBL$86-$400; HS SGL/DBL$125-$450.

Days Inn (82749 Overseas Hwy., 33036; 664-3681, Fax 664-9020, 800-325-2525) 36 rooms and efficiencies, free breakfast, outdoor pool, a/c, TV, wheelchair access, NS rooms, laundry facilities, children free with parents, senior rates, CC. SGL/DBL$45-$55.

Drop Anchor Inn (Overseas Hwy., 33036; 664-4863) 12 rooms and efficiencies, outdoor heated pool, in-room refrigerators, beach, no pets, children free with parents, a/c, TV, CC. A 1/2-mile from Theater of the Sea, 15 miles from John Pennekamp Coral Reef State Park. SGL/DBL$70-$90.

Gamefish Resort (Overseas Hwy., 33036; 664-5568) 18 rooms and efficiencies, outdoor pools, a/c, TV, beach, CC. SGL/DBL$65-$95.

Harbor Lights Motel (84951 Overseas Hwy., 33036; 664-3611, 800-327-7070) 33 rooms and efficiencies, outdoor pool, a/c, TV, children free with parents, no pets, laundry facilities, CC. SGL/DBL$65-$110.

Howard Johnson Holiday Isle Resort (84001 Overseas Hwy., 33036; 664-2711, 800-I-GO-HOJO, 800-327-7070) 180 rooms, restaurant, lounge, entertainment, outdoor pool, exercise center, no pets, children free with parents, wheelchair access, NS rooms, TV, a/c, VCRs, laundry facilities, beach, airport transportation, senior rates, meeting facilities, CC. LS SGL/DBL$70-$85; HS SGL/DBL$105-$135.

Islander Motel (Mile Marker 82.1, 33036; 664-2031) 114 rooms and efficiencies, outdoor pool, a/c, TV, laundry facilities, no pets, laundry facilities, children free with parents, meeting facilities, CC. LS SGL/DBL$60-$79; HS SGL/DBL$68-$92.

Kon Tiki Resort (Islamorada 33036; 664-4702) 19 rooms suites, outdoor pool, a/c, TV, in-room coffee makers, beach, no pets, CC. SGL/DBL$50-$60, STS$80-$125.

La Siesta Resort (Islamorada 33036; 664-2132, 800-222-1693) 51 rooms, outdoor pool, a/c, TV, no pets, children free with parents, laundry facilities, CC. SGL/DBL$110-$200.

Pelican Cove Resort (Islamorada 33036; 664-4435, Fax 664-5431, 800-445-4690) 63 rooms and efficiencies, restaurant, lounge, outdoor heated pool, tennis courts, whirlpools, in-room refrigerators, NS rooms, a/c, TV, children free with parents, no pets, senior rates, CC. LS SGL/DBL$115-$330; HS SGL/DBL$165-$490.

Plantation Yacht Resort and Marina (87000 Overseas Hwy., 33036; 852-2381, 800-356-3215, 800-432-3454 in Florida) 56 rooms, restaurant, lounge, entertainment, outdoor pool, tennis courts, beach, a/c, TV, NS rooms, wheelchair access, no pets, senior rates, CC. LS SGL/DBL$65-$85; HS SGL/DBL$95-$135.

The Ragged Edge Resort (243 Treasure Harbor Rd., 33036; 304-852-5389) 10 rooms and 1- and 2-bedroom efficiencies, restaurant, outdoor pool, a/c, TV, no pets, NS rooms, children free with parents, CC. SGL/DBL$65-$85.

Shoreline Motel (Overseas Hwy., 33036; 664-2321, 800-327-7070) 71 rooms and suites, restaurant, lounge, entertainment, outdoor pool, beach, a/c, TV, NS rooms, wheelchair access, children free with parents, no pets, laundry facilities, senior rates, CC. SGL/DBL$110-$175, STS$230-$395.

Sunset Inn Resort (82200 Hwy. 1, 33036; 664-4427, 800-666-4427) 28 rooms and efficiencies, outdoor pool, a/c, TV, in-room refrigerators and coffee makers, laundry facilities, no pets, children free with parents, senior rates, CC. LS SGL/DBL$65-$105; HS SGL/DBL$105-$125.

Jacksonville

Area Code 905

North Jacksonville

Admiral Benbow Inn (14691 Duval Rd., 32218; 741-4254, 800-451-1986) 120 rooms, outdoor pool, children free with parents, a/c, TV, laundry facilities, kitchenettes, VCRs, pets OK, airport transportation, children free with parents, NS rooms, CC. SGL/DBL$40-$50.

Best Western Inn (10888 Harts Rd., 32218; 751-5600, Fax 757-4311, 800-528-1234) 124 rooms, outdoor pool, children free with parents, a/c, TV, NS rooms, laundry facilities, wheelchair access, pets OK, meeting facilities, senior rates, CC. 7 miles from shopping mall and Riverwalk, 12 miles from the Gator Bowl. SGL/DBL$30-$55.

Days Inn (1181 Airport Rd., 32218; 741-4000, Fax 741-0609, 800-325-2525) 64 rooms, free breakfast, outdoor pool, a/c, TV, children free with parents, wheelchair access, NS rooms, no pets, laundry facilities, senior rates, CC. 14 miles from the Gator Bowl, 20 miles from Fernandina beach, 6 miles from Florida Junior College. SGL/DBL$35-$75.

Days Inn (1057 Broward Rd., 32218; 757-0990, 800-325-2525) 189 rooms, restaurant, lounge, entertainment, outdoor pool, children stay free with parents, local transportation, fax service, a/c, TV, no pets, meeting facilities, senior rates, CC. 6 miles from the Convention Center, 7 miles from the Jacksonville airport. SGL/DBL$40-$85.

Hampton Inn (1170 Airport Entrance Rd., 32218; 741-4980, Fax 741-4186, 800-HAMPTON) 113 rooms, restaurant, free breakfast, pool, exercise center, children under 18 free with parents, NS rooms, wheelchair access, in-room computer hookups, pets OK, fax service, TV, a/c, free local calls, meeting facilities, senior rates, CC. SGL/DBL$45-$60.

Kings Inn Motel (8016 Arlington Expressway, 32211; 725-3343, 800-727-3343) 95 rooms, restaurant, lounge, outdoor pool, whirlpools, a/c, TV, pets OK, children free with parents, laundry facilities, CC. SGL/DBL$26-$41.

La Quinta Inn (812 Dunn Ave., 32218; 751-6960, Fax 751-9769, 800-531-5900) 129 rooms, restaurant, lounge, outdoor heated pool, complimentary newspaper, free local calls, airport courtesy car, pets OK, a/c, TV, children free with parents, fax service, laundry service, meeting facilities, senior rates, CC. Within 10 miles of the downtown area and Gator Bowl, 5 miles from the Jacksonville airport. SGL/DBL$45.

Motel 6 North (10885 Harts Rd., 32218; 751-2344) 126 rooms, outdoor pool, a/c, TV, NS rooms, laundry facilities, pets OK, senior rates, CC. 2 miles from the Jacksonville Zoo, 3 miles from the Jacksonville airport. SGL/DBL$24-$28.

Sky Center Inn (2101 Dixie Clipper Dr., 322118; 741-4747, Fax 741-0002) 192 rooms and suites, restaurant, lounge, outdoor pool, exercise center, airport transportation, children free with parents, a/c, TV, NS rooms, room service, gift shop, wheelchair access, laundry facilities, no pets, CC. SGL/DBL$55-$110.

Super 8 Motel North (10901 Harts Rd., 32218; 751-3888, Fax 751-3888 ext 404, 800-848-8888) 62 rooms and suites, restaurant, children free with parents, free local calls, a/c, TV, in-room refrigerators and microwaves, fax service, NS rooms, wheelchair access, meeting facilities, senior rates, CC. 8 miles from the Gator Bowl and Jacksonville Landing, 7 miles from the Jacksonville airport. SGL/DBL$35-$55.

Airport Area

Holiday Inn Airport (1-95 and Airport Rd., 32229; 741-4404, Fax 741-4907, 800-HOLIDAY, 800-465-4329) 489 rooms and suites, restaurant, free breakfast, lounge, entertainment, outdoor pool, exercise center, lighted tennis court, children stay free with parents, wheelchair access, NS rooms, gift shop, car rental desk, fax service, a/c, TV, room service, pets OK, airport transportation, room service, senior rates, 14 meeting rooms, meeting facilities, CC. 11 miles from the downtown area, 2 miles from the Jacksonville airport, 17 miles from the Gator Bowl. SGL/DBL$50-$59.

Howard Johnson Lodge (1153 Airport Rd., 32229; 741-4600, Fax 741-4424, 800-I-GO-HOJO) 180 rooms, restaurant, lounge, outdoor pool, children free with parents, wheelchair access, NS rooms, airport transportation, fax service, TV, a/c, laundry facilities, senior rates, meeting facilities, CC. 1 mile from the Jacksonville airport, 14 miles from the Gator Bowl, 10 miles from the downtown area. SGL/DBL$35-$50.

Red Roof Inn (14701 Airport Entrance Rd., 32218; 741-4488, 800-843-7663) 109 rooms and suites, NS rooms, fax service, wheelchair access, complimentary newspaper, children free with parents, a/c, TV, free local calls, senior rates, CC. 2 miles from the golf course, 1 mile from the Jacksonville airport, 10 miles from the Gator Bowl. SGL/DBL$30-$35.

Arlington Area

Holiday Inn University Area East (5865 Arlington Expressway, 32211; 724-3410, Fax 727-7606, 800-874-3000, 800-342-2357 in Florida) 270 rooms, restaurant, lounge, free breakfast, outdoor pool, exercise center, whirlpools, lighted tennis courts, children stay free with parents, wheelchair access, a/c, TV, NS rooms, fax service, room service, airport transportation, pets OK, 18 meeting rooms, meeting facilities for 1,200, senior rates, CC. 4.5 miles from the Convention Center, 20 miles from the Jacksonville airport, 2 miles from the Gator Bowl. SGL/DBL$68.

Kings Inn (8016 Arlington Expressway, 32211; 725-3343, 800-727-3343) 130 rooms, restaurant, lounge, outdoor pool, a/c, TV, in-room refrigerators and microwaves, NS rooms, pets OK, wheelchair access, senior rates, CC. SGL/DBL$29-$37.

Ramada Inn East (6237 Arlington Expressway, 32211; 725-5093, 800-2-RAMADA) 143 rooms and suites, restaurant, lounge, entertainment, outdoor pool, wheelchair access, NS rooms, airport transportation, a/c, TV, local transportation, children free with parents, pets OK, meeting facilities, senior rates, CC. 3 miles of the downtown area, Gator Bowl and Civic Auditorium, 6 miles from Jacksonville Landing and the Riverwalk. SGL$35-$60, DBL$40-$70, STS$80-$125.

Mayport and the Beaches

Comfort Inn Oceanfront (1515 North 1st St., 32250; 241-2311, Fax 249-3830, 800-CLARION, 800-654-8776 in Florida) 178 rooms and suites, restaurant, lounge, outdoor heated pool, beach, a/c, TV, in-room refrigerators and microwaves, no pets, children free with parents, NS rooms, wheelchair access, senior rates, CC. SGL/DBL$60-$90.

Days Inn (1031 South 1st St., 32250; 249-7231, Fax 249-7924, 800-325-2525) 155 rooms and suites, restaurant, lounge, entertainment, outdoor pool, tennis courts, in-room refrigerators and microwaves, wheelchair access, NS rooms, fax service, children stay free with parents, no pets, a/c, TV, senior rates, 4 meeting rooms, CC. Near the Gator Bowl, 6 miles from the Mayport Naval Air Station. SGL/DBL$45-$85.

Holiday Inn Oceanfront (1617 North 1st St., 32250; 249-9071, Fax 241-4321, 800-HOLIDAY) 150 rooms, restaurant, lounge, lighted tennis courts, kitchenettes, children stay free with parents, a/c, TV, in-room microwaves, kitchenettes, no pets, wheelchair access, NS rooms, fax service, room service, 2,500 square feet of meeting space. 8 miles from the Mayo Clinic and Mayport Naval Base. SGL/DBL$60-$125.

Ramada Resort (1201 North 1st St., 32250; 241-5333, Fax 241-1862, 800-2-RAMADA) 138 rooms and suites, restaurant, lounge, entertainment, outdoor pool, wheelchair access, kitchenettes, a/c, TV, children free with parents, no pets, NS rooms, 3 meeting rooms, meeting facilities for 750, senior rates, CC. 15 miles from the Gator Bowl and downtown area. SGL$40-$60, DBL$50-$70.

Southside

Best Inns of America (8220 Dix Ellis Trail, 32256; 739-3323, Fax 739-3323 ext 305, 800-237-8466) 110 rooms, restaurant, free breakfast, outdoor pool, children stay free with parents, NS rooms, wheelchair access, fax service, a/c, TV, pets OK, 2 meeting rooms, senior rates, CC. 10 miles from the Gator Bowl, 11 miles from the Civic Auditorium, 25 miles from the Jacksonville airport. SGL$35-$45.

Best Western Bradbury Suites (8277 Western Way Circle, 32256; 737-4477, Fax 739-1649, 800-800-528-1234) 111 1-bedroom suites, restaurant, free breakfast, lounge, entertainment, outdoor pool, laundry service, airport courtesy car, a/c, TV, in-room refrigerators, no pets, children free with parents, wheelchair access, NS rooms, meeting facilities, senior rates, CC. 5 miles from the Mayo Clinic, 10 miles from Jacksonville Beach, 2 miles from the Mall of America. SGL/DBL$55-$70.

Budgetel (3199 Hartley Rd., 32257; 268-9999, Fax 268-9611, 800-428-3438) 164 rooms and suites, restaurant, free breakfast, outdoor pool, children stay free with parents, NS rooms, wheelchair access, in-room computer hookups, fax service, free local calls, in-room refrigerators, microwaves and coffee makers, meeting facilities, senior rates, CC. Near the Orange Park Mall, 9 miles from the Gator Bowl, 10 miles from the downtown area. SGL/DBL$36-$45.

Comfort Inn South (3233 Emerson St., 32207; 398-3331, 800-221-2222) 155 rooms, outdoor pool, a/c, TV, pets OK, children free with parents, NS rooms, wheelchair access, senior rates, CC. 3 miles from the downtown area, 18 miles to Atlantic beaches, 3 miles from Jacksonville Landing and St. Johns Riverwalk. SGL/DBL$40-$105.

Comfort Suites Jacksonville (8333 Dix Ellis Trail, 32256; 739-1155, Fax 731-0752, 800-CLARION, 800-228-5150) 128 rooms, outdoor pool, exercise center, whirlpool, wheelchair access, NS rooms, a/c, TV, children free with parents, in-room refrigerators, VCRs, in-room computer hookups, no pets, meeting facilities, senior rates, CC. 9 miles from the downtown area and Gator Bowl, 27 miles from the Jacksonville airport. SGL/DBL$56-$65.

Courtyard by Marriott (4600 San Pablo Rd., 32224; 223-1700, Fax 223-1026, 800-321-2211) 121 rooms and suites, restaurant, lounge, outdoor heated pool, whirlpools, children stay free with parents, a/c, TV, in-room refrigerators and coffee makers, local transportation, laundry facilities, pets OK, NS rooms, wheelchair access, meeting facilities, senior rates, CC. SGL/DBL$55-$110.

Days Inn (5649 Cagle Rd., 32216; 733-3890, 800-325-2525) 120 rooms, restaurant, lounge, free breakfast, outdoor pool, wheelchair access, children stay free with parents, fax service, a/c, TV, pets OK, NS rooms, senior rates, CC. 6 miles from the Gator Bowl and Convention Center, 4 miles from the downtown area and River Walk, 12 miles from the Mayo Clinic. SGL$30-$45, DBL$45-$50.

Doubletree Club Hotel (4700 Salisbury Rd., 32256; 281-9700, Fax 281-1957, 800-528-0444) 167 rooms, free breakfast, outdoor heated pool, whirlpools, exercise center, local transportation, in-room computer hookups, wheelchair access, in-room refrigerators, a/c, TV, no pets, 4 meeting rooms, meeting facilities for 100, senior rates, CC. 6 miles from the downtown area, 24 miles from the Jacksonville airport. SGL/DBL$120-$130.

Econolodge Central (5221 West University Blvd., 32216; 737-1690, Fax 448-5638, 800-4-CHOICE) 180 rooms, restaurant, outdoor heated pool, children free with parents, no pets, NS rooms, wheelchair access, a/c, TV, meeting facilities, senior rates, CC. 3.5 miles from the downtown area, 13 miles from Atlantic beaches, SGL/DBL$30-$46.

Economy Inns of America (4300 Salisbury Rd., 32216; 281-0198, 800-826-0778, 800-423-3018 in Florida) 124 rooms and suites, free breakfast, heated pool, free local calls, satellite TV, wheelchair access, a/c, TV, pets OK, local transportation, NS rooms, senior rates, CC. 30 miles from the Jacksonville airport, 8 miles from the downtown area. SGL/DBL$33, STS$56.

Embassy Suites (9300 Baymeadows Rd., 32256; 731-3555, Fax 731-4972, 800-EMBASSY) 210 2-room suites, restaurant, lounge, free breakfast, indoor heated pool, sauna, whirlpool, exercise center, sauna, lighted tennis courts, gift shop, NS rooms, a/c, TV, children free with parents, no pets, wheelchair access, room service, laundry service, airport transportation, in-room refrigerators, game room, 20 meeting rooms, senior rates, CC. 8 miles from Jacksonville Landing, 12 miles from Atlantic beaches. STS$79-$124.

Hampton Inn (4690 Salisbury Rd., 32256; 281-0443, Fax 281-0144, 800-426-7866) 130 rooms, free breakfast, outdoor pool, children stay free with parents, NS rooms, wheelchair access, in-room computer hookups, fax service, in-room refrigerators, free local calls, a/c, TV, meeting facilities, senior rates, CC. 9 miles from the downtown area, 10 miles from the Gator Bowl and Jacksonville Landing, 25 miles from the Jacksonville airport. SGL$42-$45, DBL$49-$52.

Holiday Inn (9150 Baymeadows Rd., 32256; 737-1700, Fax 737-0207, 800-HOLIDAY) 250 rooms and suites, restaurant, lounge, outdoor pool, exercise center, gift shop, children stay free with parents, wheelchair access, NS rooms, fax service, in-room refrigerators, room service, a/c, TV, laundry service, no pets, 8 meeting rooms, meeting facilities for 600, senior rates, CC. 25 miles from the Jacksonville airport, 9 miles from the downtown area, 1 mile to Jacksonville Landing. SGL/DBL$69-$74.

Homewood Suites (8737 Baymeadows Rd., 32556; 733-9299, Fax 448-5889, 800-225-5466) 1- and 2-bedroom suites, free breakfast, outdoor heated pool, exercise center, kitchenettes, fax service, complimentary newspaper, a/c, TV, local transportation, in-room microwaves and coffee makers, pets OK, children free with parents, laundry service, NS rooms, meeting facilities for 30, senior rates, CC. 12 miles from the Gator Bowl, 10 miles from Jacksonville Landing, 24 miles from the Jacksonville airport. 1BR$68-$99, 2BR$95-$139.

The Inn At Baymeadows (8050 Baymeadows Circle, 32256; 739-0739, Fax 739-0207, 800-831-8183, 800-826-8889 in Florida) 100 rooms and suites, free breakfast, restaurant, outdoor pool, exercise center, tennis courts, airport transportation, wheelchair access, NS rooms, a/c, TV, kitchenettes, room service, no pets, meeting facilities, senior rates, CC. SGL$65-$155.

La Quinta Inn (8255 Dix Ellis Trail, 32256; 731-9940, Fax 731-3854, 800-531-5900) 106 rooms, restaurant, lounge, free breakfast, outdoor heated pool, complimentary newspaper, free local calls, fax service, a/c, TV, children free with parents, pets OK, laundry service, meeting facilities, senior rates, CC. Within 10 miles of the Museum of Science and Industry, University of North Florida and Deerwood Center Mall, 25 miles from the Jacksonville airport. SGL/DBL$45-$53.

Marina Hotel at St. Johns Place (1515 Prudential Dr., 32207; 396-5100, Fax 396-7154, 800-342-4605) 325 rooms and suites, restaurant, lounge, outdoor pool, lighted tennis courts, in-room refrigerators, gift shop, a/c, TV, children free with parents, wheelchair access, NS rooms, 16 meeting rooms, senior rates, CC. SGL/DBL$55-$75.

Motel 6 (8285 Dix Ellis Trail, 32256; 731-8400) 109 rooms, outdoor pool, no pets, a/c, TV, children free with parents, wheelchair access, senior rates, CC. 8 miles from Jacksonville Landing and the River Walk, 18 miles from Atlantic beaches, 27 miles from the Jacksonville airport. SGL/DBL$26-$36.

Quality Inn (4660 Salisbury Rd., 32256; 281-0900, Fax 281-0417, 800-221-2222) 184 rooms, outdoor pool, sauna, in-room computer hookups, complimentary newspaper, children free with parents, a/c, TV, wheelchair access, room service, laundry service, NS rooms, 4 meeting rooms, senior rates, CC. 1 mile from the downtown area, 8 miles from the Gator Bowl and Jacksonville Landing, 12 miles from the Naval Base. SGL/DBL$48-$65.

Ramada Inn South (5624 Cagle Rd., 32216; 737-8000, Fax 448-8624, 800-2-RAMADA) 144 rooms and suites, restaurant, lounge, entertainment, outdoor pool, children free with parents, wheelchair access, NS rooms, a/c, TV, airport transportation, pets OK, 7 meeting rooms, meeting facilities for 250, senior rates, CC. 5 miles from the downtown area, Gator Bowl and Convention Center. SGL/DBL$34-$48.

Ramada Inn Mandarin Conference Center (3130 Hartley Rd., 32257; 268-8080, Fax 262-8718, 800-2-RAMADA) 153 rooms, restaurant, free breakfast, lounge, entertainment, outdoor pool, wheelchair access, NS rooms, free parking, a/c, TV, pets OK, children free with parents, room service, laundry facilities, 11 meeting rooms, meeting facilities for 500, senior rates, CC. SGL/DBL$48-$75.

Residence Inn by Marriott (8365 Dix Ellis Trail, 32256; 733-8088, Fax 731-8354, 800-331-3131) 112 efficiencies, free breakfast, outdoor heated pool, whirlpools, exercise center, in-room refrigerators, coffee makers and microwaves, laundry facilities, TV, a/c, VCRs, complimentary newspaper, local transportation, fireplaces, children free with parents, NS rooms, wheelchair access, meeting facilities, CC. 18 miles from the Atlantic beach. SGL/DBL$90-$125.

TraveLodge (8765 Baymeadows Rd., 32256; 731-7317, Fax 737-8836, 800-578-7878) 120 rooms, restaurant, lounge, free breakfast, outdoor pool, complimentary newspaper, laundry service, in-room refrigerators and microwaves, a/c, TV, children free with parents, pets OK, fax service, room service, meeting facilities for 50, senior rates, CC. 12 miles from the downtown area and Convention Center. SGL/DBL$40-$50.

Marriott Hotel (4670 Salisbury Rd., 32256; 296-2222, 800-228-9290) 256 rooms and suites, restaurant, lounge, entertainment, indoor and outdoor pools, whirlpools, exercise center, in-room computer hookups, no pets, in-room refrigerators, a/c, VCRs, gift shop, in-room refrigerators, children free with parents, TV, NS rooms, wheelchair access, meeting facilities, senior rates, CC. 7 miles from the downtown area, 15 miles from Atlantic beaches, 24 miles from the Jacksonville airport. SGL/DBL$120-$275.

Westside and Cecil Field

Holiday Inn (6802 Commonwealth Ave., 32205; 781-6000, Fax 781-2784, 800-HOLIDAY) 178 rooms, restaurant, lounge, outdoor pool, exercise center, children free with parents, wheelchair access, a/c, TV, NS rooms, fax service, room service, laundry service, meeting facilities for 400, senior rates, CC. 7 miles from the Gator Bowl, 5 miles from the Civic Center. SGL/DBL$65-$105.

Hospitality Inn Bed and Breakfast (7071 103rd St., 32210; 777-5700, 800-321-0052) 103 rooms, free breakfast, outdoor pool, exercise center, in-room coffee makers, a/c, TV, VCRs, pets OK, wheelchair access. SGL/DBL$45-$55.

House On Cherry Street (1844 Cherry St., 32205; 384-1999) 4 rooms, free breakfast, airport courtesy car, antique furnishings, children over 8 welcome, a/c, TV, no pets, NS rooms, CC. SGL/DBL$70-$80.

Judge Gray's House (2814 St. Johns Ave., 32205; 388-4248) 3 rooms, free breakfast, private baths, no children, laundry service, a/c, TV, no pets, NS, CC. 1.5 miles from the downtown area, 11 miles from the Jacksonville airport. SGL$50, DBL$55.

Ramada Inn West (510 South Lane Ave., 32205; 786-0502, Fax 786-3447, 800-2-RAMADA) 207 rooms, restaurant, lounge, entertainment, outdoor pool, children stay free with parents, wheelchair access, NS rooms, airport transportation, a/c, TV, pets OK, 8 meeting rooms, meeting facilities for 370, senior rates, CC. 6 miles from the downtown area, 8 miles from the Gator Bowl, 5 miles from Jacksonville Landing. SGL$28-$39, DBL$29-$45.

The Willows on the St. Johns River (1849 Willow Branch Terrace, 32205; 387-9152) 2 rooms, free breakfast, outdoor pool, TV, a/c, no pets. SGL/DBL$80.

Other Locations

The Archibald (125 West 2nd St., 32206; 387-1389) 5 rooms, free breakfast, TV, a/c, pets OK, major credit cards. SGL/DBL$69-$76.

Econo Lodge (5959 Youngerman Circle East, 32244; 777-0160, 800-4-CHOICE) 101 rooms, outdoor pool, children free with parents, no pets, senior rates, NS rooms, wheelchair access, a/c, TV, CC. 1 mile from the Orange Park Mall, 12 miles from the downtown area, 30 miles to Atlantic beaches. SGL/DBL$44-$53.

Hampton Inn (6135 Youngerman Circle, 32244; 777-5313, Fax 778-1545, 800-426-7866) 122 rooms, free breakfast, outdoor pool, children stay free with parents, TV, a/c, no pets, NS rooms, wheelchair access, in-room computer hookups, fax service, free local calls, meeting facilities, senior rates, CC. 15 miles from the Gator Bowl. SGL$42, DBL$47.

Hospitality Inn (901 North Main St., 32202; 355-3744) 222 rooms, rooms, children free with parents, free breakfast, TV, a/c, pets OK, major credit cards. SGL/DBL$45-$80.

La Quinta Inn (8555 Blanding Blvd., 32244; 778-9539, Fax 779-5214, 800-531-5900) 122 rooms, restaurant, lounge, free breakfast, heated pool, complimentary newspaper, free local calls, fax service, a/c, TV, children free with parents, pets OK, laundry service, meeting facilities, senior rates, CC. 30 miles from Jacksonville airport, within 10 miles of the Osborne Convention Center, Gator Bowl and Civic Auditorium. SGL/DBL$42-$48.

Motel 6 South (6017 Youngerman Circle, 32244; 772-8228, 505-891-6161) 126 rooms, outdoor pool, free local calls, children free with parents, NS rooms, wheelchair access, a/c, TV, CC. SGL/DBL$30-$40.

Omni Jacksonville Hotel (245 Water St., 32202; 355-6664, Fax 354-2970, 800-843-6664) 354 rooms and suites, restaurant, lounge, entertainment, outdoor heated pool, exercise center, lighted tennis courts, airport transportation, in-room refrigerators, NS rooms, wheelchair access, children free with parents, no pets, a/c, TV, 16 meeting rooms, meeting facilities for 870, CC. 19 miles from the beaches, 18 miles from the Jacksonville airport. SGL/DBL$120-$159, STS$350.

Plantation Manor Inn (1630 Copeland St., 32204; 384-3724) 3 rooms, free breakfast, TV, a/c, no pets. SGL/DBL$70.

Red Roof Inn (6099 Youngerman Circle, 32244; 777-1000, Fax 777-1005) 109 rooms, free breakfast, a/c, TV, children free with parents, pets OK, NS rooms, wheelchair access, CC. 13 miles from the Gator Bowl, 2 miles from the Orange Park Mall, 28 miles from the Jacksonville airport. SGL/DBL$30-$43.

Jasper

Area Code 904

Scottish Inn (Route 3, 32052; 792-1234, 800-251-1962) 56 rooms, restaurant, outdoor pool, a/c, TV, wheelchair access, free local calls, pets OK, NS rooms, children free with parents, free local calls, senior rates, CC. 18 miles from the Memorial Park, 30 miles from Okefenokee Swamp. SGL/DBL$30-$35.

Jennings
Area Code 904

Econo Lodge (I-75 and Hwy. 143, 32053; 928-5500, 800-55-ECONO) 70 rooms, outdoor pool, children free with parents, no pets, NS rooms, wheelchair access, a/c, TV, senior rates, CC. 8 miles from the factory outlet mall, 18 miles from the Valdosta airport. SGL/DBL$26-$45.

Holiday Inn (I-75 and Hwy. 143, 32053; 938-3501, Fax 938-3501, 800-HOLIDAY) 120 rooms, restaurant, lounge, outdoor pool, tennis courts, airport transportation, children free with parents, wheelchair access, a/c, TV, NS rooms, pets OK, in-room computer hookups, fax service, room service, laundry service, meeting facilities, senior rates, CC. 28 miles from the Stephen Foster Memorial, 8 miles from the factory outlet mall. SGL/DBL$40.

Jennings House Inn (Jennings 32053; 938-3305) 16 rooms, restaurant, outdoor pool, pets OK, a/c, TV, children free with parents, NS rooms, CC. SGL/DBL$20-$25.

Jensen Beach
Area Code 407

Beach Club on Hutchinson Island (10740 South Ocean Dr., 34957; 239-3100, Fax 239-3131, 800-877-8787) 2-bedroom villas, outdoor pool, beach, a/c, TV, laundry facilities, children free with parents, no pets, in-room refrigerators, microwaves and coffee makers, senior rates, CC. 2BR$175-$225.

Courtyard by Marriott (10978 South Ocean Dr., 34957; 229-1000, Fax 229-0253, 800-331-3131) 110 rooms and suites, free breakfast, outdoor pool, in-room refrigerators, microwaves and coffee makers, VCRs, no pets, complimentary newspaper, children free with parents, kitchenettes, a/c, TV, NS rooms, beach, in-room computer hookups, wheelchair access, 2 meeting rooms, senior rates, CC. SGL/DBL$60-$120.

Holiday Inn Oceanside (3793 Northeast Ocean Blvd., 34957; 225-3000, Fax 225-1956, 800-992-474 in Florida) 181 rooms, restaurant, lounge, outdoor heated pool, lighted tennis courts, beach, children free with parents, wheelchair access, a/c, TV, NS rooms, fax service, room service, gift shop, game room, laundry service, in-room refrigerators, no pets, 3 meeting rooms, senior rates, CC. 2 miles from the Elliott Museum. LS SGL/DBL$75-$110; HS SGL/DBL$100-$150.

Hutchinson Inn Resort (9750 South Ocean Dr., 34957; 229-2000, Fax 229-8875) 21 rooms, free breakfast, outdoor heated pool, tennis courts, beach, kitchenettes, no pets, a/c, TV, VCRs, in-room refrigerators, microwaves and coffee makers, children free with parents, beach, NS rooms, CC. SGL/DBL$60-$110.

Juno Beach
Area Code 407

Holiday Inn Oceanside Lodge and Suites (930 Hwy. 1, 33408; 626-1531, Fax 626-1531, 800-HOLIDAY) 46 rooms and 2-room suites, restaurant, free breakfast, lounge, outdoor pool, tennis courts, beach, children free with parents, wheelchair access, NS rooms, in-room refrigerators and microwaves, TV, a/c, beach, free local calls, laundry facilities, senior rates, meeting facilities for 200, CC. SGL/DBL$80-$160, STS$160-$170.

Jupiter
Area Code 407

Rental & Reservation Services

Bed and Breakfasts of the Palm Beaches (Jupiter 33458; 746-2545).

ааа

Comfort Inn (810 Hwy. 1, 33477; 575-2936, 800-221-2222) 53 rooms, free breakfast, outdoor heated pool, whirlpools, no pets, a/c, TV, children free with parents, NS rooms, wheelchair access, senior rates, CC. 16 miles from the Palm Beach airport, 1 mile from Carlin Park and Jupiter Dinner Theater. SGL/DBL$45-$115.

Comfort Suites Intracoastal (18903 Southeast Federal Hwy., 33477; 747-9085, 800-221-2222) 36 rooms and suites, free breakfast, outdoor pool, whirlpools, no pets, a/c, TV, children free with parents, NS rooms, wheelchair access, senior rates, laundry facilities, CC. 19 miles from the Palm Beach airport, 1 mile from Atlantic beaches, 1.5 miles from Jupiter Theater and Park. SGL/DBL$60-$135.

Hilton Jupiter Beach Resort (5 Hwy. A1A North, 33477; 746-2511, Fax 747-1714, 800-HILTONS) 193 rooms and suites, restaurant, lounge, entertainment, outdoor heated pool, exercise center, lighted tennis courts, children free with parents, NS rooms, wheelchair access, room service, gift shop, beach, local transportation, laundry facilities, a/c, TV, no pets, 10 meeting rooms, 4,500 square feet of meeting and exhibition space, meeting facilities for 500, senior rates, CC. 12 miles from the Palm Beach airport. SGL/DBL$90-$275; HS SGL/DBL$140-$385.

Wellesley Inn (34 Fisherman's Wharf, 33477; 575-7201, Fax 575-1169, 800-444-8888) 105 rooms, free breakfast, outdoor heated pool, pets OK, a/c, TV, children free with parents, laundry facilities, in-room refrigerators and microwaves, wheelchair access, NS rooms, senior rates, CC. SGL/DBL$40-$100.

Kendall

Area Code 305

Howard Johnson (10201 South Dixie Hwy., 33156; 666-2531, Fax 662-2904, 800-662-4656, 800-I-GO-HOJO) 50 rooms, restaurant, lounge, outdoor pool, children free with parents, wheelchair access, NS rooms, pets OK, car rental desk, TV, a/c, laundry facilities, senior rates, meeting facilities, CC. 14 miles from the Miami airport, 1 mile from the downtown area. SGL/DBL$70-$80.

Miami-Dadeland Marriott (9090 South Dadeland Blvd., 33156; 670-1035, Fax 670-7540, 800-228-9290, 800-331-3131) 302 rooms and suites, restaurant, lounge, outdoor pool, jacuzzi, sauna, exercise center, gift shop, car rental desk, barber and beauty shop, game room, in-room refrigerators, VCRs, children free with parents, a/c, TV, NS rooms, wheelchair access, meeting facilities, senior rates, CC. SGL/DBL$159, 1BR$250, 2BR$475.

Ramada Inn (7600 North Kendall Dr., 33156; 595-6000, 800-2-RAMADA, 800-228-2828) 95 rooms and suites, free breakfast, outdoor pool, wheelchair access, NS rooms, free parking, a/c, TV, pets OK, children free with parents, room service, laundry service, meeting facilities, senior rates, CC. SGL/DBL$79-$90.

Key Biscayne
Area Code 305

Key Islander Executive Suites (290 Sunrise Dr., 33149; 361-2464, Fax 361-6273) 7 rooms and suites, outdoor pool, a/c, TV, NS rooms, kitchenettes, VCRs, in-room microwaves, pets OK, wheelchair access, CC. 1BR$550W-$600W, 2BR$650W.

Sheraton Royal Biscayne Beach Resort (555 Ocean Dr., 33149; 361-5775, Fax 361-0360, 800-325-3535) 190 rooms and suites, restaurant, lounge, entertainment, outdoor heated pool, exercise center, tennis courts, NS rooms, a/c, room service, TV, children free with parents, beach, wheelchair access, meeting facilities for 500, 8,000 square feet of meeting and exhibition space, meeting facilities for 500, senior rates, CC. SGL/DBL$125-$235.

Silver Sands Motel (301 Ocean Dr., 33149; 361-5441, Fax 361-2487) 56 rooms and efficiencies, restaurant, lounge, outdoor heated pool, in-room refrigerators, microwaves and coffee makers, no pets, a/c, TV, kitchenettes, children free with parents, laundry facilities, NS rooms, CC. LS SGL/DBL$79-$169; HS SGL/DBL$115-$205.

Sonesta Beach Hotel (350 Ocean Dr., 33149; 361-2021, Fax 361-3069, 800-SONESTA) 292 rooms and suites, restaurant, lounge, entertainment, outdoor pool, whirlpools, sauna, exercise center, tennis courts, jacuzzi, beach, children free with parents, American Plan available, gift shop, beauty shop, a/c, TV, VCRs, laundry facilities, NS rooms, room service, senior rates, 12 meeting rooms, meeting facilities for 700, 7,200 square feet of meeting and exhibition space, CC. 12 miles from the Miami airport. LS SGL/DBL$185-$230; HS SGL/DBL$235-$275.

Key Colony Beach
Area Code 305

Rental & Reservation Services

DelCane Realty (12701 Overseas Hwy., 33050; 743-0772, 800-874-3798) rental condominiums, duplexes and private homes.

Island Rentals (Marathon 33050; 289-0999, 800-462-6081) rental condominiums and private homes.

Key Colony Beach Realty and Rentals (1 7th St., 33051; 743-6226, 800-766-5033) rental condominiums, duplexes and private homes.

Reed Realty (9499 Overseas Hwy., 33050; 743-5181) rental condominiums and private homes.

Sarah's Island Realty (Key Colony Beach 33051; 289-0999, 800-462-6081) rental condominiums and private homes.

□□□

Continental Inn (1121 West Ocean Dr., 33051; 289-0104) 42 efficiencies, outdoor pool, beach, a/c, TV, kitchenettes, no pets, children free with parents, in-room refrigerators, CC. LS SGL/DBL$79-$109; HS SGL/DBL$104-$144.

Key Colony Beach Motel (441 East Ocean Dr., 33051; 289-0411) 40 rooms, outdoor pool, beach, a/c, TV, children free with parents, no pets, CC. LS SGL/DBL$50-$65; HS SGL/DBL$65-$80.

Key Colony Beach Boatels (Key Colony Beach 33051; 289-0821) 20 1- and 2-bedroom efficiencies, a/c, TV, wheelchair access, children free with parents, pets OK, CC. 1BR/2BR$65-$135.

Key Colony Point Condominiums (Key Colony Beach 33051; 743-7701, Fax 743-0807, 800-356-7701) 18 2- and 3-bedroom condominiums, beach, outdoor pool, tennis courts, a/c, TV, no pets, in-room refrigerators and microwaves, children free with parents, laundry facilities, CC. 2BR/3BR$935W-$1,140W.

Key Largo
Area Code 305

Rental & Reservation Services

Accommodations Center Rentals (Mile Marker 100, 33070; 453-9819, 800-732-2006) rental condominiums and apartments.

Freewheeler Vacations Realty (Islamorada 33036; 664-2075, Fax 664-2884) rental homes.

Ganim Realty (82205 Overseas Hwy., Islamorada, 33036; 664-4577, 800-741-0541) rental condominiums, private homes, apartments and townhouses.

Great Miami Reservation Systems (12555 Biscayne Blvd., 33180; 800-821-2183) hotel and condominium reservations.

Sunchaser Realty Rentals (99801 Overseas Hwy., 33037; 451-3335; Fax 451-3101, 800-654-7384) rental condominiums, cottages and private homes.

Tan Keys Accommodations (451-1013, 800-826-5397) rental condominiums, cottages and motels.

□□□

Anchorage Resort and Yacht Club (107800 Overseas Hwy., 33037; 451-0500) 30 rooms, outdoor pool, children free with parents, a/c, TV, no pets, CC. LS SGL/DBL$85-$130; HS SGL/DBL$100-$140.

Bay Cove Motel (99446 Overseas Hwy., 33037; 451-1686) 10 rooms and efficiencies, children free with parents, a/c, TV, NS rooms, kitchenettes, no pets, CC. LS SGL/DBL$30-$70; HS SGL/DBL$35-$75.

Bay Harbor Lodge (97702 Overseas Hwy., 33037; 852-5695) 15 rooms and efficiencies, kitchenettes, no pets, children free with parents, a/c, TV, CC. LS SGL/DBL$40-$62; HS SGL/DBL$45-$78.

Best Western Suites of Key Largo (201 Ocean Dr., 33037; 451-5081, Fax 451-4173, 800-528-1234, 800-462-6079, 40 rooms and suites, free breakfast, outdoor pool, children free with parents, a/c, NS rooms, TV, VCRs, laundry facilities, wheelchair access, water view, no pets, meeting facilities, senior rates, CC. Half a block from John Pennekamp Coral Reef State Park. SGL/DBL$95-$170.

Gilbert's Resort and Marina (107900 Overseas Hwy., 33037; 451-1133, Fax 451-2955, 800-457-1233) 36 rooms and efficiencies, restaurant, outdoor pool, kitchenettes, children free with parents, a/c, TV, no pets, CC. SGL/DBL$50-$65.

Holiday Inn (99701 Overseas Hwy., 33037; 451-2121, Fax 451-5592, 800-HOLIDAY) 132 rooms, restaurant, lounge, outdoor heated pool, children free with parents, wheelchair access, a/c, TV, NS rooms, fax service, room service, in-room refrigerators, no pets, laundry service, meeting facilities for 75, senior rates, CC. SGL/DBL$75-$125.

Howard Johnson Resort (Overseas Hwy., 33037; 451-1400, 800-I-GO-HOJO) 100 rooms, restaurant, lounge, outdoor pool, children free with parents, wheelchair access, NS rooms, TV, a/c, laundry facilities, gift shop, in-room refrigerators, senior rates, meeting facilities for 75, local transportation, CC. SGL/DBL$90-$250.

The Hungry Pelican Motel (Key Largo 33037; 451-3576) 10 rooms and efficiencies, kitchenettes, a/c, TV, laundry facilities, no pets, CC. LS SGL/DBL$35-$65; HS SGL/DBL$40-$70.

Key Largo Beach Resort (103800 Overseas Hwy., 33037; 453-9393, Fax 453-0093, 800-932-9332) 120 rooms and suites, restaurant, lounge, entertainment, outdoor heated pool, whirlpools, beach, children free with parents, a/c, TV, no pets, in-room coffee makers, kitchenettes, senior rates, CC. LS SGL/DBL$80-$165; HS SGL/DBL$140-$275.

Kona Kai Bayfront Resort (97802 South Overseas Hwy., 33037; 852-7200, 800-365-STAY) 10 rooms and 1- and 2-bedroom apartments, outdoor pool, tennis courts, spa, kitchenettes, children free with parents, laundry facilities, CC. LS SGL/DBL$49-$79; HS SGL/DBL$57-$84.

Marina Del Mar Bayside (99470 Overseas Hwy., 33037; 451-4450, 800-451-3483) 56 rooms and suites, restaurant, free breakfast, lounge, outdoor pool, jacuzzis, exercise center, free local calls, a/c, TV, kitchenettes, no pets, senior rates, CC. LS SGL/DBL$70-$100; HS SGL/DBL$100-$145.

Marina Del Mar Resort and Marina (527 Caribbean Dr., 33037; 451-4107, Fax 451-9650, 800-451-3483) 76 rooms and 2- and 3-bedroom suites, restaurant, free breakfast, lounge, entertainment, outdoor pool, lighted tennis courts, exercise center, whirlpools, a/c, TV, in-room refrigerators, NS rooms, no pets, laundry facilities, CC. LS SGL/DBL$70-$100; HS SGL/DBL$110-$160.

Ocean Drive Apartments (Mile Marker 9.5, 33037; 221-6711, 800-332-7717) 6 1-bedroom apartments, children free with parents, no pets, a/c, TV, laundry facilities, CC. 1BR$85.

Ocean Pointe at Key Largo (500 Burton Dr., 33037; 853-3000, 800-882-9464) 112 1- and 2-bedroom suites, outdoor pool, lighted tennis courts, no pets, in-room refrigerators and microwaves, laundry facilities, children free with parents, CC. 1BR$140, 2BR$180.

Port Largo Resort and Marina (99751 Overseas Hwy., 33037; 451-3939, Fax 451-5592, 800-932-9332) 57 rooms and suites, restaurant, lounge, outdoor pool, jacuzzi, children free with parents, laundry facilities, a/c, TV, no pets, senior rates, CC. SGL/DBL$90-$114, STS$180-$225.

Port Largo Villas (Mile Marker 100, 33037; 800-476-1917) 2-bedroom villas, outdoor pool, tennis courts, a/c, TV, children free with parents, laundry facilities, in-room refrigerators, microwaves and coffee makers, no pets, senior rates, CC. LS 2BR$180-$1,000W; HS 2BR$210-$1,500W.

Sheraton Key Largo (97000 South Overseas Hwy., 33037; 852-5553, Fax 852-5533, 800-325-3535, 800-826-1006 in Florida) 200 rooms and suites, restaurant, lounge, entertainment, outdoor heated pool, exercise center, beach, whirlpools, lighted tennis courts, in-room refrigerators and coffee makers, beach, NS rooms, a/c, room service, TV, children free with parents, wheelchair access, no pets, meeting facilities for 300, 7,000 square feet of meeting and exhibition space, senior rates, CC. 5 miles from John Pennekamp Coral Reef State Park, 12 miles from Theater of the Sea. SGL/DBL$145-$255.

Tropic Vista Motel (Mile Marker 90.7, 33037; 800-537-3253) 24 rooms and efficiencies, outdoor pool, children free with parents, in-room refrigerators, NS rooms, a/c, TV, laundry facilities, pets OK, kitchenettes, wheelchair access, CC. 15 miles from John Pennekamp Coral Reef State Park. SGL/DBL$43-$95.

Key West

Area Code 305

Rental & Reservation Services

Check-In Reservation Services (7282 55th Ave. East, Bradenton 34205; 867-7760, 800-237-1033) rental condominiums and apartments.

Great Miami Reservation Systems (12555 Biscayne Blvd., 33180; 800-821-2183) hotel and condominium reservations.

H.D.S. Enterprises (148 South Federal Hwy., Boca Raton, 33432; 347-8754, 800-242-0437) rental condos, apartments and private homes.

Old Town Resorts (1319 Duval St., 33040; 294-5539, Fax: 294-8272, 800-354-4455) rental condominiums and private homes.

Property Management of Key West (1213 Truman Ave., 33040; 296-7744, Fax 296-4870).

□□□

Artist House (534 Eaton St., 33040; 296-3977, 800-582-7882) 6 rooms and suites, free breakfast, NS rooms, a/c, TV, fireplaces, children over 10 welcome, CC. SGL/DBL$125-$250.

The Banyan Resort (323 Whitehead St., 33040; 296-7786, Fax 294-1107, 800-225-0639) 38 rooms and 2-bedroom suites, outdoor pool, whirlpools, kitchenettes, no pets, in-room refrigerators, a/c, TV, VCRs, NS rooms, wheelchair access, CC. SGL/DBL$115-$220.

Best Western Hibiscus Motel (1313 Simonton St., 33040; 296-6711, 800-528-1234, 800-972-5100, 800-228-7364 in Florida) 61 rooms and efficiencies, free breakfast, outdoor heated pool, whirlpools, children free with parents, a/c, NS rooms, TV, laundry facilities, wheelchair access, local transportation, in-room refrigerators, water view, no pets, airport courtesy car, meeting facilities, senior rates, CC. In Old Towne and near golf course. SGL/DBL$90-$195.

Best Western Key Ambassador Resort Inn (3755 South Roosevelt Blvd., 33040; 296-3500, Fax 296-9961, 800-432-4315, 800-528-1234) 100 rooms, free breakfast, outdoor heated pool, children free with parents, a/c, NS rooms, TV, laundry facilities, wheelchair access, in-room refrigerators, pets OK, meeting facilities, senior rates, CC. SGL/DBL$80-$195.

Blue Marlin Motel (1320 Simonton St., 33040; 294-2585, 800-826-5303) 53 rooms and efficiencies, outdoor heated pool, kitchenettes, no pets, children free with parents, NS rooms, a/c, TV, in-room refrigerators, CC. In Old Towne, 2.5 miles from the Key West airport. SGL/DBL$70-$145.

Colours (410 Fleming St., 33040; 294-6977) 12 rooms, free breakfast, outdoor pool, no children, no pets, a/c, TV, CC. LS DBL$80-$120; HS DBL$100-$140.

Comfort Inn (3824 North Roosevelt Blvd., 33040; 294-3773, Fax 294-3773, 800-221-2222, 800-695-5150) 100 rooms, restaurant, free breakfast, lounge, entertainment, outdoor pool, a/c, TV, children free with parents, NS rooms, antique furnishings, in-room refrigerators, wheelchair access, game room, senior rates, CC. SGL/DBL$150-$190.

Curry Mansion Inn (511 Caroline St., 33040; 294-5349, Fax 294-4093) 15 rooms, outdoor pool, kitchenettes, pets OK, in-room refrigerators, children free with parents, a/c, TV, VCRs, NS rooms, CC. LS SGL/DBL$125-$175; HS SGL/DBL$170-$190.

Days Inn (3852 North Roosevelt Blvd., 33040; 294-3742, 800-325-2525) 134 rooms and suites, restaurant, free breakfast, outdoor pool, a/c, TV, wheelchair access, NS rooms, pets OK, laundry facilities, senior rates, CC. 4 miles from the historic district, 1.5 miles from the Key West airport. SGL/DBL$80-$190, STS$250.

Duval House (815 Duval St., 33040; 294-1666) 28 rooms and suites, free breakfast, in-room refrigerators, TV, a/c, no pets, antique furnishings, CC. In Old Towne. LS SGL/DBL$85-$120; HS SGL/DBL$120-$190.

Eaton Lodge (511 Eaton St., 33040; 294-3800) 13 rooms and 1-bedroom suites, free breakfast, no children, no pets, a/c, TV, CC. LS DBL$75-$105; HS DBL$105-$150, 1BR$220.

Econo Lodge Resort (3820 North Roosevelt Blvd., 33040; 294-5511, 800-55-ECONO, 800-KEE-WEST) 143 rooms and suites, restaurant, lounge, entertainment, outdoor pool, children free with parents, laundry facilities, no pets, NS rooms, wheelchair access, kitchenettes, a/c, TV, senior rates, CC. 1.5 miles from the Key West airport, 2 miles from the Gulf beaches, 3 miles from Old Towne. SGL/DBL$90-$290.

Eden House (1015 Fleming St., 33040; 296-6868) 38 rooms and suites, restaurant, outdoor pool, no pets, children free with parents, a/c, TV, NS rooms, wheelchair access, CC. LS DBL$45-$145; HS DBL$75-$195.

Fairfield Inn by Marriott (2400 North Roosevelt Blvd., 33040; 296-5700, Fax 296-5700, 800-228-9290, 800-843-5888 in Florida) 125 rooms, outdoor heated pool, children free with parents, NS rooms, free cable TV, kitchenettes, free local calls, laundry service, a/c, wheelchair access, no pets, meeting facilities, fax service, senior rates, CC. 2 miles from the Key West airport, 1.5 miles from the historic district, 2 miles from the Hemingway House and Museum. SGL/DBL$65-$150.

Galleon Resort (617 Front St., 33040; 296-7711, 800-544-3030) 96 efficiencies, outdoor heated pool, whirlpools, sauna, exercise center, a/c, TV, beach, wheelchair access, NS rooms, children free with parents, no pets, senior rates, CC. SGL/DBL$150-$375.

Hampton Inn (2801 North Roosevelt Blvd., 33040; 294-2917, Fax 296-0221, 800-426-7866) 158 rooms and suites, free breakfast, outdoor pool, whirlpools, children free with parents, NS rooms, wheelchair access, in-room computer hookups, fax service, TV, a/c, free local calls, gift shop, pets OK, meeting facilities, senior rates, CC. 2 miles from Old Towne. LS SGL/DBL$80-$110; HS SGL/DBL$135-$170.

Heron House (512 Simonton St., 33040; 294-9227, Fax 294-5692) 3 homes, free breakfast, outdoor pool, whirlpools, children over 16 welcome, in-room refrigerators, no pets, a/c, TV, NS rooms, CC. In Old Towne. LS SGL/DBL$65-$125; HS SGL/DBL$105-$195.

Holiday Inn Beachside (3841 North Roosevelt Blvd., 33040; 294-2572, Fax 296-5659, 800-HOLIDAY) 222 rooms, restaurant, lounge, outdoor pool, whirlpools, lighted tennis courts, no pets, in-room refrigerators, children free with parents, wheelchair access, car rental desk, a/c, TV, NS rooms, fax service, room service, beach, laundry service, meeting facilities for 700, senior rates, CC. 1 mile from the Key West airport. SGL/DBL$80-$250.

Holiday Inn La Concha Hotel (430 Duval St., 33040; 296-2991, Fax 294-3283, 800-745-2191, 800-HOLIDAY) 160 rooms, restaurant, lounge, entertainment, outdoor pool, children free with parents, wheelchair access, a/c, gift shop, TV, no pets, NS rooms, fax service, room service, laundry service, meeting facilities, senior rates, CC. In Old Towne, 3 miles from the Key West airport. SGL/DBL$117-$500.

Howard Johnson (3031 North Roosevelt Blvd., 33040; 296-6595, Fax 296-8351, 800-I-GO-HOJO) 64 rooms, restaurant, lounge, outdoor pool, children free with parents, wheelchair access, NS rooms, no pets, fax service, TV, a/c, VCRs, laundry facilities, senior rates, meeting facilities, CC. 1 mile from the Key West airport, 2 miles from the downtown area. SGL/DBL$100-$200.

Hyatt Key West Resort and Marina (601 Front St., 33040; 296-9900, Fax 292-1038, 800-228-9000) 120 rooms and suites, restaurant, lounge, entertainment, outdoor pool, whirlpools, exercise center, TV, a/c, 24-hour room service, NS rooms, no pets, wheelchair access, 1,000 square feet of meeting and exhibition space, senior rates, CC. 2 block from the downtown area, 10 miles from the Key West airport. LS SGL/DBL$180-$255; HS SGL/DBL$265-$370.

Island City House (810 Eaton St., 33040; 294-5720, 800-634-8230) 24 rooms, free breakfast, outdoor heated pool, whirlpools, no pets, children free with parents, a/c, TV, CC. SGL/DBL$85-$265.

Key Lodge Motel (1004 Duval St., 33040; 296-9915, 800-458-1296) 24 rooms and efficiencies, outdoor heated pool, pets OK, in-room refrigerators, a/c, TV, children free with parents, CC. In Old Towne. SGL/DBL$130-$148.

Key West Bed and Breakfast (415 Williams St., 33040; 296-7274) 8 rooms, free breakfast, whirlpools, sauna, no children, a/c, TV, no pets. SGL$85, DBL$125.

Key Wester Resort Inn and Villas (3675 South Roosevelt Blvd., 33040; 296-5671, 800-327-7072, 800-432-7413 in Florida) 93 rooms and 2-bedroom efficiencies, restaurant, outdoor pool, sauna, lighted tennis courts, no pets, a/c, TV, kitchenettes, children free with parents, NS rooms, senior rates, CC. LS SGL/DBL$60-$70; HS SGL/DBL$125-$135.

La Mer Bed and Breakfast (506 South St., 33040; 296-5611, Fax 294-8272, 800-354-4455) 11 rooms, free breakfast, children over 12 welcome, TV, a/c, no pets, CC. SGL/DBL$110-$245.

La Pensione (809 Truman Ave., 33040; 292-9923, Fax 296-6509) 7 rooms, free breakfast, outdoor pool, TV, a/c, no pets, CC. SGL/DBL$135-$160.

La Te Da (1125 Duval St., 33040; 294-8435) 18 rooms and suites, outdoor pool, no children, no pets, a/c, TV, CC. In Old Towne. LS SGL/DBL$48-$128; HS SGL/DBL$178-$183.

Marquesa Hotel (600 Fleming St., 33040; 292-1919, 800-869-4631) 15 rooms, restaurant, free breakfast, outdoor heated pool, a/c, TV, no pets, NS rooms, CC. LS SGL/DBL$115-$165; HS SGL/DBL$185-$260.

Marriott's Casa Marina Resort (1500 Reynolds St., 33040; 296-3535; Fax 296-9960, 800-228-9290) 312 rooms and 2-bedroom suites, free breakfast, outdoor heated pool, whirlpools, saunas, lighted tennis courts, airport transportation, in-room refrigerators, a/c, VCRs, children free with parents, TV, antique furnishings, NS rooms, wheelchair access, meeting facilities, Modified American Plan available, no pets, senior rates, CC. 3 miles from the Key West airport. SGL/DBL$165-$250; HS SGL/DBL$250-$695.

Merlinn Guesthouse (811 Simonton St., 33040; 296-3336, Fax 296-3524) 18 rooms, outdoor heated pool, pets OK, a/c, TV, CC. LS SGL/DBL$65-$115; HS SGL/DBL$90-$180.

Ocean Key House Suite Resort and Marina (Zero Duval St., 33040; 296-7701, Fax 292-7685, 800-328-9815) 100 rooms and 1- and 2-bedroom suites, pool, in-room refrigerators, microwaves and coffee makers, NS rooms, a/c, TV, CC. In Old Towne, 3.5 miles from the Key West airport. SGL/DBL$135, 1BR$215-$295, $259-$300.

Pegasus International Hotel (501 Southard St., 33040; 294-9323, Fax 294-4741, 800-397-8148) 25 rooms, outdoor pool, NS rooms, children free with parents, laundry facilities, no pets, CC. LS SGL/DBL$62-$115; HS SGL/DBL$137-$202.

Pelican Landing Resort and Motel (915 Eisenhower Dr., 33040; 296-7583, Fax 296-7792, 800-527-8108) 32 rooms and suites, outdoor pool, children free with parents, no pets, a/c, TV, NS rooms, senior rates, CC. 1.5 miles from the Key West airport, 10 blocks from Old Towne. SGL/DBL$125, STS$225-$475.

Pier House Inn and Beach Club (1 Duval St., 33040; 294-9541, Fax 294-9541, 800-327-8340, 800-432-3414 in Florida) 120 rooms and suites, restaurant, lounge, entertainment, outdoor pool, whirlpools, sauna, gift shop, exercise center, beauty shop, a/c, TV, VCRs, children free with parents, NS rooms, airport transportation, no pets, CC. In Old Towne, 4 miles from the Key West airport. LS SGL/DBL$195-$295; HS SGL/DBL$265-$450.

Quality Inn (3850 North Roosevelt Blvd., 33040; 294-6681, Fax 294-5618, 800-221-2222) 148 rooms and suites, restaurant, outdoor pool, exercise center, children free with parents, a/c, TV, wheelchair access, room service, laundry service, no pets, kitchenettes, in-room coffee makers, NS rooms, meeting facilities, senior rates, CC. LS SGL/DBL$60-$150; HS SGL/DBL$130-$295.

Ramada Inn (3420 North Roosevelt Blvd., 33040; 294-5541, Fax 294-7932, 800-22-RAMADA) 104 rooms and suites, restaurant, lounge, entertainment, outdoor heated pool, wheelchair access, NS rooms, free parking, a/c, TV, children free with parents, room service, pets OK, in-room refrigerators, laundry facilities, local transportation, car rental desk, meeting facilities, senior rates, CC. LS SGL/DBL$50-$120; HS SGL/DBL$140-$250.

The Reach Resort (1435 Simonton St., 33040; 296-5000, Fax 296-2830, 800-874-4118) 150 rooms, restaurant, lounge, entertainment, outdoor heated pool, sauna, exercise center, children free with parents, no pets, a/c, TV, in-room refrigerators and coffee makers, beach, NS rooms, CC. In Old Towne, 4 miles from the Key West airport. SGL/DBL$155-$475.

Santa Maria Motel (1401 Simonton St., 33040; 296-5678, Fax 294-0010, 800-821-5397) 51 rooms and efficiencies, restaurant, lounge, outdoor heated pool, a/c, TV, NS rooms, no pets, wheelchair access, senior rates, CC. In Old Towne, 4 miles from the Key West airport. SGL/DBL$95-$155.

Seascape (420 Olivia St., 33040; 296-7776) 5 rooms, free breakfast, no children, no pets, a/c, TV, CC. LS SGL/DBL$59-$69; HS SGL/DBL$79-$94.

South Beach Ocean Front Motel (508 South St., 33040; 296-5611, Fax 294-8272, 800-354-4455) 47 rooms, outdoor pool, beach, kitchenettes, no pets, a/c, TV, children free with parents, NS rooms, senior rates, CC. LS SGL/DBL$65-$115; HS SGL/DBL$115-$205.

Southernmost Motel (1319 Duval St., 33040; 296-6577, Fax 294-8272, 800-354-4455) 127 rooms, outdoor heated pool, whirlpools, in-room refrigerators, no pets, a/c, TV, NS rooms, children free with parents, CC. LS SGL/DBL$65-$130; HS SGL/DBL$100-$185.

Watson House (525 Simonton St., 33040; 294-6712) 3 rooms and suites, free breakfast, TV, a/c, VCRs, in-room refrigerators, no pets, CC. SGL/DBL$95-$360.

Whispers At The Gideon Lowe House (409 William St., 33040; 294-5956) 6 rooms, free breakfast, a/c, TV, NS, no children, no pets, CC. LS SGL/DBL$69-$75; HS SGL/DBL$95-$105.

Kissimmee

Area Code 407

Rental & Reservation Services

Century 21 Rentals-A-Paradise, Inc. (3018 Ave. C, Holmes Beach 34217; 778-4800, 800-237-2252) rental condos and apartments.

Check-In Reservation Services (7282 55th Ave. East, Bradenton 34205; 867-7760, 800-237-1033) rental condos and apartments.

Luxury Florida Vacation Villas (1004 North Hoagland Blvd., 34741; 933-2701, 800-780-2701) rental condos and apartments.

Phoenix Properties (600 North Thacker Ave., 34742; 870-8011, Fax 870-9001, 800-828-7127) rental condominiums and private homes.

□□□

A-1 Motel (4030 West Vine St., 34741; 847-9270, Fax 870-8790, 800-662-1920 in Florida) 57 rooms, efficiencies and suites, outdoor pool, in-room refrigerators and coffee makers, airport courtesy car, a/c, TV, children free with parents, NS rooms, CC. SGL/DBL$25-$29, EFF$35.

Adventure Motel (4501 West Irlo Bronson Memorial Hwy., 34746; 396-0808, Fax 396-8023) 48 rooms and efficiencies, a/c, TV, wheelchair access, children free with parents, no pets, in-room refrigerators, senior rates, CC. SGL/DBL$35-$75.

Aloha Motel (4643 West Irlo Bronson Memorial Hwy. 34746; 396-1340) 48 rooms, outdoor pool, children free with parents, a/c, TV, wheelchair access, laundry facilities, CC. SGL/DBL$30-$65.

Ambassador Motel (4107 West Vine St., 34741; 847-7171, Fax 847-7677) 48 rooms, outdoor pool, a/c, TV, CC. SGL/DBL$24-$36.

Best Western Eastgate (5565 West Irlo Bronson Memorial Hwy., 34746; 396-0707, Fax 396-6644, 800-528-1234) 403 rooms, restaurant, lounge, outdoor heated pool, whirlpools, tennis courts, in-room refrigerators, local transportation, pets OK, gift shop, children free with parents, a/c, NS rooms, TV, laundry facilities, wheelchair access, meeting facilities, senior rates, CC. 3 miles from Walt Disney World and MGM Studios, 18 miles from downtown Orlando. SGL/DBL$45-$75.

Best Western Kissimmee (2261 West Irlo Bronson Memorial Hwy., 34746; 846-2221, Fax 846-1095, 800-528-1234, 800-944-0062) 281 rooms, restaurant, lounge, outdoor heated pool, children free with parents, a/c, NS rooms, gift shop, TV, laundry facilities, local transportation, wheelchair access, kitchenettes, in-room refrigerators and microwaves, no pets, 3,300 square feet of meeting and exhibition space, meeting facilities for 300, senior rates, CC. 12 miles from Walt Disney World. LS SGL/DBL$36-$46; HS SGL/DBL$70-$90.

Best Western Maingate Inn (8600 West Irlo Bronson Memorial Hwy., 34747; 396-0100, Fax 396-6718, 800-327-9151, 800-528-1234) 299 rooms, restaurant, lounge, outdoor pool, children free with parents, gift shop, game room, a/c, TV, NS rooms, laundry facilities, wheelchair access, no pets, meeting facilities, senior rates, CC. 4 miles from Walt Disney World, 15 miles from Universal Studios. SGL/DBL$40-$75.

Best Western (4694 West Irlo Bronson Memorial Hwy., 34746; 396-1780, Fax 396-6249, 800-528-1234) 299 rooms, restaurant, free breakfast, lounge, outdoor pool, gift shop, children free with parents, a/c, NS rooms, TV, laundry facilities, airport transportation, wheelchair access, pets OK, meeting facilities, senior rates, CC. SGL/DBL$60-$70.

Caribbean Villas (2003 Trinidad Ct., 34741; 846-4405, Fax 846-2018, 800-327-4730) 150 2- and 3-bedroom condos, outdoor pool, whirlpools, a/c, TV, in-room refrigerators, microwaves and coffee makers, children free with parents, a/c, TV, laundry facilities, CC. 2BR$85, 3BR$105.

Casa Rosa Inn (4600 West Irlo Bronson Memorial Hwy., 34746; 396-2020, 800-432-0665 in Florida) 54 rooms, efficiencies and suites, outdoor pool, in-room refrigerators, a/c, no pets, CC. SGL/DBL$25, EFF$30.

Central Motel (4698 West Irlo Bronson Memorial Hwy., 34746; 396-2333, 800-247-1883 in Florida) 48 rooms, outdoor pool, no pets, a/c, TV, children free with parents, NS rooms, in-room refrigerators, senior rates, CC. SGL/DBL$25-$50.

Comfort Inn Maingate (7571 West Irlo Bronson Memorial Hwy., 34746; 396-7500, Fax 870-2010, 800-CLARION, 800-432-0887 in Florida) 281 rooms and suites, restaurant, lounge, outdoor pool, children free with parents, in-room refrigerators, local transportation, laundry facilities, a/c, TV, NS rooms, senior rates, CC. 20 miles from the Orlando airport, 15 miles from Sea World. SGL/DBL$40-$85.

Comfort Suites (4018 West Vine St., 32741; 870-2000, Fax 870-2010, 800-228-5150) 225 rooms and suites, restaurant, free breakfast, lounge, outdoor pool, whirlpools, in-room refrigerators, no pets, a/c, TV, children free with parents, local transportation, NS rooms, wheelchair access, senior rates, CC. 6 miles from Walt Disney World, 25 miles from the Orlando airport. SGL/DBL$60-$100.

Concord Apartments (3199 West Vine St., 34741; 363-7670, Fax 800-866-9128, 800-999-6896) 198 condominiums outdoor pool, a/c, TV, in-room refrigerators and coffee makers, children free with parents, wheelchair access, senior rates, CC. SGL/DBL$69-$199.

Continental Motel (4650 West Irlo Bronson Memorial Hwy., 34746; 396-2030, Fax 396-2639, 800-344-1030) 38 rooms and efficiencies, outdoor pool, children free with parents, in-room refrigerators and microwave, no pets, laundry facilities, CC. SGL/DBL$25, EFF$30.

Days Inn (2095 East Irlo Bronson Hwy., 34743; 846-7136, 800-325-2525) 122 rooms, restaurant, outdoor pool, a/c, TV, wheelchair access, NS rooms, no pets, laundry facilities, senior rates, CC. A 1/2-mile from the Astro Training Camp. SGL/DBL$30-$100.

Days Inn (I-4 and Hwy. 27, 34742; 424-2596, Fax 424-4324, 800-325-2525) 121 rooms, restaurant, outdoor pool, a/c, TV, gift shop, children free with parents, wheelchair access, NS rooms, pets OK, laundry facilities, senior rates, CC. SGL/DBL$40-$84.

Days Inn (5820 West Irlo Bronson Memorial Hwy., 34746; 396-7900, Fax 396-1789, 800-325-2525) 605 rooms, restaurant, lounge, outdoor pool, a/c, TV, wheelchair access, NS rooms, no pets, laundry facilities, game room, local transportation, kitchenettes, gift shop, senior rates, meeting facilities, CC. SGL/DBL$50-$200.

Days Inn (4104 West Irlo Bronson Memorial Hwy., 34741; 846-4714, Fax 932-2699, 800-325-2525) 226 rooms, free breakfast, outdoor pool, a/c, TV, wheelchair access, NS rooms, laundry facilities, children free with parents, airport transportation, senior rates, CC. 25 miles from Orlando airport, 1 block from the shopping mall. SGL/DBL$29-$110.

Days Inn West (7980 West Irlo Bronson Memorial Hwy., 34746; 396-1000, 800-325-2525, 800-432-9926) 366 rooms, restaurant, lounge, outdoor pool, a/c, TV, wheelchair access, NS rooms, children free with parents, pets OK, local transportation, laundry facilities, senior rates, meeting facilities for 75, CC. 10 miles from Universal Studios, 8 miles from Sea World. SGL/DBL$30-$40.

Days Suites (5840 West Irlo Bronson Memorial Hwy., 34746; 396-7969, Fax 396-8103, 800-325-2525, 800-327-9126) 604 suites, restaurant, lounge, outdoor heated pool, airport transportation, kitchenettes, a/c, TV, wheelchair access, gift shop, game room, children free with parents, in-room refrigerators, boutiques, NS rooms, no pets, laundry facilities, senior rates, CC. 8 miles from Sea World, 12 miles from Universal Studios. SGL/DBL$80-$160.

Dayspring Villas (2737 Poinciana Blvd., 34746; 396-6010, 800-726-4265) 3-bedroom villas, outdoor pool, exercise center, whirlpools, NS rooms, no pets, a/c, TV, in-room refrigerators, microwave and coffee makers, wheelchair access, children free with parents, CC. 3BR$99.

Economy Inn (5367 West Irlo Bronson Memorial Hwy., 34746; 396-4020, 800-826-0778) 197 rooms, free breakfast, outdoor pool, free local calls, wheelchair access, a/c, children free with parents, TV, NS rooms, senior rates, CC. 3 miles from Walt Disney World. SGL/DBL$48-$53.

Econo Lodge (4311 West Irlo Bronson Memorial Hwy., 34746; 396-7100, 800-365-6935, 800-55-ECONO) 173 rooms, outdoor heated pool, children free with parents, no pets, NS rooms, laundry facilities, local transportation, game room, wheelchair access, a/c, TV, senior rates, CC. 8 miles from Walt Disney World, 25 miles from the Orlando airport. LS SGL/DBL$30-$50; HS SGL/DBL$45-$65.

Econo Lodge Hawaiian Village (7514 West Irlo Bronson Memorial Hwy., 34746; 396-7700, Fax 396-2000, 800-365-6935, 800-55-ECONO) 443 rooms and suites, restaurant, lounge, entertainment, outdoor heated pool, children free with parents, no pets, laundry facilities, NS rooms, wheelchair access, game room, a/c, TV, 2 meeting rooms, 2,770 square feet of meeting and exhibition space, meeting facilities for 225, senior rates, CC. 1 mile from Walt Disney World, 2 miles from Sea World, 20 miles from the Orlando airport, 10 miles from Universal Studios. LS SGL/DBL$35-$50; HS SGL/DBL$50-$70.

Econo Lodge Maingate West (8620 West Irlo Bronson Memorial Hwy., 34746; 396-9300, 800-55-ECONO) 133 rooms, restaurant, outdoor pool, whirlpools, exercise center, gift shop, game room, VCRs, children free with parents, no pets, laundry facilities, NS rooms, wheelchair access, a/c, TV, senior rates, CC. 4 miles from Walt Disney World, 20 miles from the Orlando airport. SGL/DBL$35-$65.

Econo Lodge (4985 West Irlo Bronson Memorial Hwy., 34746; 396-4343, 800-4-CHOICE) 164 rooms, restaurant, free breakfast, outdoor pool, whirlpools, gift shop, game room, children free with parents, no pets, laundry facilities, NS rooms, wheelchair access, a/c, TV, senior rates, CC. 20 miles from the Orlando airport, 4 miles from Walt Disney World, 1 mile from Fort Liberty. SGL/DBL$35-$70.

Embassy Motel (4880 West Irlo Bronson Memorial Hwy., 34746; 396-1144, 800-325-4872, 800-432-0153 in Florida) 126 rooms and efficiencies, outdoor pool, no pets, a/c, TV, children free with parents, NS rooms, laundry facilities, senior rates, CC. SGL/DBL$30-$55.

Famous Host Inn (5875 West Irlo Bronson Memorial Hwy., 34746; 396-8883, Fax 396-8907, 800-441-5477) 121 rooms, outdoor pool, airport courtesy car, wheelchair access, laundry facilities, a/c, TV, children free with parents, CC. SGL/DBL$40.

Feel Like Home (Kissimmee 34745; 933-7070, 800-726-0434) 15 2- and 3-bedroom villas, outdoor pool, a/c, TV, children free with parents, in-room refrigerators and microwaves, no pets, laundry facilities, CC. 2BR$105, 3BR$125.

Flamingo Motel (801 East Vine St., 34744; 846-1935, 800-780-7617) 40 rooms and suites, outdoor pool, in-room refrigerators, no pets, a/c, TV, in-room microwaves, NS rooms, CC. SGL/DBL$70-$140.

Four Winds Motel (4596 West Irlo Bronson Memorial Hwy., 34746; 396-4011, Fax 239-8976, 800-826-5830) 48 rooms and 2-bedroom efficiencies, outdoor pool, in-room refrigerators and microwaves, a/c, TV, no pets, NS rooms, children free with parents, senior rates, CC. SGL/DBL$30-$50.

Gala Vista Motor Inn (5995 West Irlo Bronson Memorial Hwy., 34746; 396-4300, Fax 432-0694, 800-223-1548) 200 rooms, outdoor pool, airport courtesy car, a/c, TV, children free with parents, wheelchair access, no pets, laundry facilities, CC. SGL/DBL$39-$69.

Gator Motel (4576 West Irlo Bronson Memorial Hwy., 34746; 396-0127) 38 rooms, outdoor pool, in-room refrigerators, no pets, a/c, TV, children free with parents, NS rooms, CC. SGL/DBL$25-$55.

Gemini Motel (4624 West Irlo Bronson Memorial Hwy., 34746; 396-2151) 84 rooms and efficiencies, outdoor pool, no pets, in-room refrigerators and microwaves, a/c, TV, NS rooms, CC. SGL/DBL$22-$50.

Golden Link Motel (4914 West Irlo Bronson Memorial Hwy., 34746; 396-0555, 800-654-3957 in Florida) 84 rooms, outdoor heated pool, in-room refrigerators, no pets, a/c, TV, laundry facilities, NS rooms, CC. SGL/DBL$25-$50.

Hampton Inn Main Gate (3104 Pkwy. Blvd., 34746; 396-8484, Fax 396-7344, 800-243-844, 800-426-7866) 164 rooms and suites, free breakfast, outdoor pool, exercise center, children free with parents, NS rooms, wheelchair access, in-room computer hookups, fax service, TV, a/c, free local calls, no pets, meeting facilities, senior rates, CC. SGL/DBL$60-$87.

Hilton Inn Gateway (7470 Hwy. 192 West, 34746; 396-4400, Fax 396-4320, 800-327-9170, 800-HILTONS) 500 rooms and suites, restaurant, lounge, entertainment, outdoor pool, whirlpools, sauna, exercise center, children free with parents, NS rooms, in-room refrigerators and microwaves, no pets, car rental desk, in-rom computer hookups, wheelchair access, room service, laundry facilities, a/c, TV, local transportation, 7 meeting rooms, 6,800 square feet of meeting and exhibition space, meeting facilities for 980, senior rates, CC. 2 miles from Walt Disney World, 15 miles from Universal Studios, 10 miles from Sea World. SGL/DBL$85-$165.

HoJo Inn (6051 West Irlo Bronson Memorial Hwy., 34747; 396-1748, Fax 649-8642, 9800-288-4678, 800-I-GO-HOJO) 367 rooms, restaurant, lounge, outdoor heated pool, whirlpools, children free with parents, wheelchair access, NS rooms, TV, gift shop, fax service, in-room coffee makers, a/c, laundry facilities, senior rates, meeting facilities, CC. 2 miles from Walt Disney World, 9 miles from Sea World, 15 miles from the Orlando airport, 2 blocks from Old Towne Shopping Center. SGL/DBL$40-$80.

Holiday Inn (2145 East Irlo Bronson Memorial Hwy., 34744; 846-4646, 800-HOLIDAY) 149 rooms, restaurant, lounge, outdoor pool, exercise center, children free with parents, wheelchair access, a/c, TV, local transportation, pets OK, in-room refrigerators, NS rooms, fax service, room service, laundry service, 2,500 square feet of meeting and exhibition space, meeting facilities for 250, senior rates, CC. 16 miles from Walt Disney World, 20 miles from the Orlando airport, 18 miles from Sea World. SGL/DBL$40-$70.

Holiday Inn Maingate (7300 Irlo Bronson Memorial Hwy., 34747; 396-7300, Fax 396-7555, 800-HOLIDAY) 529 rooms, restaurant, lounge, outdoor heated pool, exercise center, children under 19 free with parents, wheelchair access, a/c, TV, NS rooms, in-room refrigerators, microwaves and coffee makers, car rental desk, gift shop, VCRs, fax service, room service, laundry service, meeting facilities, senior rates, CC. 3 miles from Walt Disney World, 8 miles from Sea World, 3 blocks from shopping mall. SGL/DBL$85-$125.

Holiday Inn Maingate West (7601 Black Lake Rd., 34747; 396-1100, Fax 396-0689, 800-HOLIDAY) 287 rooms, restaurant, lounge, outdoor heated pool, exercise center, children under 19 free with parents, wheelchair access, a/c, TV, NS rooms, local transportation, VCRs, gift shop, game room, fax service, room service, laundry service, 1,500 square feet of meeting and exhibition space, 2 meeting rooms, meeting facilities for 100, senior rates, CC. 8 miles from Sea World, 10 miles from Universal Studios, 1.5 miles from

Walt Disney World, 20 miles from the Orlando airport. SGL/DBL$65-$125.

Holiday Inn Maingate East (5678 West Irlo Bronson Memorial Hwy., 34746; 396-4488, Fax 396-8915, 800-366-5437) 670 rooms and suites, restaurant, lounge, outdoor heated pool, exercise center, children free with parents, wheelchair access, a/c, TV, pets OK, NS rooms, in-room refrigerators, microwaves and coffee makers, car rental desk, gift shop, VCRs, local transportation, fax service, room service, laundry service, meeting facilities, senior rates, CC. SGL/DBL$70-$105.

Holiday Villas (2928 Vineland Rd., 34741; 397-0700, Fax 397-0566, 800-344-3959) 190 efficiencies, free breakfast, outdoor heated pool, lighted tennis courts, whirlpools, sauna, a/c, TV, airport transportation, no pets, children free with parents, wheelchair access, meeting facilities, senior rates, CC. SGL/DBL$150-$170.

Homewood Suites At The Parkway (3100 Pkwy. Blvd., 34746; 396-2229, Fax 396-2229, 800-255-4543, 800-225-5466) 156 rooms and 1- and 2-bedroom suites, outdoor heated pool, whirlpools, exercise center, laundry facilities, in-room refrigerators, airport transportation, children free with parents, wheelchair access, a/c, TV, fireplaces, 950 square feet of meeting and exhibition space, meeting facilities for 25, senior rates, CC. 1.5 miles from Walt Disney World, 8 miles from Sea World, 9 miles from Universal Studios, 11 miles from the Orlando airport. SGL/DBL$89-$138, 1BR$109-$149, 2BR$149-$189.

Howard Johnson (2323 West Irlo Bronson Memorial Hwy., 32744; 846-4900, Fax 846-4900, 800-I-GO-HOJO) 200 rooms, restaurant, free breakfast, lounge, outdoor pool, children free with parents, wheelchair access, NS rooms, game room, in-room refrigerators, local transportation, TV, a/c, pets OK, laundry facilities, senior rates, 1,300 square feet of meeting and exhibition space, meeting facilities for 60, CC. 16 miles from the Orlando airport, 3 miles from the downtown area, 1 mile from Universal Studios. SGL/DBL$30-$90.

Howard Johnson Fountain Park Plaza (5150 West Hwy. 192, 32714; 396-1111, Fax 396-1607, 800-I-GO-HOJO) 401 rooms and suites, restaurant, lounge, outdoor heated pool, whirlpools, sauna, tennis courts, exercise center, room service, gift shop, in-room refrigerators, children free with parents, wheelchair access, local transportation, NS rooms, TV, a/c, laundry facilities, senior rates,

3 meeting rooms, 1,600 square feet of meeting and exhibition space, meeting facilities for 150, CC. 3 miles from Walt Disney World, 8 miles from Sea World, 23 miles from the Orlando airport. SGL/DBL$70-$100.

Howard Johnson Main Gate West (7600 West Irlo Bronson Memorial Hwy., 34746; 396-2500, Fax 396-2096, 800-432-4335, 800-I-GO-HOJO) 207 rooms, restaurant, lounge, outdoor pool, children free with parents, wheelchair access, gift shop, game room, NS rooms, TV, local transportation, no pets, a/c, laundry facilities, senior rates, meeting facilities, CC. 25 miles from the Orlando airport. SGL/DBL$50-$85.

Hyatt Orlando (6375 Irlo Bronson Memorial Hwy., 34746; 406-396-1234, Fax 396-5090, 800-233-1234) 924 rooms and suites, restaurant, lounge, entertainment, indoor and outdoor heated pools, whirlpools, exercise center, lighted tennis courts, room service, in-room refrigerators, local transportation, no pets, TV, a/c, NS rooms, wheelchair access, senior rates, 22 meeting rooms, 20,000 square feet of meeting and exhibition space, meeting facilities for 2,800, CC. 20 miles from the Orlando airport, 2 miles from Walt Disney World, 7 miles from Sea World. SGL/DBL$80-$120.

Inns of America (2945 Entry Point Blvd., 34746; 396-7743, Fax 396-4979, 800-826-0778, 800-423-3081 in Florida) 117 rooms and suites, outdoor heated pool, NS rooms, a/c, TV, VCRs, in-room refrigerators, wheelchair access, pets OK, CC. 1 mile from Walt Disney World. SGL/DBL$38-$50.

Key Motel (4810 West Irlo Bronson Memorial Hwy., 34747; 396-6200, Fax 396-6084) 48 rooms and efficiencies, outdoor pool, pets OK, a/c, TV, children free with parents, laundry facilities, airport courtesy car, CC. SGL/DBL$18-$55.

King's Motel and Apartments (4836 West Irlo Bronson Memorial Hwy., 34746; 396-4762, Fax 932-2500, 800-327-9071) 122 rooms and apartments, outdoor pool, laundry facilities, kitchenettes, pets OK, TV, a/c, VCRs, senior rates, CC. SGL/DBL$36-$50.

Knights Inn (7475 West Irlo Bronson Memorial Hwy., 34746; 396-4200, 800-843-5644) 145 rooms and efficiencies, restaurant, outdoor pool, wheelchair access, NS rooms, TV, a/c, in-room refrigerators and microwaves, fax service, VCRs, local transporation, children free with parents, pets OK, senior rates, CC. 1 mile from Walt

Disney World, 15 miles from Sea World, 23 miles from the Orlando airport. SGL/DBL$45-$56.

Knights Inn (2880 Poinciana Blvd., 34746; 396-8186, 800-722-7220, 800-843-5644) 126 rooms and efficiencies, outdoor pool, wheelchair access, NS rooms, TV, a/c, in-room refrigerators and microwaves, pets OK, fax service, VCRs, senior rates, CC. 22 miles from the Orlando airport, 5 miles from Walt Disney World, 23 miles from Church Street Station. SGL/DBL$36-$50.

Largo Vista Vacation Condominiums (180 Royal Palm Dr., 34743; 348-5247, Fax 348-5083, 800-458-6005) 40 2- and 3-bedroom villas, outdoor pool, whirlpools, a/c, TV, children free with parents, laundry facilities, in-room refrigerators, microwaves and coffee makers, no pets, CC. 2BR/3BR$69-$175.

Larson Lodge Kissimmee (2009 West Vine St., 32741; 846-2713, Fax 846-8695, 800-624-5905) 200 rooms and efficiencies, restaurant, lounge, outdoor pool, whirlpools, lighted tennis courts, local transportation, laundry facilities, a/c, TV, pets OK, in-room refrigerators, NS rooms, children free with parents, 3,300 square feet of meeting and exhibition space, meeting facilities for 1,300, senior rates, CC. SGL/DBL$40-$65.

Larson Lodge Main Gate (6075 Spacecoast Pkwy., 34746; 846-2713, Fax 396-6965, 800-327-9074) 128 rooms and efficiencies, restaurant, lounge, outdoor pool, whirlpools, pets OK, a/c, TV, children free with parents, CC. SGL/DBL$35-$85.

Lifetime of Vacation Resort (7770 West Hwy. 192, 34741; 396-3000, 800-527-9132) 100 condominiums, outdoor pool, a/c, TV, wheelchair access, children free with parents, in-room refrigerators, microwaves and coffee makers, no pets, laundry facilities, senior rates, CC. SGL/DBL$90-$100.

Luxury Florida Vacation Villas (714 North Bermuda Ave., 34741; 933-2701, Fax 933-7075, 800-780-2701) 5 2- and 3-bedroom condominiums, outdoor pool, in-room refrigerators, microwaves and coffee makers, laundry facilities, a/c, TV, no pets, children free with parents, CC. 2BR$65-$75, 3BR$85-$119.

Motel 6 (7455 West Irlo Bronson Memorial Hwy., 34747; 396-6422, 505-891-6161) 148 rooms, pool, free local calls, children free with parents, NS rooms, wheelchair access, a/c, TV, CC. 1 mile from Walt Disney World, 15 miles from Sea World. SGL/DBL$28-$39.

Motel 6 (5731 West Irlo Bronson Memorial Hwy., 34746; 396-6333, 505-891-6161) 351 rooms, outdoor pool, free local calls, children free with parents, NS rooms, wheelchair access, a/c, TV, CC. 4 miles from Walt Disney World, 15 miles from Sea World. SGL/DBL$28-$35.

Olympic Inn (4669 West Irlo Bronson Memorial Hwy., 34746; 396-1890, Fax 396-8336, 800-523-8729) 97 rooms, outdoor heated pool, laundry facilities, pets OK, in-room refrigerators, a/c, TV, children free with parents, senior rates, CC. SGL/DBL$25-$45.

Orange Lake Country Club (8505 West Irlo Bronson Memorial Hwy., 32741; 239-0000, Fax 239-1039, 800-877-OLCC) 368 rooms, villas and suites, restaurant, lounge, outdoor pool, tennis courts, exercise center, no pets, American Plan available, a/c, TV, VCRs, kitchenettes, NS rooms, wheelchair access, 3 meeting rooms, senior rates, CC. SGL/DBL$85-$120.

Palm Motel (4519 West Irlo Bronson Memorial Hwy., 33746; 396-0744, 800-231-6362, 800-433-7031 in Florida) 39 rooms, outdoor pool, airport courtesy car, a/c, TV, children free with parents, laundry facilities, NS rooms, in-room refrigerators, no pets, CC. SGL/DBL$30-$75.

Park Inn International (4960 West Irlo Bronson Memorial Hwy., 34746; 396-1376, Fax 396-0716, 800-327-0072, 800-432-0276 in Florida) 197 rooms and efficiencies, outdoor pool, whirlpools, a/c, TV, VCRs, gift shop, in-room refrigerators and microwaves, no pets, NS rooms, CC. 4 miles from Walt Disney World, 20 miles from the Orlando airport, 10 miles from Universal Studios and Sea World. SGL/DBL$30-$60.

Piccadilly Motor Inn (4736 West Irlo Bronson Memorial Hwy., 34746; 396-0400, Fax 396-0079, 800-432-4095 in Florida) 125 rooms, restaurant, outdoor pool, airport courtesy car, a/c, TV, NS rooms, wheelchair access, children free with parents, laundry facilities, CC. SGL/DBL$30-$39.

Polynesian Isles Resort (3045 Polynesian Isles Blvd., 396-2006, Fax 396-0062, 800-424-1943) 112 condominiums, outdoor pool, a/c, TV, in-room refrigerators and microwaves, children free with parents, laundry facilities, pets OK, CC. SGL/DBL$100-$165.

Poinciana Golf and Racquet Club (500 East Cypress Pkwy., 34759; 933-0770, Fax 870-5412, 800-331-7743) 90 1- , 2- , and 3-bedroom condos and villas, outdoor pool, tennis courts, a/c, TV, wheelchair access, in-room refrigerators, microwaves and coffee makers, laundry facilities, children free with parents, no pets, 1,000 square feet of meeting and exhibition space, meeting facilities for 150, senior rates, CC. 20 miles from Walt Disney World, 30 miles from the Orlando airport. 1BR$70, 2BR$80.

Polynesian Isles Resort (3045 Polynesian Isles Blvd., 34744; 396-2006, Fax: 396-0062, 800-424-1943) 111 2-bedroom condominiums, outdoor pool, a/c, TV, in-room refrigerators and coffee makers, children free with parents, no pets, laundry facilities, NS rooms, CC. 2BR$790W.

Quality Inn and Suites (2039 East Irlo Bronson Memorial Hwy., 34744; 846-7814, Fax 846-1863, 800-221-2222) 114 rooms and suites, restaurant, outdoor pool, exercise center, whirlpools, no pets, children free with parents, a/c, TV, game room, in-room refrigerators, wheelchair access, airport transportation, room service, laundry service, NS rooms, meeting facilities, senior rates, CC. 14 miles from Walt Disney World, 8 miles from the Orlando airport. SGL/DBL$30-$77.

Quality Inn Maingate West (8660 West Irlo Bronson Memorial Hwy., 34747; 396-4500, 800-221-2222) 230 rooms and suites, restaurant, outdoor pool, exercise center, children free with parents, a/c, TV, wheelchair access, room service, laundry service, no pets, NS rooms, meeting facilities, senior rates, CC. 10 miles from Sea World, 27 miles from the Orlando airport, 4.5 miles from Walt Disney World. SGL/DBL$35-$80.

Quality Inn (7675 West Irlo Bronson Hwy., 34747; 396-4000, 800-221-2222, 800-568-3352) 200 rooms and suites, restaurant, outdoor pool, exercise center, children free with parents, a/c, TV, wheelchair access, room service, no pets, laundry service, NS rooms, meeting facilities, senior rates, CC. 1 mile from Walt Disney World, 1.5 miles from Universal Studios, 10 miles from Sea World. SGL/DBL$36-$89.

Quality Inn Lake Cecile (4944 West Irlo Bronson Memorial Hwy., 34746; 396-4455, 800-221-2222) 222 rooms and suites, restaurant, lounge, outdoor pool, exercise center, no pets, children free with parents, a/c, TV, wheelchair access, room service, laundry service, NS rooms, meeting facilities, senior rates, CC. 25 miles from the Orlando airport, 14 miles from Universal Studios, 4 miles from Walt Disney World. SGL/DBL$40-$80.

Quality Inn Maingate East (5876 West Irlo Bronson Memorial Hwy., 34746; 396-8040, Fax 396-6766, 800-221-2222, 800-848-4148) 225 rooms and suites, restaurant, free breakfast, lounge, outdoor pool, exercise center, whirlpools, in-room refrigerators and microwaves, children free with parents, a/c, TV, wheelchair access, room service, laundry service, NS rooms, meeting facilities, senior rates, CC. 20 miles from the Orlando airport. SGL/DBL$50-$260.

Radisson Westgate Vacation Villas (2770 Old Lake Wilson Rd., 34746; 396-8523, Fax 352-2237, 800-768-2341, 800-333-3333) 438 villas, restaurant, free breakfast, lounge, entertainment, outdoor pool, exercise center, whirlpools, in-room refrigerators, microwaves and coffee makers, laundry facilities, children free with parents, VCRs, wheelchair access, free parking, NS rooms, TV, a/c, children free with parents, senior rates, CC. SGL/DBL$85-$195.

Radisson Inn Maingate (7501 West Irlo Bronson Memorial Hwy., 34746; 396-1400, Fax 396-0660, 800-333-3333) 580 rooms and suites, restaurant, lounge, entertainment, outdoor heated pool, whirlpools, lighted tennis courts, in-room refrigerators, microwaves and coffee makers, children free with parents, VCRs, wheelchair access, local transportation, free parking, NS rooms, TV, a/c, no pets, 3,600 square feet of meeting and exhibition space, 8 meeting rooms, meeting facilities for 900, senior rates, CC. 1 mile from Walt Disney World, 7 miles from Sea World, 25 miles from the Orlando airport. SGL/DBL$45-$65.

Ramada Inn (5055 West Hwy. 192, 34746; 396-2212, Fax 396-0253, 800-2-RAMADA) 107 rooms and suites, restaurant, lounge, outdoor pool, wheelchair access, NS rooms, free parking, a/c, TV, local transportation, game room, children free with parents, room service, laundry facilities, meeting facilities, senior rates, CC. 3 miles from Walt Disney World, 15 miles from Sea World. SGL/DBL$45-$65.

Ramada Inn (4559 West Hwy. 192, 34746; 396-1212, Fax 396-7926, 800-2-RAMADA) 114 rooms and suites, restaurant, lounge, outdoor pool, wheelchair access, NS rooms, free parking, a/c, TV, children free with parents, local transportation, pets OK, kitchenettes, room service, laundry facilities, meeting facilities, senior rates, CC. 18 miles from Universal Studios, 15 miles to Sea World, 5 miles from MGM Studios and Walt Disney World. SGL/DBL$40-$63.

Ramada Hotel Resort (2900 Pkwy. Blvd., 34746; 396-7000, Fax 396-6792, 800-2-RAMADA) 718 rooms and suites, restaurant, lounge, outdoor pool, lighted tennis courts, Modified American Plan available, in-room refrigerators, no pets, wheelchair access, NS rooms, free parking, a/c, TV, local transportation, children free with parents, room service, laundry facilities, 4,500 square feet of meeting and exhibition space, 4 meeting rooms, senior rates, CC. 1.5 miles from Walt Disney World, 25 miles from the Orlando airport. SGL/DBL$75-$133.

Ramada Resort Maingate (2950 Reedy Creek Blvd., 34746; 800-2-RAMADA) 400 rooms, restaurant, lounge, outdoor heated pool, lighted tennis courts, exercise center, wheelchair access, NS rooms, free parking, gift shop, game room, local transportation, a/c, TV, children free with parents, in-room refrigerators, no pets, room service, laundry facilities, 5,000 square feet of meeting and exhibition space, 6 meeting rooms, meeting facilities for 200, senior rates, CC. 1 mile from Walt Disney World, 20 miles from the Orlando airport, 10 miles from Universal Studios. SGL/DBL$65-$120.

Ramada Inn Limited Disney Area East (2225 East Irlo Bronson Hwy., 34744; 931-1000, Fax 846-0060, 800-2-RAMADA) 289 rooms and suites, restaurant, free breakfast, wheelchair access, NS rooms, free parking, a/c, TV, children free with parents, local transportation, game room, room service, laundry facilities, meeting facilities, senior rates, CC. 15 miles from Walt Disney World, 20 miles from Universal Studios. SGL/DBL$45-$110.

Ramada Inn Westgate (9200 West Hwy. 192, 34742; 424-2621, Fax 396-6418, 800-365-6935, 800-2-RAMADA) 198 rooms, restaurant, lounge, outdoor heated pool, in-room refrigerators, no pets, wheelchair access, NS rooms, free parking, gift shop, game room, a/c, TV, children free with parents, room service, laundry facilities, meeting facilities, senior rates, CC. 5 miles from Walt Disney World. SGL/DBL$30-$50.

Record Motel (4651 West Hwy. 192, 34746; 396-8400, Fax 396-8415, 800-874-4555) 57 rooms, outdoor heated pool, laundry facilities, no pets, in-room refrigerators, a/c, TV, children free with parents, NS rooms, senior rates, CC. SGL/DBL$23-$45.

Red Roof Inn (4970 Kyng's Heath Rd., 32741; 396-0065, Fax 396-0065, 800-843-7663) 102 rooms and efficiencies, outdoor pool, whirlpools, in-room computer hookups, NS rooms, fax service, wheelchair access, complimentary newspaper, children free with parents, pets OK, a/c, TV, free local calls, senior rates, CC. 8 miles from Sea World, 15 miles from the Florida Mall, 18 miles from the Orlando airport, 10 miles from the factory outlet mall. SGL/DBL$35-$65.

Residence Inn Marriott (4786 North Irlo Bronson Memorial Hwy., 34746; 396-2056, Fax 396-2901, 800-468-3027, 800-468-3012, 800-228-9290) 160 suites, free breakfast, outdoor heated pool, whirlpools, in-room refrigerators, coffee makers and microwaves, laundry facilities, TV, a/c, VCRs, complimentary newspaper, fireplaces, local transportation, children free with parents, NS rooms, wheelchair access, no pets, fireplaces, 1,100 square feet of meeting and exhibition space, meeting facilities for 80, CC. 18 miles from the Orlando airport, 5 miles from Walt Disney World, 8 miles from Sea World. SGL/DBL$115-$190.

Resort World (2794 North Poinciana Blvd., 34746; 396-8300, 800-423-8604) 300 1- , 2- , and 3-bedroom villas, restaurant, outdoor pool, a/c, TV, wheelchair access, no pets, in-room refrigerators and coffee makers, senior rates, CC. 1BR$142, 2BR$175, 3BR$208.

Riviera Motel (2248 East Irlo Bronson Memorial Hwy., 34744; 847-9494) 28 rooms and efficiencies, outdoor pool, a/c, TV, airport courtesy car, children free with parents, CC. SGL/DBL$25-$65.

Roadway Inn (5245 West Irlo Bronson Memorial Hwy., 34746; 396-7700, Fax 396-0293, 800-228-2000, 800-424-4777) 200 rooms, restaurant, lounge, outdoor pool, wheelchair access, NS rooms, children free with parents, a/c, TV, meeting facilities, senior rates, CC. 3.5 miles from Walt Disney World. LS SGL/DBL$35-$50; HS SGL/DBL$64-$74.

Sevilla Inn (4640 West Spacecoast Pkwy., 34746; 396-4135, Fax 396-4942, 800-367-1363) 50 rooms, outdoor heated pool, no pets, in-room refrigerators, NS rooms, a/c, TV, laundry facilities, CC. SGL/DBL$25-$50.

Sheraton Lakeside Inn (7769 West Irlo Bronson Memorial Hwy., 34746; 239-7919, Fax 239-7919, 800-325-3535) 651 rooms and suites, restaurant, lounge, entertainment, outdoor pool, exercise center, lighted tennis courts, NS rooms, a/c, room service, in-room computer hookups, local transportation, in-room refrigerators, no pets, TV, children free with parents, wheelchair access, meeting facilities for 100, 2 meeting rooms, 1,550 square feet of meeting and exhibition space, senior rates, CC. 22 miles from the Orlando airport, 10 miles from Sea World, 2 miles from Walt Disney World. SGL/DBL$60-$120.

Shoney's Inn (4156 West Vine St., 34741; 870-7374, 800-222-2222) 130 rooms, restaurant, outdoor pool, a/c, TV, children free with parents, complimentary newspaper, NS rooms, free local calls, wheelchair access, local transportation, in-room refrigerators, fax service, senior rates, 1,000 square feet of meeting and exhibition space, meeting facilities for 90, CC. 22 miles from the Orlando airport, 8 miles from Walt Disney World. SGL/DBL$48-$68.

Sleep Inn (8536 West Irlo Bronson Hwy., 34746; 396-1600, 800-221-2222) 104 rooms, free breakfast, outdoor pool, wheelchair access, no pets, NS rooms, children free with parents, in-room refrigerators and microwaves, airport transportation, laundry facilities, in-room computer hookups, senior rates, a/c, TV, meeting facilities, CC. 4.5 miles from Walt Disney World, 10 miles from Sea World, 27 miles from the Orlando airport. SGL/DBL$30-$75.

Snow White Village (4567 Seven Dwarfs Lane, 34746; 396-0084) 49 villas, outdoor pool, whirlpools, a/c, TV, no pets, children free with parents, CC. SGL/DBL$65-$95.

Sol Orlando (4748 West Irlo Bronson Hwy., 34746; 397-0555, Fax 397-0553, 800-292-9765) 150 efficiencies and suites, restaurant, lounge, outdoor heated pool, whirlpools, lighted tennis courts, exercise center, game room, in-room coffee makers, a/c, TV, laundry facilities, NS rooms, wheelchair access, Modified American Plan available, senior rates, 1,600 square feet of meeting and exhibition space, meeting facilities for 120, CC. 5 miles from Walt Disney World, 12 miles from Sea World, 15 miles from Universal Studios, 18 miles from the Orlando airport. SGL/DBL$115-$195.

Sun Motel (5020 West Irlo Bronson Memorial Hwy., 34746; 396-2673, 800-541-2674) 106 rooms, outdoor pool, a/c, TV, wheelchair access, NS rooms, no pets, airport courtesy car, CC. 4 miles from Walt Disney World, 25 miles from the Orlando airport. SGL/DBL$26-$30.

Sunrise Motel (801 West Vine St.; 846-3224, Fax 932-4092) 24 rooms and efficiencies, outdoor pool, in-room refrigerators, a/c, TV, no pets, NS rooms, CC. SGL/DBL$35-$75.

TraveLodge Flags (2407 West Irlo Bronson Memorial Hwy., 34741; 933-2400, Fax 933-1474, 800-578-7878) 131 rooms, free breakfast, outdoor pool, wheelchair access, complimentary newspaper, laundry service, TV, a/c, free local calls, fax service, NS rooms, in-room refrigerators and microwaves, gift shop, children free with parents, kitchenettes, no pets, meeting facilities, senior rates, CC. SGL/DBL$30-$70.

TraveLodge Hotel Maingate East (5711 West Irlo Bronson Memorial Hwy., 32741; 396-4111, Fax 396-0570, 800-327-1128, 800-578-7878) 446 rooms, restaurant, lounge, entertainment, free breakfast, outdoor pool, exercise center, wheelchair access, complimentary newspaper, laundry service, TV, a/c, free local calls, fax service, NS rooms, in-room refrigerators and microwaves, car rental desk, local transportation, children free with parents, 4,500 square feet of meeting and exhibition space, meeting facilities for 250, senior rates, CC. 4 miles from Walt Disney World, 25 miles from the Orlando airport. SGL/DBL$60-$120.

TraveLodge Maingate West (7785 West Hwy. 192, 32741; 396-1828, Fax 396-1305, 800-423-4336, 800-578-7878) 200 rooms, outdoor pool, wheelchair access, complimentary newspaper, laundry service, TV, a/c, VCRs, free local calls, fax service, game room, no pets, NS rooms, in-room refrigerators and microwaves, children free with parents, meeting facilities, senior rates, CC. 25 miles from the Orlando airport, 2 miles from Walt Disney World. SGL/DBL$45-$70.

TraveLodge Suites (5399 West Irlo Bronson Memorial Hwy., 34746; 396-7666, 800-578-7878) 156 suites, outdoor pool, whirlpools, wheelchair access, complimentary newspaper, laundry service, TV, a/c, free local calls, no pets, fax service, NS rooms, in-room refrigerators and microwaves, gift shop, game room, airport transportation, children free with parents, meeting facilities, senior rates, CC. 10 miles from Universal Studios, 5 miles from MGM Studios. SGL/DBL$50-$125.

Tropicana Motel (4131 West Vine St., 34741; 847-4707, Fax 847-0980, 800-333-6044) 54 rooms, outdoor pool, a/c, TV, children free with parents, NS rooms, airport courtesy car, CC. 7 miles from Walt Disney World, 20 miles from the Orlando airport. SGL/DBL$25-$30.

Viking Motel (4539 West Irlo Bronson Memorial Hwy., 34746; 396-8860, Fax 396-8860) 49 rooms and efficiencies, outdoor pool, a/c, TV, pets OK, children free with parents, CC. SGL/DBL$33-$66.

Villas At Somerset (2701 North Poinciana Blvd., 34746; 397-0700) 130 rooms and villas, outdoor heated pool, exercise center, sauna, whirlpools, a/c, TV, VCRs, no pets, NS rooms, wheelchair access, laundry facilities, CC. SGL/DBL$125-$225.

Wilson World Hotel Main Gate (7491 West Spacecoast Pkwy., 34746; 396-6000, Fax 396-7393, 800-669-6753) 442 rooms and suites, restaurant, lounge, entertainment, indoor and outdoor heated pools, whirlpools, local transportation, a/c, TV, VCRs, in-room refrigerators, no pets, wheelchair access, children free with parents, senior rates, 2 meeting rooms, 1,750 square feet of meeting and exhibition space, meeting facilities for 120, CC. 1 mile from Walt Disney World, 22 miles from the Orlando airport. SGL/DBL$70-$90.

Wynfield Inn (5335 West Irlo Bronson Memorial Hwy., 34746; 396-2121, Fax 396-1142, 800-468-8374) 216 rooms, outdoor heated pool, no pets, laundry facilities, in-room refrigerators, a/c, TV, children free with parents, NS rooms, CC. SGL/DBL$55-$80.

La Belle

Area Code 813

Port Labelle Inn and Country Club (1 Oxbow Dr., 33935; 675-4411, Fax 675-3996, 800-282-3375) 50 rooms and suites, restaurant, outdoor pool, whirlpools, exercise center, a/c, TV, no pets, children free with parents, laundry facilities, in-room refrigerators, CC. SGL/DBL$49, STS$99.

Rivers Edge Motel (285 North River Rd., 33935; 675-6061) 8 rooms, a/c, TV, children free with parents, pets OK, CC. SGL/DBL$45.

Lady Lake
Area Code 904

Lake Griffin Marina (5620 Beltsville Rd., 32159; 753-3241) 11 rooms, outdoor pool, a/c, TV, wheelchair access, children free with parents, NS rooms, meeting facilities, CC. LS SGL/DBL$25-$45; HS SGL/DBL$25-$55.

Lake Buena Vista
Area Code 407

Best Western Buena Vista Suites (14450 International Dr., 32830; 239-8588, Fax 239-1401, 800-528-1234, 800-537-7737) 280 2-room suites, restaurant, free breakfast, lounge, outdoor heated pool, whirlpools, exercise center, children free with parents, game room, gift shop, a/c, NS rooms, TV, VCRs, in-room refrigerators, microwaves and coffee makers, laundry facilities, wheelchair access, pets OK, meeting facilities, senior rates, CC. SGL/DBL$99-$150.

Best Western Inn (1850 Hotel Plaza Blvd., 32830; 828-4444, Fax 828-8192, 800-528-1234, 800-624-4109) 630 rooms, restaurant, lounge, entertainment, outdoor heated pool, spa, tennis courts, in-room refrigerators and coffee makers, children free with parents, a/c, NS rooms, TV, laundry facilities, local transportation, wheelchair access, pets OK, meeting facilities, senior rates, CC. SGL/DBL$56-$85.

Buena Vista Palace at Walt Disney World Village (Disney Village, 32830; 827-2727, Fax 827-6034, 800-327-2990) 1,028 rooms and suites, restaurant, lounge, outdoor heated pool, exercise center, tennis courts, in-room microwaves and coffee makers, laundry facilities, airport transportation, a/c, TV, room service, NS rooms, no pets, senior rates, 90,000 square feet of meeting and exhibition space, meeting facilities for 2,400, CC. At Walt Disney World. SGL/DBL$130-$245.

Comfort Inn (8442 Palm Pkwy., 32830; 239-7300, 800-221-2222, 800-999-7300) 204 rooms, restaurant, lounge, outdoor pool, gift shop, laundry facilities, a/c, TV, pets OK, game room, gift shop, local transportation, children free with parents, NS rooms, wheelchair access, senior rates, CC. 2 miles from Walt Disney World. SGL/DBL$40-$70.

Disney Beach Club Resort (1800 Epcot Resorts Blvd., 32830; 934-8000, Fax 934-3850) 584 rooms and suites, restaurant, lounge, entertainment, indoor and outdoor heated pools, whirlpools, lighted tennis courts, exercise center, sauna, in-room refrigerators, game room, gift shop, barber and beauty shop, laundry facilities, no pets, NS rooms, children free with parents, in-room computer hookups, room service, senior rates, CC. At Walt Disney World. SGL/DBL$200-$300.

Disney Caribbean Beach Resort (900 Cayman Way, 32830; 934-3400, Fax 934-3288) 2,112 rooms and suites, restaurant, lounge, indoor and outdoor pools, boutiques, local transportation, beach, a/c, TV, NS rooms, children free with parents, no pets, wheelchair access, meeting facilities, CC. SGL/DBL$90-$120.

Disney's Contemporary Resort (Lake Buena Vista 32830; 934-7639, Fax 352-3202, 800-647-7900) 1,053 rooms and suites, restaurant, lounge, entertainment, outdoor heated pool, sauna, lighted tennis court, airport transportation, no pets, children free with parents, in-room refrigerators and microwaves, a/c, TV, NS rooms, local transportation, senior rates, CC. At Walt Disney World. SGL/DBL$195-$270.

Disney's Dixie Landings Resort (Lake Buena Vista 32830; 934-7639, Fax 352-3202, 800-647-7900) 2,048 rooms, restaurant, lounge, indoor and outdoor pools, whirlpools, in-room refrigerators, children free with parents, a/c, TV, no pets, laundry facilities, local transportation, senior rates, CC. SGL/DBL$95-$125.

Disney's Grand Floridian (4001 Grand Floridian Way, 32830; 824-3000) 906 rooms and suites, restaurant, lounge, entertainment, outdoor heated pool, whirlpools, lighted tennis courts, in-room refrigerators, barber and beauty shop, gift shop, complimentary newspaper, room service, laundry facilities, children free with parents, a/c, TV, VCRs, no pets, NS rooms, in-room computer hookups, wheelchair access, senior rates, CC. At Walt Disney World. SGL/DBL$245-$465.

Disney Inn Resort (1950 West Palm Magnolia Dr., 32830; 824-2200, Fax 824-3229) 288 rooms and suites, restaurant, lounge, outdoor pool, exercise center, game room, laundry facilities, gift shop, airport transportation, no pets, NS rooms, wheelchair access, children free with parents, meeting facilities, CC. SGL/DBL$200-$250, STS$555-$770.

The Disney Inn (Lake Buena Vista, 32830; 934-7639, Fax 352-3202, 800-647-7900) 288 rooms, restaurant, lounge, outdoor heated pool, lighted tennis courts, exercise center, a/c, TV, children free with parents, NS rooms, wheelchair access, local transportation, no pets, CC. SGL/DBL$185-$225.

Disney's Polynesian Resort (1662 Old South Rd., 32830; 934-7639, Fax 352-3202, 800-647-7900) 841 rooms and suites, restaurant, lounge, indoor and outdoor pools, lighted tennis courts, a/c, TV, no pets, NS rooms, wheelchair access, children free with parents, in-room refrigerators, laundry facilities, local transportation, senior rates, CC. At Walt Disney World. SGL/DBL$195-$285.

Disney's Village Resort (1901 Buena Vista Dr., 32830; 934-7639, Fax 352-3202, 800-647-7900) 324 1-, 2-, and 3-bedroom villas and suites, restaurant, lounge, entertainment, outdoor pool, exercise center, game room, beach, in-room refrigerators, children free with parents, a/c, TV, no pets, NS rooms, local transportation, meeting facilities, CC. SGL/DBL$195-$285.

Disney Yacht Club Resort (1700 Epcot Resort Blvd., 32830; 934-7000) 635 rooms, restaurant, lounge, entertainment, outdoor pool, lighted tennis courts, game room, exercise center, whirlpools, sauna, wheelchair access, NS rooms, TV, a/c, children free with parents, no pets, barber and beauty shop, gift shop, airport transportation, laundry facilities, CC. At Walt Disney World. SGL/DBL$230-$290, STS$400-$800.

Dixie Landings (1251 Dixie Dr., 32830; 934-6000) 2,048 rooms and suites, restaurant, lounge, entertainment, outdoor pool, lighted tennis courts, gift shop, airport transportation, game room, a/c, TV, NS rooms, wheelchair access, no pets, senior rates, CC. SGL/DBL$95-$120.

Doubletree Club Hotel (8688 Palm Pkwy., 32830; 239-8500, Fax 239-8591, 800-528-0444, 800-222-TREE) 167 rooms and suites, restaurant, free breakfast, outdoor heated pool, exercise center, whirlpools, no pets, a/c, NS rooms, local transportation, in-room refrigerators, wheelchair access, TV, 4 meeting rooms, meeting facilities for 100, senior rates, CC. 2 miles from Walt Disney World, 18 miles from the Orlando airport. SGL/DBL$80-$100.

Fantasy World Club Villas (Lake Buena Vista 32830; 396-1808, Fax 396-6737, 800-874-8047, 800-432-7038 in Florida) 2-bedroom townhouses, restaurant, outdoor pool, lighted tennis courts, a/c, TV, in-room refrigerators, microwaves and coffee makers, children free with parents, laundry facilities, no pets, CC. 2BR$160.

Guest Quarters Suite Resort Walt Disney World Village (2305 Hotel Plaza Blvd., 32830; 924-1000, Fax 934-1011, 800-424-2900) 229 1- and 2-room suites, restaurant, outdoor pool, lighted tennis courts, exercise center, sauna, whirlpools, TV, a/c, in-room refrigerators, microwaves and coffee makers, no pets, local transportation, laundry service, fax service, NS rooms, wheelchair access, 9 meeting rooms, senior rates, CC. SGL/DBL$140-$200.

Hilton At The World Disney World Village (Hotel Plaza Blvd., 32830; 827-4000, Fax 827-6380, 800-782-4414, 800-HILTONS) 814 rooms and suites, restaurant, lounge, entertainment, outdoor heated pool, exercise center, sauna, lighted tennis courts, in-room refrigerators, children free with parents, NS rooms, wheelchair access, room service, laundry facilities, a/c, TV, local transportation, 29 meeting rooms, senior rates, CC. SGL/DBL$180-$215.

Holiday Inn (13351 Hwy. 535, 32830; 239-4500, Fax 239-8463, 800-HOLIDAY) 507 rooms, restaurant, lounge, outdoor pool, exercise center, children free with parents, wheelchair access, a/c, TV, no pets, in-room computer hookups, NS rooms, fax service, in-room refrigerators, microwaves and coffee makers, local transportation, room service, laundry service, meeting facilities, senior rates, CC. 15 miles from the Orlando airport, 6 miles from the Convention Center, .5 miles from Walt Disney World. SGL/DBL$100-$140.

Howard Johnson (1805 Hotel Plaza Blvd., 32830; 828-8888, Fax 827-4623, 800-I-GO-HOJO, 800-223-9930) 323 rooms, restaurant, lounge, outdoor heated pool, exercise center, whirlpools, in-room refrigerators, children free with parents, wheelchair access, NS rooms, free local calls, in-room refrigerators, microwaves and coffee makers, game room, local transportation, TV, VCRs, no pets, a/c, laundry facilities, senior rates, 4 meeting rooms, CC. 15 miles from the downtown area, 9 miles from Universal Studio, 19 miles from the Orlando airport. SGL/DBL$60-$160.

Howard Johnson Park Square (8501 Palm Pkwy., 32830; 239-6900, Fax 239-1287, 800-I-GO-HOJO, 800-635-8684) 308 rooms and 2-room suites, restaurant, lounge, outdoor heated pool, whirlpools, children free with parents, wheelchair access, NS rooms, TV, a/c, laundry facilities, in-room refrigerators and microwaves, gift shop, game room, car rental desk, no pets, senior rates, meeting facilities, CC. A 1/4-mile from Walt Disney World, 20 miles from the downtown area, 15 miles from the Orlando airport. SGL/DBL$75-$150.

Royal Plaza Hotel (Lake Buena Vista 32830; 828-2828, 800-248-7890) 396 rooms and suites, restaurant, lounge, entertainment, outdoor heated pool, sauna, whirlpools, lighted tennis courts, a/c, TV, children free with parents, no pets, gift shop, barber and beauty shop, local transportation, in-room refrigerators, senior rates, 13,000 square feet of meeting and exhibition space, 12 meeting rooms, meeting facilities for 900, CC. SGL/DBL$145-$160, STS$405-$550.

TraveLodge Hotel Walt Disney World Village (2000 Hotel Plaza Blvd., 32830; 828-2424, Fax 828-2424, 800-578-7878) 325 rooms, restaurant, lounge, free breakfast, outdoor pool, wheelchair access, no pets, free newspaper, laundry service, TV, a/c, free local calls, fax service, NS rooms, in-room refrigerators and coffee makers, local transportation, children free with parents, 4 meeting roms, senior rates, CC. LS SGL/DBL$150-$340; HS SGL/DBL$250-$550.

Vistana Resort Villas and Tennis (13800 Vistana Dr., 32830; 239-3100, Fax 239-3131, 800-877-8787) 820 rooms and 2-bedroom suites, restaurant, lounge, indoor and outdoor heated pools, lighted tennis courts, exercise center, in-room refrigerators, game room, whirlpools, a/c, TV, VCRs, Modified American Plan available, no pets, NS rooms, CC. SGL/DBL$175-$275.

Walt Disney World Dolphin and Sheraton Dolphin Towers (1500 Epcot Resort Blvd., 32830; 934-4000, Fax 934-4099, 800-227-1500) 1,509 rooms and suites, restaurant, lounge, indoor and outdoor heated pools, lighted tennis courts, whirlpools, sauna, NS rooms, no pets, wheelchair access, game room, airport transportation, a/c, TV, children free with parents, laundry facilities, 46 meeting rooms, 200,000 square feet of meeting and exhibition space, senior rates, CC. At Walt Disney World. SGL/DBL$210-$350.

Walt Disney World Swan Resort (1200 Epcot Resort Blvd., 32830; 934-3000, Fax 934-4499, 800-228-3000, 800-248-SWAN in Florida)

758 rooms, restaurant, lounge, entertainment, outdoor heated pool, whirlpools, lighted tennis courts, beach, gift shop, game room, beauty shop, no pets, a/c, TV, airport transportation, NS rooms, children free with parents, room service, 31 meeting rooms, senior rates, CC. At Walt Disney World, 30 miles from the Orlando airport. SGL/DBL$225-$345.

Lake City
Area Code 904

Best Western Inn (Lake City 32055; 752-3801, Fax 755-4846, 800-528-1234) 82 rooms and suites, restaurant, free breakfast, outdoor pool, whirlpools, sauna, game room, children free with parents, a/c, NS rooms, TV, laundry facilities, wheelchair access, pets OK, meeting facilities, senior rates, CC. A 1/2-mile from the Florida Sports Hall of Fame. SGL/DBL$26-$65.

Comfort Inn (I-75 and Hwy. 90, 32056; 755-1344, 800-221-2222) 104 rooms, outdoor pool, a/c, TV, children free with parents, NS rooms, wheelchair access, no pets, senior rates, CC. SGL/DBL$45-$60.

Cypress Inn (Hwy. 90, 32056; 752-9369) 48 rooms and efficiencies, outdoor pool, in-room refrigerators and microwaves, pets OK, a/c, TV, laundry facilities, kitchenettes, children free with parents, CC. SGL/DBL$25-$40.

Days Inn (Lake City 32055; 752-9350, 800-329-7466) 120 rooms, restaurant, outdoor pool, a/c, TV, wheelchair access, NS rooms, laundry facilities, in-room refrigerators, pets OK, senior rates, CC. 1 mile from the Florida Sports Hall of Fame, a 1/2-mile from the shopping center, 15 miles from the Stephen Foster Memorial and Itchetucknee Springs State Park. SGL/DBL$30-$40.

Driftwood Motel (Lake City 32055; 755-3545) 20 rooms, a/c, TV, pets OK, NS rooms, senior rates, CC. SGL/DBL$25-$30.

Econo Lodge (5500 West Hwy. 90, 32055; 752-7891, 800-446-6900, 800-55-ECONO) 62 rooms, restaurant, outdoor pool, children free with parents, pets OK, NS rooms, wheelchair access, laundry facilities, a/c, TV, senior rates, CC. 15 miles from the North Florida Farmers Market, 3 miles from the downtown area, 2 blocks from the Florida Sports Hall of Fame. SGL/DBL$30-$65.

Econo Lodge South (Route 3, 32055; 755-9311, 800-4-CHOICE) 60 rooms, outdoor pool, children free with parents, no pets, laundry service, NS rooms, wheelchair access, a/c, TV, senior rates, CC. SGL/DBL$35.

Friendship Inn (Lake City 32056; 755-5203, 800-424-4777) 44 rooms, restaurant, a/c, TV, NS rooms, children free with parents, laundry facilities, pets OK, wheelchair access, senior rates, CC. 14 miles from the Stephen Foster Memorial, 1 mile from the Florida Sports Hall of Fame, 1 mile from the golf course. SGL/DBL$25-$40.

Gateway Inn Motel (Hwy. 90 West, 32055; 755-1707) 52 rooms, a/c, TV, no pets, NS rooms, children free with parents, CC. SGL/DBL$20-$25.

Holiday Inn (I-90 and Hwy. 90, 32056; 752-3901, 800-HOLIDAY) 224 rooms, restaurant, lounge, outdoor heated pool, lighted tennis courts, children free with parents, wheelchair access, a/c, TV, NS rooms, fax service, room service, pets OK, laundry service, meeting facilities for 350, senior rates, CC. A 1/4-mile from the Florida Sports Hall of Fame, 7 miles from the regional airport, 14 miles from the Stephen Foster Memorial. SGL/DBL$45-$50.

Howard Johnson (Hwy. 90 West, 32056; 752-6262, Fax 752-8251, 800-I-GO-HOJO) 91 rooms, restaurant, lounge, outdoor pool, children free with parents, wheelchair access, NS rooms, TV, a/c, laundry facilities, senior rates, meeting facilities, CC. SGL/DBL$33-$65.

Knights Inn (Box 201, Route 13, 32055; 752-7720) 100 rooms and suites, pets OK, wheelchair access, NS rooms, free parking, a/c, TV, children free with parents, room service, laundry facilities, meeting facilities, senior rates, CC. 20 miles from Itchetucknee Springs State Park, a 1/2-mile from the Florida Sports Hall of Fame. SGL/DBL$35-$55.

Motel 6 (Hwy. 90 and Hall of Fame Dr., 32055; 755-4664, 505-891-6161) 120 rooms, outdoor pool, free local calls, children free with parents, NS rooms, wheelchair access, a/c, TV, CC. A 1/2-mile from the golf course and the Florida Sports Hall of Fame, 20 miles from the Itchetucknee Springs State Park. SGL/DBL$22-$26.

Quality Inn (5600 Hwy. 90 West, 32055; 752-7550, 800-221-2222) 120 rooms, outdoor pool, whirlpools, pets OK, children free with parents, a/c, TV, wheelchair access, room service, laundry service, NS rooms, meeting facilities, senior rates, CC. SGL/DBL$30-$45.

Piney Woods Lodge (Lake City 32055; 752-8334) 280 rooms, restaurant, outdoor pool, children free with parents, no pets, a/c, TV, CC. SGL/DBL$19-$40.

Ramada Inn (Exit 82, Interstate 75, 32055; 752-7550, 800-2-RAMADA) 28 rooms and suites, wheelchair access, NS rooms, free parking, a/c, TV, children free with parents, pets OK, room service, laundry facilities, meeting facilities, senior rates, CC. A 1/2-mile from the Florida Sports Hall of Fame, 20 miles from the Itchetucknee Springs State Park. SGL/DBL$30-$48.

Rodeway Inn (Lake City 32055; 752-7720, 800-228-2000) 100 rooms, whirlpools, pets OK, wheelchair access, NS rooms, children free with parents, a/c, TV, senior rates, CC. SGL/DBL$25-$32.

Scottish Inns (Hwy 90, 32055; 755-0230, 800-251-1962) 34 rooms, restaurant, a/c, TV, wheelchair access, pets OK, NS rooms, children free with parents, free local calls, senior rates, CC. A 1/2-mile from the Florida Sports Hall of Fame, 22 miles from the Itchetucknee Springs State Park, 14 miles from the Stephen Foster Memorial. SGL/DBL$26-$33.

Super 8 Motel (I-75 and Hwy. 47, 32055; 752-6450, 800-848-8888) 95 rooms, restaurant, lounge, outdoor pool, children free with parents, free local calls, a/c, TV, in-room refrigerators and microwaves, fax service, NS rooms, wheelchair access, meeting facilities, senior rates, CC. 5 miles from the Florida Sports Hall of Fame. SGL/DBL$34-$45.

TraveLodge (Hwy. 90 West and I-75, 32055; 755-9306, Fax 755-9505, 800-578-7878) 50 rooms and suites, restaurant, lounge, free breakfast, no pets, wheelchair access, complimentary newspaper, laundry service, TV, a/c, free local calls, fax service, NS rooms, in-room refrigerators and microwaves, children free with parents, meeting facilities, senior rates, CC. 3 blocks from the Florida Sports Hall of Fame. SGL/DBL$30-$50.

Lake Helen

Area Code 904

Clausers Bed and Breakfast (201 East Kicklighter Rd., 32744; 228-0310) 2 rooms, free breakfast, a/c, TV, CC. SGL/DBL$50-$85.

Lake Placid

Area Code 813

Best Western Inn and Conference Center (2175 Hwy. 27 South, 33852; 465-3133, 800-528-1234) 99 rooms, restaurant, lounge, entertainment, outdoor heated pool, children free with parents, a/c, NS rooms, TV, laundry facilities, wheelchair access, no pets, meeting facilities, senior rates, CC. SGL/DBL$40-$100.

Lake Wales

Area Code 813

Chalet Suzanne (Lake Wales 33853; 676-6011, Fax 676-1814, 800-288-6011) 30 rooms and efficiencies, restaurant, lounge, outdoor pool, whirlpools, a/c, TV, laundry facilities, NS rooms, meeting facilities, CC. SGL/DBL$95-$185.

Econo Lodge (501 South Hwy. 27, 33853; 676-7963, 800-55-ECONO) 48 rooms, restaurant, outdoor pool, children free with parents, no pets, NS rooms, wheelchair access, a/c, TV, senior rates, CC. SGL/DBL$42-$50.

Emerald Motel (530 South Scenic Hwy., 33853; 676-3310) 19 rooms, outdoor pool, a/c, TV, pets OK, NS rooms, children free with parents, in-room refrigerators, CC. SGL/DBL$25-$45.

Prince of Wales Motel (513 South Scenic Hwy., 33853; 676-1246) 22 rooms and efficiencies, laundry facilities, a/c, TV, in-room refrigerators and microwaves, pets OK, children free with parents, CC. SGL/DBL$20-$45.

River Ranch Guest Ranch (24700 Hwy. 60 East, 33853; 692-1321, Fax 692-9134, 800-654-8575) 192 rooms, efficiencies and 1- and 2-bedroom cottages, restaurant, outdoor pool, exercise center, a/c,

TV, in-room refrigerators, microwaves and coffee makers, no pets, children free with parents, senior rates, CC. SGL/DBL$72-$180.

Royal Inn (1747 Hwy. 27 North, 33853; 676-2511) 56 rooms, restaurant, lounge, outdoor pool, spa, exercise facilities, children free with parents, laundry facilities, no pets, CC. LS SGL/DBL$28-$38; HS SGL/DBL$38-$44.

Super 8 Motel (541 West Central Ave., 33853; 676-7925, Fax 676-6662, 800-800-8000) 66 rooms and suites, children free with parents, free local calls, a/c, TV, in-room refrigerators and microwaves, laundry facilities, fax service, NS rooms, wheelchair access, meeting facilities, senior rates, CC. 35 miles from Universal Studios and Sea World, 28 miles from Walt Disney World. SGL/DBL$30-$78.

Lake Worth

Area Code 407

Holiday Inn West Palm Beach (7859 Lake Worth Rd., 33467; 968-5000, Fax 968-2451, 800-HOLIDAY, 800-325-8193, 800-824-2545 in Florida) 114 rooms, restaurant, lounge, outdoor heated pool, exercise center, children free with parents, wheelchair access, a/c, TV, NS rooms, fax service, room service, laundry service, VCRs, in-room refrigerators, pets OK, meeting facilities for 160, senior rates, CC. 5 miles from the Palm Beach airport, 8 miles from Atlantic beaches, 4 miles from the South Florida Fairgrounds, 1 block from the shopping mall. LS SGL/DBL$55; HS SGL/DBL$85.

Lakeland

Area Code 813

Best Western Inn (3311 Hwy. 98 North, 33805; 688-7972, Fax 688-8377, 800-528-1234) 120 rooms, restaurant, lounge, entertainment, outdoor pool, exercise center, in-room coffee makers, no pets, children free with parents, a/c, NS rooms, TV, laundry facilities, game room, wheelchair access, meeting facilities, senior rates, CC. A 1/2-mile from shopping mall, 3 miles from the Civic Center. SGL/DBL$55-$80.

Days Inn (508 East Memorial Blvd., 33801; 683-7471, 800-325-2525) 80 rooms, outdoor pool, a/c, TV, wheelchair access, NS rooms, pets OK, children free with parents, laundry facilities, senior rates, CC.

30 miles from Busch Gardens and Walt Disney World. SGL/DBL$30-$65.

Econo Lodge (1817 East Memorial Blvd., 33801; 688-9221, 800-55-ECONO) 65 rooms and efficiencies, free breakfast, outdoor pool, children free with parents, pets OK, laundry facilities, NS rooms, wheelchair access, a/c, TV, senior rates, CC. 33 miles from the Tampa airport, 1 mile from the Detroit Tigers Training Camp. SGL/DBL$35-$55.

Holiday Inn (4645 North Socrum Loop Rd., 33809; 858-1411, Fax 858-2977, 800-HOLIDAY) 160 rooms, restaurant, lounge, outdoor pool, exercise center, children free with parents, wheelchair access, a/c, pets OK, in-room refrigerators, TV, NS rooms, fax service, room service, laundry service, meeting facilities for 250, senior rates, CC. 5 miles from the Civic Center, 2 miles from the shopping mall, 1 mile from the golf course and Lakeland Regional Hospital. SGL/DBL$55-$76.

Holiday Inn (910 East Memorial Blvd., 33801; 682-0101, Fax 683-0815, 800-HOLIDAY) 130 rooms, restaurant, lounge, outdoor pool, exercise center, children free with parents, wheelchair access, a/c, TV, NS rooms, fax service, beach, room service, laundry service, meeting facilities for 250, senior rates, CC. SGL/DBL$57-$77.

Holiday Inn South (3405 South Florida Ave., 33803- 8123-646-5731, 800-HOLIDAY) 172 rooms and suites, restaurant, free breakfast, lounge, entertainment, outdoor pool, exercise center, whirlpools, pets OK, children free with parents, wheelchair access, local transportation, a/c, TV, NS rooms, fax service, in-room refrigerators and microwaves, room service, laundry service, meeting facilities, senior rates, CC. 2 miles from the regional airport and Civic Center, 1 mile from Florida Southern College, SGL/DBL$60-$70.

Lake Morton Bed and Breakfast (817 South Blvd., 33801; 688-6788) 3 suites, free breakfast, no pets, a/c, TV, NS, CC. SGL/DBL$30-$50.

Motel 6 (Hwy. 98 North, 33805; 682-0643, 505-891-6161) 124 rooms, outdoor pool, free local calls, children free with parents, NS rooms, wheelchair access, a/c, TV, CC. 5 miles from the Civic Center, 6 miles from Florida Southern College, 1 mile from Tigertown Stadium. SGL/DBL$30-$38.

Passport Inn (740 East Main St., 33801; 688-5506, 800-251-1962) 57 rooms, outdoor pool, a/c, TV, NS rooms, wheelchair access, free local calls, in-room refrigerators and microwaves, pets OK, children free with parents, senior rates, CC. 6 blocks from the Lakeland Civic Center. SGL/DBL$40-$56.

Ramada Inn (3260 Hwy. 98 North, 33805; 688-8080, Fax 687-9799, 800-2-RAMADA) 153 rooms, restaurant, lounge, outdoor pool, whirlpools, wheelchair access, NS rooms, free parking, a/c, TV, children free with parents, no pets, room service, laundry facilities, in-room refrigerators, 6 meeting rooms, meeting facilities for 200, senior rates, CC. SGL/DBL$50-$68.

Red Carpet Inn (1539 East Memorial Blvd., 33801; 683-7821, 800-251-1962) 42 rooms, restaurant, lounge, pool, children free with parents, in-room refrigerators, no pets, TV, a/c, NS rooms, meeting facilities, senior rates, CC. 10 miles from Cypress Gardens and the regional airport. SGL/DBL$29-$39.

Scottish Inn (244 North Florida Ave., 33801; 687-2530, 800-251-1962) 50 rooms, restaurant, outdoor a/c, TV, no pets, wheelchair access, NS rooms, children free with parents, free local calls, senior rates, CC. A 1/4-mile from the Civic Center, 17 miles from Cypress Gardens. SGL/DBL$26-$45.

Sheraton Lakeland Hotel and Conference Center (414 South Florida Ave., 33818; 647-3000, Fax 644-0467, 800-325-3535) 140 rooms and suites, restaurant, lounge, entertainment, outdoor heated pool, exercise center, sauna, whirlpools, NS rooms, a/c, room service, TV, VCRs, no pets, children free with parents, wheelchair access, in-room refrigerators, 9 meeting rooms, meeting facilities for 800, 8,500 square feet of meeting and exhibition space, senior rates, CC. 40 miles from the Tampa airport, 15 miles from Cypress Gardens. SGL/DBL$60-$100.

Sunset Motel (2301 New Tampa Hwy., 33801; 683-6464) 12 rooms, outdoor pool, a/c, TV, no pets, CC. SGL/DBL$32-$50.

Lantana

Area Code 407

Knights Inn South (1255 Hypoluxo Rd., 33462; 585-3970, Fax 586-3028, 800-843-5644) 131 rooms and efficiencies, restaurant, outdoor pool, wheelchair access, NS rooms, TV, a/c, in-room refrigerators and microwaves, fax service, VCRs, senior rates, CC. 10 miles from the Palm Beach airport, 2 miles from John Prince Park, 15 miles from Lion Country Safari. SGL/DBL$50-$60.

Motel 6 (3120 Hwy. 98 North, 33463; 585-5833) 154 rooms, outdoor pool, free local calls, children free with parents, NS rooms, wheelchair access, a/c, TV, CC. 5 miles from Atlantic beaches. SGL/DBL$29-$36.

Largo
Area Code 813

Bardmoor Country Club (10801 Starkey Rd., 34647; 393-5997) 50 condominiums, restaurant, outdoor pool, tennis courts, exercise center, a/c, TV, wheelchair access, no pets, laundry facilities, children free with parents, CC. LS SGL/DBL$425W-$550W; HS SGL/DBL$625W-$700W.

Le Versailles Courts (10464 106th Ave. North, 34643; 391-6045) 8 rooms and apartments, outdoor pool, whirlpools, laundry facilities, no pets, a/c, TV, local transportation, children free with parents, CC. SGL/DBL$120-$250.

Lauderdale-By-The-Sea
Area Code 305

Beach Apartments (4337 El Mar Dr., 33308; 776-5074, Fax 776-0070) 17 rooms, efficiencies and 1- and 2-bedroom apartments, outdoor pool, in-room refrigerators and microwaves, children free with parents, no pets, wheelchair access, laundry facilities, CC. SGL/DBL$25-$40, EFF$28-$48, 1BR$38-$55, 2BR$50-$75.

Captain's Quarters (4644 El Mar Dr., 33308; 771-3919, Fax 771-2959, 800-843-3344) 30 rooms and efficiencies, outdoor pool, a/c, TV, laundry facilities, children free with parents, no pets, CC. SGL/DBL$60, EFF$75.

Fort Lauderdale Inn (5727 North Federal Hwy., 33308; 491-2500, Fax 491-7945, 800-458-110) 156 rooms, restaurant, lounge, entertainment, outdoor heated pool, sauna, no pets, children free with parents, NS rooms, a/c, TV, laundry facilities, in-room refrigerators, 6 meeting rooms, senior rates, CC. SGL/DBL$45-$75.

High Noon (4424 El Mar Dr., 33308; 776-1124) 18 rooms, efficiencies, 1-bedroom apartments and suites, outdoor pool, kitchenettes, children free with parents, a/c, CC. SGL/DBL$47-$98, EFF$52-$119, 1BR$57-$131, STS$88-$198.

Howard Johnson Motor Lodge (4660 Ocean Dr., 33308; 776-5660, Fax 776-4689, 800-327-5919, 800-I-GO-HOJO) 150 rooms, efficiencies and apartments, restaurant, lounge, entertainment, outdoor heated pool, exercise center, beach, in-room refrigerators and coffee makers, kitchenettes, no pets, children free with parents, wheelchair access, NS rooms, TV, a/c, laundry facilities, senior rates, meeting facilities for 110, CC. 10 miles from the Ft. Lauderdale-Hollywood airport and the downtown area, 8 miles from the Broward Convention Center. SGL/DBL$65-$190.

Howard Johnson Motor Lodge (5001 North Federal Hwy., 33308; 771-8100, Fax 776-7980, 800-I-GO-HOJO) 107 rooms, restaurant, lounge, outdoor pool, children free with parents, wheelchair access, NS rooms, complimentary newspaper, TV, a/c, laundry facilities, senior rates, meeting facilities, CC. 11 miles from the Ft. Lauderdale-Hollywood airport, 7 miles from Port Everglades, a 1/2-mile from the golf course. SGL/DBL$50-$100.

Little Inn by the Sea (4546 El Mar Dr., 33308; 772-2450, Fax 938-9354) 29 rooms and efficiencies, free breakfast, outdoor heated pool, beach, in-room refrigerators and coffee makers, no pets, a/c, TV, complimentary newspaper, CC. SGL/DBL$60-$120.

Pier Point Resort (4324 El Mar Dr., 33308; 776-5121, Fax 491-9084, 800-776-5121) 98 rooms, efficiencies and 1-bedroom apartments, outdoor pool, tennis, a/c, TV, laundry facilities, wheelchair access, children free with parents, no pets, NS rooms, senior rates, CC. SGL/DBL$50-$90, EFF$60-$100, 1BR$90-$135.

Ramada Beach Resort (4060 Galt Ocean Dr., 33308, 565-6611, Fax 564-7730, 800-2-RAMADA) 220 rooms and suites, restaurant, lounge, outdoor heated pool, exercise center, wheelchair access, NS rooms, a/c, TV, children free with parents, in-room refrigerators, no pets, room service, laundry facilities, meeting facilities for 350, senior rates, CC. 20 miles from the Ft. Lauderdale-Hollywood airport. SGL/DBL$60-$160.

Sand Dollar Motel (4308 El Mar Dr., 33308; 776-4940) 10 rooms, efficiencies and 1-bedroom apartments, outdoor pool, tennis courts, whirlpools, a/c, TV, pets OK, kitchenettes, children free with parents, laundry facilities, CC. SGL/DBL$28-$60, EFF$32-$74, 1BR$36-$76.

Shore Haven Motor Inn (4433 Ocean Dr., 33308; 776-5555, Fax 776-0828, 800-552-1959) 68 rooms, efficiencies and 1-bedroom apartments, outdoor pool, tennis courts, a/c, TV, children free with parents, no pets, laundry facilities, CC. SGL/DBL$31, 1BR$42.

Villa Caprice Ocean Resort Motel (4110 El Mar Dr., 33308; 776-4123, Fax 776-2026) 21 rooms and 1- and 2-bedroom apartments, outdoor heated pool, in-room refrigerators and microwaves, a/c, TV, no pets, NS rooms, senior rates, CC. SGL/DBL$80-$230.

Villas By The Sea (4456 El Mar Dr., 33308; 776-3550, Fax 772-3835, 800-247-8963) 148 rooms, efficiencies and 1- and 2-bedroom apartments, restaurant, free breakfast, lounge, outdoor pool, tennis courts, in-room refrigerators, beach, children free with parents, no pets, NS rooms, senior rates, CC. SGL/DBL$90-$120, STS$140-$225.

Leesburg
Area Code 904

Budget Host (1225 North 14th St., 34748; 787-3534, Fax 787-0060, 800-283-4678) 50 rooms, restaurant, outdoor pool, laundry facilities, kitchenettes, pets OK, limousine service, NS rooms, airport transportation, wheelchair access, a/c, TV, children free with parents, senior rates, CC. SGL/DBL$47-$55.

Days Inn (1308 North 14th St., 34748; 787-1210, Fax 365-0163, 800-325-2525) 130 rooms, lounge, entertainment, free breakfast, outdoor pool, in-room microwaves, pets OK, a/c, TV, wheelchair access, children free with parents, NS rooms, laundry facilities, senior rates, CC. 1 mile from Lake Griffin State Park. SGL/DBL$40-$60.

Econo Lodge (1115 West North Blvd., 34748; 742-2323, 800-826-0778, 800-423-3018 in Florida) 61 rooms and suites, hot tub, restaurant, outdoor pool, whirlpools, children free with parents, no pets,

NS rooms, kitchenettes, wheelchair access, a/c, TV, senior rates, CC. SGL/DBL$35-$85.

Scottish Inn (1321 North 14th St., 34748; 787-3343, 800-251-1962) 28 rooms, outdoor pool, pets OK, a/c, TV, wheelchair access, NS rooms, children free with parents, free local calls, senior rates, CC. 3.5 miles from the airport, 31 miles from Silver Springs. SGL/DBL$29-$40.

Super 8 Motel (1392 North Blvd. West, 34748) 787-6363, 800-848-8888) 53 rooms and suites, restaurant, outdoor heated pool, pets OK, children free with parents, free local calls, a/c, TV, in-room refrigerators and microwaves, fax service, NS rooms, wheelchair access, meeting facilities, senior rates, CC. 3 miles from Lake Griffin State Park, 35 miles from Sea World. SGL/DBL$35-$60.

Lehigh Acres
Area Code 813

Rental & Reservation Services

Century 21/Lehigh Realty (1240 West Homestead Rd., 33936; 369-6166) rental condominiums.

Realty World Rentals (30 Colorado Rd., 33936; 369-5841) rental condominiums, apartments and private homes.

□□□

Admiral Lehigh Golf and Resort (225 East Joel Blvd., 33936; 369-2131) 121 rooms, villas and 1- and 2-bedroom suites, restaurant, lounge, entertainment, outdoor heated pools, whirlpools, lighted tennis courts, children free with parents, in-room refrigerators, no pets, Modified American Plan available, a/c, TV, senior rates, CC. SGL/DBL$55-$145.

Little Torch Key
Area Code 305

Little Palm Island (Little Torch Key 33042; 872-2524, Fax 872-4843, 800-GET-LOST) 28 rooms and villas, restaurant, lounge, entertainment, a/c, TV, American Plan available, children over 12 welcome, airport transportation, gift shop, CC. SGL/DBL$465.

Live Oak
Area Code 904

Best Western Inn (Live Oak 32060; 362-6000, 800-528-1234) 64 rooms, outdoor pool, children free with parents, a/c, NS rooms, TV, laundry facilities, wheelchair access, in-room refrigerators, pets OK, meeting facilities, senior rates, CC. Near the Suwanee River, 25 miles from river rafting. SGL/DBL$40-$45.

Econo Lodge (Hwy. 129, 32060; 362-7459, 800-55-ECONO) 52 rooms, outdoor pool, hot tubs, children free with parents, no pets, laundry facilities, in-room refrigerators, NS rooms, wheelchair access, a/c, TV, senior rates, CC. SGL/DBL$35-$75.

Scottish Inns (827 West Howard St., 32060; 362-7828, 800-251-1962) 24 rooms, restaurant, no pets, a/c, TV, wheelchair access, NS rooms, children free with parents, free local calls, senior rates, CC. 10 miles from the Florida Sheriffs Boys Ranch, 6 miles from the golf course, 20 miles from the Florida Sports Hall of Fame. SGL/DBL$25-$40.

Longboat Key
Area Code 813

Rental & Reservation Services

Longboat Accommodations (4030 Gulf of Mexico Dr., 34228; 383-9505, 800-237-9505) rental condominiums and private homes.

□□□

Beach Castle Motel (5310 Gulf of Mexico Dr., 34228; 383-2639) 19 rooms and 1- and 2-bedroom suites, outdoor heated pool, whirlpools, beach, no pets, a/c, TV, children free with parents, NS rooms, CC. LS SGL/DBL$500W-$810W; HS SGL/DBL$750W-$1,050W.

Cedars East Tennis Club and Resort (545 Cedars Ct. 34228; 383-4621, 800-433-4621) 61 1-, 2-, and 3-bedroom rooms and suites, restaurant, lounge, outdoor pool, tennis courts, beach, in-room refrigerators and coffee makers, a/c, TV, children free with parents, senior rates, pets OK, CC. 1BR$750W, 2BR$800W.

Colony Beach and Tennis Resort (1620 Gulf of Mexico Dr., 34228; 383-6464, Fax 383-7549, 800-237-9443) 232 rooms and 1- and 2-bedroom apartments, restaurant, lounge, outdoor heated pool, whirlpools, sauna, lighted tennis courts, exercise center, in-room coffee makers, airport transportation, room service, no pets, children free with parents, a/c, TV, NS rooms, room service, 7 meeting rooms, meeting facilities for 300, senior rates. CC. 10 miles from the Sarasota airport. LS SGL/DBL$250; HS SGL/DBL$300-$355.

Diplomat Resort (3155 Gulf of Mexico Dr., 34228; 383-3791) 50 1- and 2-bedroom condominiums, outdoor heated pool, beach, a/c, TV, children free with parents, no pets, laundry facilities, wheelchair access, CC. SGL/DBL$115-$185.

Hilton Beach Resort (4711 Gulf of Mexico Dr., 34228; 383-2451, Fax 383-7979, 800-HILTONS) 102 rooms and 1- and 2-bedroom suites, restaurant, lounge, entertainment, outdoor pool, exercise center, tennis court, beach, in-room refrigerators and coffee makers, no pets, local transportation, children free with parents, NS rooms, wheelchair access, room service, laundry facilities, a/c, TV, 4 meeting rooms, senior rates, CC. 4 miles from the Sarasota airport, SGL/DBL$100-$430.

Holiday Beach Resort (4765 Gulf of Mexico Dr., 34228; 383-3704, Fax 383-0546) 22 rooms and efficiencies, outdoor heated pool, laundry facilities, children free with parents, no pets, NS rooms, wheelchair access, CC. SGL/DBL$100-$150.

Holiday Inn Holidome (4949 Gulf of Mexico Dr., 34228; 383-3771, Fax 383-7871, 800-HOLIDAY) 146 rooms, restaurant, lounge, indoor heated pool, exercise center, whirlpools, sauna, lighted tennis courts, children free with parents, wheelchair access, a/c, TV, NS rooms, gift shop, beach, fax service, room service, in-room refrigerators and microwaves, VCRs, pets OK, laundry service, 4 meeting rooms, meeting facilities for 400, kitchenettes, senior rates, CC. SGL/DBL$90-$180, STS$215-$280.

Holiday Lodge Resort (4235 Gulf of Mexico Dr., 34228; 383-3788) 29 rooms and 2-bedroom cottages, outdoor heated pool, whirlpools, in-room refrigerators and coffee makers, a/c, TV, laundry facilities, no pets, airport transportation, children stay free with parents, CC. SGL/DBL$355W-$470W.

Little Gulf Cottages (5330 Gulf of Mexico Dr., 34228; 383-0881, 800-333-7335) 16 1- and 2-bedroom cottages, outdoor pool, tennis courts, a/c, TV, kitchenettes, children free with parents, in-room refrigerators and microwaves, no pets, CC. 1BR$500W-$550W, 2BR$575-$800W.

The Resort at Longboat Key Club (301 Gulf of Mexico Dr., 34228; 383-8821, Fax 383-0359, 800-237-8821) 221 rooms and 1- and 2-bedroom suites, restaurant, lounge, entertainment, outdoor pool, whirlpools, sauna, airport transportation, a/c, TV, no pets, in-room refrigerators, microwaves and coffee makers, beach, wheelchair access, car rental desk, laundry service, 5 meeting rooms, meeting facilities for 150, senior rates, CC. 5 miles from the downtown area, 12 miles from the Sarasota airport. SGL/DBL$195-$285, STS$275-$500.

Sand Cay Beach Resort (4725 Gulf of Mexico Dr., 34228; 383-5044, 800-843-4459) 60 rooms and efficiencies, outdoor pool, tennis courts, beach, in-room refrigerators, microwaves and coffee makers, no pets, laundry facilities, wheelchair access, a/c, TV, children free with parents, CC. 2BR$660W-$825W.

Sea Club I (4141 Gulf of Mexico Dr., 34228; 383-2431) 24 efficiencies and 1- and 2-bedroom villas, outdoor heated pool, a/c, TV, laundry facilities, children free with parents, no pets, beach, CC. SGL/DBL$75-$120.

Sea Horse Beach Resort (3453 Gulf of Mexico Dr., 34228; 383-2417) 35 1- and 2-bedroom efficiencies, restaurant, outdoor pool, laundry facilities, a/c, TV, children free with parents, no pets, wheelchair access, 1BR$130, 2BR$170.

Silver Sands Apartments (5841 Gulf of Mexico Dr., 34228; 383-3731, 800-245-3731) 37 1- and 2-bedroom apartments, outdoor pool, a/c, TV, no pets, children free with parents, kitchenettes, laundry facilities, CC. LS SGL/DBL$42-$116; HS SGL/DBL$73-$163.

Sun N' Sea Cottage Apartments (4651 Gulf of Mexico Dr., 34228; 383-5588) 1- and 2-bedroom efficiencies, beach, no pets, kitchenettes, a/c, TV, children free with parents, CC. LS SGL/DBL$40-$90; HS SGL/DBL$60-$100.

Twin Shores Resort (3740 Gulf of Mexico Dr., 34228; 383-1646) 16 rooms, a/c, TV, children free with parents, no pets, CC. LS SGL/DBL$50-$65; HS SGL/DBL$65-$80.

Longwood
Area Code 407

Quality Inn North (2025 West Hwy. 434, 32750; 862-4000, 800-221-2222) 196 rooms and suites, restaurant, lounge, entertainment, outdoor pool, exercise center, children free with parents, a/c, TV, wheelchair access, room service, laundry service, pets OK, NS rooms, meeting facilities, senior rates, CC. SGL/DBL$52-$69.

Macclenny
Area Code 904

Days Inn (1499 South 6th St., 32063; 259-5100, 800-325-2525) 43 rooms and suites, restaurant, pets OK, a/c, TV, wheelchair access, NS rooms, VCRs, children free with parents, laundry facilities, senior rates, CC. 25 miles from the Gator Bowl, 35 miles from Okefenokee Swamp, 6 miles from the Northeast Florida Hospital. SGL/DBL$30-$55.

Econo Lodge (I-10 and Hwy. 121, 32063; 259-3000, 800-55-ECONO) 53 rooms, outdoor pool, whirlpools, laundry facilities, children free with parents, pets OK, NS rooms, wheelchair access, a/c, TV, VCRs, senior rates, meeting facilities, CC. 30 miles from the Okefenokee Swamp, 35 miles from downtown Jacksonville. SGL/DBL$32-$65.

Madeira Beach
Area Code 813

Rental & Reservation Services

Best Beach Rentals and Sale (20045 Gulf Blvd., Indian Rocks Beach, 34635; 595-5700, Fax 593-1095, 800-523-2882) rental condominiums, villas and private homes.

Excel Travel Service (14955 Gulf Blvd., 33708; 391-5512, Fax 393-8885, 800-733-4004) rental condominiums.

Suncoast Resort Properties (12817 Gulf Blvd., 33708; 398-1295) rental condominiums and private homes.

□□□

Anchorage Motel (14080 Gulf Blvd., 33708; 393-4546) 15 rooms and efficiencies, outdoor pool, beach, a/c, TV, children free with parents, pets OK, laundry facilities, CC. LS SGL/DBL$43-$58; HS SGL/DBL$56-$73.

Golden Sun Apartments (14105 Gulf Blvd., 33708; 393-5512, 800-733-4004) 120 condominiums, outdoor pool, beach, a/c, TV, children free with parents, no pets, CC. LS SGL/DBL$250W-$650W; HS SGL/DBL$350W-$800W.

Holiday Inn (15208 Gulf Blvd., 33708; 392-2275, 800-HOLIDAY) 147 rooms, restaurant, lounge, entertainment, outdoor heated pool, tennis courts, no pets, children free with parents, wheelchair access, beach, a/c, TV, NS rooms, fax service, room service, laundry service, meeting facilities for 50, senior rates, CC. 15 miles from the St. Petersburg-Clearwater airport, 1 mile from the Boardwalk, 10 miles from the Florida Suncoast Dome. LS SGL/DBL$65-$130; HS SGL/DBL$105-$160.

Madeira Vista Condominiums (1480 Gulf Blvd., 33708; 393-9660) 35 condominiums, outdoor pool, beach, a/c, children free with parents, TV, wheelchair access, no pets, laundry facilities, CC. LS SGL/DBL$450W; HS SGL/DBL$770W.

Redington Sun Apartments (Madeira Beach 33708; 398-2674) 8 1-, 2-, and 3-bedroom apartments, outdoor pool, kitchenettes, a/c, TV, children free with parents, pets OK, CC. 1BR$500W-$550W, 2BR$600W-$650W, 3BR$700W-$800W.

Sandy Shores Condominiums (12924 Gulf Blvd., 33708; 392-1281) 51 rooms, outdoor pool, children free with parents, in-room refrigerators, microwaves and coffee makers, pets OK, laundry facilities, senior rates, CC. LS SGL/DBL$250W-$350W.

Sea Dawn Motel (13733 Gulf Blvd., 33708; 391-7500) 8 rooms and efficiencies, outdoor pool, a/c, TV, kitchenettes, children free with parents, NS rooms, pets OK, CC. SGL/DBL$25-$60.

Shoreline Island Resort Motel (14200 Gulf Blvd., 33708; 397-6641, 800-635-8373) 49 efficiencies and 1- and 2-bedroom apartments, outdoor heated pool, laundry facilities, in-room refrigerators and microwaves, no pets, NS rooms, children free with parents, a/c, TV, CC. SGL/DBL$60-$145.

Skyline Motel and Apartments (139999 Gulf Blvd., 33708; 391-5817) 18 rooms and efficiencies, outdoor pool, a/c, TV, in-room refrigerators and coffee makers, no pets, laundry facilities, CC. LS SGL/DBL$26-$35; HS SGL/DBL$55-$70.

Surf Song Resort (12960 Gulf Blvd., 33708; 391-0284, Fax 393-8364, 800-237-4816) 38 condos, a/c, TV, in-room refrigerators, microwaves and coffee makers, children free with parents, laundry facilities, CC. LS SGL/DBL$230W-$515W; HS SGL/DBL$355W-$740W.

Madison
Area Code 904

Days Inn (Madison 32340; 973-3330, Fax 973-3542, 800-325-2525) 62 rooms and apartments, restaurant, outdoor pool, free breakfast, a/c, TV, wheelchair access, NS rooms, laundry facilities, children free with parents, no pets, senior rates, CC. 18 miles from the Suwanee River State Park, 7 miles from North Florida Junior College. SGL/DBL$35-$45.

Friendship Inn (Route 1, 32340; 973-2504, 800-424-4777) 32 rooms, outdoor pool, a/c, TV, NS rooms, children free with parents, wheelchair access, laundry facilities, pets OK, senior rates, CC. 13 miles from the Suwanee River State Park. SGL/DBL$40-$50.

Mainland
Area Code 407

Rental & Reservation Services

Julia Switlick Rentals (504 Oak Lane, 32751; 339-6473) rental condominiums and apartments.

□□□

Lake of the Woods Resort (Mainland 32751; 834-7631) 35 rooms and efficiencies, outdoor pool, whirlpools, in-room refrigerators, microwaves and coffee makers, in-room computer hookups, a/c,

TV, children free with parents, NS, no pets, laundry facilities, senior rates, CC. SGL/DBL$45-$75.

Thurston House (851 Lake Ave., 32751; 539-1911) 4 rooms, free breakfast, TV, a/c, NS, antique furnishings, no pets, CC. SGL/DBL$70-$80.

Manalapan
Area Code 407

Ritz-Carlton Palm Beach (100 South Ocean Blvd., 33462; 533-6000, Fax 588-4201, 800-241-3333) 270 rooms and suites, restaurant, lounge, entertainment, outdoor pool, exercise center, whirlpools, sauna, boutiques, barber and beauty shop, airport transportation, no pets, 24-hour room service, wheelchair access, a/c, TV, NS rooms, wheelchair access, children free with parents, 9 meeting rooms, 10,000 square feet of meeting and exhibition space, senior rates, CC. SGL/DBL$300-$500, STS$870-$3,000.

Marathon
Area Code 305

Rental & Reservation Services

Carico Real Estate (9141 Overseas Hwy., 33050; 743-7636, 800-940-7636) rental condominiums and private homes.

Land and Sea Vacations (6805 Overseas Hwy., 33050; 743-6494, 800-327-4836) rental private homes, condominiums and villas.

Reed Realty (9499 Overseas Hwy., 33050; 743-5181, 800-366-5181) rental condominiums and private homes.

❑❑❑

Banana Bay Resort (4590 Overseas Hwy., 33050; 743-3648, Fax 743-2670, 800-448-6636) 60 rooms, restaurant, lounge, outdoor pool, beach, whirlpools, exercise center, in-room refrigerators, no pets, a/c, TV, laundry facilities, meeting facilities, CC. LS SGL/DBL$65-$105; HS SGL/DBL$95-$175.

Blue Waters Motel (2222 Overseas Hwy., 33050; 743-4832) 16 apartments, outdoor pool, a/c, TV, no pets, CC. LS SGL/DBL$60-$75; HS SGL/DBL$65-$80.

Bonefish Bay Motel (12565 Overseas Hwy., 33050; 289-0565, 800-336-0565) 14 efficiencies, outdoor pool, no pets, airport transportation, a/c, TV, NS rooms, kitchenettes, children free with parents, CC. EFF$59, 1BR$69.

Buccaneer Resort (2600 Overseas Hwy., 33050; 743-9071, Fax 743-5470, 800-237-3329) 76 rooms, villas and cottages, restaurant, outdoor pool, beach, tennis courts, a/c, TV, children free with parents, no pets, CC. SGL/DBL$49-$65, STS$149-$159.

Coco Plum Beach and Tennis Club (109 Coco Plum Dr., 33050; 743-0242, 800-228-1587, 800-325-6117 in Florida) 20 2-bedroom villas, beach, outdoor pool, tennis courts, no pets, a/c, TV, in-room refrigerators, microwaves and coffee makers, children free with parents, CC. 2BR$110-$350.

Conch Key Cottages (Marathon 33050; 289-1377, Fax 743-8207, 800-330-1577) 10 cottages and 1-bedroom apartments, pool, beach, pets OK, a/c, TV, in-room refrigerators, microwaves and coffee makers, children free with parents, CC. SGL/DBL$87-$155.

Faro Blanco Marine Resort (1996 Overseas Hwy., 33050; 743-9018, Fax 743-2918, 800-759-3276) 83 rooms, condominiums and houseboats, restaurant, outdoor pool, a/c, TV, children free with parents, NS rooms, wheelchair access, in-room refrigerators, laundry facilities, no pets, CC. SGL/DBL$69-$99.

Hawk's Cay Resort and Marina (Mile Marker 61, 33050; 743-7000, 800-327-7775, 800-432-2242) 193 rooms and 2-bedroom efficiencies, restaurant, free breakfast, lounge, entertainment, outdoor heated pool, whirlpools, lighted tennis courts, no pets, gift shop, in-room refrigerators, wheelchair access, laundry facilities, children stay free with parents, a/c, TV, meeting facilities for 200, senior rates, CC. LS SGL/DBL$140-$215; HS SGL/DBL$210-$335.

Holiday Inn (13201 Overseas Hwy., 33050; 289-0222, Fax 743-5460, 800-224-5053, 800-HOLIDAY) 134 rooms, restaurant, lounge, outdoor pool, exercise center, children free with parents, wheelchair access, gift shop, a/c, TV, NS rooms, fax service, room service, laundry service, meeting facilities for 75, senior rates, CC. 5 miles from the Dolphin Research Center and Sombrero Beach, 15 miles from Bahia Honda State Park. SGL/DBL$55-$65.

Howard Johnson Resort (13351 Overseas Hwy., 33050; 743-8550, Fax 743-8832, 800-I-GO-HOJO) 80 rooms, restaurant, lounge, outdoor pool, in-room refrigerators, pets OK, children free with parents, wheelchair access, NS rooms, TV, a/c, laundry facilities, senior rates, meeting facilities, CC. SGL/DBL$50-$155.

Kingsail Resort Motel (7050 Overseas Hwy., 33050; 743-5246, Fax 743-8896, 800-423-7474) 43 rooms, efficiencies and 1- and 2-bedroom apartments, outdoor pool, no pets, kitchenettes, children free with parents, laundry facilities, a/c, TV, CC. SGL/DBL$48, 1BR$61, 2BR$159.

Rainbow Bend Fishing Resort (Mile Marker 58, 33050; 289-1505, Fax 743-0257) 18 rooms and 1- and 2-bedroom efficiencies, restaurant, free breakfast, outdoor pool, local transportation, beach, pets OK, children free with parents, a/c, TV, senior rates, CC. SGL/DBL$120-$205.

Sombrero Resort and Lighthouse Marina (19 Sombrero Blvd., 33050; 743-2250, Fax 743-2998, 800-433-8660) 124 rooms and 1- and 2-bedroom suites, restaurant, lounge, entertainment, outdoor pool, sauna, lighted tennis courts, children free with parents, no pets, fax service, laundry facilities, meeting facilities, senior rates, CC. SGL/DBL$115, STS$240-$280.

Marco Island

Area Code 813

Rental & Reservation Services

The Vacation Shoppe (11595 Kelly Rd., Ft. Myers, 33908; 454-1400, Fax 466-3299) rental condominiums, apartments and townhouses.

Vacations in Paradise Rentals (800-237-8906) rental condominiums and apartments.

□□□

Beach Club of Marco (901 South Collier Island, 33937; 394-8860, Fax 394-5176, 800-323-8860, 800-237-8402 in Florida) 52 rooms and

2-bedroom efficiencies, outdoor pool, laundry facilities, no pets, in-room coffee makers, a/c, TV, beach, CC. SGL/DBL$90-$190.

The Boat House Motel (1180 Edington Place, 33937; 642-2400, 800-528-6345) 19 rooms, restaurant, outdoor pool, laundry facilities, airport transportation, antique furnishings, pets OK, a/c, TV, children free with parents, wheelchair access, senior rates, CC. SGL/DBL$100-$120.

Eagle's Nest (410 South Collier Blvd., 33937; 481-3636, Fax 642-1599, 800-237-8906) 96 1- and 2-bedroom condominiums, restaurant, outdoor pool, lighted tennis courts, whirlpools, sauna, game room, beach a/c, TV, children free with parents, wheelchair access, no pets, CC. SGL/DBL$260-$285.

Florida Pavilion Club Condominium (1170 Edington Place, 33937; 394-3345, Fax 394-7472) 20 1- and 2-bedroom efficiencies, restaurant, outdoor heated pool, a/c, TV, no pets, wheelchair access, laundry facilities, CC. SGL/DBL$135-$215.

Hilton Beach Resort (560 South Collier Blvd., 33937; 394-5000, Fax 394-5251, 800-443-4550, 800-237-1247 in Florida) 294 rooms and suites, restaurant, lounge, entertainment, outdoor pool, exercise center, lighted tennis courts, whirlpools, game room, beach, children free with parents, NS rooms, wheelchair access, room service, in-room refrigerators and coffee makers, gift shop, no pets, laundry facilities, a/c, TV, meeting facilities, senior rates, CC. 25 miles from the Naples airport, 42 miles from the Fort Myers airport. SGL/DBL$100-$285.

Marco Bay Resort (1001 North Barfield Dr., 33937; 394-8881, Fax 394-8909, 800-228-0661, 800-282-6833 in Florida) 140 rooms, restaurant, lounge, outdoor heated pool, whirlpools, exercise center, in-room refrigerators, microwaves and coffee makers, local transportation, no pets, a/c, TV, children free with parents, NS rooms, senior rates. SGL/DBL$85-$155.

Marriott's Marco Island Resort (400 South Collier Blvd., 33937; 394-2511, 800-228-9290) 736 rooms and suites, restaurant, lounge, outdoor heated pool, whirlpools, tennis courts, local transportation, in-room refrigerators, microwaves and coffee makers, boutiques, barber and beauty shop, gift shop, no pets, a/c, VCRs, children free with parents, TV, NS rooms, wheelchair access, meeting facilities, senior rates, CC. SGL/DBL$125-$250.

Radisson Suite Beach Resort (600 South Collier Blvd., 33937; 394-4100, Fax 394-0418, 800-333-3333) 214 rooms and 1- and 2-bedroom suites, restaurant, lounge, entertainment, outdoor heated pool, exercise center, whirlpools, lighted tennis courts, wheelchair access, in-room refrigerators, microwaves and coffee makers, children free with parents, gift shop, game room, VCRs, free parking, NS rooms, TV, a/c, no pets, beach, senior rates, CC. SGL/DBL$85-$170.

Marianna

Area Code 904

Best Value Sandusky (918 West Lafayette St., 32446; 482-4973, 800-322-8029) 25 rooms, a/c, TV, senior rates, CC. SGL/DBL$37-$44.

Best Western Marianna Inn (Marianna 32446; 526-5666, 800-528-1234) 80 rooms, restaurant, outdoor pool, pets OK, children free with parents, a/c, NS rooms, TV, laundry facilities, wheelchair access, meeting facilities, senior rates, CC. 10 miles from Caverns State Park, 11 miles from Lake Seminole. SGL/DBL$38-$48.

Comfort Inn (I-10 and Hwy. 71, 32446; 526-5600, 800-221-2222) 80 rooms, free breakfast, outdoor pool, a/c, TV, children free with parents, pets OK, NS rooms, wheelchair access, laundry facilities, senior rates, CC. 5 miles from the Battle of Marianna site, 8 miles from Caverns State Park, 6 miles from Chipola Junior College. SGL/DBL$45-$62.

Econo Lodge (1119 West Lafayette St., 32446; 526-3710, 800-55-ECONO) 54 rooms, outdoor pool, children free with parents, no pets, NS rooms, wheelchair access, a/c, TV, senior rates, CC. SGL/DBL$32-$40.

Holiday Inn (4655 Hwy. 90 East, 32446; 526-3251, Fax 482-6223, 800-HOLIDAY) 80 rooms, restaurant, free breakfast, lounge, outdoor pool, pets OK, children free with parents, wheelchair access, a/c, TV, NS rooms, fax service, room service, laundry service, meeting facilities for 100, senior rates, CC. 3.5 miles from Florida Caverns State Park, 6 miles from Sunland Training Center. SGL/DBL$45-$55.

TraveLodge (4132 West Lafayette St., 32446; 526-4311, 800-578-7878) 58 rooms, outdoor pool, wheelchair access, complimentary newspaper, laundry service, TV, a/c, free local calls, fax service, NS rooms, in-room refrigerators and microwaves, children free with parents, no pets, meeting facilities, senior rates, CC. 6 miles from the regional airport, 25 miles from Lake Seminole, 6 miles from Florida Caverns State Park. SGL/DBL$35-$65.

Marineland
Area Code 904

Quality Inn Marineland (9507 Ocean Shore Blvd., 32084; 471-1222, Fax 461-0156, 800-221-2222, 800-824-4218 in Florida) 124 rooms and suites, restaurant, lounge, outdoor pool, exercise center, no pets, in-room refrigerators and coffee makers, beach, children free with parents, a/c, TV, wheelchair access, VCRs, room service, laundry service, NS rooms, meeting facilities, senior rates, CC. 19 miles from St. Augustine. SGL/DBL$50-$100.

Melbourne
Area Code 407

Comfort Inn (8298 North Wickham Rd., 32904; 255-0077, 800-221-2222) 134 rooms and suites, lounge, free breakfast, outdoor pool, a/c, TV, children free with parents, NS rooms, wheelchair access, no pets, airport transportation, in-room refrigerators, senior rates, CC. 7 miles from Atlantic beaches, 8 miles from the regional airport, 4 miles from the Brevard Performing Arts Center. SGL/DBL$50-$88.

Courtyard by Marriott (2101 West New Haven Ave., 32904; 724-6400, 800-228-9290) 146 rooms, restaurant, lounge, outdoor heated pool, whirlpools, exercise center, in-room refrigerators, microwaves and coffee makers, a/c, VCRs, no pets, complimentary newspaper, children free with parents, kitchenettes, TV, NS rooms, wheelchair access, meeting facilities, senior rates, CC. SGL/DBL$55-$80.

Days Inn (4455 West New Haven Ave., 32904; 724-5840, 800-325-2525) 235 rooms, free breakfast, outdoor pool, lighted tennis courts, a/c, TV, wheelchair access, NS rooms, no pets, laundry facilities, children free with parents, senior rates, CC. 5 miles from the airport, 3 miles from the shopping mall, 5 miles from the dog track. SGL/DBL$40-$55.

Econo Lodge West (4504 West New Haven Ave., 32904; 724-5450, 800-4-CHOICE) 48 rooms, children under 12 free with parents, no pets, senior rates, NS rooms, wheelchair access, a/c, TV, CC. 8 miles from Atlantic beaches, 6 miles from the regional airport. SGL/DBL$30-$65.

Hilton at Rialto Place Airport (200 Rialto Place, 32901; 768-0200, Fax 984-2528, 800-HILTONS) 241 rooms and suites, restaurant, lounge, entertainment, outdoor pool, exercise center, lighted tennis courts, whirlpools, children free with parents, NS rooms, wheelchair access, room service, local transportation, laundry facilities, pets OK, in-room refrigerators, car rental desk, a/c, TV, 9 meeting rooms, senior rates, CC. 40 miles from the Kennedy Space Center, 50 miles from Walt Disney World. SGL/DBL$110-$120.

Holiday Inn (420 South Harbor City Blvd., 32901; 723-5320, Fax 724-0581, 800-HOLIDAY) 100 rooms, restaurant, lounge, indoor heated pool, children free with parents, wheelchair access, a/c, TV, NS rooms, in-room refrigerators and microwaves, fax service, room service, laundry service, meeting facilities for 50, senior rates, CC. 7 miles from the dog track, 3 miles to Atlantic beaches. SGL/DBL$55-$65.

Holiday Inn Riverfront West (4500 West New Haven Ave., 32904; 724-2050, 800-HOLIDAY) 100 rooms, restaurant, lounge, entertainment, outdoor pool, children free with parents, wheelchair access, a/c, TV, NS rooms, pets OK, fax service, room service, laundry service, meeting facilities for 50, senior rates, CC. 3 miles from the regional airport, 2 miles from the shopping mall, 6 miles to Atlantic beaches. SGL/DBL$50-$85.

Melbourne Harbor Suites (1207 East New Haven Ave., 32901; 723-4251, 800-242-4251, 800-226-4251 in Florida) 51 1-bedroom suites, restaurant, free breakfast, outdoor pool, a/c, TV, NS rooms, children free with parents, laundry facilities, wheelchair access, kitchenettes, CC. 1BR$65.

Ramada Inn Riverfront of Melbourne (964 Harbor City Blvd., 32905; 724-4422, 800-2-RAMADA) 121 rooms, restaurant, lounge, outdoor pool, wheelchair access, NS rooms, free parking, local transportation, a/c, TV, VCRs, no pets, in-room coffee makers, children free with parents, room service, laundry facilities, meeting facilities, senior rates, CC. 1 mile from the Melbourne airport, 3 miles to Atlantic beaches. SGL/DBL$45-$70.

Shoney's Inn (4431 West New Haven Ave., 32904; 768-8439, 800-222-2222) 119 rooms, restaurant, outdoor pool, a/c, TV, children free with parents, complimentary newspaper, NS rooms, free local calls, wheelchair access, fax service, senior rates, meeting facilities, CC. SGL/DBL$45-$65.

Topper Motel (58 Harbor City Blvd., 32935; 254-9956) 11 rooms, outdoor pool, children free with parents, a/c, TV, no pets, CC. SGL/DBL$25-$34.

Merritt Island
Area Code 407

Holiday Inn Merritt Island (260 East Merritt Island Causeway, 32952; 452-7711, 800-HOLIDAY) 128 rooms, restaurant, lounge, entertainment, outdoor pool, tennis courts, children free with parents, wheelchair access, a/c, TV, NS rooms, fax service, room service, laundry service, in-room computer hookups, no pets, meeting facilities for 400, senior rates, CC. 5 miles from Atlantic beaches, 8 miles from Port Canaveral Cruise Terminals, 19 miles from the Melbourne airport. SGL/DBL$70-$88.

Mexico Beach
Area Code 904

The Surfside Motel (Hwy. 98, 32410; 648-5771) 1- and 2-bedroom efficiencies, a/c, TV, beach, children free with parents, no pets, CC. 1BR/2BR$35-$58.

Miami
Area Code 305

Rental & Reservation Services

Central Reservation Service (305-950-0232, Fax 305-274-1357, 800-950-0232) rental hotel rooms.

Great Miami Reservation Systems (12555 Biscayne Blvd., 33180; 800-821-2183) hotel and condominium reservations.

Downtown Miami

Best Western Marina Park Hotel (340 Biscayne Blvd., 33132; 371-4400, Fax 372-2862, 800-528-1234) 200 rooms and suites, restaurant, lounge, outdoor pool, NS rooms, no pets, children stay free with parents, fax service, water view, a/c, TV, meeting facilities, senior rates. Across from the Port of Miami. CC. SGL$85-$125.

Biscayne Bay Marriott Hotel and Marina (1633 North Bayshore Dr., 33132; 374-3900, Fax 375-0597) 605 rooms and suites, free breakfast, outdoor heated pool, whirlpools, exercise center, jacuzzi, in-room refrigerators, a/c, VCRs, children free with parents, a/c, TV, NS rooms, car rental desk, complimentary newspaper, beauty shop, gift shop, boutiques, wheelchair access, 19 meeting rooms, meeting facilities, senior rates, CC. 8 miles from the Miami airport. SGL/DBL$125-$375.

Days Inn Downtown Medical Center (1050 Northwest 14th St., 33136; 324-0200, Fax 545-8482, 800-325-2525) 212 rooms, restaurant, outdoor pool, gift shop, airport courtesy car, laundry service, free parking, a/c, TV, children stay free with parents, local transportation, no pets, wheelchair access, NS rooms, fax service, senior rates, CC. 1 mile from the Miami Arena, a 1/2-mile from the Orange Bowl. SGL/DBL$50-$80.

Dupont Plaza Hotel (300 Biscayne Blvd., 33131; 358-2541, Fax 377-4049, 800-327-3480, 800-432-9076 in Florida) 442 rooms and 1- and 2-bedroom suites, restaurant, lounge, outdoor pool, car rental desk, a/c, TV, NS rooms, in-room refrigerators, room service, no pets, airport transportation, senior rates, meeting facilities, CC. 8 miles from the Orange Bowl, 6 miles from the Miami airport. SGL/DBL$100, STS$150-$450.

Everglades Hotel (944 Biscayne Blvd., 33132; 379-5461, Fax 577-8445) 365 rooms, restaurant, outdoor pool, a/c, TV, wheelchair access, children free with parents, no pets, CC. SGL/DBL$85-$95.

Grand Prix Hotel (1717 North Bayshore Dr., 33132; 372-0313, Fax 539-9228, 800-872-7749) 176 rooms and suites, restaurant, lounge, entertainment, outdoor heated pool, exercise center, whirlpools, children free with parents, in-room refrigerators and coffee makers, local transportation, game room, gift shop, a/c, TV, NS rooms, senior rates, meeting facilities. SGL/DBL$125-$325.

Hampton Inn (2500 Brickell Ave., 33139; 854-2070, Fax 854-2070, 800-426-7866) 70 rooms, free breakfast, outdoor pool, children stay free with parents, NS rooms, pets OK, wheelchair access, in-room computer hookups, a/c, fax service, free local calls, meeting facilities, senior rates, CC. 4 miles from the Orange Bowl, 3 miles from the University of Miami. SGL/DBL$83-$90.

Holiday Inn Civic Center (1170 Northwest 11th St., 33136; 324-0800, Fax 547-1820, 800-HOLIDAY) 174 rooms and suites, restaurant, lounge, outdoor pool, exercise center, children free with parents, wheelchair access, a/c, TV, NS rooms, airport transportation, no pets, fax service, room service, laundry service, meeting facilities, senior rates, CC. SGL/DBL$65-$75, STS$115.

Hotel Intercontinental Miami (100 Chopin Plaza, 33131; 577-1000, Fax 372-4440, 800-327-3005) 600 rooms and suites, restaurant, lounge, heated pool, exercise center, a/c, TV, 24-hour room service, in-room refrigerators and coffee makers, laundry facilities, children free with parents, no pets, antique furnishings, game room, wheelchair access, NS rooms, meeting facilities, senior rates, CC. 10 miles from the Miami airport, 6 miles from the Orange Bowl. SGL/DBL$175-$275, STS$450-$3,000.

Holiday Inn (200 Southeast 2nd Ave., 33131; 374-3000, Fax 374-3000 ext 1504, 800-HOLIDAY) 256 rooms, restaurant, lounge, outdoor pool, room service, children stay free with parents, NS rooms, game room, gift shop, wheelchair access, laundry service, a/c, TV, no pets, fax service, meeting facilities for 200, senior rates, CC. 1.5 miles from the Orange bowl and Jackson Memorial Hospital, 3 miles from Atlantic beaches, 5 miles from the Miami airport. SGL/DBL$70-$130, STS$180-$250.

Howard Johnson (100 Southeast 4th St., 33131; 374-5100, Fax 381-9826, 800-I-GO-HOJO) 135 rooms and suites, restaurant, lounge, outdoor pool, exercise center, complimentary newspaper, children stay free with parents, wheelchair access, a/c, TV, laundry facilities, NS rooms, in-room refrigerators, no pets, meeting facilities, senior rates, CC. SGL/DBL$110-$180.

Howard Johnson (1100 Biscayne Blvd., 33132; 358-3080, Fax 358-3080 ext 1613, 800-I-GO-HOJO) 115 rooms, restaurant, lounge, outdoor pool, children stay free with parents, NS rooms, a/c, TV, wheelchair access, complimentary newspaper, room service, local transportation, laundry service, senior rates, CC. 8 miles from the Miami airport, a 1/2-mile from downtown. SGL/DBL$60-$110.

Hyatt Regency Miami (400 Southeast 2nd Ave., 33131; 358-1234, Fax 374-1728, 800-228-9000) 615 rooms and suites, restaurant, lounge, outdoor pool, gift shop, laundry service, no pets, a/c, TV, NS, in-room refrigerators, wheelchair access, 30 meeting rooms, 100,000 square feet of meeting and exhibition space, senior rates, CC. 8 miles from the Miami airport, near the Riverfront Exhibition Hall and Conference Center. SGL/DBL$135-$190.

Miami River Inn (118 Southwest River Dr., 33130; 325-0045, Fax 325-9227, 800-HOTEL89) 40 1- and 2-bedroom apartments, outdoor pool, sauna, whirlpool, kitchenettes, children free with parents, antique furnishings, a/c, TV, laundry facilities, wheelchair access, no pets, meeting facilities, senior rates, CC. 6 miles from the Miami airport, 3 miles from the Orange Bowl. 1BR$250W, 2BR$350W.

Miami Sun Hotel (226 Northeast 1st Ave., 33132; 375-0786, Fax 375-0726, 800-322-0786) 88 roOms and suites, restaurant, lounge, hot tub, laundry facilities, a/c, TV, NS rooms, room service, children free with parents, wheelchair access, senior rates, CC. 5 miles from the Miami airport, 12 miles from the University of Miami. SGL/DBL$42-$60.

Omni International Hotel (1601 Biscayne Blvd., 33132; 374-0000, Fax 374-0020, 800-843-6664) 531 rooms and suites, restaurant, lounge, entertainment, outdoor heated pool, tennis, exercise center, beauty shop, game room, gift shop, boutiques, in-room refrigerators, wheelchair access, a/c, TV, laundry facilities, NS rooms, 21 meeting rooms, 43,000 square feet of meeting and exhibition space, 8 miles from the Miami airport. SGL/DBL$125.

Royalton Hotel (131 Southeast 1st St., 33131; 374-7451) 84 rooms, lounge, a/c, TV, gift shop, NS rooms, fax service, senior rates, meeting facilities, CC. SGL/DBL$43-$58.

Sheraton Biscayne Bay Hotel (495 Brickell Ave., 33131; 373-6000, Fax 372-9808, 800-325-3535) 598 rooms and suites, restaurant, lounge, entertainment, outdoor heated pool, NS rooms, wheelchair access, game room, gift shop, in-room refrigerators, car rental desk, airport courtesy car, a/c, TV, 9 meeting rooms, 10,000 square feet of meeting and exhibition space, meeting facilities for 500, senior rates, CC. Near the Orange Bowl, Bayside Marketplace and Miami Seaquarium. SGL/DBL$130-$180, STS$250-$350.

Airport Area

Airport Regency Hotel (1000 Northwest 42nd St., 33126; 441-1600, Fax 443-0766, 800-367-1039, 800-432-1192 in Florida) 175 rooms, restaurant, lounge, entertainment, outdoor heated pool, airport courtesy car, a/c, TV, laundry service, gift shop, NS rooms, meeting facilities, senior rates, CC. 1 mile from the airport. SGL$75-$85, DBL$85-$95.

Best Western Airport (1550 Northwest LeJeune Rd., 33126; 871-2345, Fax 871-2811, 800-528-1234) 208 rooms, restaurant, lounge, outdoor pool, children free with parents, a/c, NS rooms, TV, laundry facilities, wheelchair access, game room, in-room refrigerators, airport courtesy car, pets OK, meeting facilities, senior rates, CC. SGL/DBL$80-$195.

Budgetel Inn Airport (3501 Northwest LeJeune Rd., 33142; 871-1777, Fax 871-8080, 800-428-3438) 152 rooms and suites, restaurant, free breakfast, outdoor pool, children stay free with parents, wheelchair access, NS rooms, in-room computer hookups, fax service, airport transportation, free local calls, a/c, TV, in-room refrigerators and microwaves, meeting facilities, senior rates, CC. 3 miles from the Orange Bowl, a 1/2-mile from the Merchandise Mart, 4 miles from the downtown area. SGL/DBL/STS$54-$65.

Days Inn (3401 Northwest LeJeune Rd., 33142; 871-4221, Fax 871-3933, 800-325-2525) 155 rooms and suites, restaurant, outdoor pool, airport courtesy car, wheelchair access, NS rooms, fax service, children stay free with parents, complimentary newspaper, car rental desk, senior rates, meeting facilities. CC. 4 miles from the Miami Arena, 3 miles from the Orange Bowl, 10 miles from the downtown area. SGL$45-$79, DBL$49-$89, STS$60-$109.

Days Inn (7250 Northwest 11th St., 33126; 261-4230, Fax 261-0969, 800-325-2525) 103 rooms, restaurant, lounge, entertainment, outdoor pool, car rental desk, complimentary newspaper, airport courtesy car, wheelchair access, NS rooms, fax service, children stay free with parents, a/c, TV, senior rates, CC. 2 miles from the Miami airport, downtown area and Orange Bowl. SGL$45-$60, DBL$50-$70.

Holiday Inn (1101 Northwest 57th Ave., 33126; 266-0000, Fax 266-9179, 800-HOLIDAY) 266 rooms, restaurant, lounge, outdoor pool, exercise center, children under 19 free with parents, wheelchair access, a/c, TV, NS rooms, fax service, room service, laundry service, meeting facilities, senior rates, CC. 1 block from the shopping mall, 10 miles from Atlantic beaches, 4 miles from the University of Miami. SGL/DBL$85-$135.

Holiday Inn Airport LeJeune Center (950 Northwest LeJeune Rd., 33126; 446-9000, Fax 441-0725, 800-HOLIDAY) 300 rooms and suites, restaurant, lounge, free breakfast, entertainment, outdoor pool, whirlpool, room service, no pets, children free with parents, a/c, TV, gift shop, airport transportation, complimentary newspaper, meeting facilities for 400, senior rates, CC. 1 mile from the Miami airport, 6 miles from the downtown area and the University of Miami, 2 miles from the Expo Center. SGL/DBL$100-$195.

Howard Johnson Lodge (1980 Northwest LeJeune Rd., 33126; 871-4370, Fax 871-4370 ext 135, 800-I-GO-HOJO) 64 rooms, restaurant, outdoor pool, children stay free with parents, NS rooms, a/c, TV, wheelchair car rental desk, access, free parking, airport transportation, senior rates, meeting facilities, CC. A 1/4-mile from the Miami airport, 6 miles from the downtown area. SGL$49-$74, DBL$59-$105.

Marriott Airport Hotel (1201 Northwest LeJeune Rd., 33126; 649-5000, Fax 642-3369, 800-228-9290) 782 rooms and suites, restaurant, lounge, entertainment, outdoor pool, exercise center, whirlpools, lighted tennis courts, airport courtesy car, free parking, NS rooms, a/c, TV, laundry service, barber and beauty shop, pets OK, wheelchair access, gift shop, meeting facilities, senior rates, CC. 8 miles from the downtown area and the Orange Bowl. SGL/DBL$60-$175.

Marriott Residence Inn (1212 Northwest 82nd Ave., 33126; 591-2211, Fax 591-0902, 800-331-3131) 237 suites, kitchens, in-room refrigerators, outdoor pool, airport transportation, free parking, laundry room, fireplaces, wheelchair access, NS rooms, pets OK, VCRs, a/c, TV, meeting facilities for 60, senior rates, CC. 10 miles from the downtown area, 7 miles from the Orange Bowl, two miles from the Miami airport. SGL/DBL$125.

Miami Airport Hilton and Marina (5101 Blue Lagoon Dr., 33126; 262-1000, Fax 267-5726, 800-HILTONS) 500 rooms and 1- and 2-bedroom suites, restaurant, lounge, entertainment, outdoor heated pool, exercise center, lighted tennis courts, whirlpools, saunas, pets OK, 24-hour room service, a/c, TV, wheelchair access, gift shop, airport courtesy car, NS rooms, 22 meeting rooms, meeting facilities for 1,500, senior rates, CC. 8 miles from the downtown area and Port of Miami. SGL/DBL$110-$185, DBL$130-$205, 1BR$400, 2BR$500.

Miami Airport Hotel (Miami Airport, 33159; 871-1400, Fax 871-0800, 800-327-1276) 334 rooms and suites, restaurant, lounge, entertainment, outdoor pool, exercise center, whirlpools, sauna, lighted tennis court, a/c, TV, pets OK, wheelchair access, NS rooms, meeting facilities, senior rates, CC. SGL/DBL$120-$160, STS$196-$600.

Hotel Miami Airport (Northwest 20th St., 33159; 871-4100, Fax 871-0800, 800-327-1276, 800-421-0694 in Florida) 260 rooms, restaurant, outdoor pool, whirlpools, exercise center, jacuzzi, sauna, gift shop, a/c, TV, no pets, room service, barber and beauty shop, children free with parents, NS rooms, complimentary newspaper, laundry service, kitchenettes, meeting facilities, senior rates, CC. SGL/DBL$110-$159.

Quality Inn Airport (2373 Northwest LeJeune Ave., 33142; 871-3230, 800-221-2222) 160 rooms and suites, restaurant, lounge, outdoor pool, exercise center, children free with parents, a/c, TV, wheelchair access, room service, laundry service, no pets, airport courtesy car, NS rooms, meeting facilities, senior rates, CC. 1 block from the Miami airport. SGL/DBL$60-$95.

Ramada Renaissance Hotel Airport (3941 Northwest 22nd St., 33142; 871-1700, Fax 871-4830, 800-228-2828) 273 rooms, restaurant, lounge, outdoor heated pool, exercise center, gift shop, children stay free with parents, wheelchair access, local transportation, NS rooms, a/c, TV, 8 meeting rooms, meeting facilities for 450, CC. 2 miles from the Merchandise Mart, 4 miles from the Orange Bowl, 6 miles from the Port of Miami. SGL/DBL$75-$158.

Radisson Mart Plaza (711 Northwest 72nd Ave., 33126; 261-3800, Fax 261-7665, 800-333-3333) 334 rooms, restaurant, lounge, outdoor pool, whirlpools, exercise center, lighted tennis courts, boutiques, room service, a/c, TV, laundry facilities, beauty shop, airport courtesy car, NS rooms, pets OK, wheelchair access, children stay free with parents, meeting facilities, CC. SGL/DBL$120-$145, STS$155-$500.

Sheraton River House (3900 Northwest 21st St., 33142; 871-3800, Fax 871-0447, 800-325-3535) 408 rooms and suites, restaurant, lounge, entertainment, outdoor pool, exercise center, lighted tennis courts, complimentary newspaper, NS rooms, wheelchair access, airport courtesy car, a/c, TV, room service, pets OK, 15,000 square feet of meeting and exhibition space, 18 meeting rooms, meeting facilities for 800, 15,000 square feet of meeting and exhibition space, senior rates, CC. In the downtown area near the Port of Miami and the Brickell Financial District. SGL/DBL$100-$500.

Hotel Sofitel Miami (5800 Blue Lagoon Dr., 33126; 264-4888, Fax 262-9049, 800-258-4888, 800-221-4542 in Florida) 282 rooms and suites, restaurant, lounge, entertainment, outdoor heated pool, exercise center, lighted tennis courts, sauna, whirlpools, complimentary newspaper, a/c, TV, pets OK, gift shop, airport transportation, children free with parents, NS rooms, meeting facilities for 900, senior rates, CC. SGL/DBL$139-$189.

North Miami

Park Plaza International (7707 Northwest 103rd St., 33016; 825-1000, Fax 556-6785, 800-437-PARK) 262 rooms, restaurant, outdoor pool, spa, sauna, exercise center, lighted tennis courts, NS rooms, a/c, TV, gift shop, airport courtesy car, complimentary newspaper, meeting facilities for 1,000, senior rates, CC. Near Westland Mall, 8 miles from Joe Robbie Stadium, 9 miles from the Orange Bowl and the airport. SGL/DBL$77-$145.

Wellesley Inn (7925 Northwest 154th St., 33016; 721-8274, Fax 828-2257, 800-444-8888) 100 rooms and suites, restaurant, free breakfast, outdoor heated pool, in-room refrigerators, wheelchair access, pets OK, a/c, TV, NS rooms, children stay free with parents, complimentary newspaper, fax service, senior rates, meeting facilities, CC. SGL/DBL$55-$90.

South Miami

Quality Inn South (14501 South Dixie Hwy., 33176; 251-2000, 800-221-2222) 126 rooms, restaurant, lounge, children free with parents, outdoor heated pool, exercise center, pets OK, kitchenettes, a/c, TV, room service, laundry service, wheelchair access, NS rooms, senior rates, CC. 11 miles from the Miami airport, 6 miles from the University of Miami, 13 miles from the downtown area. SGL/DBL$60-$100.

from the University of Miami, 13 miles from the downtown area. SGL/DBL$60-$100.

Other Locations

Days Inn (660 Northwest 81st St., 33150; 756-5121, Fax 756-1291, 800-325-2525) 125 rooms, restaurant, outdoor pool, no pets, wheelchair access, NS rooms, children stay free with parents, a/c, TV, senior rates, meeting facilities, CC. 10 miles from the Miami airport and Jai Alai fronton, 8 miles from the Orange Bowl. SGL$49-$58, DBL$59-$68.

Doral Hotel and Country Club (4400 Northwest 87th Ave., 33178; 592-2000, Fax 594-4682, 800-327-6334) 639 rooms and suites, restaurant, lounge, entertainment, outdoor pool, lighted tennis courts, exercise center, a/c, TV, boutiques, in-room refrigerators, room service, game room, laundry service, wheelchair access, local transportation, NS rooms, 35 meeting rooms, meeting facilities, senior rates, CC. 10 miles from the downtown area, 7 miles from the Miami airport. SGL/DBL$245-$345, STS$360-$1,500.

Holiday Inn Calder (21485 Northwest 27th Ave., 33156; 621-5801, Fax 624-8202, 800-HOLIDAY) 214 rooms and suites, restaurant, lounge, entertainment, outdoor heated pool, wheelchair access, a/c, TV, in-room refrigerators, NS rooms, children free with parents, gift shop, room service, laundry service, no pets, meeting facilities for 400, senior rates, CC. 14 miles from the Miami airport, a 1/2-mile from Joe Robbie Stadium, 10 miles from Atlantic beaches. SGL/DBL$60-$120.

Holiday Inn Cutler Ridge (10775 Caribbean Blvd., 33189; 253-9960, 800-HOLIDAY) 120 rooms, restaurant, lounge, outdoor pool, exercise center, children free with parents, wheelchair access, a/c, TV, NS rooms, fax service, room service, laundry service, no pets, meeting facilities for 75, senior rates, CC. 8 miles from Fairchild Gardens, 1 block from the Cutler Ridge Shopping Center, 3 miles from the Metro Zoo. SGL/DBL$50-$66.

Holiday Inn Golden Glades (148 Northwest 167th St., 33169; 949-1441, Fax 956-9693, 800-HOLIDAY) 184 rooms, restaurant, lounge, outdoor pool, a/c, TV, children free with parents, laundry service, no pets, meeting facilities for 200, senior rates, CC. 12 miles from the Miami airport, 2 miles from the shopping center, 3 miles from Calder Race Track. SGL/DBL$65-$75.

Howard Johnson (12210 Biscayne Blvd., 33181; 891-7350, 891-7350 ext 103, 800-I-GO-HOJO) 96 rooms and suites, restaurant, lounge, outdoor heated pool, gift shop, free breakfast, children stay free with parents, NS rooms, wheelchair access, car rental desk, a/c, TV, fax service, meeting facilities, senior rates, CC. 12 miles from the airport, 6 miles from the downtown area and the Miami Dolphin Stadium, 7 miles from the Bayside Marketplace. SGL/DBL$65-$85.

Howard Johnson Lodge (16500 Northwest 2nd Ave., 33169; 945-2621, Fax 945-2621 ext 196, 800-I-GO-HOJO) 248 rooms, restaurant, lounge, two pools, exercise center, children stay free with parents, NS rooms, wheelchair access, laundry service, in-room refrigerators and microwaves, a/c, TV, meeting facilities for 200, senior rates, CC. 12 miles from the Miami airport, 15 miles from the downtown area. SGL/DBL$54-$75, STS$105.

Miami Beach

Area Code 305

Rental & Reservation Services

Budget Reservation Services (Miami Beach 33119; 532-7273) rental hotel rooms.

Miami Beach Resort Hotel Association (407 Lincoln Rd., 33119; 800-964-6835) rental hotel rooms.

❑❑❑

The Adrian Hotel (1060 Ocean Dr., 33139; 538-0007, Fax 532-3048, 800-332-6835) 117 rooms and efficiencies, restaurant, lounge, boutiques, a/c, TV, room service, NS rooms, senior rates, CC. SGL/DBL$70-$80.

The Alexander All-Suite Hotel (5225 Collins Ave., 33140; 865-6500, Fax 864-8525, 800-327-6121) 150 1- and 2-bedroom suites, restaurant, lounge, entertainment, outdoor heated pool, jacuzzi, exercise center, a/c, TV, complimentary newspaper, gift shop, beauty shop, antique furnishings, children free with parents, no pets, kitchenettes, NS rooms, wheelchair access, senior rates, 4,800 square feet of meeting and exhibition space, meeting facilities for

250, CC. 12 miles from the Miami airport, 8 miles from the Convention Center. 1BR$225-$495, 2BR$420-$1,250.

Atlantic Beach Hotel (3400 Collins Ave., 33140; 672-6539) 45 rooms and suites, lounge, free breakfast, in-room refrigerators and microwaves, a/c, TV, NS rooms, laundry facilities, senior rates, CC. SGL/DBL$40-$60.

Avalon Hotel (700 Ocean Dr., 33139; 538-0133, Fax 534-0258, 800-933-3306) 108 rooms and suites, restaurant, lounge, free breakfast, a/c, TV, NS rooms, children free with parents, laundry facilities, wheelchair access, no pets, in-room refrigerators, senior rates, CC. SGL/DBL$55-$145.

Beach Paradise Hotel (600 Ocean Dr., 33134; 531-0021, Fax 674-0206, 800-258-8886) 50 rooms and suites, restaurant, lounge, free breakfast, in-room refrigerators, children free with parents, NS rooms, a/c, TV, room service, laundry facilities, CC. SGL/DBL$55-$160.

The Beacon Hotel (720 Ocean Dr., 33139; 531-5891, Fax 674-8976, 800-541-4477) 80 rooms and suites, restaurant, lounge, no pets, children free with parents, kitchenettes, laundry facilities, beach, a/c, TV, NS rooms, wheelchair access, senior rates, CC. SGL/DBL$75-$210.

Bentley Hotel (510 Ocean Dr., 33139; 538-1700, Fax 532-4865) 40 rooms, restaurant, lounge, a/c, TV, NS rooms, in-room refrigerators, no pets, CC. SGL/DBL$55-$95.

Betsy Ross Hotel (1440 Ocean Dr., 33139; 531-3934, 800-755-4601) 80 rooms and suites, restaurant, lounge, outdoor pool, a/c, TV, children free with parents, laundry facilities, no pets, wheelchair access, NS rooms, in-room refrigerators, beach, senior rates, CC. SGL/DBL$90-$130, STS$130-$165.

Boulevard Hotel and Cafe (740 Ocean Dr., 33139; 532- 0376, Fax 674-8179) 40 rooms and suites, restaurant, lounge, outdoor pool, beauty shop, a/c, TV, in-room refrigerators, laundry facilities, room service, NS rooms, CC. SGL/DBL$75-$225.

Cardozo Hotel (1300 Ocean Dr., 33139; 535-6500) 41 rooms and suites, restaurant, lounge, a/c, TV, children free with parents, in-room refrigerators, room service, NS rooms, no pets, CC. SGL/DBL$135-$225.

The Castle Beach Club (5445 Collins Ave., 33140; 865-1500, 800-327-0555) 300 rooms and suites, restaurant, lounge, heated pool, exercise facilities, spa, tennis courts, beach, laundry facilities, room service, gift shop, complimentary newspaper, car rental desk, children free with parents, in-room refrigerators, pets OK, NS rooms, senior rates, 16,000 square feet of meeting and exhibition space, CC. SGL/DBL$105-$125.

Clarion Crystal Beach Suite Hotel (6985 Collins Ave., 33141; 865-9555, Fax 866-3514, 800-221-2222, 800-428-8604) 56 1-bedroom suites, outdoor pool, exercise center, whirlpools, in-room refrigerators, microwaves and coffee makers, VCRs, kitchenettes, no pets, NS rooms, laundry facilities, children free with parents, senior rates, meeting facilities, a/c, TV, CC. 2 miles from the Convention Center, 11 miles from the Miami airport. SGL/DBL$115-$190.

Days Inn Beachfront (100 21st St., 33139; 538-6631, 800-325-2525) 171 rooms, a/c, TV, wheelchair access, NS rooms, laundry facilities, children free with parents, beach, room service, senior rates, CC. SGL/DBL$80-$100.

Days Inn Central (7450 Ocean Terrace, 33141; 866-1631, Fax 868-4617, 800-325-2525) 93 rooms and suites, restaurant, lounge, outdoor pool, a/c, TV, children free with parents, room service, in-room refrigerators, NS rooms, fax service, senior rates, CC. 16 miles from the Seaquarium, 25 miles from Joe Robbie Stadium. SGL/DBL$35-$80, STS$89.

Days Inn Oceanside (4299 Collins Ave., 33140; 673-1513, Fax 538-0727, 800-325-2525) 133 rooms, restaurant, lounge, heated pool, in-room refrigerators, children stay free with parents, room service, laundry service, free local calls, local transportation, no pets, wheelchair access, NS rooms, senior rates, CC. 5 miles from the Orange Bowl, 9 miles from the Miami Port Cruise Terminal, 12 miles from the Miami airport. SGL/DBL$90-$120.

Dezerland Surfside Hotel (8701 Collins Ave., 33154; 865-6661) 220 suites, restaurant, lounge, outdoor pool, beach, whirlpools, a/c, TV, NS rooms, children free with parents, pets OK, in-room refrigerators, laundry facilities, senior rates, CC. SGL/DBL$60-$115.

Doral Ocean Beach Resort (4833 Collins Ave., 33140; 532-3600, 800-22-DORAL) 420 rooms and suites, restaurants, lounge, entertainment, heated pool, jacuzzis, sauna, lighted tennis courts, spa, exercise facilities, a/c, TV, NS rooms, game room, gift shop, beauty salon, in-room refrigerators, laundry service, boutiques, 24-hour room service, local transportation, car rental desk, meeting facilities, senior rates, CC. 12 miles from the Miami airport, 10 miles from the downtown area and Port of Miami. SGL/DBL$120-$200.

Eden Rock Hotel and Marina (4525 Collins Ave., 33140; 531-0000, Fax 531-6955, 800-327-8337) 395 rooms and suites, restaurant, lounge, entertainment, outdoor heated pool, beauty shop, laundry facilities, room service, wheelchair access, gift shop, TV, a/c, NS rooms, CC. SGL/DBL$120-$185, STS$180-$575.

Essex House Travelodge Hotel (1001 Collins Ave., 33139; 534-2700, Fax 532-3827, 800-525-9055) 57 rooms and suites, restaurant, free breakfast, children free with parents, laundry facilities, airport transportation, a/c, TV, NS rooms, pets OK, wheelchair access, beach, senior rates, CC. SGL/DBL$75-$175.

Fountainebleau Hilton Resort and Spa (4441 Collins Ave., 33140; 538-2000, Fax 534-7821, 800-HILTONS) 1,206 rooms and suites, restaurant, lounge, entertainment, indoor and outdoor pools, exercise center, spa, lighted tennis courts, a/c, TV, NS rooms, wheelchair access, beauty shop, game room, gift shop, in-room refrigerators, boutiques, meeting facilities for 4,500, CC. 16 miles from the Miami airport, 10 miles from the Port of Miami. SGL/DBL$140-$310.

Governor Hotel (435 21st St., 33139; 532-2100, Fax 532-9139) 126 rooms, restaurant, lounge, outdoor pool, beach, a/c, TV, kitchenettes, NS rooms, wheelchair access, in-room refrigerators, children free with parents, senior rates, CC. SGL/DBL$55-$125.

Holiday Inn Oceanside Convention Center (2201 Collins Ave., 33139; 534-1511, Fax 534-0966, 800-HOLIDAY) 351 rooms and suites, restaurant, lounge, outdoor pool, exercise facilities, lighted tennis courts, whirlpools, barber and beauty shop, gift shop, car rental desk, complimentary newspaper, children stay free with parents, beach, wheelchair access, NS rooms, fax service, room service, no pets, laundry service, meeting facilities for 350, senior rates. 10 miles from the Bayside Mall, 6 blocks from the Convention Center and Performing Arts Center. SGL/DBL$103-$130.

Hotel 100 (100 Lincoln Rd., 33139; 531-6885, 800-327-1039) 210 rooms and suites, lounge, outdoor heated pool, laundry facilities, in-room refrigerators, a/c, TV, kitchenettes, car rental desk, room service, CC. SGL/DBL$95-$195.

Howard Johnson (6261 Collins Ave., 33140; 868-1200, Fax 868-3003, 800-I-GO-HOJO) 150 rooms, restaurant, lounge, outdoor pool, children free with parents, wheelchair access, NS rooms, TV, a/c, laundry facilities, room service, senior rates, meeting facilities, CC. 2.5 miles from the Miami Beach Convention Center, 12 miles from the Miami Airport, 19 miles from the Joe Robbie Stadium. SGL/DBL$75-$120.

Howard Johnson (4000 Alton Rd., 33140; 532-4411, Fax 534- 6540, 800-I-GO-HOJO) 140 rooms and suites, restaurant, lounge, out-door heated pool, children stay free with parents, wheelchair access, NS rooms, pets OK, airport transportation, a/c, TV, free parking, meeting facilities, senior rates, CC. 6 miles from the Miami airport, 4 miles from the downtown area, 1 mile from the golf course and the Miami Beach Convention Center. SGL/DBL$65-$85, STS$140-$235.

The International Inn On The Bay (2301 Normandy Dr., 33141; 866-7661, 800-848-0924) 60 rooms and efficiencies, restaurant, free breakfast, outdoor pool, room service, children free with parents, laundry facilities, in-room refrigerators and microwaves, kitchen-ettes, a/c, TV, NS rooms, wheelchair access, CC. SGL/DBL$42-$57, EFF$52-$67.

Leslie Hotel (1244 Ocean Dr., 33139; 534-2135, 800-338-9076) 47 rooms, free breakfast, in-room refrigerators, a/c, TV, NS rooms, children free with parents, laundry facilities, wheelchair access, senior rates, CC. SGL/DBL$104-$255.

Lido Spa Hotel (40 Island Ave., 33139; 538-4621, Fax 534-3680, 800-327-8363) 106 rooms and suites, restaurant, lounge, entertain-ment, heated pool, whirlpools, jacuzzi, sauna, beauty shop, bou-tiques, laundry service, a/c, TV, room service, children free with parents, in-room refrigerators, airport courtesy car, car rental desk, NS rooms, wheelchair access, CC. SGL/DBL$110-$150.

The Ocean Pavilion (5601 Collins Ave., 33140; 865- 6511, Fax 868-5779) 120 1- and 2-bedroom apartments, restaurant, heated pool, gift shop, boutiques, beauty shop, a/c, TV, laundry facilities, NS rooms, wheelchair access, CC. 1BR$120-$140, 2BR$135-$145.

Quality Inn Shawnee Beach (4343 Collins Ave., 33140; 532-2311, 800-832-8332, 800-221-2222) 475 rooms and suites, restaurant, lounge, outdoor pool, exercise center, whirlpools, no pets, children free with parents, a/c, TV, wheelchair access, room service, laundry service, NS rooms, meeting facilities, senior rates, CC. 12 miles from the Miami airport, 2 miles from the Convention Center, 6 miles from the Port of Miami. SGL/DBL$125-$225.

Ramada Resort Deauville (6701 Collins Ave., 33141; 865- 8511, Fax 865-8154, 800-2-RAMADA) 550 rental rooms and suites, restaurant, lounge, entertainment, outdoor pool, tennis courts, jacuzzi, exercise center, boutiques, wheelchair access, NS rooms, airport transportation, free parking, pets OK, beach, wheelchair access, a/c, TV, game room, gift shop, room service, laundry facilities, meeting facilities, senior rates. CC. 15 miles from the Miami Port Cruise Terminal, 20 miles from the Miami airport. SGL/DBL$110-$140, STS$150-$295.

The Rodney Ocean Suites (9365 Collins Ave., 33154; 864-2232, Fax 864-3045, 800-327-1412) 100 rooms and suites, restaurant, heated pool, in-room refrigerators, NS rooms, a/c, TV, children free with parents, laundry facilities, wheelchair access, senior rates, CC. SGL/DBL$46-$75, STS$54-$80.

The Roney Plaza Apartment Hotel (2301 Collins Ave., 33139; 531-8811, Fax 538-7141, 800-432-4317) 400 rooms and suites, restaurant, outdoor pool, exercise facilities, beach, tennis courts, a/c, TV, airport transportation, children free with parents, meeting facilities, senior rates, CC. SGL/DBL$186.

Sagamore Resort Hotel (1671 Collins Ave., 33139; 538-7211, Fax 674-0371) 128 rooms and suites, restaurant, lounge, entertainment, heated pool, room service, laundry service, in-room refrigerators, local transportation, wheelchair access, NS rooms, senior rates, CC. SGL/DBL$60-$85.

Seacoast Towers Suite Hotel (5151 Collins Ave., 33140; 865-5152, Fax 868-4090) 150 rooms and 2-bedroom suites, restaurant, outdoor heated pool, lighted tennis courts, barber and beauty shop, local transportation, NS rooms, wheelchair access, in-room refrigerators and coffee makers, children free with parents, no pets, laundry facilities, senior rates, CC. SGL/DBL$125-$310.

Seville Beach Hotel (2901 Collins Ave., 33140; 532-2511, 800-327-1641) 326 rooms and suites, restaurant, lounge, outdoor heated pool, whirlpools, exercise center, a/c, TV, beauty shop, gift shop, room service, in-room refrigerators, NS rooms, children free with parents, no pets, senior rates, CC. SGL/DBL$125-$500.

Sovereign Hotel (4385 Collins Ave., 33140; 531-5371, 800-327-4733) 112 one-bedroom apartments, outdoor heated pool, kitchenettes, a/c, TV, NS rooms, children free with parents, no pets, laundry facilities, senior rates, CC. SGL/DBL$54-$135.

Surfcomber Motel (1717 Collins Ave., 33139; 532-7715, Fax 532-7280, 800-336-4264) 194 rooms and efficiencies, restaurant, lounge, entertainment, outdoor heated pool, exercise center, in-room refrigerators, laundry facilities, gift shop, a/c, TV, children free with parents, NS rooms, no pets, meeting facilities, CC. $70-$200.

Waldorf Towers Hotel (860 Ocean Dr., 33139; 531-7684, Fax 672-6836, 800-44-UTELL) 42 rooms and suites, restaurant, lounge, laundry service, in-room refrigerators, room service, a/c, TV, car rental desk, wheelchair access, NS rooms, senior rates, meeting facilities, CC. SGL/DBL$110-$200.

Miami Springs
Area Code 305

Courtyard by Marriott (3929 Northwest 79th Ave., 33166, 477-8118, Fax 599-9636, 800-331-3131) 145 rooms and suites, free breakfast, outdoor pool, exercise center, in-room refrigerators, microwaves and coffee makers, a/c, VCRs, no pets, complimentary newspaper, airport courtesy car, children free with parents, kitchenettes, TV, NS rooms, wheelchair access, meeting facilities, senior rates, CC. SGL/DBL$110-$140.

Executive Club Corporate Apartments (8290 Lake Dr., 33166; 477-1515, Fax 477-5428) 114 1- and 2-bedroom apartments, outdoor pool, exercise center, sauna, whirlpools, lighted tennis courts, a/c, TV, laundry facilities, in-room microwaves, NS rooms, senior rates, CC. 1BR$87, 2BR$88.

Fairfield Inn West Airport (3959 Northwest 79th St., 33166; 599-5200, Fax 599-5200, 800-228-2800) 135 rooms, free breakfast, outdoor heated pool, a/c, TV, children stay free with parents, NS rooms, no pets, airport courtesy car, wheelchair access, meeting rooms, senior rates, CC. 4 miles from the Miami airport and International Mall, 10 miles from the downtown area, 2 miles from the Merchandise Mart. SGL/DBL$60-$75.

Hampton Inn Airport (5125 Northwest 36th St., 33166; 887-2153, 800-HAMPTON) 110 rooms, free breakfast, pool, exercise center, children under 18 free with parents, NS rooms, wheelchair access, in-room computer hookups, fax service, TV, a/c, pets OK, free local calls, meeting facilities, senior rates, CC. 1 mile from the Miami airport, 5 miles from the downtown area. SGL/DBL$40-$65.

Howard Johnson (7330 Northwest 36th St., 33166; 592-5440, Fax 477-8155, 800-I-GO-HOJO) 124 rooms, free breakfast, outdoor pool, exercise center, children free with parents, NS rooms, wheelchair access, airport transportation, in-room computer hookups, fax service, TV, a/c, free local calls, meeting facilities, senior rates, CC. 3 miles from the Miami airport, 7 miles from the downtown area. SGL/DBL$48-$85.

Holiday Inn North Airport (1111 South Poinciana Blvd., 33166; 885-1941, Fax 884-1881, 800-HOLIDAY) restaurant, lounge, entertainment, children stay free with parents, wheelchair access, car rental desk, gift shop, NS rooms, fax service, room service, airport transportation, meeting facilities for 200. 10 miles from the downtown area and Miami Port Cruise Terminal, 4 blocks from the Jai Alai fronton. SGL$75, DBL$85.

La Quinta Inn Airport (7401 Northwest 36th St., 33166; 599-9902, Fax 594-0552, 800-531-5900) 165 rooms, restaurant, lounge, heated pool, complimentary newspaper, free local calls, fax service, laundry service, pets OK, a/c, TV, wheelchair access, NS rooms, airport transportation, children free with parents, free parking, meeting facilities, senior rates, 2 miles from the Miami airport, 14 miles from Joe Robbie Stadium. CC. SGL/DBL$65-$75.

Miami Airways Apartment Motel (5001 Northwest 36th St., Miami FL 33166; 883-4700, Fax 888-8072, 800-824-9910) 88 rooms and 1- and 2-bedroom suites, restaurant, lounge, outdoor pool, airport courtesy car, a/c, TV, NS rooms, laundry facilities, in-room refrigerators and microwaves, wheelchair access, kitchenettes, senior rates, CC. SGL$36-$42, DBL$42-$45, STS$50-$55.

Travelodge Miami Airport (5301 Northwest 36th St., 33166; 871-6000, Fax 871-4971, 800-578-7878) 267 rooms, restaurant, lounge, free breakfast, outdoor pool, tennis courts, exercise center, airport transportation, wheelchair access, complimentary newspaper, laundry service, TV, a/c, free local calls, fax service, NS rooms, in-room refrigerators and microwaves, children free with parents, no pets, meeting facilities, senior rates, CC. 10 miles from the downtown area and Port of Miami. SGL/DBL$60-$90.

Wellesley Inn (8436 Northwest 36th St., 33166; 592-4799, Fax 471-8461, 800-444-8888) 106 rooms and suites, free breakfast, outdoor pool, wheelchair access, laundry facilities, in-room refrigerators, a/c, TV, NS rooms, pets OK, fax service, senior rates, CC. SGL/DBL$75-$105.

Middleburg
Area Code 904

The Inn At Ravines (2932 Ravines Rd., 32068; 282-1111) 40 rooms and suites, restaurant, lounge, outdoor pool, whirlpools, lighted tennis courts, laundry facilities, children free with parents, rooms service, no pets, a/c, TV, NS rooms, 3 meeting rooms, senior rates, CC. SGL/DBL$70-$120.

Milton
Area Code 904

Adventures Unlimited (Milton 32570; 623-6197) 14 cottages and cabins, restaurant, a/c, TV, children free with parents, no pets, CC. SGL/DBL$25-$65.

Mount Dora
Area Code 904

Comfort Inn (3600 Hwy. 441 West, 32757; 383-3400, 800-221-2222) 62 rooms, outdoor pool, exercise center, sauna, no pets, a/c, TV, children free with parents, NS rooms, wheelchair access, senior rates, CC. 45 miles from the Miami airport. SGL/DBL$40-$90.

Econo Lodge (300 Hwy. 441 North, 32757; 383-2181, 800-4-CHOICE) 45 rooms, restaurant, lounge, outdoor pool, children free with parents, NS rooms, wheelchair access, a/c, TV, no pets, meeting facilities, kitchenettes, senior rates, CC. SGL/DBL$35-$60.

Lakeside Inn of Mt. Dora (100 North Alexander, 32757; 383-4101, Fax 735-2642, 800-556-5016) 87 rooms, restaurant, lounge, entertainment, outdoor heated pool, lighted tennis courts, a/c, TV, children free with parents, Modified American Plan available, NS rooms, no pets, VCRs, in-room refrigerators, wheelchair access, 5 meeting rooms, senior rates, CC. LS SGL/DBL$65-$155; HS SGL/DBL$80-$155.

Naples

Area Code 813

Rental & Reservation Services

Glacid Properties (1600 Wellesley Circle; 353-1211) rental condominiums and apartments.

The Vacation Shoppe (11595 Kelly Rd., Fort Myers 33908; 454-1400, Fax 466-3299) rental condos, apartments and townhouses.

□□□

Best Western Naples Inn (2329 9th St., 33940; 261-1148, 800-243-1148, 800-528-1234) 80 rooms, restaurant, lounge, free breakfast, outdoor heated pool, children free with parents, a/c, NS rooms, TV, laundry facilities, in-room refrigerators, microwaves and coffee makers, VCRs, no pets, wheelchair access, senior rates, CC. 1 block from the shopping mall. SGL/DBL$50-$110.

Comfort Inn and Executive Suites (3860 Tollgate Blvd., 33939; 353-950, 800-221-2222) 140 rooms and suites, restaurant, lounge, free breakfast, outdoor pool, whirlpools, no pets, a/c, TV, in-room refrigerators, children free with parents, gift shop, game room, in-room computer hookups, NS rooms, wheelchair access, senior rates, CC. 5 miles from the airport, 7 miles to Gulf beaches, 8 miles from the Naples Dinner Theater. SGL/DBL$40-$190.

Comfort Inn (1221 5th Ave. South, 33940; 649-5800, 800-221-2222, 800-382-7941) 100 rooms, outdoor pool, a/c, TV, children free with parents, in-room refrigerators, NS rooms, wheelchair access, no pets, senior rates, CC. 4 miles from the Naples airport, 1 block from the shopping mall, a 1/2-mile to Gulf beaches. SGL/DBL$45-$135.

Cove Inn Resort (1191 8th St. South, 33940; 262-7161) 102 rooms and suites, restaurant, lounge, outdoor heated pool, in-room refrigerators, children free with parents, no pets, a/c, TV, NS rooms, wheelchair access, senior rates, CC. SGL/DBL$110-$260.

Days Inn Lodge (1925 Davis Blvd., 33942; 774-3117, Fax 775-5333, 800-325-2525) 158 rooms and apartments, restaurant, free breakfast, outdoor heated pool, whirlpools, kitchenettes, in-room refrigerators, a/c, TV, wheelchair access, NS rooms, no pets, laundry facilities, senior rates, CC. 1 mile from Gulf beaches, 25 miles from regional airport. SGL/DBL$50-$90.

Edgewater Beach Hotel (1901 Gulf Shore Blvd. North, 33940; 262-6511, Fax 262-1234, 800-821-0199, 800-282-3766 in Florida) 124 1- and 2-bedroom suites, restaurant, lounge, entertainment, outdoor heated pool, exercise center, tennis courts, in-room refrigerators and microwaves, no pets, a/c, TV, children free with parents, room service, NS rooms, wheelchair access, senior rates, CC. LS SGL/DBL$100-$300; HS SGL/DBL$200-$500.

Fairways Resort (103 Palm River Blvd., 33942; 597-8181, Fax 597-5413, 800-835-1311) 12 rooms, efficiencies and 1-bedroom apartments, outdoor heated pool, whirlpools, a/c, TV, VCRs, no pets, in-room refrigerators, NS rooms, children free with parents, kitchenettes, senior rates. LS SGL/DBL$36-$55; HS SGL/DBL$75-$85.

Hampton Inn (3210 Tamiami Trail, 33940; 261-8000, Fax 261-7802, 800-426-7866) 107 rooms and 2-bedroom suites, free breakfast, outdoor heated pool, exercise center, children free with parents, NS rooms, wheelchair access, in-room computer hookups, fax service, TV, a/c, in-room refrigerators and microwaves, no pets, free local calls, meeting facilities, senior rates, CC. 3 miles from Gulf beaches, 1 mile from the shopping mall, 2 miles from the Philharmonic Center. SGL/DBL$45-$95.

Holiday Inn (1100 9th St., 33940; 262-7146, Fax 261-3809, 800-HOLIDAY) 137 rooms, restaurant, lounge, outdoor pool, exercise center, children free with parents, wheelchair access, a/c, TV, NS rooms, fax service, room service, laundry service, in-room coffee makers, no pets, meeting facilities for 137, senior rates, CC. 5 miles from the regional airport, a 1/2-mile from Gulf beaches. SGL/DBL$50-$115.

Howard Johnson Lodge (221 9th St. South, 33939; 262-6181, Fax 262-0318, 800-I-GO-HOJO) 100 rooms and suites, pool, children free with parents, wheelchair access, NS rooms, TV, a/c, laundry facilities, in-room refrigerators and microwaves, local transportation, no pets, senior rates, meeting facilities, CC. 3 miles from the Naples airport, 9 blocks from Gulf beaches. SGL/DBL$40-$125.

The Inn at Pelican Bay (800 Vanderbilt Beach Rd., 33963; 597-8777, Fax 597-8012) 100 rooms, outdoor heated pool, whirlpools, in-room computer hookups, no pets, a/c, TV, children free with parents, VCRs, room service, NS rooms, meeting facilities, senior rates, CC. SGL/DBL$65-$135.

Inn By The Sea Bed and Breakfast (287 11th Ave. South, 33940; 649-4124) 5 rooms and suites, free breakfast, NS, no pets, airport transportation, a/c, TV, children free with parents, CC. LS SGL/DBL$115-$170.

The Inn Of Naples (4055 Tamiami Trail, 33963; 649-5500, Fax 649-5500, 800-237-8858) 64 rooms and 1-bedroom suites, restaurant, free breakfast, outdoor heated pool, whirlpools, children free with parents, in-room refrigerators and coffee makers, a/c, TV, VCRs, no pets, NS rooms, senior rates, CC. LS SGL/DBL$65-$95; HS SGL/DBL$120-$155.

La Playa Beach and Racquet Inn (9891 Gulfshore Blvd. North, 33963; 597-3123, Fax 597-6278, 800-282-4423 in Florida, 800-237-6883) 137 rooms and 1- and 2-bedroom suites, restaurant, lounge, outdoor heated pool, tennis courts, kitchenettes, children free with parents, NS rooms, wheelchair access, no pets, laundry facilities, airport transportation, beach, CC. LS SGL/DBL$80-$135; HS SGL/DBL$125-$175.

Naples Bath and Tennis Club (4995 Airport Rd., 33942; 261-5777, Fax 649-2045, 800-225-9692) 40 1- , 2- , and 3-bedroom condominiums, restaurant, lounge, outdoor heated pool, whirlpools, in-room refrigerators, microwaves and coffee makers, children free with parents, laundry facilities, no pets, CC. 15 miles from the Naples airport. 1BR$90-$100, 2BR$115-$135, 3BR$150-$165.

Naples Beach Hotel and Golf Club (851 Gulfshore Blvd. North, 33940; 261-2222, Fax 261-8019, 800-237-7600, 800-282-7601 in Florida) 315 rooms and suites, restaurant, lounge, entertainment, outdoor heated pool, tennis courts, children free with parents, a/c, TV, kitchenettes, beach, gift shop, airport transportation, game room, NS rooms, wheelchair access, in-room computer hookups, meeting facilities, senior rates, CC. 7 miles from Gulf beaches. LS SGL/DBL$70-$135; HS SGL/DBL$150-$250.

Park Shore Resort Hotel (600 Neapolitan Way, 33940; 262-2222, Fax 263-0946, 800-752-4544, 800-548-2077 in Florida) 103 rooms and 1- and 2-bedroom suites, restaurant, lounge, outdoor pool, whirlpools, laundry facilities, in-room refrigerators, children free with parents, local transportation, no pets, a/c, TV, NS rooms, CC. LS SGL/DBL$75-$85; HS SGL/DBL$165-$190.

Port of the Islands Resort and Marina (25000 East Tamiami Trail, 33940; 394-3103, Fax 394-4335, 800-237-4173) 185 rooms and efficiencies, restaurant, lounge, entertainment, outdoor heated pool, lighted tennis courts, exercise center, in-room coffee makers, children free with parents, no pets, NS rooms, laundry facilities, CC. SGL/DBL$75-$95.

Quality Inn Golf and Country Club (4100 Golden Gate Pkwy., 33940; 455-1010, 800-221-2222) 153 rooms and 1- and 2-bedroom suites, restaurant, lounge, outdoor pool, exercise center, whirlpools, tennis courts, no pets, kitchenettes, children free with parents, a/c, TV, wheelchair access, room service, laundry service, NS rooms, meeting facilities, senior rates, CC. 6 miles from Gulf beaches, 18 miles from the dog track, 4 miles from the Naples airport. SGL/DBL$45-$210.

Quality Inn Gulfcoast (2555 North Tamiami Trail, 33940; 261-6046, Fax 261-5742, 800-221-2222, 800-330-0046 in Florida) 113 rooms and 1- and 2-bedroom suites, restaurant, lounge, entertainment, outdoor heated pool, exercise center, tennis courts, no pets, in-room refrigerators and coffee makers, children free with parents, a/c, TV, wheelchair access, room service, laundry service, NS rooms, meeting facilities, senior rates, CC. 1 mile from Atlantic beaches, 5 miles from the Naples Theater, 2 miles from the Naples airport. LS SGL/DBL$45-$60; HS SGL/DBL$85-$100.

Registry Resort (475 Seagate Dr., 33940; 597-3232, Fax 597-3147) 474 rooms and suites, restaurant, lounge, entertainment, indoor and outdoor heated pool, whirlpools, lighted tennis courts, a/c, TV, local transportation, no pets, in-room refrigerators, gift shop, NS rooms, wheelchair access, children free with parents, beach, 38,000 square feet of meeting and exhibition space, CC. LS SGL/DBL$160-$240; HS SGL/DBL$290-$465.

The Ritz-Carlton Hotel (280 Vanderbilt Beach Rd., 33963; 598-3300, Fax 598-6690, 800-241-3333) 463 rooms and suites, restaurant, lounge, entertainment, outdoor heated pool, exercise center, sauna, whirlpools, beach, VCRs, 24-hour room service, a/c, TV, NS rooms, wheelchair access, gift shop, airport transportation, children free with parents, no pets, in-room computer hookups, 13,000 square feet of meeting and exhibition space, 19 meeting rooms, senior rates, CC. 25 miles from the Fort Myers airport. SGL/DBL$130-$490.

Stoney's Courtyard Inn (2630 North Tamiami Trail, 33940; 261-3870, Fax 261-4932, 800-432-3870) 76 rooms and 1-bedroom suites, free breakfast, outdoor heated pool, laundry facilities, pets OK, in-room refrigerators, NS rooms, a/c, TV, children free with parents, CC. SGL/DBL$75-$110.

Spinnaker Inn (6600 Dudley Dr., 33940; 434-0444, Fax 434-0414) 110 rooms and efficiencies, outdoor pool, pets OK, in-room refrigerators, a/c, TV, children free with parents, CC. SGL/DBL$35-$77.

Super 8 Motel (I-75 and Alligator Alley, 33942; 455-0808, Fax 455-7124, 800-800-8000) 104 rooms and suites, free breakfast, outdoor heated pool, children free with parents, free local calls, a/c, TV, in-room refrigerators and microwaves, fax service, NS rooms, wheelchair access, no pets, meeting facilities, senior rates, CC. SGL/DBL$40-$90.

Tides Motor Inn (1801 Gulfshore Blvd. North, 33963; 262-6196, Fax 597-6278, 800-237-6883, 800-282-4423 in Florida) 36 rooms and 1-bedroom suites, free breakfast, outdoor heated pool, beach, airport transportation, a/c, TV, NS rooms, no pets, CC. SGL/DBL$125-$130, STS$165-$185.

Trail's End Motel (309 9th St. South, 33963; 262-6336, Fax 262-3381, 800-247-5307) 49 rooms, outdoor pool, no pets, a/c, in-room refrigerators and microwaves, children free with parents, NS rooms, wheelchair access, laundry facilities, TV, CC. SGL/DBL$30.

The Tropics In Olde Naples (312 8th Ave. South, 33940; 262-5194, Fax 262-4876, 800-637-6036) 60 rooms and 1- and 2-bedroom suites, free breakfast, outdoor heated pool, laundry facilities, children free with parents, no pets, NS rooms, senior rates, CC. 2 blocks from the Cambier Tennis and Recreation Center. SGL/DBL$90-$165.

Vanderbilt Beach Motel (9225 Gulfshore Drive North, 33963; 597-3144, Fax 597-2199, 800-243-9076) 66 rooms and 1- and 2-bedroom suites, restaurant, free breakfast, heated pool, tennis courts, beach, in-room coffee makers, a/c, TV, NS rooms, kitchenettes, no pets, VCRs, in-room refrigerators, senior rates, CC. SGL/DBL$55-$125.

Vanderbilt Inn On The Gulf (11000 Gulfshore Drive North, 33963; 597-3151, Fax 597-3099, 800-643-8654 in Florida) 134 rooms and efficiencies, restaurant, lounge, entertainment, outdoor heated pool, beach, in-room refrigerators, a/c, TV, no pets, beach, children free with parents, room service, NS rooms, laundry facilities, senior rates, CC. SGL/DBL$80-$160.

Wellesley Inn at Naples (1555 5th Ave. South, 33942; 793-4646, Fax 793-4646, 800-444-8888) 105 rooms, restaurant, free breakfast, outdoor heated pool, in-room refrigerators, pets OK, a/c, TV, children free with parents, fax service, NS rooms, wheelchair access, senior rates, CC. SGL/DBL$40-$125.

World Tennis Center and Resort (4800 Airport Rd., 33942; 263-1900, Fax 649-7055, 800-292-6663) 107 rooms and 2-bedroom apartments, restaurant, lounge, outdoor heated pool, whirlpools, sauna, lighted tennis courts, a/c, wheelchair access, in-room refrigerators, TV, laundry facilities, pets OK, NS rooms, meeting rooms, senior rates, CC. SGL/DBL$75-145.

Naranja Lakes

Area Code 305

Econo Lodge (27707 South Dixie Hwy., 33032; 245-4330, 800-4-CHOICE) 140 rooms, children free with parents, no pets, senior rates, NS rooms, wheelchair access, a/c, TV, CC. SGL/DBL$30-$75.

Navarre & Navarre Beach
Area Code 904

Comfort Inn (8680 Navarre Pkwy., 32566; 939-1761, 800-221-2222) 63 rooms, outdoor pool, a/c, TV, children free with parents, in-room refrigerators and microwaves, pets OK, water view, laundry facilities, NS rooms, wheelchair access, senior rates, CC. 1 mile to Gulf beaches, 25 miles from the Naval Museum, 5 miles to Gulf-shore Island National Seashore. SGL/DBL$45-$90.

Holiday Inn (8375 Gulf Blvd., 32566; 939-2321, Fax 939-4786, 800-HOLIDAY) 254 rooms, restaurant, lounge, indoor pool, exercise center, whirlpools, beach, gift shop, children free with parents, wheelchair access, a/c, TV, NS rooms, fax service, room service, laundry service, 7 meeting rooms, senior rates, CC. A 1/2-mile from fishing pier, 5 miles from National Seashore Park. SGL/DBL$48-$88.

Neptune Beach
Area Code 904

Days Inn (1401 Atlantic Blvd., 32233; 249-3852, 800-325-2525) 133 rooms, restaurant, lounge, outdoor pool, a/c, TV, wheelchair access, NS rooms, no pets, laundry facilities, senior rates, CC. A 1/2-mile from Atlantic beaches, 7 miles from the Mayo Clinic, 5 miles from the Mayport Naval Station. SGL/DBL$35-$80.

New Port Richey
Area Code 813

Comfort Inn (6826 Hwy. 19 North, 34652; 842-6800, 800-221-2222) 66 rooms, outdoor pool, whirlpools, sauna, no pets, a/c, TV, children free with parents, NS rooms, wheelchair access, senior rates, CC. 18 miles to Gulf beaches, 30 miles to Busch Gardens. SGL/DBL$45-$70.

Econo Lodge (7631 Hwy. 19, 34652; 845-4990, 800-55-ECONO) 104 rooms, outdoor pool, children free with parents, NS rooms, no pets, laundry facilities, wheelchair access, a/c, TV, fax service, kitchenettes, senior rates, CC. 7 miles from the Tarpon Springs sponge docks, 1 mile from Gulf beaches, 30 miles from the Tampa airport. LS SGL/DBL$30-$38; HS SGL/DBL$40-$50.

Gulf Coast Inn (10826 Hwy. 10, 34652; 869-9999) 50 rooms and efficiencies, outdoor heated pool, sauna, whirlpools, a/c, TV, NS rooms, laundry facilities, wheelchair access, meeting facilities, senior rates, CC. SGL/DBL$45-$52.

Holiday Inn Bayside (5015 Hwy. 19, 34652; 849-8551, 800-HOLIDAY) 135 rooms, restaurant, lounge, entertainment, outdoor pool, children free with parents, wheelchair access, a/c, TV, NS rooms, fax service, room service, pets OK, laundry service, meeting facilities for 65, senior rates, CC. 1 block from the shopping mall, 6 miles from the sponge docks. SGL/DBL$50-$75.

Howard Johnson (6523 Hwy. 19, 34652; 848-3487, 800-I-GO-HOJO) 114 rooms and suites, restaurant, lounge, outdoor pool, children free with parents, wheelchair access, NS rooms, TV, a/c, no pets, laundry facilities, senior rates, meeting facilities, CC. 25 miles from Tampa airport and Busch Gardens. SGL/DBL$40-$70.

Sheraton Inn (5316 Hwy. 19, 34652; 847-9005, 800-325-3535) 160 rooms and suites, restaurant, lounge, entertainment, outdoor pool, whirlpools, NS rooms, a/c, room service, TV, children free with parents, wheelchair access, pets OK, 5 meeting rooms, meeting facilities for 550, 5,200 square feet of meeting and exhibition space, senior rates, CC. 33 miles from Tampa airport, 25 miles from Weeki Wachee. SGL/DBL$45-$55.

New Smyrna Beach

Area Code 904

Rental & Reservation Services

Check-In Reservation Services (7282 55th Ave. East, Bradenton 34205; 867-7760, 800-237-1033) rental condos and apartments.

Granstrom Real Estate Rentals (6941 South Atlantic Ave., 32169; 427-5953, Fax 423-8108) rental condominiums and private homes.

Ocean Properties (4168 South Atlantic Ave, 32169; 428-0513, 800-521-9657) rental condominiums.

Sentry Management Rentals (4309 Sea Mist Dr., 32169; 423-7796, Fax 423-1278, 800-826-8614) rental condominiums, villas and private homes.

□□□

Buena Vista Motel (500 North Causeway, 32169; 428-5565) 8 rooms and efficiencies, laundry facilities, a/c, TV, pets OK, in-room refrigerators and microwaves, CC. SGL/DBL$35-$60.

Castle Reef Condominiums (4175 South Atlantic Ave., 32169; 427-5252, 800-227-5581) 165 1- and 2-bedroom condominiums, outdoor pool, tennis courts, a/c, TV, children free with parents, laundry facilities, in-room refrigerators, microwaves and coffee makers, wheelchair access, CC. 1BR$450W-$550W, 2BR$550W-$700W.

Cedar Island Club Condominiums (855 Ladyfish Ave., 32169; 428-7461, 800-285-6104) 20 rooms and 2-bedroom condominiums, outdoor pool, whirlpools, in-room refrigerators, microwaves and coffee makers, a/c, TV, no pets, children free with parents, laundry facilities, CC. SGL/DBL$255W-$555W.

Coastal Waters Inn (3509 South Atlantic Ave., 32169; 428-3800, 800-321-7882) 40 rooms, efficiencies and 2-bedroom suites, restaurant, outdoor heated pool, gift shop, airport courtesy car, kitchenettes, no pets, a/c, TV, children free with parents, wheelchair access, senior rates, CC. SGL/DBL$50-$135.

Holiday Inn (1401 South Atlantic Blvd., 32169; 426-0020, Fax 423-3977, 800-HOLIDAY) 102 rooms and suites, restaurant, lounge, outdoor pool, exercise center, children free with parents, wheelchair access, a/c, TV, NS rooms, kitchenettes, game room, no pets, beach, fax service, room service, laundry service, meeting facilities, senior rates, CC. 20 miles from the Daytona International Speedway. SGL/DBL$65-$75.

Islander Beach Resort (1601 South Atlantic Ave., 32169; 428-3452, Fax 426-5605) 114 efficiencies, restaurant, lounge, outdoor heated pool, exercise center, wheelchair access, a/c, TV, NS rooms, beach, CC. SGL/DBL$60-$130.

Moontide Condominiums (4139 South Atlantic Ave., 32169; 428-5691) 114 1- , 2- , and 3-bedroom condominiums, outdoor pool, beach, tennis courts, a/c, TV, wheelchair access, in-room refrigerators and coffee makers, children free with parents, laundry facilities, no pets, CC. 1BR$90, 2BR$110, 3BR$135.

Mott's Indian River Landing (1210 South Riverside Dr., 32169; 428-2491, 800-541-4529) 42 1- and 2-room suites, restaurant, outdoor pool, a/c, TV, in-room refrigerators and microwaves, no pets, children free with parents, CC. 1BR$40-$50, 2BR$80.

Night Swan Bed and Breakfast (512 South Riverside Dr., 32168; 423-4940) 5 rooms, free breakfast, NS, no pets, a/c, CC. SGL/DBL$49-$89.

Oceania Suite Hotel (421 South Atlantic Ave., 32169; 423-8400, Fax 423-0254, 800-874-1931) 62 efficiencies, outdoor heated pool, beach, lighted tennis courts, wheelchair access, a/c, TV, NS rooms, children free with parents, laundry facilities, no pets, CC. SGL/DBL$120-$135.

Riverview Hotel (103 Flagler Ave., 32169; 428-5858, Fax 423-8927, 800-945-7416) 18 rooms and suites, restaurant, lounge, entertainment, outdoor pool, wheelchair access, NS rooms, children free with parents, laundry facilities, senior rates, CC. SGL/DBL$65-$100.

Sea Woods (4400 Sea Mist Dr., 32169; 423-7796, 800-826-8614) 1-, 2-, and 3-bedroom villas, outdoor pool, tennis courts, whirlpools, exercise center, a/c, TV, in-room refrigerators, microwaves and coffee makers, children free with parents, laundry facilities, CC. 1BR$375W-$425W, 2BR$400W-$550W, 3BR$500W-$650W.

Smyrna Motel (1050 North Dixie Freeway, 32169; 428-2495) 10 rooms, in-room refrigerators, kitchenettes, children free with parents, NS rooms, pets OK, a/c, TV, CC. SGL/DBL$25-$37.

Watermark Apartment (401 North Atlantic Ave., 32169; 428-3793) 2- and 3-bedroom apartments, outdoor pool, tennis courts, a/c, TV, wheelchair access, kitchenettes, no pets, laundry facilities, CC. 2BR$635W, 3BR$725W.

Niceville

Area Code 904

Blue Water Bay Resort (1950 Bluewater Blvd., 32578; 897-3613, Fax 897-2424, 800-874-2128) 240 rooms and suites, restaurant, outdoor pool, exercise center, whirlpools, lighted tennis courts, a/c, TV, children free with parents, no pets, in-room refrigerators, microwaves and coffee makers, room service, laundry facilities, 3 meeting rooms, senior rates, CC. SGL/DBL$75-$180.

Comfort Inn (101 Hwy. 85 North, 32578; 678-8077, 800-221-2222) 62 rooms, outdoor pool, whirlpools, no pets, a/c, TV, children free with parents, NS rooms, wheelchair access, senior rates, CC. 12 miles to Gulf beaches, 3 miles to Eglin Air Force Base, 5 miles to Blue Water Bay. SGL/DBL$50-$90.

Friendship Inn (626 John Sims Pkwy., 32578; 678-4164, 800-424-4777) 39 rooms, restaurant, lounge, entertainment, pool, exercise center, a/c, TV, NS rooms, children free with parents, wheelchair access, meeting facilities, senior rates, CC. 3 miles from the Pensacola airport, 20 miles from Gulf beaches. SGL/DBL$30-$50.

Nokomis

Area Code 813

Gulf Shore Beach Apartments (317 Casey Key Rd., 34275; 488-6210) 2-bedroom beach houses and apartments, a/c, TV, children free with parents, in-room refrigerators, microwaves and coffee makers, laundry facilities, wheelchair access, no pets. 2BR$290W-$660W.

La Casa Cay Beach Apartments (309 Casey Key Rd., 34275; 484-8009) 2-bedroom apartments, a/c, TV, children free with parents, kitchenettes, laundry facilities, pets OK, wheelchair access, CC. 2BR$299W-$580W.

Place To Be Resort (105 Casey Key Rd., 34275; 485-3424, 800-247-8257) 44 1- and 2-bedroom apartments, outdoor pool, beach, no pets, a/c, TV, children free with parents, in-room refrigerators and coffee makers, wheelchair access, senior rates, CC. 1BR$55-$95, 2BR$65-$100.

Sea Grape Motel (106 Casey Key Rd., 34275; 484-0071) 5 rooms, a/c, TV, children free with parents, NS rooms, laundry facilities, CC. LS SGL/DBL$36-$48; HS SGL/DBL$60-$77.

Wishing Well Beach To Bay (221 Casey Key Rd., 34275; 488-5011) 14 rooms and apartments, a/c, TV, no pets, CC. LS SGL/DBL$33-$55; HS SGL/DBL$44-$85.

North Palm Beach

Area Code 407

Comfort Inn (11320 Hwy. 1, 33408; 624-7186, 800-221-2222) 88 rooms, outdoor pool, exercise center, sauna, a/c, TV, children free with parents, NS rooms, wheelchair access, senior rates, CC. 15 miles from the Palm Beach airport, 3 miles from Palm Beach Junior College, 2 miles from MacArthur State Beach, 5 miles to Atlantic beaches. SGL/DBL$45-$110.

Econo Lodge North (757 Hwy. 1 North, 33408; 848-1424, 800-446-6900, 800-4-CHOICE) 109 rooms and efficiencies, outdoor pool, exercise center, sauna, whirlpools, children free with parents, no pets, laundry facilities, NS rooms, wheelchair access, a/c, TV, senior rates, CC. 15 miles from the West Palm Beach airport, 3 miles from Atlantic beaches. SGL/DBL$40-$78.

Ocala

Area Code 904

Budget Host Western Motel (4013 Northwest Blitchton Rd., 34475; 732-6940, 800-626-7064) 21 rooms, laundry facilities, NS rooms, wheelchair access, a/c, TV, children free with parents, pets OK, in-room refrigerators, senior rates, CC. SGL/DBL$45-$50.

Budgetel Ocala Princess (3701 Southwest 38th Ave., 34475; 237-4848, Fax 237-2281, 800-428-3438) 140 rooms and suites, restaurant, free breakfast, children free with parents, a/c, wheelchair access, NS rooms, free local calls, in-room computer hookups, fax service, VCRs, TV, meeting facilities, CC. 1 mile from the Paddock Shopping Mall, 3 miles from Silver Springs Theme Park. SGL/DBL$51-$62.

Comfort Inn (4040 West Silver Springs Blvd., 34482, 629-8850, 800-221-2222) 50 rooms, restaurant, outdoor pool, a/c, TV, children free with parents, NS rooms, wheelchair access, senior rates, CC. 35 miles from the Gainesville airport, 8 miles from Wild Waters and the Don Garlits Museum. SGL/DBL$30-$60.

Days Inn (3811 Northwest Blitchton Rd., 32675; 629-7041, Fax 629-0126, 800-329-7466) 64 rooms, restaurant, lounge, outdoor pool, children free with parents, wheelchair access, NS rooms, TV, a/c, laundry facilities, pets OK, senior rates, meeting facilities, CC. 3 miles from the downtown area, 5 miles from the regional airport. SGL/DBL$42-$75.

Friendship Inn (723 West Pine Ave. 34474; 622-1266, 800-424-4777) 20 rooms, outdoor pool, a/c, TV, NS rooms, children free with parents, wheelchair access, senior rates, CC. 3 miles from the regional airport, 10 miles from Ocala National Forest, 1 mile from the hospital. SGL/DBL$22-$48.

Friendship Inn (2829 Northeast Silver Springs Rd., 34470; 622-7503, 800-424-4777) 26 rooms, outdoor pool, no pets, a/c, TV, NS rooms, children free with parents, wheelchair access, senior rates, CC. 5 miles from the regional airport, 10 miles from Ocala National Forest, 1 block from the golf course. SGL/DBL$22-$42.

Hampton Inn (3434 Southwest College Rd., 34474; 854-3200, Fax 854-5633, 800-HAMPTON) 152 rooms and suites, restaurant, free breakfast, outdoor pool, exercise center, children free with parents, NS rooms, wheelchair access, in-room computer hookups, fax service, pets OK, in-room refrigerators, TV, a/c, free local calls, meeting facilities, senior rates, CC. SGL/DBL$65-$85, STS$85-$135.

Hilton Hotel (3600 Southwest 36th Ave., 34474; 854-1400, Fax 854-4010, 800-922-3756, 800-HILTONS, 800-843-3756 in Florida) 200 rooms and suites, restaurant, lounge, entertainment, outdoor heated pool, whirlpools, hot tubs, lighted tennis courts, exercise center, in-room refrigerators, children free with parents, NS rooms, wheelchair access, local transportation, room service, laundry facilities, a/c, TV, 9 meeting rooms, senior rates, CC. SGL/DBL$80-$120.

Holiday Inn (3621 West Silver Springs Blvd., 34478; 629-0381, 800-HOLIDAY) 276 rooms and suites, restaurant, lounge, entertainment, outdoor heated pool, children free with parents, wheelchair access, a/c, TV, NS rooms, fax service, pets OK, room service, laundry service, 5 meeting rooms, meeting facilities for 300, senior rates, CC. 2 miles from the regional airport and the Ocala Breeders Sales Pavilion, 8 miles from Silver Springs. SGL/DBL$40-$45.

Howard Johnson Park Square Inn (3712 Southwest 38th Ave., 34474; 237-8000, Fax 237-0580, 800-I-GO-HOJO) 179 rooms, rooms, restaurant, lounge, outdoor heated pool, spa, children free with parents, wheelchair access, NS rooms, TV, a/c, in-room refrigerators, pets OK, laundry facilities, senior rates, meeting facilities, CC. 2 miles from the Ocala airport, 4 miles from the downtown. SGL/DBL$40-$70.

Quality Inn (3767 Northwest Blitchton Rd., 32675; 732-2300, Fax 351-0153, 800-221-2222) 119 rooms and suites, restaurant, lounge, entertainment, outdoor pool, exercise center, children free with parents, a/c, TV, VCRs, wheelchair access, no pets, room service, laundry service, NS rooms, meeting facilities, senior rates, CC. 2 miles from the shopping center. LS SGL/DBL$30-$40; HS SGL/DBL$35-$50.

Ramada Steinbrenner's Yankee Inn (3810 Northwest Blitchton Rd., 34482; 732-3131, Fax 732-5692, 800-2-RAMADA) 133 rooms and suites, restaurant, lounge, entertainment, outdoor pool, whirlpools, jacuzzi, gift shop, wheelchair access, NS rooms, free parking, a/c, TV, children free with parents, room service, laundry facilities, airport transportation, in-room refrigerators, 6 meeting rooms, meeting facilities for 650, senior rates, CC. 20 miles from the Jai Alai fronton, 8 miles from Wild Waters Theme Park. SGL/DBL$40-$85.

Red Carpet Inn (4020 Northwest Blitchton Rd., 34482; 732-2510, 800-251-1962) 140 rooms, pets OK, children free with parents, TV, a/c, NS rooms, meeting facilities, senior rates, CC. SGL/DBL$22-$30.

Scottish Inns (3520 West Silver Springs Blvd., 34470; 629-7961, 800-251-1962) 55 rooms, outdoor pool, pets OK, in-room refrigerators, a/c, TV, wheelchair access, NS rooms, children free with parents, free local calls, senior rates, CC. 8 miles from Silver Springs and Wild Waters. SGL/DBL$22-$26.

Seven Sisters Inn (820 Southeast Fort King St., 34471; 867-1170) 5 rooms and suites, free breakfast, no pets, a/c, TV, children over 12 welcome, NS, wheelchair access, CC. SGL/DBL$75-$105.

Sleep Inn (I-75 and Hwy. 200, 32675; 800-221-2222) 120 rooms, free breakfast, outdoor pool, wheelchair access, NS rooms, children free with parents, no pets, a/c, TV, meeting facilities, senior rates, CC. 4 miles from the downtown area. SGL/DBL$30-$60.

Southland Motel (1260 East Silver Springs Blvd., 32671; 351-0113) 12 rooms, outdoor pool, a/c, TV, children free with parents, no pets, CC. SGL$19-$25.

TraveLodge South (1626 Southwest Pine Ave., 32671; 622-4121, 800-578-7878) 68 rooms, free breakfast, outdoor pool, wheelchair access, complimentary newspaper, laundry service, TV, a/c, free local calls, fax service, NS rooms, in-room refrigerators and microwaves, children free with parents, meeting facilities, senior rates, CC. 5 miles from the Ocala airport and Silver Springs. SGL/DBL$32-$44.

Ocoee

Area Code 407

Colony Plaza Hotel (2600 West Hwy. 50, 34761; 656-3333, Fax 656-2232, 800-821-0136) 300 rooms, restaurant, lounge, entertainment, outdoor pool, tennis courts, a/c, TV, NS rooms, wheelchair access, gift shop, local transportation, children free with parents, laundry facilities, no pets, senior rates, CC. LS DBL$65; HS SGL/DBL$65-$80.

Holiday Inn West (10945 West Colonial Dr., 34761; 656-5050, 800-465-4329, 800-HOLIDAY) 169 rooms, restaurant, lounge, outdoor pool, exercise center, children free with parents, wheelchair access, a/c, TV, no pets, NS rooms, fax service, room service, laundry service, meeting facilities for 60, senior rates, CC. 8 miles from the factory outlet mall, 1 mile from the Florida Auto Auction. SGL/DBL$44-$55.

Okeechobee

Area Code 813

Days Inn (2200 Southeast Hwy. 441, 34974; 763-8003, Fax 467-2738, 800-329-7466) 88 rooms and efficiencies, outdoor pool, a/c, TV, pets OK, laundry facilities, children free with parents, NS rooms, in-room refrigerators and coffee makers, no pets, senior rates, meeting facilities, CC. 1 block from the Lake Okeechobee Canal. SGL/DBL$40-$45.

Ohio Motel (507 North Parrott Ave., 34972; 763-1148) 24 rooms, a/c, TV, in-room refrigerators, no pets, senior rates, CC. SGL/DBL$28-$54.

Orange City
Area Code 904

Comfort Inn (445 South Volusia Ave., 32763; 775-7444, 800-221-2222) 60 rooms, a/c, TV, children free with parents, NS rooms, wheelchair access, senior rates, CC. 25 miles from the Daytona airport, 1.5 miles from Blue Springs Park, 8 miles from Stetson University. LS SGL/DBL$32-$64; HS SGL/DBL$32-$130.

Days Inn (2501 North Volusia Ave., 32763; 775-4522, 800-325-2525) 37 rooms and 2-bedroom efficiencies, outdoor pool, kitchenettes, children free with parents, a/c, TV, wheelchair access, NS rooms, no pets, laundry facilities, senior rates, CC. 3 miles from Blue Springs State Park, 5 miles from Stetson University. SGL/DBL$38-$70.

Orange Park
Area Code 904

Best Western Inn (300 Park Ave. North, 32073; 264-1211, Fax 269-6756, 800-528-1234) 200 rooms and suites, restaurant, lounge, entertainment, outdoor pool, exercise center, children free with parents, a/c, TV, NS rooms, laundry facilities, wheelchair access, pets OK, 4 meeting rooms, senior rates, CC. 2 miles from shopping mall, 3 miles from Jacksonville Naval Air Station. SGL/DBL$50-$70.

Club Continental (Orange Park 32073; 264-6070, Fax 264-4044) 22 rooms and suites, restaurant, free breakfast, pool, tennis courts, kitchenettes, a/c, TV, NS rooms, no pets, CC. SGL/DBL$55-$100, STS$135.

Comfort Inn (341 Park Ave., 32073; 264-3297, 800-221-2222) 120 rooms, restaurant, lounge, entertainment, outdoor pool, a/c, TV, children free with parents, NS rooms, wheelchair access, senior rates, CC. 15 miles from the Jacksonville airport, 1 mile from the dog track, 20 miles from the Gator Bowl. SGL/DBL$30-$50.

Days Inn (4280 Eldridge Ave., 32073; 269-8887, 800-325-2525) 62 rooms, restaurant, free breakfast, a/c, TV, wheelchair access, NS rooms, pets OK, children free with parents, laundry facilities, senior rates, CC. 2 blocks from the Orange Park Kennel Club and shopping mall, 15 miles from Jackson Landing and the Gator Bowl. SGL/DBL$30-$55.

Econo Lodge (141 Park Ave., 32073; 264-5107, 800-4-CHOICE) 107 rooms, restaurant, outdoor pool, children free with parents, no pets, NS rooms, laundry facilities, fax, wheelchair access, a/c, TV, senior rates, CC. 25 miles from the Jackson airport, 1 mile from the shopping mall and Jacksonville Naval Air Station. SGL/DBL$30-$75.

Holiday Inn (150 Park Ave., 32073; 264-9513, 800-HOLIDAY) 302 rooms, restaurant, lounge, outdoor pool, exercise center, gift shop, children free with parents, wheelchair access, a/c, TV, NS rooms, fax service, room service, laundry service, 4 meeting rooms, meeting facilities for 300, senior rates, CC. 2 miles from the Naval Air Station, 35 miles from the Jacksonville airport, 35 miles from Atlantic beaches, SGL/DBL$58-$65.

Orlando

Area Code 407

Rental & Reservation Services

Best Beach Rentals and Sales (20045 Gulf Blvd., Indian Rocks Beach, 34635; 595-5700, Fax 593-1095, 800-523-2882) rental condominiums, villas and private homes.

Century 21 Rentals; A Paradise, Inc. (3018 Ave. C, Holmes Beach 34217; 778-4800, 800-237-2252) rental condos and apartments.

Check-In Reservation Services (7282 55th Ave. East, Bradenton 34205; 867-7760, 800-237-1033) rental condos and apartments.

Concord Resorts (5728 Major Blvd., 32819; 363-7670, Fax 363-9128 and 800-866-9128, 800-999-6896) rental condominiums and homes.

Condo Rentals of Daytona (Daytona Beach, 32116; 255-2233, 800-447-3685).

Great Miami Reservation Systems (12555 Biscayne Blvd., 33180; 800-821-2183) hotel and condominium reservations.

❑❑❑

Bed and Breakfast of Orlando (532 Pinar Dr., 32825; 277-4903) 9 rooms, free breakfast, NS, no pets, a/c, TV, CC. SGL$39, DBL$50.

Best Western Plaza International (8738 International Dr., 32819; 345-8195, Fax 352-8196, 800-654-7160, 800-528-1234) 669 rooms and 1-bedroom suites, restaurant, lounge, outdoor heated pool, whirlpools, children free with parents, airport transportation, gift shop, game room, a/c, NS rooms, TV, laundry facilities, wheelchair access, pets OK, meeting facilities, senior rates, CC. 8 miles from Walt Disney World and Sea World, 3 miles from Universal Studios. SGL/DBL$60-$80, STS$100-$105.

Best Western Inn (2014 West Colonial Dr., 32804; 841-8600, 800-528-1234) 111 rooms, restaurant, lounge, outdoor pool, children free with parents, a/c, NS rooms, TV, laundry facilities, wheelchair access, pets OK, meeting facilities, senior rates, CC. 2 miles from the Fairground, 18 miles from Walt Disney World, 5 miles from the Naval Training Center. SGL/DBL$40-$100.

Budgetel Inn (2051 Consulate Dr., 32821; 240-0500, Fax 428-3438, 800-428-3438) 120 rooms, restaurant, free breakfast, children free with parents, a/c, wheelchair access, NS rooms, free local calls, in-room refrigerators and microwaves, fax service, VCRs, TV, meeting facilities, CC. 6 miles from the Orlando airport and the Orange County Convention Center, 1 mile from the Florida Mall, 8 miles from Sea World. SGL/DBL$45-$53.

Clarion Plaza Hotel (9700 International Dr., 32819; 352-9100, Fax 351-9111, 800-366-9700, 800-CLARION) 810 rooms, restaurant, lounge, entertainment, free breakfast, outdoor pool, whirlpools, local transportation, in-room refrigerators, airport transportation, no pets, gift shop, game room, NS rooms, children free with parents, senior rates, 22 meeting rooms, 26,000 square feet of meeting and exhibition space, a/c, TV, CC. 12 miles from the Orlando airport, 8 miles from Walt Disney World, 2 miles from Sea World and Universal Studios, 1 block from the Convention Center. SGL/DBL$80-$100.

Colonial Plaza Inn (2801 East Colonial Dr., 32803; 2741, Fax 896-9858, 800-321-2323) 225 rooms and suites, restaurant, outdoor heated pool, whirlpools, laundry facilities, a/c, TV, children free with parents, no pets, senior rates, CC. SGL/DBL$51, STS$65-$99.

Comfort Inn (8421 South Orange Blossom Trail, 32809; 855-6060, Fax 859-5132, 800-221-2222) 204 rooms, restaurant, lounge, outdoor pool, a/c, TV, VCRs, children free with parents, NS rooms, wheelchair access, in-room refrigerators, no pets, kitchenettes, local transportation, senior rates, CC. 1 block from the shopping mall. SGL/DBL$40-$100.

Comfort Inn International (5825 International Dr., 32819; 351-4100, Fax 352-2991, 800-327-1366, 800-221-2222) 161 rooms, restaurant, lounge, entertainment, outdoor pool, a/c, TV, children free with parents, NS rooms, no pets, local transportation, in-room refrigerators, wheelchair access, senior rates, CC. 9 miles from Walt Disney World, 10 miles from the Orlando airport. SGL/DBL$40-$100.

Comfort Inn West (3956 West Colonial Dr., 291-1452, 800-221-2222) 80 rooms and suites, outdoor pool, a/c, TV, children free with parents, free local calls, no pets, NS rooms, wheelchair access, senior rates, CC. 3 miles from the downtown area, 18 miles from Walt Disney World and the Orlando airport. SGL/DBL$35-$250.

Comfort Suites (9350 Turkey Lake Rd., 32819; 351-5050, 800-221-2222) 214 rooms, restaurant, free breakfast, free breakfast, lounge, outdoor pool, whirlpools, sauna, no pets, in-room refrigerators and microwaves, game room, a/c, TV, children free with parents, NS rooms, wheelchair access, senior rates, CC. 5 miles from Walt Disney World, 2 miles from Sea World, Universal Studios and the Convention Center. SGL/DBL$60-$120.

Comfort Inn (830 Lee Rd., 32810; 629-4000, 800-221-2222) 145 rooms, outdoor pool, exercise center, no pets, a/c, TV, children free with parents, NS rooms, wheelchair access, senior rates, CC. 18 miles from the Orlando airport, 3 miles from the Citrus Bowl and Rollins College. SGL/DBL$55-$90.

Condo Lodge Vacation Villas (97611 South Orange Blossom Trail, 32809; 800-866-2660) 2-bedroom/2-bath villas, outdoor pool, tennis courts, whirlpools, in-room refrigerators, microwaves and coffee makers, complimentary newspaper, a/c, TV, children free with parents, laundry facilities, no pets, CC. 2BR$89, 3BR$109.

Courtyard by Marriott (8600 Austrian Ct., 32819; 351-2244, Fax 351-3306, 800-331-3131) 151 rooms and suites, free breakfast, outdoor heated pool, in-room refrigerators, microwaves and coffee makers, VCRs, no pets, in-room computer hookups, local transportation, in-room refrigerators, complimentary newspaper, children free with parents, kitchenettes, a/c, TV, NS rooms, wheelchair access, meeting facilities, senior rates, CC. SGL/DBL$70-$86.

Courtyard by Marriott Airport (7155 North Frontage Rd., 32812; 240-7200, Fax 240-8962, 800-331-3131) 149 rooms and suites, free breakfast, outdoor pool, in-room refrigerators, microwaves and coffee makers, VCRs, no pets, complimentary newspaper, children free with parents, kitchenettes, a/c, TV, NS rooms, wheelchair access, meeting facilities, senior rates, CC. SGL/DBL$50-$110.

The Courtyard at Lake Lucerne (211 North Lucerne Circle East, 32801; 648-5188, 800-331-3131) 22 rooms and suites, free breakfast, antique furnishings, a/c, TV, NS rooms, local transportation, kitchenettes, senior rates, CC. SGL/DBL$65-$150.

Davis Park Motel (221 East Colonial Dr., 32801; 425-9065, Fax 423-7647, 800-468-3550) 75 rooms and apartments, restaurant, outdoor pool, a/c, TV, laundry facilities, NS rooms, pets OK, kitchenettes, children free with parents, senior rates, CC. SGL/DBL$40-$49.

Days Inn (12490 Apopka-Vineland Rd., 32836; 249-4646, Fax 239-8469, 800-325-2525) 145 rooms, restaurant, lounge, outdoor pool, pets OK, a/c, TV, wheelchair access, NS rooms, game room, gift shop, laundry facilities, senior rates, meeting facilities, CC. 12 miles from the Orlando airport. SGL/DBL$60-$135.

Days Inn (7335 Sandlake Rd., 32819; 351-1900, Fax 352-2690, 800-325-2525) 685 rooms and suites, restaurant, lounge, indoor and outdoor pool, beach, gift shop, game room, a/c, TV, wheelchair access, NS rooms, no pets, laundry facilities, children free with parents, laundry facilities, senior rates, CC. 3 miles from Sea World, 2 miles from the Convention Center, 7 miles from Walt Disney World. SGL/DBL$45-$80.

Days Inn (7200 International Dr., 32819; 351-1200, 800-325-2525) 243 rooms, free breakfast, outdoor heated pool, local transportation, pets OK, a/c, TV, wheelchair access, NS rooms, laundry facilities, children free with parents, local transportation, game room, senior rates, CC. 2 miles from Universal Studios, 3 miles from Sea World, 7 miles from Walt Disney World, 2 miles from the shopping center. SGL/DBL$50-$81.

Days Inn (1851 West Landstreet Rd., 32809; 859-7700, Fax 851-6266, 800-325-2525) 422 rooms, efficiencies and suites, restaurant, outdoor heated pool, a/c, TV, wheelchair access, NS rooms, laundry facilities, children free with parents, local transportation, gift shop, in-room refrigerators, kitchenettes, pets OK, senior rates, CC. 5 miles from the Orlando airport and Convention Center, 10 miles from Walt Disney World. SGL/DBL$35-$80; HS SGL/DBL$100-$180.

Days Inn (9990 International Dr., 32819; 352-8700, 800-325-2525) 221 rooms, restaurant, free breakfast, outdoor pool, a/c, TV, wheelchair access, NS rooms, children free with parents, local transportation, no pets, laundry facilities, senior rates, CC. A 1/4-mile from Sea World, 11 miles from the Orlando airport, 2 blocks from the Convention Center. SGL/DBL$65-$80.

Days Inn (4919 Colonial Dr., 32808; 299-8180, Fax 299-2857, 800-325-2525) 214 rooms, restaurant, lounge, free breakfast, outdoor pool, car rental desk, children free with parents, local transportation, a/c, TV, wheelchair access, NS rooms, no pets, laundry facilities, senior rates, CC. 15 miles from Walt Disney World and the downtown area, 8 miles from Sea World, 1 block from the Central Florida Fairgrounds. SGL/DBL$30-$110.

Days Inn (11639 East Colonial Dr., 32817; 282-2777, 800-325-2525) 100 rooms, efficiencies and suites, free breakfast, outdoor pool, children free with parents, a/c, TV, wheelchair access, kitchenettes, NS rooms, no pets, laundry facilities, senior rates, CC. 10 miles from the downtown area, 30 miles from Walt Disney World, 15 miles from the Orlando airport. SGL/DBL$40-$60.

Days Inn (4049 South Orange Blossom Trail, 32809; 843-1350, Fax 649-1949, 800-325-2525) 180 rooms and suites, outdoor pool, a/c, TV, wheelchair access, NS rooms, no pets, laundry facilities, senior rates, CC. SGL/DBL$25-$150.

Days Inn (2500 West 33rd, 32809; 841-3731, 800-325-2525) 200 rooms, restaurant, outdoor pool, a/c, TV, wheelchair access, children free with parents, NS rooms, pets OK, laundry facilities, senior rates, CC. 10 miles from Walt Disney World, 1 mile from the Citrus Bowl, 2 miles from the downtown area, 6 miles from Sea World. SGL/DBL$30-$75.

Days Inn (5827 Caravan Ct. 32819; 351-3800, Fax 363-0907, 800-325-2525) 262 rooms, efficiencies and suites, restaurant, lounge, free breakfast, outdoor pool, whirlpools, local transportation, gift shop, in-room refrigerators, no pets, a/c, TV, wheelchair access, NS rooms, laundry facilities, children free with parents, senior rates, CC. 2 miles from the Convention Center, 5 miles from the Citrus Bowl. LS SGL/DBL$40-$80; HS SGL/DBL$90-$130.

Days Inn (2323 McCoy Rd., 32809; 859-6100, 800-325-2525) 720 rooms, restaurant, outdoor pool, gift shop, pets OK, a/c, TV, wheelchair access, NS rooms, laundry facilities, senior rates, CC. SGL/DBL$30-$80.

Days Inn Lake Buena Vista Village (12799 Apopka-Vineland Rd., 32819; 239-4441, Fax 239-0325, 800-325-2525) 203 rooms, restaurant, lounge, outdoor pool, a/c, TV, VCRs, local transportation, wheelchair access, NS rooms, no pets, laundry facilities, senior rates, CC. 3.5 miles from Walt Disney World, 12 miles from the Orlando airport. SGL/DBL$60-$90.

Delta Orlando Resort (5715 Major Blvd., 32819; 351-3340, Fax 351-5117) 800 rooms and suites, restaurant, lounge, entertainment, indoor and outdoor heated pools, sauna, whirlpools, lighted tennis courts, sauna, a/c, TV, NS rooms, gift shop, in-room coffee makers, laundry facilities, pets OK, children free with parents, room service, senior rates, 14 meeting rooms, meeting facilities for 1,100, CC. 15 miles from the Orlando airport, 10 miles from the Expo Center, 1 block from Universal Studios. SGL/DBL$120-$150.

Economy Inns of America (8222 Jamaican Ct., 32819; 345-1172, 800-826-0778) 121 rooms, free breakfast, outdoor heated pool, free local calls, wheelchair access, a/c, children free with parents, TV, NS rooms, senior rates, CC. 4 blocks from the Mercado Shopping Mall. SGL/DBL$40-$60.

Econo Lodge (11731 East Colonial Dr., 32817; 273-1500, 800-4-CHOICE) 111 rooms, outdoor pool, children free with parents, no pets, laundry facilities, NS rooms, wheelchair access, a/c, TV, senior rates, meeting facilities, CC. SGL/DBL$30-$68.

Econo Lodge (5870 South Orange Blossom Trail, 32809; 859-5410, 800-55-ECONO) 48 rooms, outdoor pool, children free with parents, no pets, NS rooms, wheelchair access, a/c, TV, senior rates, CC. 10 miles from Sea World, 7 miles from the Orlando airport, 12 miles from Walt Disney World. SGL/DBL$28-$55.

Econo Lodge (9401 South Orange Blossom Trail, 32821; 851-1050, 800-55-ECONO) 48 rooms, outdoor pool, children free with parents, no pets, laundry facilities, NS rooms, wheelchair access, a/c, TV, senior rates, CC. 12 miles from Walt Disney World, 5 miles from the Orlando airport, 8 miles from Universal Studios. SGL/DBL$28-$66.

Econo Lodge Orlando Central (3300 West Colonial Dr., 32808; 293-7221, Fax 293-1166, 800-55-ECONO, 800-723-2666) 103 rooms, restaurant, lounge, outdoor pool, children free with parents, no pets, laundry facilities, local transportation, NS rooms, wheelchair access, a/c, TV, senior rates, meeting facilities, CC. 2 miles from the downtown area and Church Street Station. SGL/DBL$45-$65.

Embassy Suites Plaza International (8250 Jamaican Ct., 32819; 345-8250, Fax 352-1463, 800-327-9797) 246 2-room suites, indoor and outdoor heated pools, whirlpool, exercise center, sauna, room service, laundry service, in-room refrigerators, microwaves and coffee makers, wheelchair access, game room, gift shop, complimentary newspaper, no pets, free local calls, NS rooms, in-room computer hookups, local transportation, meeting facilities, CC. 10 miles from the Orlando airport, 8 miles from Walt Disney World, 1 mile from the Orange County Convention Center. SGL/DBL$125-$155.

Embassy Suites (8978 International Dr., 32819; 352-1400, Fax 363-1120, 800-EMBASSY) 245 2-room suites, indoor and outdoor heated pools, whirlpool, exercise center, sauna, room service, laundry service, wheelchair access, complimentary newspaper, free local calls, NS rooms, in-room refrigerators, microwaves and coffee makers, no pets, local transportation, 5,000 square feet of meeting and exhibition space, senior rates, CC. 8 miles from the Orlando airport and Walt Disney World, 2 miles from Sea World, 5 miles from the Florida Mall. SGL/DBL$130-$180.

Embassy Suites Resort (8100 Lake Ave., 32836; 239-1144) 280 suites, restaurant, lounge, free breakfast, lounge, heated pool, whirlpool, exercise center, sauna, room service, laundry service, wheelchair access, gift shop, airport transportation, in-room refrigerators, complimentary newspaper, free local calls, NS rooms, gift shop, local transportation, meeting facilities, CC. 1 mile from Walt Disney World, 7 miles from the Universal Studios, 12 miles from the Orlando airport. SGL/DBL$65-$105.

Enclave Suites at Orlando (6165 Carrier Dr., 32819; 351-1155, Fax 351-2001, 800-457-0077 in Florida) 321 suites, restaurant, lounge, free breakfast, outdoor pool, lighted tennis courts, exercise center, whirlpools, sauna, game room, laundry facilities, local transportation, children free with parents, a/c, TV, wheelchair access, senior rates, CC. SGL/DBL$100-$160.

Fairfield Inn by Marriott (8342 Jamaican Ct., 32819; 363-1944, 800-228-2800) 135 rooms, free breakfast, outdoor heated, outdoor pool, children free with parents, NS rooms, game room, free cable TV, free local calls, laundry service, a/c, wheelchair access, fax service, senior rates, CC. 8 miles from Walt Disney World, 2 miles from Sea World, 1 mile from the Orange County Convention Center, 10 miles from the Orlando airport. SGL/DBL$45-$70.

Fairfield Inn by Marriott (1850 Landstreet Rd., 32809; 240-8400, 800-228-2800) 132 rooms, outdoor pool, children free with parents, NS rooms, in-room computer hookups, free cable TV, free local calls, laundry service, a/c, wheelchair access, fax service, meeting facilities, senior rates, CC. 10 miles from Walt Disney World, 5 miles from the Orlando airport, a 1/2-mile from the Orlando Mall. SGL/DBL$37-$58.

Floridian of Orlando (7299 Republic Dr., 32819; 351-5009, Fax 363-7807, 800-445-7299, 800-237-0730 in Florida) 296 rooms, restaurant, lounge, outdoor heated pool, laundry facilities, gift shop, airport transportation, a/c, TV, NS rooms, wheelchair access, children free with parents, 4 meeting rooms, senior rates, CC. SGL/DBL$69-$99.

Gateway Inn (7050 Kirkman Rd., 32819; 352-2000, Fax 363-1835, 800-327-3808, 800-432-1179 in Florida) 354 rooms and suites, restaurant, lounge, entertainment, outdoor heated pool, a/c, TV, NS rooms, in-room refrigerators, room service, local transportation, game room, children free with parents, wheelchair access, pets OK, meeting facilities, senior rates, CC. LS SGL/DBL$52-$68; HS SGL/DBL$80-$95.

Guest Quarters Suite Hotel at Orlando (International Airport, 32882; 240-5555, Fax 240-1300, 800-424-2900) 150 1- and 2-room suites, restaurant, lounge, outdoor pool, exercise center, whirlpools, TV, a/c, in-room refrigerators and microwaves, no pets, local transportation, laundry service, fax service, NS rooms, wheelchair access, meeting facilities for 100, CC. SGL/DBL$80-$100.

Hampton Inn (5621 Windhover Dr., 32819; 351-6716, Fax 363-1711, 800-HAMPTON) 120 rooms, restaurant, free breakfast, outdoor pool, children free with parents, NS rooms, wheelchair access, in-room computer hookups, fax service, TV, a/c, free local calls, meeting facilities, senior rates, CC. SGL/DBL$45-$80.

Hampton Inn (7110 South Kirkman Rd., 32819; 345-1112, Fax 345-1112, 800-763-1100, 800-426-7866) 170 rooms, restaurant, free breakfast, outdoor heated pool, exercise center, children free with parents, NS rooms, wheelchair access, in-room computer hookups, fax service, TV, a/c, free local calls, gift shop, in-room refrigerators and microwaves, no pets, meeting facilities, senior rates, CC. SGL/DBL$55-$85.

Harley Hotel (151 East Washington St., 32801; 841-3220, Fax 841-3220, 800-321-2323) 281 rooms and suites, restaurant, lounge, entertainment, outdoor heated pool, exercise center, a/c, TV, in-room refrigerators, NS rooms, local transportation, children free with parents, in-room refrigerators, no pets, senior rates, CC. SGL/DBL$55-$85.

Hawthorne Suites Hotel (6435 Westwood Blvd., 32821; 351-6000, Fax 351-1977, 800-527-1133) 150 1- and 2-bedroom apartments, free breakfast, outdoor heated pool, exercise center, whirlpools, kitchenettes, laundry facilities, game room, airport transportation, in-room refrigerators, a/c, TV, children free with parents, no pets, senior rates, CC. 12 miles from the Orlando airport, 4 miles from Walt Disney World, a 1/2-mile from Sea World, 1 mile from the Convention Center. SGL/DBL$115-$185.

Heritage Inn (9861 International Dr., 32819; 352-0008, Fax 352-5449, 800-447-1890) 150 rooms, restaurant, lounge, entertainment, outdoor heated pool, laundry facilities, local transportation, a/c, TV, in-room refrigerators and coffee makers, children free with parents, no pets, NS rooms, senior rates, CC. SGL/DBL$60-$110.

Hilton at Walt Disney World Village (1751 Hotel Plaza Blvd., 32817; 827-4000, 800-HILTONS) 813 rooms and suites, restaurant, lounge, entertainment, outdoor heated pool, exercise center, lighted tennis courts, spa, local transportation, children free with parents, NS rooms, wheelchair access, room service, laundry facilities, a/c, TV, meeting facilities, senior rates, CC. 18 miles from the Orlando airport, 7 miles from the Orange County Civic Center. SGL/DBL$125-$250.

Holiday Inn (3330 West Colonial Dr., 32808; 299-6710, Fax 578-2023, 800-HOLIDAY) 128 rooms, restaurant, free breakfast, lounge, outdoor pool, exercise center, children free with parents, wheelchair access, a/c, TV, NS rooms, free local calls, kitchenettes, fax service, room service, laundry service, meeting facilities for 75, senior rates, CC. 7 miles from Universal Studios, 5 miles from Church Street Station, 20 miles from Walt Disney World. SGL/DBL$85-$135.

Holiday Inn (8750 East Colonial Dr., 32817; 282-3900, 282-0416, 800-HOLIDAY) 118 rooms, restaurant, free breakfast, lounge, outdoor pool, exercise center, children free with parents, wheelchair access, a/c, TV, NS rooms, in-room refrigerators and microwaves, no pets, free local calls, fax service, room service, laundry service, meeting facilities for 25, senior rates, CC. 6 miles from the University of Central Florida, 5 miles from the golf course, 9 miles from the Orlando airport. SGL/DBL$125-$275.

Holiday Inn (626 Lee Rd., 32810; 645-5600, Fax 740-7912, 800-HOLIDAY) 201 rooms, restaurant, lounge, entertainment, outdoor pool, exercise center, game room, local transportation, Modified American Plan available, children free with parents, wheelchair access, a/c, TV, NS rooms, fax service, room service, laundry service, no pets, 4 meeting rooms, meeting facilities for 200, senior rates, CC. 2 miles from Maitland Center, 3 miles from Rollins College, 5 miles from the Church Street Station. SGL/DBL$70-$90.

Holiday Inn (304 West Colonial Dr., 32801; 843-8700, 800-523-3405, 800-HOLIDAY) 276 rooms, restaurant, lounge, outdoor pool, exercise center, gift shop, room service, children free with parents, wheelchair access, NS rooms, TV, a/c, laundry facilities, senior rates, meeting facilities for 500, 6,400 square feet of meeting and exhibition space, CC. A 1/2-mile from Church Street Station, 7 miles from University Studios, 2 blocks from the Expo Center. SGL/DBL$40-$105.

Holiday Inn (5905 South Kirkman Rd., 32819; 351-3333, 800-HOLIDAY) 256 rooms, restaurant, lounge, outdoor pool, exercise center, children free with parents, wheelchair access, a/c, TV, game room, gift shop, NS rooms, no pets, in-room refrigerators and coffee makers, local transportation, VCRs, fax service, room service, laundry service, 13,000 square feet of meeting and exhibition space, senior rates, CC. At Universal City, 6 miles from Sea World, 5 miles from the Convention Center. SGL/DBL$80-$120.

Holiday Inn (6323 International Dr., 32819; 351-4430, Fax 345-0742, 800-HOLIDAY) 217 rooms and suites, indoor and outdoor heated pool, children free with parents, wheelchair access, a/c, TV, NS rooms, fax service, local transportation, free local calls, room service, game room, in-room refrigerators and microwaves, no pets, laundry service, meeting facilities, senior rates, CC. 8 miles from Walt Disney World and MGM Studios, 1.5 miles from the outlet mall, 8 miles from the Citrus Bowl. SGL/DBL$40-$70.

Holiday Inn (6515 International Dr., 32819; 351-3500, Fax 351-5727, 800-HOLIDAY) 650 rooms, restaurant, lounge, entertainment, outdoor heated pool, exercise center, whirlpools, in-room refrigerators and coffee makers, local transportation, children free with parents, wheelchair access, a/c, TV, NS rooms, fax service, no pets, room service, laundry service, meeting facilities, senior rates, CC. 5 miles from Sea World, 8 miles from Walt Disney World. SGL/DBL$100-$140.

Holiday Inn Central Park (7900 South Orange Blossom Trail, 32809; 859-7900, Fax 859-7442, 800-HOLIDAY) 266 rooms, restaurant, lounge, outdoor pool, exercise center, children free with parents, wheelchair access, a/c, TV, NS rooms, fax service, room service, laundry service, meeting facilities for 275, airport transportation, no pets, senior rates, CC. 1 block from the Florida Mall, 5 miles from the Orlando airport, 6 miles from the Citrus Bowl. SGL/DBL$50-$60.

Holiday Inn Centroplex (929 West Colonial Dr., 32804; 843-1360, Fax 839-3333, 800-HOLIDAY) 154 rooms, restaurant, lounge, outdoor pool, whirlpools, jacuzzi, car rental desk, children free with parents, wheelchair access, a/c, TV, NS rooms, fax service, room service, pets OK, laundry service, meeting facilities for 75, senior rates, CC. 4 miles from the Citrus Bowl and Tinker Field, 20 miles from Orlando airport and Walt Disney World. SGL/DBL$40-$85.

Holiday Inn International Airport (5750 TG Lee Blvd., 32822; 851-6400, Fax 240-3717, 800-HOLIDAY) 291 rooms, restaurant, lounge, outdoor pool, exercise center, tennis court, children free with parents, wheelchair access, airport transportation, in-room coffee makers, no pets, a/c, game room, TV, NS rooms, fax service, room service, laundry service, 7 meeting rooms, meeting facilities for 400, senior rates, CC. 1 mile from the Orlando airport, 5 miles from the Orlando Central Business Park. SGL/DBL$53-$60.

Holiday Inn University (12125 High Tech Ave., 32817; 275-9000, Fax 382-0019, 800-HOLIDAY) 250 rooms and suites, restaurant, lounge, entertainment, outdoor pool, whirlpools, sauna, in-room refrigerators, children free with parents, wheelchair access, car rental desk, no pets, a/c, TV, NS rooms, fax service, room service, laundry service, meeting facilities for 600, senior rates, CC. 1 block from the University of Central Florida, 15 miles from Church Street Station and the Orlando airport. SGL/DBL$75-$95, STS$135.

Howard Johnson (3835 McCoy Rd., 32813; 859-2711, Fax 859-0423, 800-I-GO-HOJO) 340 rooms and suites, restaurant, lounge, outdoor pool, exercise center, whirlpools, sauna, local transportation, gift shop, no pets, children free with parents, game room, beauty shop, car rental desk, a/c, TV, wheelchair access, room service, laundry service, NS rooms, meeting facilities, senior rates, CC. 12 miles from Walt Disney World, 9 miles from Sea World, 3 miles from the Florida Mall. SGL/DBL$40-$85.

Howard Johnson (8820 South Orange Blossom Trail, 32809; 851-8200, Fax 855-753, 800-I-GO-HOJO) 195 rooms, restaurant, free breakfast, lounge, outdoor pool, children free with parents, wheelchair access, NS rooms, TV, game room, a/c, laundry facilities, senior rates, meeting facilities, CC. SGL/DBL$45-$85.

Howard Johnson Hotel (8020 International Dr., 32819; 351-1730, 800-I-GO-HOJO) 150 rooms, restaurant, lounge, outdoor pool, children free with parents, wheelchair access, NS rooms, TV, a/c, room service, gift shop, fax service, laundry facilities, senior rates, meeting facilities for 200, CC. SGL/DBL$40-$75.

Howard Johnson Lodge (8700 South Orange Blossom Trail, 32809; 851-2330, Fax 855-6747, 800-I-GO-HOJO) 192 rooms, restaurant, lounge, entertainment, outdoor pool, in-room refrigerators and microwaves, no pets, children free with parents, game room, wheelchair access, NS rooms, TV, a/c, laundry facilities, senior rates, meeting facilities for 150, game room, CC. 6 miles from Orlando airport, a 1/2-mile from the Florida Mall, 8 miles from the downtown area. SGL/DBL$45-$85.

Howard Johnson Lodge (6603 International Dr., 32819; 351-2900, 800-I-GO-HOJO) 176 rooms, restaurant, lounge, outdoor pool, children free with parents, wheelchair access, NS rooms, TV, a/c, no pets, fax service, laundry facilities, senior rates, meeting facilities,

CC. 1 mile from Universal Studios, 11 miles from the Orlando airport, 10 miles from Church Street Station. SGL/DBL$39-$69.

Howard Johnson Resort Hotel (5905 International Dr., 32819; 351-2100, 800-327-1366, 800-I-GO-HOJO) 303 rooms, restaurant, lounge, entertainment, outdoor heated pool, children free with parents, wheelchair access, NS rooms, TV, a/c, laundry facilities, local transportation, car rental desk, beauty shop, game room, senior rates, 10 meeting rooms, CC. 7 miles from Walt Disney World and MGM Studios, 3 miles from Sea World, 10 miles from the Orlando airport. SGL/DBL$40-$100.

Hyatt Regency Grand Cypress (1 Grand Cypress Blvd., 32836; 239-1234, Fax 239-3800, 800-228-9000) 750 rooms and suites, restaurant, lounge, entertainment, outdoor pool, whirlpools, exercise center, sauna, game room, room service, TV, a/c, NS rooms, wheelchair access, senior rates, 27 meeting rooms, 57,000 square feet of meeting and exhibition space, CC. SGL/DBL$85-$350.

Hyatt Regency International Airport (9300 Airport Blvd., 32877; 825-1234, Fax 856-1672, 800-228-9000) 443 rooms and suites, restaurant, lounge, entertainment, outdoor pool, whirlpools, exercise center, lighted tennis courts, local transportation, room service, in-room refrigerators and coffee makers, children free with parents, boutiques, no pets, in-room computer hookups, TV, a/c, NS rooms, wheelchair access, senior rates, 35,000 square feet of meeting and exhibition space, CC. At the Orlando airport. SGL/DBL$95-$220.

International Gateway Inn (5859 American Way, 32819; 345-8880, Fax 363-9366) 193 rooms, restaurant, outdoor heated pool, children free with parents, a/c, TV, in-room refrigerators, laundry facilities, game room, pets OK, NS rooms, senior rates, CC. LS SGL/DBL$40-$56; HS SGL/DBL$66-$85.

International Inn (6327 International Dr., 32809; 351-4444, Fax 352-5806, 800-999-6327) 315 rooms and suites, restaurant, lounge, outdoor heated pool, pets OK, wheelchair access, NS rooms, children free with parents, a/c, TV, in-room refrigerators, gift shop, senior rates, CC. SGL/DBL$55-$65.

La Quinta Airport (7931 Daetwyler Dr., 32812; 857-9215, 800-531-5900) 130 rooms, restaurant, free breakfast, outdoor heated pool, exercise center, complimentary newspaper, free local calls, fax service, laundry service, NS rooms, wheelchair access, airport transportation, no pets, a/c, meeting facilities, senior rates, CC. 3 miles from the Orlando airport, 20 miles from Walt Disney World. SGL/DBL$55-$65.

Las Palmas Inn (6233 International Dr., 32819; 351-3900, Fax 352-5597, 800-327-2114) 262 rooms and suites, restaurant, lounge, outdoor heated pool, a/c, TV, children free with parents, in-room refrigerators, no pets, NS rooms, 6 meeting rooms, senior rates, CC. SGL/DBL$45-$56.

Marriott Airport (7499 Augusta National Dr., 32822; 851-9000, Fax 856-9926, 800-331-3131) 484 rooms and suites, free breakfast, outdoor pool, exercise center, lighted tennis courts, whirlpools, in-room refrigerators, a/c, VCRs, children free with parents, TV, NS rooms, wheelchair access, game room, gift shop, airport courtesy car, no pets, 24 meeting rooms, senior rates, CC. 20 miles from Walt Disney World, 15 miles from Sea World, 40 miles from Port Canaveral. SGL/DBL$60-$185.

Marriott International (8001 International Dr., 32819; 351-2420, Fax 345-5611, 800-331-3131) 1,076 rooms and suites, restaurant, lounge, entertainment, outdoor heated pool, lighted tennis courts, exercise center, whirlpools, airport transportation, game room, in-room refrigerators and microwaves, no pets, a/c, VCRs, children free with parents, TV, NS rooms, wheelchair access, 24 meeting rooms, 27,000 square feet of meeting and exhibition space, meeting facilities for 1,000, senior rates, CC. 10 miles from Walt Disney World, 20 miles from the downtown area and Church Street Station, 2 miles from the Orange Country Convention Center. SGL/DBL$70-$115.

Marriott's Orlando World Center (8701 World Center Dr., 32821; 239-4200, Fax 239-5777, 800-228-9290) 1,500 rooms and suites, restaurant, lounge, entertainment, outdoor pool, exercise center, whirlpools, sauna, lighted tennis courts, game room, local transportation, in-room refrigerators, car rental desk, VCRs, gift shop, children free with parents, a/c, TV, NS rooms, wheelchair access, 143,000 square feet of meeting and exhibition space, meeting facilities for 12,000, senior rates, CC. 2 miles from Walt Disney World, 20 miles from the Orlando airport, 5 miles from the Orange County Convention Center. SGL/DBL$180-$210, STS$300-$450.

Motel 6 (5909 American Way, 32819; 351-6500, 505-891-6161) 36 rooms, outdoor pool, free local calls, children under 17 free with parents, NS rooms, wheelchair access, a/c, TV, CC. 1 mile from the factory outlet mall, 5 miles from the downtown area and Church Street Station, 6 miles from the Florida Mall, 12 miles from the Orlando airport. SGL/DBL$30-$36.

Omni International Hotel at Centroplex (400 West Livingston, 32801; 843-6664, Fax 839-4982, 800-843-6664) 288 rooms and suites, restaurant, lounge, entertainment, outdoor pool, sauna, exercise center, whirlpools, lighted tennis courts, no pets, in-room refrigerators, gift shop, car rental desk, airport transportation, laundry service, wheelchair access, NS rooms, a/c, TV, senior rates, 10 meeting rooms, 81,000 square feet of meeting and exhibition space, meeting facilities for 1,700, CC. 1 block from the Orlando Arena, 12 miles from the Orlando airport and 25 miles from Walt Disney World. SGL/DBL$95-$200.

Parc Corniche Condominiums (6300 Parc Corniche Dr., 32821; 239-7100, Fax 239-8501) 210 condominiums, restaurant, lounge, outdoor heated pool, whirlpools, kitchenettes, airport transportation, no pets, a/c, TV, CC. SGL/DBL$80-$130.

Park Inn (736 Lee Rd., 32810; 647-1112, Fax 740-8964, 800-437-PARK) 135 rooms and suites, restaurant, lounge, outdoor pool, laundry facilities, a/c, TV, complimentary newspaper, wheelchair access, NS rooms for 250, senior rates, CC. 25 miles from Walt Disney World, 12 miles from Universal Studios, 5 miles from the downtown area and Church Street Station. SGL/DBL$40-$85.

Peabody Orlando Hotel (9801 International Dr., 32819; 352-4000, Fax 351-0073, 800-PEABODY) 891 rooms and 2-bedroom suites, restaurant, lounge, entertainment, outdoor heated pool, lighted tennis courts, exercise center, whirlpools, airport transportation, in-room refrigerators, children free with parents, game room, airline ticket desk, car rental desk, room service, in-room refrigerators, a/c, TV, NS rooms, no pets, laundry facilities, 32 meeting rooms, meeting facilities for 3,200, 26,500 square feet of meeting and exhibition space, senior rates, CC. 1 block from the Orange County Convention Center, 10 miles from the Orlando airport and Walt Disney World, 1 mile from Sea World. SGL/DBL$165-$240.

Penta Hotel (5445 Forbes Place, 32812; 240-1000, Fax 240-1005) 300 rooms and suites, restaurant, lounge, entertainment, outdoor heated pool, exercise center, whirlpools, sauna, game room, a/c, TV, NS rooms, airport courtesy car, in-room refrigerators and microwaves, gift shop, children free with parents, no pets, wheelchair access, 10 meeting rooms, senior rates, CC. SGL/DBL$85-$145, STS$290-$345.

Quality Inn Airport (2601 McCoy Rd., 32809; 856-4663, 800-221-2222) 98 rooms and suites, restaurant, outdoor pool, exercise center, children free with parents, a/c, TV, wheelchair access, room service, laundry service, NS rooms, no pets, meeting facilities, senior rates, CC. 6 miles from Sea World, 1 mile from the Orlando airport. SGL/DBL$40-$160.

Quality Inn Plaza (7600 International Dr., 32809; 351-1600, 800-221-2222, 800-825-7600) 728 rooms and suites, restaurant, lounge, outdoor pool, exercise center, children free with parents, a/c, TV, wheelchair access, pets OK, local transportation, room service, laundry service, NS rooms, meeting facilities, senior rates, CC. 8 miles from Walt Disney World. SGL/DBL$30-$53.

Quality Inn Plaza (9000 International Dr., 32819; 345-8585, Fax 352-6839, 800-221-2222, 800-999-8585) 1,020 rooms and suites, restaurant, lounge, entertainment, outdoor pool, exercise center, local transportation, gift shop, game room, pets OK, children free with parents, a/c, TV, wheelchair access, room service, laundry service, NS rooms, meeting facilities, senior rates, CC. 5 miles from Walt Disney World. SGL/DBL$30-$60.

Quality Inn (4855 South Orange Blossom Trail, 32839; 851-3000, 800-221-2222) 138 rooms and suites, outdoor heated pool, exercise center, children free with parents, a/c, TV, kitchenettes, no pets, airport transportation, in-room refrigerators, microwaves and coffee makers, wheelchair access, room service, laundry service, NS rooms, meeting facilities, senior rates, CC. 12 miles from Walt Disney World, 8 miles from the Orlando airport. SGL/DBL$70-$160.

Quality Suites Universal Studio (7400 Canada Ave., 32819; 363-0332, 800-221-2222) 154 suites, free breakfast, pool, exercise center, whirlpools, children free with parents, a/c, TV, wheelchair access, in-room refrigerators, VCRs, in-room computer hookups, no pets, laundry service, NS rooms, meeting facilities, senior rates, 10 miles from Walt Disney World and the Orlando airport, 1 mile from the Convention Center. CC. SGL/DBL$60-$110.

Radisson Hotel Airport (5555 Hazeltine National Dr., 32812; 856-0100, Fax 855-7991, 800-333-3333) 346 rooms and suites, restaurant, lounge, entertainment, outdoor pool, exercise center, in-room refrigerators, microwaves and coffee makers, no pets, VCRs, wheelchair access, free parking, NS rooms, TV, a/c, children free with parents, senior rates, CC. SGL/DBL$100-$120.

Radisson Inn (8686 Palm Pkwy., 32836; 239-8400, Fax 239-8025, 800-333-3333) 200 rooms and suites, restaurant, lounge, entertainment, outdoor pool, exercise center, in-room refrigerators, microwaves and coffee makers, VCRs, wheelchair access, free parking, NS rooms, pets OK, TV, a/c, children free with parents, senior rates, CC. SGL/DBL$60-$140.

Radisson Inn and Aquatic Center (8444 International Dr., 32819; 345-0505, Fax 352-5894, 800-333-3333) 300 rooms and suites, restaurant, lounge, entertainment, outdoor pool, exercise center, in-room refrigerators, microwaves and coffee makers, children free with parents, VCRs, wheelchair access, free parking, gift shop, local transportation, NS rooms, no pets, TV, a/c, 8 meeting rooms, 7,000 square feet of meeting and exhibition space, senior rates, CC. SGL/DBL$60-$85.

Ramada Inn Plaza International (8300 Jamaican Ct., 32819; 351-1660, Fax 351-1660, 800-2-RAMADA) 200 rooms and suites, restaurant, lounge, outdoor heated pool, whirlpools, NS rooms, free parking, a/c, TV, children free with parents, local transportation, room service, laundry facilities, in-room refrigerators, pets OK, meeting facilities, senior rates, CC. 8 miles from the MGM Studios, 1.5 miles from Sea World, 1 mile from the Orange County Convention Center, 10 miles from the Orlando airport. LS SGL/DBL$45-$70; HS SGL/DBL$80-$100.

Radisson Plaza Hotel (60 South Ivanhoe Blvd., 32804; 425-4455, Fax 425-4455, 800-333-3333) 337 rooms and suites, restaurant, lounge, entertainment, outdoor pool, exercise center, whirlpools, lighted tennis courts, gift shop, in-room refrigerators, microwaves and coffee makers, children free with parents, VCRs, wheelchair access, free parking, NS rooms, pets OK, laundry service, TV, a/c, children free with parents, senior rates, CC. SGL/DBL$95-$105.

Ramada Inn (8296 South Orange Blossom Trail, 32809; 240-0570, Fax 856-5507, 800-2-RAMADA) 75 rooms and suites, outdoor pool, wheelchair access, jacuzzi, fax service, car rental desk, NS rooms, free parking, a/c, TV, children free with parents, room service, local transportation, laundry facilities, meeting facilities, senior rates, CC. 15 miles from Universal Studios, 6 miles from the Orlando airport. SGL/DBL$55-$85.

Ramada Inn Resort Florida Center (7400 International Dr., 32819; 351-4600, Fax 363-0517, 800-2-RAMADA) 395 rooms, restaurant, lounge, entertainment, outdoor heated pool, exercise center, lighted tennis courts, no pets, wheelchair access, NS rooms, free parking, game room, gift shop, complimentary newspaper, barber shop, a/c, TV, children free with parents, room service, laundry facilities, 10 meeting rooms, 8,500 square feet of meeting and exhibition space, meeting facilities for 200, senior rates, CC. 2 miles from Universal Studios, 3 miles from Sea World, 10 miles from the downtown area and Walt Disney World. SGL/DBL$60-$105.

Ramada Orlando Central (3200 West Colonial Dr., 32808; 295-5270, Fax 295-5270, 800-2-RAMADA) 318 rooms and suites, restaurant, lounge, outdoor pool, wheelchair access, NS rooms, free parking, a/c, TV, barber and beauty shop, gift shop, game room, complimentary newspaper, children free with parents, kitchenettes, VCRs, pets OK, room service, laundry facilities, 5,000 square feet of meeting and exhibition space, senior rates, CC. SGL/DBL$45-$90.

Residence Inn Orlando International Cove (7975 Canada Ave., 32819; 345-0117, Fax 352-2689, 800-227-3978, 800-426-6260 in Florida) 176 rooms and suites, free breakfast, outdoor heated pool, whirlpools, in-room refrigerators, coffee makers and microwaves, laundry facilities, TV, a/c, VCRs, complimentary newspaper, local transportation, fireplaces, in-room computer hookups, children free with parents, NS rooms, wheelchair access, no pets, meeting facilities, CC. 10 miles from the Orlando airport, 9 miles from Walt Disney World, 3 miles from Universal Studios, 2 miles from the Orange County Convention Center. SGL/DBL$95-$145.

Residence Inn by Marriott (8800 Meadow Creek Dr., 32821; 239-7700, Fax 239-7605, 800-331-3131) 688 rooms and suites, restaurant, lounge, free breakfast, in-room refrigerators, coffee makers and microwaves, outdoor pool, jacuzzi, tennis courts, laundry facilities, TV, a/c, VCRs, complimentary newspaper, fireplaces, children free with parents, room service, NS rooms, wheelchair access, meeting facilities, CC. 15 miles from the Orlando airport, 4 miles from Walt Disney World, 5 miles from Sea World. SGL/DBL$99, STS$124-$199.

Rodeway Inn (8601 South Orange Blossom Trail, 32809; 859-4100, 800-424-4777) 133 rooms, restaurant, outdoor pool, wheelchair access, no pets, NS rooms, children free with parents, a/c, TV, senior rates, CC. 7 miles from Universal Studios, 6 miles from the Orlando airport, 13 miles from Walt Disney World. SGL/DBL$35-$65.

Rodeway Inn Convention Center (9956 Hawaiian Ct., 32819; 351-5100, 800-228-2000, 800-424-4777, 800-826-4847) 222 rooms and suites, outdoor pool, whirlpools, wheelchair access, NS rooms, local transportation, game room, in-room refrigerators and microwaves, no pets, children free with parents, a/c, TV, senior rates, CC. SGL/DBL$40-$70.

Scottish Inns (5735 South Orange Blossom Trail, 32809; 855-3810, 800-251-1962) 50 rooms, outdoor pool, no pets, a/c, TV, wheelchair access, NS rooms, children free with parents, free local calls, senior rates, CC. 15 miles from Walt Disney World, 10 miles from Sea World, 7 miles from Universal Studios and MGM, 7 miles from the Orlando airport. SGL/DBL$30-$60.

Sheraton Plaza Hotel at the Florida Mall (1500 Sand Lake Rd., 32809; 859-1500, Fax 855-1585, 800-325-3535) 496 rooms and suites, restaurant, lounge, outdoor pool, sauna, whirlpools, exercise center, NS rooms, a/c, room service, TV, children free with parents, gift shop, wheelchair access, laundry service, in-room refrigerators, 18 meeting rooms, 20,000 square feet of meeting and exhibition space, meeting facilities for 1,000, senior rates, CC. At the Florida Mall, 6 miles from the Orlando airport. SGL/DBL$120-$175.

Sheraton University Inn (1724 Alafaya Trail, 32806; 658-9008, Fax 381-5456, 800-325-3535) 150 rooms and suites, restaurant, lounge, entertainment, outdoor pool, exercise center, sauna, no pets, NS rooms, a/c, room service, TV, children free with parents, in-room refrigerators, laundry service, wheelchair access, 5 meeting rooms, meeting facilities for 200, 3,000 square feet of meeting and exhibition space, senior rates, CC. 12 miles from Orlando Arena, 18 miles from the Orlando airport, 25 miles from Walt Disney World. SGL/DBL$70-$80.

Sheraton World Resort (10100 International Dr., 32821; 352-1100, Fax 352-2632, 800-325-3535) 793 rooms and suites, restaurant, lounge, entertainment, outdoor heated pool, exercise center, lighted tennis courts, laundry facilities, in-room refrigerators, pets OK, NS rooms, a/c, room service, game room, local transportation, gift shop, TV, children free with parents, wheelchair access, 30 meeting rooms, meeting facilities for 1,500, 35,000 square feet of meeting and exhibition space, senior rates, CC. 1 block from Sea World, 9 miles from Walt Disney World, 12 miles from the Orlando airport. SGL/DBL$95-$125.

Sonesta Villa Resort Orlando (10000 Turkey Lake Rd., 32819; 352-8051, Fax 345-5384, 800-SONESTA) 369 1- and 2-bedroom villas, restaurant, lounge, outdoor heated pool, beach, whirlpools, sauna, lighted tennis courts, a/c, TV, in-room refrigerators, car rental desk, gift shop, NS rooms, laundry service, no pets, 24-hour room service, children free with parents, 7 meeting rooms, meeting facilities for 220, 2,500 square feet of meeting and exhibition space, senior rates. SGL/DBL$95-$160.

Stouffer Orlando Resort (6677 Sea Harbor Dr., 32821; 351-5555, Fax 351-9994, 800-327-6677 in Florida) 780 rooms and suites, restaurant, lounge, entertainment, outdoor heated pool, whirlpools, exercise center, lighted tennis courts, no pets, airport courtesy car, wheelchair access, NS rooms, complimentary newspaper, game room, boutiques, car rental desk, barber and beauty shop, TV, a/c, room service, children free with parents, fax service, in-room refrigerators, 45 meeting rooms, 36,000 square feet of meeting and exhibition space, senior rates, CC. 8 miles from the Orlando airport and the downtown area, 2 miles from the Orange County Convention Center. LS SGL/DBL$165-$225; HS SGL/DBL$180-$250.

Summerfield Suites (8480 International Dr., 32819; 359-2400, Fax 352-4631, 800-833-4353) 146 rooms and 1- and 2-bedroom suites, lounge, outdoor heated pool, whirlpools, exercise center, laundry facilities, a/c, TV, VCRs, airport transportation, no pets, NS rooms, children free with parents, 2 meeting rooms, CC. 10 miles from Walt Disney World. SGL/DBL$140-$250.

Super 8 Motel (5900 American Way, 32819; 352-8383, 800-848-8888) 111 rooms, outdoor pool, game room, pets OK, car rental desk, children free with parents, free local calls, a/c, TV, in-room refrigerators and microwaves, fax service, NS rooms, wheelchair access, meeting facilities, senior rates, CC. 9 miles from the Orlando airport, 2 blocks from Universal Studio, 11 miles from Walt Disney World, 2 miles from Sea World. SGL/DBL$40-$73.

Travelodge (7101 South Orange Blossom Trail, 32809; 851-4300, Fax 859-6723, 800-578-7878) 162 rooms, restaurant, lounge, free breakfast, outdoor pool, wheelchair access, free newspaper, laundry service, TV, a/c, free local calls, fax service, NS rooms, in-room refrigerators and microwaves, children free with parents, car rental desk, no pets, meeting facilities, senior rates, CC. 7 miles from Walt Disney World, 3 miles from the downtown area and the Citrus Bowl, 1 mile from the Florida Mall, SGL/DBL$40-$60.

TraveLodge Downtown (409 North Magnolia Ave., 32801; 423-1671, Fax 423-1523, 800-578-7878) 75 rooms, outdoor heated pool, no pets, wheelchair access, complimentary newspaper, laundry service, TV, a/c, free local calls, fax service, NS rooms, in-room refrigerators, microwaves and coffee makers, airport transportation, children free with parents, meeting facilities, senior rates, CC. 6 blocks from the Church Street Station, 1 mile from the Citrus Bowl, 4 miles from the Orlando airport and the Navy Training Center. SGL/DBL$45-$70.

TraveLodge (5858 International Dr., 32819; 859-5151, Fax 856-0567, 800-578-7878) 270 rooms, restaurant, lounge, free breakfast, outdoor pool, wheelchair access, complimentary newspaper, laundry service, TV, a/c, car rental desk, gift shop, free local calls, fax service, NS rooms, in-room refrigerators, microwaves and coffee makers, children free with parents, meeting facilities, senior rates, CC. 2 miles from the Convention Center, 1 mile to Universal Studios. SGL/DBL$33-$75.

TraveLodge (9301 South Orange Blossom Trail, 32837; 855-0308, Fax 856-9155, 800-578-7878) 144 rooms, restaurant, lounge, free breakfast, outdoor pool, wheelchair access, free newspaper, laundry service, TV, a/c, free local calls, fax service, NS rooms, in-room refrigerators, microwaves and coffee makers, no pets, game room, car rental desk, local transportation, children free with parents, meeting facilities, senior rates, CC. 1 mile from the Florida Mall, 4.5 miles from Universal Studios, 6 miles from Walt Disney World, 2.5 miles from the Orlando airport. SGL/DBL$40-$60.

Twin Towers Hotel and Convention Center (5780 Major Blvd., 32819; 351-1000, Fax 363-0106, 800-327-2110) 760 rooms and suites, restaurant, lounge, entertainment, outdoor pool, exercise center, whirlpools, sauna, laundry facilities, boutiques, beauty shop, airport transportation, car rental desk, fax service, room service, wheelchair access, NS rooms, a/c, TV, children free with parents, no pets, senior rates, 16 meeting rooms, 58,000 square feet of meeting and exhibition space, CC. At Universal Studios, 12 miles from the Orlando airport, 8 miles from the Convention Center. SGL/DBL$95-$165, STS$250-$750.

The Villas of Grand Cypress (1 North Jacaranda, 32836; 239-4700, 800-835-7377, Fax 239-7219, 800-835-7377) 146 1-, 2-, and 3-bedroom suites, restaurant, lounge, entertainment, outdoor heated pool, whirlpools, tennis courts, in-room refrigerators, local transportation, 24-hour room service, 3 meeting rooms, 7,500 square feet of meeting and exhibition space, meeting facilities for 160, senior rates, CC. 12 miles from the Orlando airport, 1 mile from Walt Disney World. 1BR$150-$350, 2BR$220-$510, 3BR$400-$800.

Wynfield Inn (6263 Westwood Blvd., 32821; 345-8000, Fax 351-5087, 800-346-1551) 300 rooms, restaurant, outdoor heated pool, local transportation, a/c, TV, in-room refrigerators, NS rooms, no pets, wheelchair access, game room, children free with parents, senior rates, CC. SGL/DBL$52-$72.

Ormond Beach

Area Code 904

Rental & Reservation Services

Daytona Beach Ocean Home Rentals (541 South Atlantic Ave., 32176; 0720, 800-666-0720) private rental homes.

Ocean Village Realty (229 Cardinal Dr., Ormond Beach 32167; 677-0662, Fax 676-0279) rental villas.

□□□

Bed and Breakfast (393 John Anderson Dr., 32175; 672-5557) 1-bedroom apartment, free breakfast, no pets, no children, a/c, TV, NS, CC. SGL/DBL$70-$105.

Argosy Motel (1255 Ocean Shore Blvd., 32176; 441-0630) 19 rooms and efficiencies, outdoor pool, beach, kitchenettes, no pets, in-room refrigerators, a/c, TV, children free with parents, senior rates, CC. SGL/DBL$30-$50, 1BR$35-$50, 2BR$45-$80.

Best Western Inn (2251 South Old Dixie Hwy., 32174; 437-3737, 800-528-1234) 100 rooms, restaurant, lounge, outdoor pool, jacuzzi, gift shop, no pets, outdoor pool, children free with parents, a/c, NS rooms, TV, laundry facilities, wheelchair access, meeting facilities, senior rates, CC. 2 miles to Atlantic beaches, a 1/2-mile from Tomoka State Park. SGL/DBL$39-$45.

Casa Del Mar Beach Resort (621 South Atlantic Ave., 32176; 672-4550, Fax 253-9935, 800-874-7420) 151 rooms and suites, restaurant, lounge, outdoor pool, whirlpools, in-room microwaves and coffee makers, game room, beach, a/c, room service, TV, NS rooms, children free with parents, no pets, laundry facilities, senior rates, CC. LS SGL/DBL$80-$115; HS SGL/DBL$105-$180.

Comfort Inn (1567 North Hwy. 1, 32174; 672-8621, 800-221-2222) 77 rooms and suites, restaurant, outdoor pool, exercise center, children free with parents, a/c, TV, wheelchair access, room service, laundry service, pets OK, NS rooms, meeting facilities, senior rates, CC. 6 miles from Atlantic beaches, 12 miles from the Daytona airport, 6 miles from the Daytona International Speedway. SGL/DBL$40-$125.

Comfort Inn on the Beach (507 South Atlantic Ave., 32176; 677-8550, Fax 673-6260, 800-456-8550) 50 rooms and 1-bedroom efficiencies, outdoor pool, a/c, TV, children free with parents, NS rooms, wheelchair access, in-room refrigerators, pets OK, kitchenettes, senior rates, CC. 15 miles from the Daytona airport. SGL/DBL$45-$80, 1BR$55-$90.

Coral Beach Motel (711 South Atlantic Ave., 32176; 677-4712) 98 rooms and 2-bedroom efficiencies, indoor and outdoor heated pools, children free with parents, a/c, TV, NS rooms, in-room computer hookups, no pets, laundry facilities, beach, senior rates, CC. SGL/DBL$50-$160.

Coral Sands Inn and Seaside Cottages (1009 Ocean Shore Blvd., 32176; 441-1831, 800-441-1831) 18 1- and 2-bedroom cottages, outdoor heated pool, beach, in-room refrigerators, microwaves and coffee makers, NS rooms, no pets, fax service, children free with parents, laundry facilities, wheelchair access, CC. 1BR$434W-$595W, 2BR$700W-$980W.

Days Inn (839 South Atlantic Ave., 32176; 677-6600, 800-325-2525) 128 rooms, suites and efficiencies, restaurant, lounge, free breakfast, outdoor pool, children free with parents, a/c, TV, wheelchair access, NS rooms, beach, no pets, laundry facilities, senior rates, CC. 6 miles from Daytona International Airport. SGL/DBL$40-$175.

Days Inn (1608 North Hwy. 1, 32174; 672-7341, Fax 672-3717, 800-325-2525) 72 rooms, free breakfast, outdoor pool, a/c, TV, wheelchair access, NS rooms, no pets, laundry facilities, senior rates, CC. 8 miles from Daytona Beach, 10 miles from the Daytona International Speedway and the Lighthouse Museum. SGL/DBL$40-$45.

Driftwood Beach Motel (675 South Atlantic Ave., 32176; 677-1331, Fax 677-0626) 44 rooms and 2-bedroom efficiencies, outdoor heated pool, beach, laundry facilities, a/c, TV, NS rooms, in-room refrigerators and microwaves, pets OK, children free with parents, laundry facilities, SGL/DBL$30-$65, 1BR$64-$95, 2BR$82-$130.

Econo Lodge on the Beach (295 South Atlantic Ave., 32176; 672-2651, 800-4-CHOICE) 58 rooms and 1-bedroom efficiencies, outdoor pool, children free with parents, no pets, NS rooms, wheelchair access, laundry facilities, kitchenettes, a/c, beach, TV, senior rates, CC. 15 miles from the Daytona International Speedway and Daytona airport. SGL/DBL$45-$75, 1BR$55-$105.

Econo Lodge (1634 North Hwy. 1, 32174; 672-6222, 800-4-CHOICE) 48 rooms, outdoor pool, children free with parents, no pets, NS rooms, wheelchair access, a/c, TV, senior rates, CC. 5 miles to Atlantic beaches, 12 miles from the Daytona airport. SGL/DBL$26-$90.

Granada Inn (51 South Atlantic Ave., 32175; 672-7550) 193 rooms, restaurant, lounge, indoor and outdoor pool, whirlpools, children free with parents, in-room refrigerators, no pets, a/c, TV, NS rooms, laundry facilities, CC. SGL/DBL$55-$105.

Holiday Inn (1614 North Hwy. 1, 32174; 672-2510, Fax 676-2510, 800-HOLIDAY) 128 rooms, restaurant, free breakfast, lounge, outdoor pool, exercise center, children free with parents, wheelchair access, a/c, TV, NS rooms, game room, fax service, room service, laundry service, meeting facilities, senior rates, CC. 12 miles from the regional airport and Peabody Auditorium, 6 miles from the Municipal Stadium. SGL/DBL$90-$120.

Howard Johnson Lodge North (1633 Hwy. 1 North, 32174, 677-7310, 800-I-GO-HOJO) 64 rooms, outdoor pool, children free with parents, wheelchair access, NS rooms, TV, a/c, laundry facilities, no pets, beach, senior rates, meeting facilities, CC. 14 miles from the Daytona International Speedway and the Daytona airport, 12 miles from the Ocean's Convention Center. LS SGL/DBL$35; HS SGL/DBL$100-$140.

Ivanhoe Beach Resort (205 South Atlantic Ave., 32176; 672-6711, Fax 676-9494, 800-874-9910) 147 rooms and suites, restaurant, heated pool, beach, in-room refrigerators, laundry facilities, no pets, a/c, TV, NS rooms, room service, game room, children free with parents, CC. LS SGL/DBL$50-$65; HS SGL/DBL$60-$145.

Jamaican Beach Motel (505 South Atlantic Ave., 32176; 677-3353, 800-336-3353) 42 rooms and efficiencies, outdoor pool, beach, children free with parents, a/c, TV, pets OK, in-room refrigerators and microwaves, laundry facilities, NS rooms, senior rates, CC. SGL/DBL$28-$55, 1BR$45-$70, 2BR$50-$75.

Mainsail Motel (281 South Atlantic Ave., 32176; 677-2131) 48 rooms and 2-bedroom efficiencies, outdoor heated pool, exercise center, sauna, a/c, TV, kitchenettes, children free with parents, NS rooms, game room, beach, no pets, laundry facilities, senior rates, CC. LS SGL/DBL$45-$60; HS SGL/DBL$70-$95.

Makai Motel (707 South Atlantic Ave., 32176; 677-8060) 100 rooms and suites, outdoor heated pool, whirlpools, in-room refrigerators, game room, laundry facilities, a/c, TV, beach, children free with parents, no pets, CC. SGL/DBL$45-$75, STS$90-$150.

Maverick (485 South Atlantic Ave., 32174; 672-3550) 138 rooms and efficiencies, restaurant, outdoor heated pool, whirlpools, sauna, children free with parents, a/c, TV, laundry facilities, beach, NS rooms, CC. SGL/DBL$90-$115.

Quality Inn (251 South Atlantic Ave., 32176; 672-8510, 800-221-2222) 157 rooms and suites, restaurant, lounge, entertainment, indoor and outdoor pools, exercise center, children free with parents, a/c, TV, wheelchair access, in-room refrigerators, no pets, kitchenettes, game room, room service, laundry service, NS rooms, meeting facilities, senior rates, CC. LS SGL/DBL$45-$80; HS SGL/DBL$100-$160.

Symphony Beach Motel (453 South Atlantic Ave., 32175; 672-7373, 800-922-7373) 30 rooms, outdoor heated pool, beach, a/c, TV, laundry facilities, in-room refrigerators, NS rooms, wheelchair access, children free with parents, no pets, senior rates, CC. LS SGL/DBL$35-$55; HS SGL/DBL$65-$115.

Traders Inn (1355 Ocean Shore Blvd., 32176; 441-1111) 49 efficiencies, outdoor heated pool, laundry facilities, beach, a/c, TV, kitchenettes, NS rooms, no pets, wheelchair access, CC. SGL/DBL$60-$80.

Osprey
Area Code 813

Holiday Inn Sarasota South (1660 South Tamiami Trail, 34229; 966-2121, 800-HOLIDAY) 148 rooms and efficiencies, restaurant, lounge, entertainment, outdoor pool, exercise center, gift shop, no pets, kitchenettes, children free with parents, wheelchair access, a/c, TV, NS rooms, fax service, room service, laundry service, meeting facilities for 250, senior rates, CC. SGL/DBL$85-$110.

Palatka
Area Code 904

Best Western Inn (119 Hwy. 17, 32131; 325-7800, 800-528-1234) 56 rooms, free breakfast, outdoor pool, children free with parents, a/c, NS rooms, TV, laundry facilities, wheelchair access, pets OK, meeting facilities, senior rates, CC. 2 miles from Ravine Gardens State Park, 1 block from the St. Johns River. SGL/DBL$45-$75.

Holiday Inn Riverfront (201 North 1st St., 32177; 328-3481, 800-HOLIDAY) 131 rooms, restaurant, lounge, entertainment, outdoor pool, pets OK, a/c, TV, NS rooms, wheelchair access, children free with parents, senior rates, CC. 2 miles from Azalea Ravine State Park, 2 miles from the downtown area. SGL/DBL$55-$65.

Palm Bay
Area Code 407

Days Inn Palm Bay (4700 Dixie Hwy., 32905; 951-0350, 800-325-2525) 120 rooms, restaurant, lounge, free breakfast, outdoor pool, a/c, TV, VCRs, wheelchair access, NS rooms, laundry facilities, in-room refrigerators and microwaves, children free with parents, no pets, senior rates, CC. 7 miles from Atlantic beaches, 37 miles from the Kennedy Space Center. SGL/DBL$30-$50.

Glen Oak Motel (6275 South Hwy. 1, 32905; 723-2713) 9 rooms and efficiencies, no pets, children free with parents, in-room refrigerators, microwaves and coffee makers, CC. SGL/DBL$35-$40.

Howard Johnson (1881 Palm Bay Rd. Northeast, 32905; 723-8181, Fax 727-7390, 800-I-GO-HOJO) 132 rooms, restaurant, free breakfast, lounge, indoor and outdoor pools, jacuzzi, children free with parents, wheelchair access, NS rooms, TV, a/c, laundry facilities, senior rates, 8 meeting roms, CC. 1 mile from the downtown area, 5 miles from the Melbourne airport, 12 miles from King Center. SGL/DBL$35-$48.

Knights Inn (1170 Malabar Road Southeast, 32905; 951-8222, 800-843-5644) 118 rooms and efficiencies, outdoor pool, wheelchair access, NS rooms, TV, a/c, in-room refrigerators and microwaves, fax service, VCRs, pets OK, senior rates, CC. 8 miles from the Melbourne airport, 30 miles from Port Canaveral, 10 miles from Atlantic beaches, 2 miles from downtown. SGL/DBL$30-$45.

Palm Beach

Area Code 407

Beachcomber Apartment Motel (3024 South Ocean Blvd., 33480; 585-4648, 800-833-7122) 50 1- and 2-bedroom apartments, outdoor pool, beach, a/c, TV, laundry facilities, beach, children free with parents, wheelchair access, kitchenettes, senior rates, CC. SGL/DBL$45-$195.

Brazilian Court Hotel (300 Brazilian Ave., 33480; 655-7740, Fax 655-0801, 800-351-5656) 134 rooms and suites, restaurant, lounge, entertainment, outdoor pool, in-room refrigerators, a/c, TV, wheelchair access, NS rooms, 24-hour room service, 6 meeting rooms, senior rates, CC. SGL/DBL$185-$290, STS$525-$850.

The Breakers (1 South County Rd., 33480; 659-8444, Fax 659-9403, 800-833-3141) 568 rooms and suites, restaurant, lounge, entertainment, outdoor heated pool, whirlpools, no pets, children free with parents, Modified American Plan available, in-room refrigerators, boutiques, barber and beauty shop, game room, beach, a/c, TV, VCRs, in-room computer hookups, wheelchair access, 18 meeting rooms, meeting facilities for 1,100, 9,500 square feet of meeting and exhibition space, senior rates, CC. 6 miles from the Palm Beach airport. LS SGL/DBL$75-$125; HS SGL/DBL$185-$260.

The Chesterfield Hotel Deluxe (363 Coconut Row, 33480; 659-5800, Fax 659-6706, 800-243-7871) 58 rooms and suites, restaurant, lounge, outdoor heated pool, whirlpools, airport transportation, game room, room service, a/c, TV, wheelchair access, NS rooms, meeting facilities, senior rates, CC. 1 mile from the downtown area, 6 miles from the Palm Beach airport. SGL/DBL$175-$250, STS$325-$700.

Colony Hotel (155 Harmon Ave., 33480; 655-5430, Fax 832-7318, 800-521-5525) 119 rooms and 2-bedroom villas, restaurant, outdoor pool, exercise center, whirlpools, a/c, TV, wheelchair access, room service, in-room refrigerators, microwaves and coffee makers, pets OK, children free with parents, VCRs, laundry service, NS rooms, complimentary newspapers, senior rates. SGL/DBL$80-$110, 2BR$200-$275.

Hawaiian Ocean Inn (3550 South Ocean Blvd., 33480; 582-5631, 800-457-5631) 58 rooms and 2-bedroom apartments, restaurant, lounge, outdoor heated pool, beach, kitchenettes, a/c, TV, pets OK, children free with parents, airport transportation, laundry service, in-room refrigerators and microwaves, VCRs, CC. LS SGL/DBL$60-$75; HS SGL/DBL$90-$100.

Heart of Palm Beach Hotel (160 Royal Palm Way, 33480; 655-5600, Fax 832-1201, 800-523-LESS) 88 rooms and efficiencies, restaurant, lounge, outdoor heated pool, American Plan available, pets OK, room service, children free with parents, in-room refrigerators, a/c, TV, VCRs, meeting facilities, senior rates, CC. SGL/DBL$60-$190.

Hilton Oceanside Hotel (2842 South Ocean Blvd, 33480; 586-6542, Fax 585-0188, 800-HILTONS) 134 rooms and suites, restaurant, lounge, entertainment, outdoor pool, exercise center, tennis courts, sauna, jacuzzi, children free with parents, NS rooms, wheelchair access, room service, laundry facilities, a/c, TV, 2 meeting rooms, meeting facilities for 250, senior rates, CC. 6 miles from the Palm Beach airport. SGL/DBL$210-$260, STS$475-$950.

Howard Johnson Motor Lodge (2870 South County Rd., 33480; 582-2581, Fax 582-7189, 800-I-GO-HOJO) 98 rooms, outdoor heated pool, children free with parents, wheelchair access, NS rooms, fax service, TV, a/c, laundry facilities, in-room refrigerators, pets OK, senior rates, meeting facilities, CC. 6 miles from the Palm Beach airport. SGL/DBL$65-$120.

The Ocean Grand (2800 South Ocean Blvd., 33480; 582-2800, Fax 547-1557, 800-432-2335) 210 rooms and suites, restaurant, lounge, entertainment, outdoor heated pool, exercise center, whirlpools, saunas, children free with parents, no pets, a/c, TV, beach, 24-hour room service, in-room refrigerators, beach, NS rooms, wheelchair access, kitchenettes, 19 meeting rooms, meeting facilities for 600, 22,000 square feet of meeting and exhibition space, senior rates, CC. 15 miles from the Palm Beach airport, 5 miles from the downtown area. LS SGL/DBL$145-$270; HS SGL/DBL$300-$480.

Plaza Inn (215 Brazilian Ave., 33480; 832-8666, Fax 835-8776) 50 rooms, free breakfast, restaurant, lounge, entertainment, outdoor heated pool, whirlpools, in-room refrigerators, room service, pets OK, children free with parents, meeting facilities for 80, TV, a/c, CC. SGL/DBL$75-$165.

Sea Lord Hotel (2315 South Ocean Blvd., 33480; 582-1461) 40 rooms and 1-bedroom apartments, restaurant, outdoor heated pool, a/c, TV, in-room refrigerators, NS rooms, children free with parents, no pets, kitchenettes, CC. SGL/DBL$55-$190.

Palm Beach Gardens
Area Code 407

Holiday Inn (4431 PGA Blvd., 33410; 622-2260, Fax 624-1043, 800-HOLIDAY) 280 rooms, restaurant, lounge, outdoor pool, hot tubs, children free with parents, wheelchair access, a/c, TV, airport courtesy car, NS rooms, fax service, room service, laundry service, 5 meeting rooms, meeting facilities for 300, senior rates, CC. 2 miles from the Gardens Mall. SGL/DBL$80-$120.

Marriott Hotel (4000 RCA Blvd., 33410; 622-8888, Fax 622-0052, 800-331-3131) 279 rooms and suites, lounge, entertainment, outdoor pool, tennis courts, sauna, whirlpools, gift shop, in-room refrigerators, VCRs, children free with parents, a/c, TV, NS rooms, wheelchair access, 10 meeting rooms, senior rates, CC. 15 miles from the Palm Beach airport, a 1/2-mile from the Gardens Mall. SGL/DBL$68-$145.

PGA National Resort (400 Avenue of the Champions, 33418; 627-2000, Fax 622-0261, 800-633-9150) 335 rooms and suites, restaurant, lounge, entertainment, outdoor heated pool, saunas, whirlpools, lighted tennis courts, in-room computer hookups, wheelchair access, NS rooms, a/c, TV/ VCRs, children free with parents, no pets, senior rates, 21 meeting rooms, 30,000 square feet of meeting and exhibition space, CC. 8 miles from West Palm Auditorium, 15 miles from the Palm Beach airport. LS SGL/DBL$100-$130; HS SGL/DBL$265-$300.

Radisson Suite Hotel (4350 PGA Blvd., 33410; 622-1000, Fax 622-0551, 800-333-3333) 160 1- and 2-bedroom suites, restaurant, lounge, entertainment, outdoor pool, exercise center, in-room refrigerators, microwaves and coffee makers, children free with parents, in-room computer hookups, no pets, VCRs, wheelchair access, NS rooms, TV, a/c, senior rates, 6 meeting rooms, 4,400 square feet of meeting and exhibition space, CC. SGL/DBL$110-$180.

Palm Beach Shores
Area Code 407

Best Western Inn (123 South Ocean Dr., 33404; 844-0233, Fax 844-9885, 800-528-1234) 50 rooms, restaurant, lounge, entertainment, pool, children free with parents, a/c, NS rooms, TV, laundry facilities, wheelchair access, airport courtesy car, water view, beach, no pets, meeting facilities, senior rates, CC. 5 miles from golf course, 6 blocks from tennis courts. SGL/DBL$64-$86.

Days Inn Oceanfront Resort (2700 North Ocean Dr., 33404; 848-8661, Fax 844-0999, 800-325-2525) 165 rooms, restaurant, lounge, outdoor pool, pets OK, a/c, TV, wheelchair access, NS rooms, laundry facilities, children free with parents, beach, senior rates, CC. 8 miles from the Palm Beach airport. SGL/DBL$39-$120.

Embassy Resorts Hotel (181 Ocean Ave., 33404; 863-4000, 800-EMBASSY) 257, 2-room suites, restaurant, lounge, entertainment, outdoor heated pool, free breakfast, whirlpool, exercise center, sauna, room service, in-room refrigerators, microwaves and coffee makers, pets OK, children free with parents, local transportation, laundry service, wheelchair access, complimentary newspaper, free local calls, NS rooms, 4 meeting rooms, CC. 11 miles from the Palm Beach airport, 6 miles from the Jai Alai fronton. SGL/DBL$200-$400.

Quality Resort Oceanfront (3800 North Ocean Dr., 33404; 848-5502, 800-221-2222, 800-765-5502) 124 rooms and suites, restaurant, outdoor pool, exercise center, whirlpools, children free with parents, a/c, TV, wheelchair access, room service, laundry service, NS rooms, meeting facilities, senior rates, CC. 15 miles from the Palm Beach airport, 10 miles from the Kravis Center, 3 miles from the Port of Palm Beach. SGL/DBL$65-$225.

Sailfish Marina Resort (98 Lake Dr., 33404; 844-1724, 800-446-4577 in Florida) 15 rooms and efficiencies, restaurant, outdoor pool, no pets, a/c, TV, room service, laundry facilities, children free with parents, CC. SGL/DBL$65, EFF$75-$95.

Palm Coast
Area Code 904

Sheraton Palm Coast Resort (300 Clubhouse Dr., 32037; 445-3000, Fax 445-9685, 800-654-6538, 800-325-3535) 154 rooms and suites, restaurant, lounge, entertainment, outdoor heated pool, exercise center, lighted tennis courts, in-room coffee makers, pets OK, in-room computer hookups, NS rooms, a/c, room service, TV, children free with parents, wheelchair access, 11 meeting rooms, meeting facilities 350, 11,500 square feet of meeting and exhibition space, senior rates, CC. 27 miles from the Daytona Beach airport, 27 miles from the Daytona International Speedway. LS SGL/DBL$90-$110; HS SGL/DBL$120-$175.

Palm Harbor
Area Code 813

Econo Lodge (32000 Hwy. 19 North, 34648; 786-2529, Fax 786-7462, 800-4-CHOICE) 100 rooms and efficiencies, outdoor heated pool, children free with parents, NS rooms, wheelchair access, pets OK, a/c, TV, kitchenettes, senior rates, CC. 15 miles from the Tampa airport, 4 miles from Gulf beaches. SGL/DBL$30-$70.

Knights Inn (34106 Hwy. 19 North, 34684; 789-2002, Fax 784-6206, 800-843-5644) 115 rooms, outdoor pool, wheelchair access, NS rooms, TV, a/c, in-room refrigerators and microwaves, fax service, pets OK, VCRs, senior rates, CC. 20 miles from the Tampa airport, 30 miles from Busch Gardens, 4 miles from the Tarpon Springs sponge docks. SGL/DBL$30-$53.

Palmetto
Area Code 813

Bayshore Inn (3512 Hwy. 41 North, 34221; 722-6448) 86 rooms and efficiencies, restaurant, outdoor pool, pets OK, children free with parents, a/c, TV, CC. SGL/DBL$35-$43.

Five Oaks Inn (1102 Riverside Dr., 34221; 723-1236) 4 rooms, free breakfast, airport transportation, no children, TV, a/c, no pets, CC. SGL/DBL$65-$100.

Panacea
Area Code 904

Oaks Motel (Hwy. 98, 32346; 984-5370) 20 rooms, a/c, TV, children free with parents, pets OK, meeting facilities, CC. SGL/DBL$28-$63.

Panama City
Area Code 904

Rental & Reservation Services

Clark Realty (8801 Front Beach Rd., 32404; 234-3371, 800-321-5734) rental condominiums, apartments and private homes.

Dunes of Panama Management (7205 Thomas Drive; 234-8839, 800-874-2412) rental condominiums.

Sand Dollar Surf n' Sand Properties (9722 South Thomas Dr., 32408; 235-2205, 800-821-2205) rental condos, apartments and private homes.

St. Andrews Bay Resort Management (726 Thomas Dr., 32408; 235-4075, 800-423-1889, 800-621-2462) rental condos and apartments.

□□□

Best Western Inn (711 West Beach Dr., 32401; 763-4622, Fax 747-9522, 800-528-1234) 97 rooms, restaurant, outdoor pool, children free with parents, a/c, NS rooms, TV, laundry facilities, wheelchair access, in-room refrigerators, microwaves and coffee makers, pets

OK, meeting facilities, senior rates, CC. 1 mile from the Civic Center, 8 miles to Gulf beaches, a 1/2-mile from the downtown art district. SGL/DBL$40-$70.

Classic Inn (4903 Hwy. 98 West, 32401; 769-8899) 40 rooms, a/c, TV, in-room refrigerators and microwaves, no pets, NS rooms, CC. SGL/DBL$25-$45.

Comfort Inn (1013 East 23rd St., 32405; 769-6969, 800-228-5150, 800-221-2222) 105 rooms, outdoor pool, a/c, TV, children free with parents, NS rooms, no pets, wheelchair access, senior rates, laundry facilities, meeting facilities, CC. 3 miles from Gulf beaches and the Panama City airport, 3 blocks from the shopping mall, 10 miles from Tyndall Air Force Base, SGL/DBL$50-$78.

Days Inn (301 West 23rd St., 32405; 785-0001, 800-325-2525) 40 rooms and efficiencies, a/c, TV, wheelchair access, kitchenettes, NS rooms, children free with parents, no pets, laundry facilities, free local calls, senior rates, CC. 1 mile from the Panama City airport, 1 block from Gulf Coast Hospital, 8 miles from Gulf beaches. SGL/DBL$30-$60.

Days Inn (4111 West Hwy. 98, 32401; 784-1777, Fax 784-0178, 800-325-2525) 52 rooms, outdoor pool, pets OK, a/c, TV, wheelchair access, NS rooms, children free with parents, free local calls, kitchenettes, laundry facilities, senior rates, CC. 2 miles from the downtown area and Panama City airport, 5 miles from Gulf beaches. SGL/DBL$30-$53.

Econo Lodge (4411 West Hwy. 98, 32401; 785-2700, 800-4-CHOICE) 51 rooms, outdoor pool, children free with parents, no pets, laundry facilities, NS rooms, wheelchair access, a/c, TV, senior rates, CC. 2 miles from the Navy Base, 3 miles from the Panama City airport, 1 mile from Gulf Coast Community College. SGL/DBL$35-$90.

Holiday Inn Mall (2001 North Cove Blvd., 32405; 769-0000, Fax 763-3828, 800-HOLIDAY) 173 rooms, restaurant, lounge, indoor heated pool, whirlpools, sauna, children free with parents, wheelchair access, a/c, TV, NS rooms, free local calls, complimentary newspaper, airport courtesy car, fax service, room service, laundry service, no pets, 8 meeting rooms, meeting facilities for 350, senior rates, CC. 1 block from the Panama City Shopping Mall, 3 miles from the Panama City airport, 10 miles from the golf course. SGL/DBL$60-$85.

Howard Johnson (301 East 23rd St., 32405; 872-8585, 800-I-GO-HOJO) 44 rooms, restaurant, free breakfast, lounge, outdoor pool, whirlpools, children free with parents, wheelchair access, NS rooms, TV, a/c, laundry facilities, senior rates, meeting facilities, CC. 2 miles from the downtown area and Panama City airport, 8 miles from Tyndall Air Force Base and Gulf beaches. SGL/DBL$35-$70.

Howard Johnson Motor Lodge (4601 West Hwy. 98, 32401; 785-0222, Fax 769-3472, 800-I-GO-HOJO) 124 rooms, outdoor pool, beach, children free with parents, wheelchair access, NS rooms, TV, a/c, laundry facilities, no pets, senior rates, meeting facilities, CC. 3 miles from the Panama City airport, 10 miles from Gulf beaches, 4 miles from the downtown area. SGL/DBL$42-$75.

Las Brisas Inn (5711 East Hwy. 98, 32401; 871-2345, Fax 871-2345, 800-523-4369) 96 rooms, outdoor pool, no pets, a/c, TV, wheelchair access, children free with parents, laundry facilities, CC. SGL/DBL$45.

Ramada Inn (3001 West 10th St., 32401; 785-0561, Fax 785-3280, 800-2-RAMADA) 150 rooms, restaurant, lounge, entertainment, outdoor pool, exercise center, in-room refrigerators, no pets, wheelchair access, NS rooms, local transportation, a/c, TV, children free with parents, room service, laundry facilities, meeting facilities for 250, senior rates, CC. 3 miles from the downtown area, 5 miles from the Panama City Mall, 3.5 miles from the Panama City airport, 7 miles from Gulf beaches. SGL/DBL$50-$65.

Sleep Inn (5126 West Hwy. 98, 32401; 800-221-2222) 82 rooms, free breakfast, outdoor pool, wheelchair access, NS rooms, children free with parents, a/c, TV, meeting facilities, senior rates, CC. 2 miles from the Navy Base and the Panama City airport, 4 miles from the shopping mall. SGL/DBL$50-$75.

Super 8 Motel (207 Hwy. 231, 32405; 784-1988, Fax 784-6655, 800-800-8000) 63 rooms and suites, outdoor pool, pets OK, children free with parents, free local calls, a/c, TV, VCRs, NS rooms, wheelchair access, meeting facilities, senior rates, CC. 2 miles from the Panama City airport, 15 miles from Gulf beaches, 1 mile from the Panama City Mall. SGL/DBL$36-$47.

Panama City Beach

Area Code 904

Rental & Reservation Services

Sunbird Management Company (9850 Thomas Dr., 32408; 230-9470, 800-433-8240) rental condominiums.

ㅁㅁㅁ

Beach Colony Motel (8014 Surf Dr., 32408; 234-3604) 21 rooms and 2-bedroom efficiencies, kitchenettes, no pets, a/c, TV, in-room refrigerators, NS rooms, beach, senior rates, CC. SGL/DBL$30-$80.

Beachwalker Condominiums (17751 Back Beach Rd., 32408; 234-3990) 2-bedroom condominiums, outdoor pool, kitchenettes, a/c, TV, laundry facilities, pets OK, children free with parents, wheelchair access, CC. 2BR$65-$125.

Best Western Casa Loma (13615 Front Beach Rd., 32413; 234-1100, 800-528-1234) 101 rooms and suites, outdoor pool, beach, children free with parents, a/c, NS rooms, TV, laundry facilities, wheelchair access, kitchenettes, in-room refrigerators and microwaves, water view, beach, pets OK, kitchenettes, meeting facilities, senior rates, CC. A 1/4-mile from city fishing pier, 20 miles from the dog track, a 1/2-mile from golf course. LS SGL/DBL$60-$140; HS SGL/DBL$80-$160.

Best Western Del Coronado (11815 Front Beach Rd., 32408; 234-1600, Fax 235-0888, 800-528-1234) 106 rooms, restaurant, outdoor pool, children free with parents, a/c, NS rooms, TV, laundry facilities, wheelchair access, water view, pets OK, meeting facilities, senior rates, CC. A 1/2-mile from the golf course. SGL/DBL$65-$105.

Bikini Beach Motel (11001 West Hwy. 98, 32408; 234-3392, 800-451-5307) 78 rooms and efficiencies, restaurant, lounge, outdoor pool, laundry facilities, game room, beach, a/c, TV, NS rooms, wheelchair access, children free with parents, no pets, senior rates, CC. SGL/DBL$50-$90, STS$90-$130.

Chateau Motel (12525 West Hwy. 98, 32413; 234-2174, Fax 234-2174, 800-874-8826) 151 rooms, efficiencies, beach, outdoor pool, a/c, TV, in-room refrigerators, no pets, CC. SGL/DBL$35-$45, EFF$45-$55.

Comfort Inn and Suites (9600 South Thomas Dr., 32408; 234-6511, 800-221-2222) 210 rooms, outdoor pool, a/c, TV, children free with parents, NS rooms, wheelchair access, senior rates, CC. A 1/4-mile from the golf course, 3 miles from the Navy Base, 8 miles from the Panama City airport. SGL/DBL$50-$170.

Commodore Condominiums (4715 Thomas Dr., 32413; 235-1486) 1-, 2-, and 3-bedroom condominiums, beach, outdoor pool, whirlpools, in-room refrigerators, microwaves and coffee makers, children free with parents, no pets, laundry facilities, CC. 1BR/2BR/3BR$510W-$750W.

Days Inn (12818 Front Beach Rd., 32413; 233-3333, 800-325-2525) 188 rooms and efficiencies, outdoor pool, whirlpools, sauna, lighted tennis courts, beach, kitchenettes, a/c, TV, wheelchair access, NS rooms, children free with parents, game room, gift shop, no pets, laundry facilities, senior rates, CC. 8 miles from the Panama City airport. SGL/DBL$55-$128.

Dunes of Panama (7205 Thomas Dr., 32408; 234-6669) 2-bedroom condominiums, beach, outdoor pool, in-room refrigerators, microwaves and coffee makers, children free with parents, a/c, TV, wheelchair access, laundry facilities, no pets, CC. 2BR$125.

Edgewater Beach Resort (11212 Front Beach Rd., 32413; 235-4044, Fax 233-7599, 800-874-8686) 520 1-, 2- and 3-bedroom condos, restaurant, lounge, entertainment, outdoor pool, whirlpools, saunas, lighted tennis courts, exercise center, beach, children stay free with parents, a/c, TV, laundry facilities, no pets, senior rates, 13 meeting rooms, 12,500 square feet of meeting and exhibition space, senior rates, CC. 1BR$65-$120, 2BR$80-$135, 3BR$150-$250.

Endless Summer Condominiums (17614 Front Beach Rd., 32413; 235-3150) 1-, 2-, and 3-bedroom condominiums, outdoor pool, whirlpools, TV, a/c, in-room refrigerators, microwaves and coffee makers, children free with parents, wheelchair access, no pets, laundry facilities, CC. 1BR$75-$115, 2BR$80-$145, 3BR$165-$250.

Fiesta Motel (13623 Front Beach Rd., 32413; 235-1000, 800-833-1415) 186 rooms and efficiencies, outdoor pool, a/c, TV, children free with parents, kitchens, beach, CC. 10 miles from the Panama City airport. SGL/DBL$60-$95.

Holiday Inn Beach Resort (11127 Front Beach Rd., 32413; 234-1111, Fax 235-1907, 800-HOLIDAY) 342 rooms and suites, efficiencies, restaurant, lounge, outdoor heated pool, exercise center, whirlpools, sauna, VCRs, lighted tennis courts, game room, beach, children free with parents, wheelchair access, a/c, TV, in-room computer hookups, gift shop, no pets, in-room refrigerators, microwaves and coffee makers, NS rooms, fax service, room service, laundry service, meeting facilities for 100, senior rates, CC. 2 miles from Gulf World, 20 miles from the dog track. SGL/DBL$130-$140, STS$450-$1,000.

Horizon South II Condominiums (17462 Front Beach Rd., 32408; 234-8219, 800-334-4010) 150 1- and 2-bedroom condominiums, outdoor pool, beach tennis courts, game room, kitchen, laundry facilities, children free with parents, laundry facilities, 1BR$40, 2BR$50, 3BR$60.

Howard Johnson (9400 South Thomas Dr., 32408; 234-6521, 800-240-Gulf, 800-I-GO-HOJO) 153 rooms and suites, restaurant, lounge, outdoor pool, children free with parents, wheelchair access, NS rooms, TV, a/c, kitchenettes, laundry facilities, senior rates, meeting facilities, CC. 1 block from the golf course, 8 miles from the Panama City airport. SGL/DBL$80-$120.

The Inn At St. Thomas Square (8600 Thomas Dr., 32408; 234-0349, Fax 235-8104, 800-874-8600) 70 1- , 2- , and 3-bedroom suites, free breakfast, outdoor pool, whirlpools, lighted tennis courts, sauna, a/c, TV, laundry facilities, no pets, in-room refrigerators, children free with parents, senior rates, CC. LS SGL/DBL$35-$100; HS SGL/DBL$55-$160.

La Brisa Inn (9424 West Hwy. 98, 32401; 235-1122, 800-523-4369) 60 rooms and efficiencies, a/c, TV, laundry facilities, kitchenettes, no pets, children free with parents, NS, senior rates, CC. SGL/DBL$28-$55.

Marriott's Bay Point Resort (4200 Marriott Dr., 32408; 234-3307, Fax 233-1308, 800-874-7105, 800-228-9290) 355 rooms and suites, restaurant, lounge, indoor and outdoor heated pools, whirlpools, exercise center, lighted tennis courts, kitchenettes, a/c, TV, in-room refrigerators, children stay free with parents, beach, gift shop, NS rooms, room service, game room, no pets, in-room computer hookups, laundry service, senior rates, 22 meeting rooms, 40,000 square feet of meeting and exhibition space, CC. 8 miles from the Panama City airport. LS SGL/DBL$75; HS SGL/DBL$125.

Moondrifter Condominiums I (8815 Thomas Dr., 32407; 234-9741) 1-bedroom condominiums, beach, outdoor pool, a/c, TV, in-room refrigerators, microwaves and coffee makers, laundry facilities, no pets, children free with parents, CC. 1BR$70-$100.

Moonspinner Condominiums II (4425 Thomas Dr., 32408; 234-8900, 800-223-3947) 115 condominiums, outdoor pool, whirlpools, lighted tennis courts, beach, kitchenettes, a/c, TV, CC. LS SGL/DBL$475W-$650W; HS SGL/DBL$820W-$1,100W.

Nautical Watch Condominiums (6205 Thomas Dr., 32408; 234-6876) 1-bedroom condominiums, beach, outdoor pool, laundry facilities, wheelchair access, NS rooms, children free with parents, no pets, in-room refrigerators, microwaves and coffee makers, CC. 1BR$55-$85.

Passport Inn (5003 West Hwy. 98, 32401; 769-2010, 800-251-1962) 44 rooms, restaurant, outdoor pets OK, outdoor pool, a/c, TV, NS rooms, wheelchair access, free local calls, children free with parents, senior rates, CC. 5 miles from the Gulf beaches, 4 miles from the Panama City airport. SGL/DBL$30-$55.

Pier 99 Waterfront Motel (9900 South Thomas Dr., 32407; 234-6657, 800-874-6657) 100 rooms, kitchen, outdoor pool, beach, a/c, laundry facilities, wheelchair access, no pets, CC. SGL/DBL$30-$95.

Pinnacle Port Condominiums (23224 Front Beach Rd., 32413; 234-8813, 800-874-8824) 200 1- and 2-bedroom suites, indoor and outdoor heated pools, sauna, lighted tennis courts, a/c, TV, kitchenettes, no pets, laundry facilities, senior rates, CC. LS SGL/DBL$80-$105; HS SGL/DBL$115-$180.

Quality Inn Beachfront (15285 Front Beach Rd., 32413; 234-6636, 800-221-2222) 120 rooms and suites, outdoor pool, exercise center, tennis courts, children free with parents, a/c, TV, wheelchair access, room service, laundry service, NS rooms, no pets, senior rates, CC. 15 miles from the Panama City airport, 2.5 miles from Shipwreck Island Water Park. SGL/DBL$40-$125.

Ramada Inn Beachside Resort (12907 Front Beach Rd., 32407; 234-1700, Fax 235-2700, 800-2-RAMADA) 147 rooms, restaurant, lounge, outdoor pool, beach, in-room refrigerators and coffee makers, a/c, TV, pets OK, children stay free with parents, NS rooms, senior rates, meeting facilities for 900, CC. 1 mile from the golf course. SGL/DBL$60-$155.

Red Carpet Inn (10811 Front Beach Rd., 32407; 234-2811, 800-251-1962) 20 rooms, restaurant, lounge, outdoor pool, children free with parents, kitchenettes, no pets, TV, a/c, NS rooms, meeting facilities, senior rates, CC. SGL/DBL$40-$78.

Scottish Inn (4907 Hwy. 98 West, 32401; 769-2432, 800-251-1962) 31 rooms, outdoor pool, pets OK, a/c, TV, wheelchair access, NS rooms, children free with parents, free local calls, senior rates, CC. 3 miles from the golf course. SGL/DBL$24-$48.

Seachase Condominiums (17351 Front Beach Rd., 32408; 235-1300, 800-457-2051) 2-bedroom condominiums and townhouses, outdoor pool, beach, kitchenettes, no pets, a/c, TV, laundry facilities, senior rates, CC. 2BR$400W-$820W.

Shalimar Plaza Motel (17545 Front Beach Rd., 32408; 234-2133, 800-232-2435) 74 1- and 2-bedroom efficiencies, restaurant, outdoor pool, tennis courts, beach, children free with parents, a/c, TV, CC. SGL/DBL$40-$90.

Sugar Beach Condominiums (8727 Thomas Dr., 32413; 234-2102, 800-45-SUGAR) 1- , 2- , and 3-bedroom condominiums, outdoor pool, beach, a/c, TV, children free with parent, in-room refrigerators, microwaves and coffee makers, laundry facilities, no pets, CC. 1BR$99-$116, 2BR$110-$120, 3BR$125-$165.

Sunset Inn (8109 Surf Dr., 32408; 234-7370) 50 rooms and 2-bedroom efficiencies, outdoor pool, beach, laundry facilities, in-room refrigerators and microwaves, a/c, TV, no pets, senior rates, CC. SGL/DBL$30-$90.

Sunswept Condominiums (6829 Thomas Dr., 32407; 233-1231, 800-272-6370) 1-bedroom condominiums, outdoor pool, beach, a/c, TV, wheelchair access, kitchenettes, children free with parents, CC. 1BR$100, 2BR$200.

Surf High Inn (10611 Front Beach Rd., 32407; 234-2129) 32 rooms and 2-bedroom efficiencies, outdoor pool, beach, kitchenettes, a/c,

TV, children free with parents, NS rooms, pets OK, laundry facilities, CC. SGL/DBL$35-$55.

Pembroke Pines

Area Code 305

Grand Palms Golf and Country Club (110 Grand Palms Dr., 33027; 431-8800, Fax 435-5988, 800-327-9246) 137 rooms and suites, restaurant, outdoor pool, exercise center, lighted tennis courts, a/c, TV, laundry facilities, children free with parents, no pets, 5 meeting rooms, meeting facilities for 600, senior rates, CC. 20 miles from the Ft. Lauderdale-Hollywood airport, 23 miles from the Broward Convention Center. LS SGL/DBL$65; HS SGL/DBL$85

Pensacola

Area Code 904

Best Western Village Inn (8240 North Davis Hwy., 32561; 479-1099, Fax 479-9320, 800-528-1234) 94 rooms and suites, free breakfast, in-room refrigerators, outdoor pool, children free with parents, a/c, NS rooms, TV, laundry facilities, wheelchair access, pets OK, meeting facilities, senior rates, CC. 11 miles from Gulf beaches, 4 miles from the Pensacola airport. SGL/DBL$45-$66.

Comfort Inn (6919 Pensacola Blvd., 32505; 478-4499, 800-228-5150, 800-221-2222) 120 rooms, outdoor pool, a/c, TV, in-room refrigerators and microwaves, pets OK, children free with parents, NS rooms, wheelchair access, senior rates, CC. 10 miles from the Pensacola airport, 13 miles from Gulf beaches. SGL/DBL$32-$58.

Comfort Inn Naval Air Station (3 New Warrington Rd., 32506; 455-3233, 800-228-5150, 800-221-2222) 102 rooms, restaurant, free breakfast, lounge, entertainment, outdoor pool, a/c, TV, no pets, children free with parents, NS rooms, in-room refrigerators and microwaves, wheelchair access, senior rates, CC. 6 miles from the dog track, 8 miles from the Pensacola airport, 12 miles to Gulf beaches. LS SGL/DBL$36-$56; HS SGL/DBL$50-$60.

Days Inn (7051 Pensacola Blvd., 32505; 476-9090, 800-325-2525) 80 rooms and suites, restaurant, free breakfast, outdoor pool, a/c, TV, wheelchair access, children free with parents, pets OK, NS rooms, laundry facilities, senior rates, meeting facilities, CC. 5 miles from the Naval Air Station, 3 miles from the Five Flags Speedway, 2 miles from the shopping mall. SGL/DBL$40-$60.

Days Inn (710 North Palafox St., 32501; 438-4922, 800-325-2525) 156 rooms and suites, restaurant, outdoor pool, a/c, TV, wheelchair access, NS rooms, children free with parents, pets OK, laundry facilities, airport transportation, senior rates, CC. SGL/DBL$38-$68.

Econo Lodge (7194 Pensacola Blvd., 32505; 479-8600, 800-446-6900, 800-4-CHOICE) 60 rooms, restaurant, outdoor pool, children free with parents, no pets, NS rooms, wheelchair access, a/c, TV, senior rates, CC. 5 miles from the Pensacola airport, 10 miles from Fort Pickens and the State Park, 3 miles from the Five Flag Speedway. SGL/DBL$34-$56.

Executive Inn (6954 Pensacola Blvd., 32505; 478-4015) 36 rooms, outdoor pool, no pets, in-room refrigerators and microwaves, a/c, TV, children free with parents, NS rooms, senior rates, CC. SGL/DBL$30-$40.

Hampton Inn (7330 Plantation Rd., 32504; 477-3333, 800-426-7866) 124 rooms, outdoor pool, children free with parents, NS rooms, wheelchair access, in-room computer hookups, fax service, in-room refrigerators, local transportation, microwaves and coffee makers, TV, a/c, no pets, free local calls, meeting facilities, senior rates, CC. 1 block from the shopping mall, 15 miles from Gulf beaches, 4 miles from the Pensacola airport, 6 miles from the downtown area. SGL/DBL$45-$54.

Hilton Hotel (200 East Gregory St., 32501; 433-3336, Fax 432-7572, 800-HILTONS) 212 rooms and suites, restaurant, lounge, entertainment, outdoor heated pool, exercise center, children free with parents, NS rooms, wheelchair access, room service, local transportation, laundry facilities, a/c, TV, 8 meeting rooms, meeting facilities for 1,300, senior rates, CC. 1 block from the historic district and Civic Center, 6 miles from the Pensacola airport. SGL/DBL$65-$135.

HoJo Inn (4126 Mobile Hwy., 32506; 456-5731, 800-I-GO-HOJO) 67 rooms, restaurant, lounge, outdoor pool, children free with parents, wheelchair access, no pets, NS rooms, TV, a/c, laundry facilities, senior rates, meeting facilities, CC. SGL/DBL$28-$48.

Holiday Inn (7200 Plantation Rd., 32504; 474-0100, 800-HOLIDAY) 152 rooms and suites, restaurant, lounge, entertainment, outdoor pool, exercise center, children free with parents, wheelchair access, a/c, TV, NS rooms, airport courtesy car, fax service, room service, laundry service, meeting facilities for 300, senior rates, CC. 10 miles from the Gulf beaches, 3 miles from the University of West Florida, 1 block from the University Mall. SGL/DBL$65-$80, STS$125.

Holiday Inn Airport Express (6501 Pensacola Blvd., 32505; 476-7200, Fax 474-0100, 800-HOLIDAY) 215 rooms and suites, free breakfast, outdoor pool, exercise center, children free with parents, wheelchair access, a/c, TV, free local calls, NS rooms, pets OK, fax service, room service, laundry service, meeting facilities for 75, senior rates, CC. 5 miles from the Pensacola airport and Civic Center, 10 miles from the NASA Museum. SGL/DBL$60-$78.

Homestead Inn (7830 Pine Forest Rd., 32506; 944-4816, 800-937-1735) 6 rooms, free breakfast, a/c, TV, fireplaces, no pets, NS, senior rates, CC. SGL/DBL$60-$80.

Hospitality Inn (4910 Mobile Hwy., 32506; 453-3333, 800-321-0052) 80 rooms and efficiencies, outdoor pool, a/c, TV, VCRs, children free with parents, pets OK, NS rooms, in-room refrigerators, microwaves and coffee makers, laundry facilities, meeting facilities, CC. SGL/DBL$55-$65.

Hospitality Inn (6900 Pensacola Blvd., 32505; 477-2333, Fax 479-3575) 124 rooms, outdoor pool, exercise center, a/c, TV, VCRs, kitchenettes, laundry facilities, children free with parents, pets OK, CC. SGL/DBL$70-$80.

Knights Inn (1953 Northcross Lane, 32514; 477-2554, 800-843-5644) 103 rooms, outdoor pool, wheelchair access, NS rooms, TV, a/c, in-room refrigerators and microwaves, pets OK, fax service, VCRs, senior rates, CC. 8 miles from the downtown area, 3 miles from the Pensacola airport and University of West Florida, 15 miles from Gulf beaches. SGL/DBL$32-$38.

La Quinta Inn (7750 North Davis Hwy., 32514; 474-0411, Fax 474-1521, 800-531-5900) 130 rooms, restaurant, outdoor pool, complimentary newspaper, free local calls, fax service, laundry service, NS rooms, in-room refrigerators, pets OK, wheelchair access, TV, a/c, meeting facilities, senior rates, CC. 15 miles from the Pensacola Naval Air Station Museum, 3 miles from the Orlando airport. SGL/DBL$45-$55.

Motel 6 (5829 Pensacola Blvd., 32505; 477-2152, 505-891-6161) 120 rooms, outdoor pool, free local calls, children free with parents, NS rooms, wheelchair access, a/c, TV, CC. SGL/DBL$28-$36.

Motel 6 (7827 North Davis Hwy., 32514; 476-5386, 505-891-6161) 106 rooms, outdoor pool, free local calls, children free with parents, NS rooms, wheelchair access, a/c, TV, CC. 1 block from University Mall. SGL/DBL$30-$36.

Motel 6 (7226 Plantation Rd., 32504; 474-1060, 505-891-6161) 80 rooms, outdoor pool, free local calls, children free with parents, NS rooms, wheelchair access, a/c, TV, CC. 1 block from the University Mall, 15 miles to Gulf beaches. SGL/DBL$28-$35.

New World Landing Inn (600 South Palafox St., 32501; 432-4111) 16 rooms and suites, restaurant, free breakfast, a/c, TV, no pets, NS rooms, meeting facilities, CC. SGL/DBL$55-$80.

Quality Inn (6911 Pensacola Blvd., 32505; 479-3800, 800-221-2222) 126 rooms and suites, restaurant, outdoor pool, exercise center, children free with parents, a/c, TV, VCRs, pets OK, wheelchair access, in-room refrigerators and microwaves, room service, laundry service, NS rooms, meeting facilities, senior rates, CC. 5 miles from the Pensacola airport, 12 miles from Gulf beaches, 11 miles from the Pensacola Naval Air Station Museum. LS SGL/DBL$32-$35; HS SGL/DBL$38-$54.

Ramada Inn Bayview (7601 Scenic Hwy., 32504; 477-7155, 800-2-RAMADA) 150 rooms and suites, restaurant, lounge, entertainment, outdoor pool, jacuzzi, exercise center, wheelchair access, NS rooms, a/c, TV, children free with parents, in-room refrigerators and microwaves, local transportation, game room, pets OK, room service, laundry facilities, meeting facilities, senior rates, CC. 13 miles from Gulf beaches, 3 miles from the Pensacola airport, 3 miles from the shopping mall. SGL/DBL$55-$75.

Ramada Inn North (6550 Pensacola Blvd., 32505; 477-0711, 800-2-RAMADA) 106 rooms and suites, restaurant, lounge, outdoor pool, wheelchair access, NS rooms, a/c, TV, children free with parents, local transportation, pets OK, in-room refrigerators, microwaves and coffee makers, room service, laundry facilities, meeting facilities, senior rates, CC. 4 miles from the Pensacola airport, 1/8 mile from golf course, 10 miles from Greyhound Race Track, 4 miles from the shopping mall. SGL/DBL$48-$59, STS$85-$105.

Red Carpet Inn (4448 Mobile Hwy., 32506; 456-7411, 800-251-1962) 50 rooms, restaurant, lounge, outdoor pool, sauna, pets OK, children free with parents, TV, a/c, NS rooms, meeting facilities, senior rates, CC. 5 miles from the Naval Station. SGL/DBL$35.

Red Roof Inn (7340 Plantation Rd., 32504; 476-7960, Fax: 479-4606, 800-843-7663) 108 rooms and suites, NS rooms, fax service, wheelchair access, complimentary newspaper, children free with parents, pets OK, in-room computer hookups, a/c, TV, free local calls, senior rates, CC. 1 block from the University Mall, 5 miles from the University of West Florida, 10 miles from the Convention Center, 6 miles from the Pensacola airport. SGL/DBL$33-$47.

Residence Inn (7230 Plantation Rd., 32504; 479-1000, 800-331-3131) 64 rooms and suites, free breakfast, outdoor pool, whirlpools, sauna, in-room refrigerators, microwaves and coffee makers, pets OK, laundry facilities, TV, a/c, VCRs, complimentary newspaper, fireplaces, children free with parents, NS rooms, wheelchair access, meeting facilities for 40, senior rates, CC. 3 miles from the Pensacola airport, 18 miles from Gulf beaches, 5 miles from the downtown area and University of West Florida. SGL/DBL$85-$110.

Rodeway Inn (8500 Pine Forest Rd., 32534; 477-9150, 800-424-4777) 100 rooms, restaurant, lounge, entertainment, outdoor pool, wheelchair access, NS rooms, children free with parents, a/c, in-room refrigerators, pets OK, TV, VCRs, senior rates, CC. 10 miles from the Pensacola airport and golf course, 2 miles from the Fairgrounds, 9 miles from the Naval Air Station Museum. SGL/DBL$36-$55.

Sabine Yacht and Racquet Club (330 Ft. Pickens Rd., 32561; 932-7290, 800-343-0344) 30 1-, 2-, and 3-bedroom villas, outdoor pool, tennis, exercise center, whirlpools, children free with parents, a/c, TV, VCRs, wheelchair access, laundry facilities, in-room refrigerators, microwaves and coffee makers, CC. 1BR$675W, 2BR$800W, 3BR$900.

Seville Inn (223 East Garden St., 32501; 433-8331, Fax 432-6849) 128 rooms and suites, restaurant, lounge, outdoor pool, pets OK, laundry facilities, a/c, TV, NS rooms, wheelchair access, senior rates, CC. SGL/DBL$45-$100.

Super 8 Motel (7220 Plantation Rd., 32504; 476-8038, Fax 474-6284, 800-800-8000) 62 rooms, outdoor pool, children free with parents, free local calls, a/c, TV, in-room refrigerators and microwaves, fax service, pets OK, NS rooms, wheelchair access, meeting facilities, senior rates, CC. 10 miles from the Pensacola airport, 15 miles from Gulf beaches. SGL/DBL$35-$55.

Pensacola Beach
Area Code 904

Rental & Reservation Services

Baars Realty (11 Via De Luna Dr., 32561; 932-9321, 800-874-9010) rental privately-owned houses, townhouses and condominiums.

Gulf Breeze Properties (41 Via De Luna Drive 32561; 932-3539, 800-334-2056) rental apartments, townhouses and private homes.

Pensacola Beach Properties (1200 Ft. Pickens Rd., 32561; 932-9341, 800-826-0614) rental condominiums and private homes.

Pensacola Beach Realty (649 Pensacola Beach Blvd., 32561; 932-5337, 800-874-9243) rental condos, townhouses and private homes.

Realty Marts (1591 Via De Luna Dr., 32561; 932-5376, 800-874-9245) rental condominiums, townhouses and private homes.

Tristan Realty (Ft. Pickens Rd., 32562; 932-7363, Fax 932-8361, 800-445-9931) rental private homes, condominiums, apartments and townhouses.

□□□

Barbary Coast Motel (24 Via De Luna, 32561; 932-2233) 24 rooms and efficiencies, outdoor pool, beach, children free with parents, in-room refrigerators, no pets, CC. SGL/DBL$45-$110.

Best Western Pensacola Beach (16 Via De Luna, 32561; 934-3300, 800-528-1234) 62 rooms and suites, free breakfast, outdoor pool, children free with parents, a/c, NS rooms, TV, kitchenettes, laundry facilities, wheelchair access, in-room refrigerators, microwaves and coffee makers, no pets, beach, meeting facilities, senior rates,

CC. A 1/2-mile from the shopping mall, 11 miles to Gulf beaches, 4 miles from the Pensacola airport. SGL/DBL$55-$105.

Clarion Suites Resort (20 Via De Luna, 32561; 932-4300, 800-221-2222, 800-874-5303) 86 rooms and suites, outdoor pool, exercise center, no pets, beach, in-room coffee makers, NS rooms, children free with parents, senior rates, meeting facilities, a/c, TV, CC. 11 miles from the Pensacola airport, 5 miles from the golf course. SGL/DBL$60-$130.

Five Flags Motel (299 Ft. Pickens Rd., 32561; 932-3586) 49 rooms, a/c, TV, children free with parents, NS rooms, laundry facilities, CC. SGL/DBL$45-$75.

Gulf Air Motel (21 Via De Luna Dr., 32561; 932-2319) 23 rooms and efficiencies, outdoor heated pool, beach, pets OK, a/c, TV, children free with parents, NS rooms, CC. SGL/DBL$33-$63.

Holiday Inn (165 Ft. Pickens Rd., 32561; 932-5361, Fax 932-7121, 800-HOLIDAY) 150 rooms, restaurant, lounge, outdoor pool, lighted tennis courts, children free with parents, wheelchair access, a/c, in-room refrigerators, TV, NS rooms, gift shop, boutiques, game room, fax service, room service, laundry service, no pets, 6 meeting rooms, meeting facilities for 250, senior rates, CC. 1 mile from the National Aviation Museum and Tiki Water Center, 12 miles from the Pensacola airport, 7 miles from the Civic Center, LS SGL/DBL$60-$90; HS SGL/DBL$90-$120.

Regency Villas (1600 Via De Luna Dr., 32561; 932-0128, 800-255-4853) 1- and 2-bedroom villas, outdoor pool, a/c, TV, in-room refrigerators, microwaves and coffee makers, children free with parents, no pets, laundry service, CC. 1BR/2BR$425W-$890W.

Perdido Key

Area Code 904

Rental & Reservation Services

Century 21 Leib and Association (14620 Perdido Key Dr., 32507; 492-0744, 800-553-1223) rental condominiums, townhouses and private homes.

□□□

Comfort Inn (13586 Perdido Key Dr., 32507; 492-2755, 800-228-5150, 800-221-2222) 100 rooms, outdoor pool, whirlpools, no pets, beach, a/c, TV, children free with parents, NS rooms, wheelchair access, senior rates, CC. 20 miles from the Pensacola airport, 1.5 miles from the golf course, 5 miles from the greyhound race track. SGL/DBL$38-$110.

Perdido Sun Condominiums (13753 Perdido Key Dr., 32507; 492-2390, 800-227-2390) 90 1- , 2- , and 3-bedroom condominiums, outdoor pool, exercise center, wheelchair access, a/c, TV, children free with parents, laundry facilities, kitchenettes, CC. 1BR/2BR/3BR$330W-$1195W.

Vista Del Mar Condominiums (13333 Johnson Beach Rd., 32507; 492-0211, 800-648-4529) 32 1- and 2-bedroom condominiums, outdoor pool, tennis, beach, a/c, TV, children free with parents, laundry facilities, in-room refrigerators, microwaves and coffee makers, no pets, senior rates, CC. 1BR$125, 2BR$145.

Perry
Area Code 904

Days Inn (2277 South Byron Butler Hwy., 32347; 584-5311, 800-325-2525) 60 rooms, restaurant, free breakfast, outdoor pool, a/c, TV, wheelchair access, NS rooms, pets OK, children free with parents, laundry facilities, senior rates, CC. 2 miles from the regional airport, 20 miles to Gulf beaches. SGL/DBL$37-$65.

Pinellas Park
Area Code 813

Days Inn Gateway (9359 Hwy. 19 North, 34666; 577-3833, Fax 576-3790, 800-325-2525) 154 rooms, restaurant, outdoor pool, a/c, TV, wheelchair access, NS rooms, pets OK, complimentary newspaper, children free with parents, laundry facilities, in-room refrigerators and microwaves, senior rates, CC. 1 mile from Gulf beaches, 8 miles from the Florida Suncoast Dome, 15 miles from the Tampa airport. SGL/DBL$35-$70.

La Mark Charles Motel (6200 North 34th St., 34664; 527-7334, 800-448-6781) 93 rooms and suites, restaurant, outdoor pool, whirlpools, laundry facilities, gift shop, in-room refrigerators, a/c, TV, kitchenettes, NS rooms, children free with parents, pets OK, senior rates, CC. SGL/DBL$55-$60, STS$65-$70.

La Quinta Inn (7500 Hwy. 19, 34665; 545-5611, Fax 544-4202, 800-531-5900) 117 rooms, restaurant, free breakfast, lounge, outdoor pool, complimentary newspaper, free local calls, fax service, laundry service, NS rooms, wheelchair access, remote control TV, a/c, meeting facilities, senior rates, CC. 5 miles from the St. Petersburg-Clearwater airport, 20 miles from Tampa Bay Downs, 14 miles from the Tampa airport. SGL/DBL$48-$68.

Plant City
Area Code 813

Days Inn (301 South Frontage St., 33566; 752-0570, Fax 754-3422, 800-325-2525) 176 rooms, restaurant, outdoor pool, a/c, TV, wheelchair access, children free with parents, pets OK, NS rooms, laundry facilities, senior rates, CC. SGL/DBL$35-$75.

Holiday Inn (2011 North Wheeler St., 33566; 754-5657, Fax 754-5657, 800-HOLIDAY) 261 rooms and efficiencies, restaurant, lounge, entertainment, outdoor pool, exercise center, children free with parents, wheelchair access, a/c, TV, NS rooms, kitchenettes, game room, laundry, pets OK, fax service, room service, 7 meeting rooms, meeting facilities for 500, senior rates, CC. LS SGL/DBL$50-$70; HS SGL/DBL$75-$85.

Plantation
Area Code 305

Amble Inn Motel (790 Southwest 40th Ave., 33317; 583-2018) 9 rooms, efficiencies and 1-bedroom apartments, outdoor pool, whirlpools, a/c, TV, kitchenettes, no pets, CC. SGL/DBL$30-$40, EFF$35-$45, 1BR$40-$60.

Holiday Inn (1711 North University Dr., 33317; 472-5600, Fax 370-3201, 800-HOLIDAY) 330 rooms and suites, restaurant, lounge, entertainment, outdoor heated pool, children free with parents, wheelchair access, a/c, TV, NS rooms, fax service, in-room computer hookups, pets OK, kitchenettes, room service, laundry service, 20 meeting rooms, meeting facilities for 1,600, senior rates, CC. A 1/4-mile from the Galleria Mall, 2 miles from Port Everglades, 12 miles from the Ft. Lauderdale-Hollywood airport, 15 miles from the Convention Center. SGL/DBL$60-$95.

Melrose Park Motel (790 Hwy. 7, 33317; 583-6650) 18 rooms, efficiencies and 1-bedroom apartments, outdoor pool, whirlpools, a/c, TV, no pets, children free with parents, CC. SGL/DBL$40-$53, EFF$38-$48, 1BR$50-$60.

Sheraton Suites (311 North University Dr., 33324; 424-3300, Fax 452-8887, 800-325-3535) 264 rooms and suites, restaurant, lounge, entertainment, outdoor heated pool, NS rooms, a/c, room service, no pets, in-room computer hookups, boutiques, TV, children free with parents, in-room microwaves and coffee makers, wheelchair access, meeting facilities for 300, 7,000 square feet of meeting and exhibition space, senior rates, CC. 1 block from the Fashion Mall, 10 miles from Atlantic beaches, 8 miles from the Ft. Lauderdale-Hollywood airport, 9 miles from the Convention Center. SGL/DBL$110-$145.

Wellesley Inn At Plantation (7901 Southwest 6th St., 33324; 473-8257, Fax 473-9804, 800-444-8888) 106 rooms, free breakfast, outdoor heated pool, a/c, TV, pets OK, children free with parents, airport transportation, in-room microwaves, NS rooms, fax service, laundry facilities, senior rates, CC. SGL/DBL$55-$100.

Pompano Beach
Area Code 305

Aqua Mar Resort (555 North Riverside Dr., 33062; 943-8800, Fax 942-7866) 27 1-bedroom apartments, outdoor pool, whirlpool, a/c, TV, in-room refrigerators and microwaves, children free with parents, CC. 1BR$40-$110.

Best Western Beachcomber Hotel and Villa (1200 South Ocean Blvd., 33062; 941-7830, Fax 942-7680, 800-231-2423, 800-231-2424) 147 rooms, suites and villas, restaurant, lounge, entertainment, outdoor heated pool, children free with parents, beach, no pets, a/c, NS rooms, TV, laundry facilities, wheelchair access, in-room microwaves, meeting facilities, senior rates, CC. A 1/2-mile from fishing pier, 1 block from the shopping mall. LS SGL/DBL$55-$125; HS SGL/DBL$85-$255.

Carib Terrace Resort Motel (522 North Ocean Blvd., 33062; 943-9130) 11 rooms, pool, a/c, TV, no pets, CC. SGL/DBL$85-$125.

Croton Arms Apartments (3237 Northeast 11th St., 33062; 941-1766, Fax 941-1775) 20 apartments, outdoor pool, in-room refrigerators, microwaves and coffee makers, a/c, TV, no pets, NS rooms, senior rates, CC. LS SGL/DBL$35-$55; HS SGL/DBL$60-$90.

Days Inn (1411 Northwest 31st Ave., 33069; 972-3700, Fax 977-3090, 800-325-2525) 172 rooms, restaurant, outdoor pool, pets OK, a/c, TV, wheelchair access, NS rooms, laundry facilities, children free with parents, senior rates, CC. 15 miles from the Sawgrass Mills Mall, 2 miles from Butterfly World, 5 miles from Atlantic beaches. SGL/DBL$32-$69.

Dolphin Apartment Motel (3215 Northeast 7th St., 33062; 941-7373, Fax 941-7388) 20 rooms, efficiencies and 1-bedroom apartments, outdoor heated pool, in-room microwaves and coffee makers, no pets, children stay free with parents, a/c, TV, kitchenettes, NS rooms, CC. SGL/DBL$45-$95.

Ebb Tide Apartments (312 Briny Ave., 33062; 941-7200) 34 rooms, efficiencies and 1-bedroom apartments, outdoor pool, in-room refrigerators, microwaves and coffee makers, children free with parents, no pets, laundry facilities, CC. SGL/DBL$40-$78, EFF$45-$100, 1BR$60-$122.

Holiday Inn (1350 South Ocean Blvd., 33062; 941-7300, Fax 941-7300, 800-HOLIDAY) 133 rooms and 1-bedroom suites, restaurant, lounge, outdoor heated pool, tennis courts, children free with parents, wheelchair access, a/c, beach, TV, NS rooms, fax service, room service, laundry service, no pets, kitchenettes, 2 meeting rooms, meeting facilities for 100, senior rates, CC. 12 miles from the Ft. Lauderdale-Hollywood airport and the Broward Convention Center, 11 miles from Port Everglades. SGL/DBL$70-$185.

Howard Johnson Resort (9 North Pompano Beach Blvd., 33062; 781-1300, Fax 782-5585, 800-223-5844, 800-I-GO-HOJO) 104 rooms and efficiencies, restaurant, lounge, entertainment, outdoor pool, children free with parents, wheelchair access, complimentary newspaper, room service, NS rooms, TV, a/c, laundry facilities, in-room refrigerators, microwaves and coffee makers, no pets, senior rates, meeting facilities, CC. 10 miles from the Ft. Lauderdale-Hollywood airport. SGL/DBL$60-$160.

Motel 6 (1201 Northwest 31st Ave., 33069; 972-6366, 505-891-6161) 127 rooms, outdoor pool, free local calls, children free with parents, NS rooms, wheelchair access, a/c, TV, CC. SGL/DBL$30-$34.

Native Son Resort (1950 South Ocean Blvd., 33062; 942-2800) 35 1- and 2-bedroom apartments, outdoor pool, tennis courts, exercise center, children free with parents, no pets, laundry facilities, wheelchair access, CC. 1BR$85-$125, 2BR$95-$135.

Ocean Ranch Hotel (1110 South Ocean Blvd., 33062; 941-7100, Fax 941-7100, 800-843-5526) 80 rooms, efficiencies and 1-bedroom apartments, restaurant, outdoor pool, tennis courts, exercise center, a/c, TV, wheelchair access, NS rooms, children free with parents, room service, no pets, laundry facilities, senior rates, CC. SGL/DBL$51, EFF$55, 1BR$63.

Palm Aire Spa Resort and Country Club (2501 North Palm Aire Dr., 33069; 972-3300, Fax 968-2744, 800-327-4960) 166 rooms and suites, restaurant, lounge, entertainment, indoor and outdoor heated pools, whirlpools, tennis courts, children free with parents, no pets, in-room computer hookups, laundry service, barber and beauty shop, local transportation, NS rooms, 16 meeting rooms, meeting facilities for 350, senior rates, CC. 12 miles from the Ft. Lauderdale-Hollywood airport. LS SGL/DBL$80-$100; HS SGL/DBL$120-$170.

Pompano Beach Motor Lodge (1112 North Ocean Blvd., 33062; 943-0630) 54 rooms and efficiencies, restaurant, lounge, outdoor pool, in-room refrigerators, a/c, TV, beach, children free with parents, no pets, CC. SGL/DBL$80-$97.

Quality Inn Oceanside (1208 North Ocean Blvd., 33062; 782-5300, Fax 946-1853, 800-221-2222) 165 rooms and suites, restaurant, lounge, outdoor pool, exercise center, children free with parents, a/c, TV, wheelchair access, room service, laundry service, in-room refrigerators, beauty shop, NS rooms, meeting facilities, senior rates, CC. 15 miles from the Pompano Beach airport, 20 miles from the Sawgrass Mills Shopping Mall, 6 miles from the Pompano Harness Race Track. SGL/DBL$100-$250.

Ronny Dee Resort Motel (717 South Ocean Blvd., 33062; 943-3020) 31 rooms, outdoor heated pool, kitchenettes, a/c, TV, no pets, children free with parents, in-room refrigerators, laundry facilities, NS rooms, CC. SGL/DBL$30-$80.

Sands Harbor Hotel and Marina (125 North Riverside Dr., 33062; 942-9100, Fax 785-5657, 800-227-3353) 56 rooms, efficiencies and suites, restaurant, lounge, outdoor pool, in-room refrigerators, a/c, TV, senior rates, CC. SGL/DBL$70-$130, STS$150-$275.

Sea Castle Resort (730 North Ocean Blvd., 33062; 941-2570, 800-331-4666) 40 rooms, outdoor heated pool, beach, in-room microwaves and coffee makers, children free with parents, a/c, TV, NS rooms, senior rates, CC. SGL/DBL$40-$120.

Sea Garden Beach and Tennis Resort (615 North Ocean Blvd., 33062; 943-6200, Fax 783-0047, 800-327-8920) 144 rooms, efficiencies and 1- and 2-bedroom apartments, restaurant, lounge, entertainment, outdoor pool, exercise center, lighted tennis courts, a/c, TV, NS rooms, children free with parents, no pets, senior rates, CC. SGL/DBL$120-$200.

Three Sisters Inn (2300 Northeast 10th St., 33062; 943-3500, Fax 943-3500) 61 rooms, free breakfast, in-room refrigerators, a/c, TV, NS rooms, children free with parents, no pets, CC. SGL/DBL$45-$70.

Traders Ocean Resort (1600 South Ocean Blvd., 33062; 941-8400, Fax 941-1024, 800-325-5220) 93 rooms, efficiencies and 1-bedroom apartments, restaurant, outdoor pool, room service, NS rooms, wheelchair access, a/c, TV, VCRs, children free with parents, laundry facilities, CC. SGL/DBL$65-$92, EFF$68-$110, 1BR$99-$205.

Ponte Vedra

Area Code 904

The Lodge at Ponte Vedra Beach (607 Ponte Vedra Blvd., 32082; 273-9500, Fax 273-0210, 800-243-4304) 66 rooms, restaurant, lounge, entertainment, outdoor heated pool, saunas, tennis courts, whirlpools, exercise center, in-room refrigerators, microwaves and coffee makers, children stay free with parents, no pets, beach, NS rooms, a/c, TV, senior rates, 3 meeting rooms, meeting facilities for 500, 1,600 square feet of meeting and exhibition space. CC. SGL/DBL$145-$235.

Marriott at Sawgrass (1000 TPC Blvd., 32082; 285-7777, Fax 285-0906, 800-228-9280, 800-331-3131) 552 rooms and suites, restaurant, lounge, entertainment, outdoor heated pool, sauna, exercise center, beach, kitchenettes, no pets, airport transportation, in-room refrigerators, microwaves and coffee makers, VCRs, children free with parents, gift shops, a/c, TV, NS rooms, wheelchair access, 8 meeting rooms, senior rates, CC. SGL/DBL$110-$500.

Ponte Vedra Inn and Club (200 Ponte Vedra Blvd., 32082; 285-1111, Fax 285-2111, 800-234-7842) 202 rooms and suites, restaurant, lounge, entertainment, outdoor heated pool, tennis courts, exercise center, whirlpools, kitchenettes, children stay free with parents, a/c, TV, in-room refrigerators, microwaves and coffee makers, beach, senior rates, 17 meeting rooms, 17,000 square feet of meeting and exhibition space, meeting facilities for 450. CC. LS SGL/DBL$90-$125; HS SGL/DBL$175-$195.

Port Charlotte

Area Code 813

Days Inn (1941 Tamiami Trail, 33952; 627-8900, 800-325-2525) 126 rooms, restaurant, lounge, entertainment, outdoor pool, exercise center, in-room refrigerators, pets OK, a/c, TV, wheelchair access, NS rooms, children stay free with parents, laundry facilities, senior rates, meeting facilities, CC. 12 miles from Gulf beaches. LS SGL/DBL$35-$55; HS SGL/DBL$85-$90.

Econo Lodge (4100 Tamiami Trail, 33952; 743-2442, 800-4-CHOICE) 60 rooms, children under 12 free with parents, senior rates, NS rooms, wheelchair access, no pets, a/c, TV, senior rates, CC. 10 miles from the Texas Rangers Training Camp, 20 miles from Gulf Beaches. SGL/DBL$30-$65.

Quality Inn (3400 Tamiami Trail, 33952; 625-4181, Fax 629-1740, 800-221-2222) 105 rooms and suites, restaurant, lounge, outdoor pool, exercise center, children free with parents, a/c, TV, wheelchair access, room service, laundry service, pets OK, in-room refrigerators, microwaves and coffee makers, NS rooms, meeting facilities, senior rates, CC. 17 miles from Gulf beaches, 2 miles from Peace River Harbor, 10 miles from Warm Mineral Springs. LS SGL/DBL$32-$53; HS SGL/DBL$55-$85.

Sand Piper Motel (3291 Tamiami Trail, 33952; 625-4016) 40 rooms and efficiencies, restaurant, outdoor pool, no pets, kitchenettes, a/c, TV, children free with parents, laundry facilities, CC. SGL/DBL$30-$80.

Port Richey
Area Code 813

Comfort Inn (11810 Hwy. 19, 34668; 863-3336, 800-221-2222) 100 rooms, outdoor pool, sauna, whirlpools, a/c, TV, no pets, children free with parents, NS rooms, laundry facilities, in-room computer hookups, wheelchair access, senior rates, CC. 14 miles from the Tarpon Springs sponge docks, 35 miles from Gulf beaches. SGL/DBL$60-$70.

Days Inn (11736 Hwy. 19, 34668; 863-1502, 800-325-2525) 156 rooms and suites, free breakfast, outdoor pool, a/c, TV, wheelchair access, children free with parents, kitchenettes, NS rooms, pets OK, laundry facilities, senior rates, CC. 15 miles from Weeki Wachee, 45 miles from the Tampa airport. SGL/DBL$55-$65.

Port St. Joe
Area Code 904

Barrier Dunes (Port St. Joe, 32456; 229-2777, 800-624-3964) 35 1-, 2-, and 3-bedroom condominiums, outdoor pool, tennis courts, beach, a/c, TV, in-room refrigerators, microwaves and coffee makers, no pets, children free with parents, CC. 1BR$400W-$600W, 2BR$650W-$700W, 3BR$600W-$800W.

Gulf Sands Motel (Hwy. 98 Northwest, 32456; 648-5711) 20 rooms, outdoor pool, a/c, TV, children free with parents, pets OK, CC. SGL/DBL$40-$55.

Port St. Lucie
Area Code 813

Best Western Port St. Lucie Suites (7900 South Hwy. 1, 34952; 878-7600, Fax 340-0422, 800-528-1234) 98 suites, free breakfast, outdoor heated pool, whirlpools, free local calls, VCRs, a/c, TV, children free with parents, NS rooms, laundry facilities, wheelchair access, no pets, meeting facilities for 60, senior rates, CC. SGL/DBL$50-$90.

Holiday Inn (10120 Hwy. 1, 34952; 337-2200, Fax 335-7872, 800-HOLIDAY) 142 rooms and suites, restaurant, lounge, entertainment, outdoor heated pool, exercise center, whirlpools, in-room refrigerators, microwaves and coffee makers, VCRs, wheelchair access, free parking, NS rooms, TV, a/c, children free with parents, no pets, meeting facilities for 150, senior rates, CC. 6 miles from the New York Mets Stadium, 1 mile from the shopping mall and golf course, 4 miles from Gulf beaches. SGL/DBL$90-$125.

Port Salerno
Area Code 407

Pirates Cove Resort (4307 Southeast Bayview St., 34992; 287-2500, Fax 220-2704, 800-332-1414) 50 rooms and suites, outdoor heated pool, a/c, TV, in-room refrigerators and microwaves, no pets, in-room computer hookups, local transportation, CC. SGL/DBL$65-$150.

Punta Gorda
Area Code 813.

Burnt Stone Marina Resort (3150 Matecumbe Key Rd., 33955; 639-4151, Fax 639-4151, 800-237-4255) 40 1- , 2- , and 3-bedroom suites, restaurant, lounge, entertainment, outdoor pool, whirlpools, children free with parents, laundry facilities, gift shop, wheelchair access, a/c, TV, senior rates, CC. SGL/DBL$125-$185.

Days Inn (26560 North Jones Loop Dr., 33950; 637-7200, Fax 637-7202, 800-325-2525) 74 rooms, restaurant, pool, a/c, TV, wheelchair access, NS rooms, pets OK, children free with parents, laundry facilities, kitchenettes, senior rates, CC. SGL/DBL$35-$100.

Holiday Inn (300 West Retta Esplanade, 33950; 639-1165, Fax 639-8116, 800-HOLIDAY) 183 rooms and suites, restaurant, lounge, entertainment, outdoor pool, exercise center, tennis courts, children free with parents, wheelchair access, a/c, TV, NS rooms, gift shop, pets OK, fax service, room service, laundry service, meeting facilities for 400, senior rates, CC. 5 miles from the regional airport, 1 block from the Civic Center, 11 miles from Texas Rangers Spring Training Camp. SGL/DBL$85-$105, STS$130-$155.

Howard Johnson (33 Tamiami Trail, 33950; 639-2167, Fax 639-1707, 800-I-GO-HOJO) 100 rooms, restaurant, lounge, outdoor heated pool, children free with parents, wheelchair access, NS rooms, TV, a/c, laundry facilities, in-room refrigerators, pets OK, senior rates, meeting facilities, CC. 1 block from the Charlotte County Auditorium. SGL/DBL$38-$100.

Motel 6 (9300 Knights Dr., 33950; 639-9585, 505-891-6161) 114 rooms, outdoor pool, free local calls, children free with parents, NS rooms, wheelchair access, a/c, TV, CC. SGL/DBL$30-$34.

Sea Cove Motel and Apartments (25000 East Marion Ave., 33950; 639-0060) 18 rooms and efficiencies, a/c, TV, NS rooms, kitchenettes, CC. SGL/DBL$45-$50.

Quincy
Area Code 904

Allison House Inn Bed and Breakfast (215 North Madison, 32351; 875-2511) 6 rooms, free breakfast, no pets, NS, private baths, a/c, TV, antique furnishings, CC. SGL/DBL$50-$70.

Redington Shores & Redington Beach
Area Code 813

Rental & Reservation Services

Best Beach Rentals and Sales (20045 Gulf Blvd., Indian Rocks Beach, 34635; 595-5700, Fax 593-1095, 800-523-2882) rental condominiums, villas and private homes.

Excel Travel Service (14955 Gulf Blvd., 33708; 391-5512, Fax 393-8885, 800-733-4004) rental condominiums.

J.C. Resort Management (17200 Gulf Blvd., 33708; 397-0441, Fax 397-8894, 800-535-7776) rental condominiums and apartments.

Suncoast Resort Rentals (16401 Gulf Blvd., 33708; 393-3425, 800-237-6586) rental condominiums and apartments.

□□□

El Morocco Resort (16333 Gulf Blvd., 33708; 391-1675) 18 rooms, outdoor pool, kitchenettes, a/c, TV, no pets, in-room refrigerators, CC. SGL/DBL$245W-$375W.

Far Horizons Motel (17248 Gulf Blvd., 33708; 393-8791) 24 apartments, outdoor pool, beach, kitchenettes, a/c, TV, wheelchair access, laundry facilities, CC. SGL/DBL$250W-$385W.

Hilton Resort (17120 Gulf Blvd., 33708; 391-4000, 800-447-7263) 125 rooms and suites, restaurant, lounge, entertainment, outdoor heated pool, beach, children free with parents, NS rooms, wheelchair access, gift shop, room service, laundry facilities, in-room coffee makers, no pets, a/c, TV, 4 meeting rooms, senior rates, CC. 14 miles from the St. Petersburg-Clearwater airport. LS SGL/DBL$80-$140; HS SGL/DBL$120-$190.

Ram Sea Condotel (17200 Gulf Blvd., 33708; 397-0441, Fax 397-8894, 800-535-7776) 60 2- and 3-bedroom condominiums, outdoor heated pool, whirlpools, children free with parents, a/c, TV, no pets, in-room refrigerators, microwaves and coffee makers, laundry facilities, beach, senior rates, CC. 16 miles from the St. Petersburg-Clearwater. 2BR$480W-$900W, 3BR$900W-$1,140W.

Sails and Gulf Terrace Motel (17004 Gulf Blvd., 33708; 391-6000) 19 rooms and 2-bedroom efficiencies, outdoor heated pool, a/c, TV, no pets, NS rooms, children free with parents, kitchenettes, CC. SGL/DBL$330W-$560W.

Saxony Apartments (16340 Gulf Blvd., 33708; 391-9828) 17 rooms, efficiencies and homes, outdoor heated pool, laundry facilities, beach, a/c, TV, no pets, kitchenettes, CC. LS SGL/DBL$365W-$635W; HS SGL/DBL$465W-$830W.

Shannon Motel (16311 Gulf Blvd., 33708; 391-4456) 18 rooms, outdoor pool, a/c, TV, pets OK, SGL/DBL$35-$55.

Tides Hotel and Bath Club (16700 Gulf Blvd., 33708; 8123-391-9681, Fax 397-2476, 800-255-3349) 160 rooms, restaurant, outdoor pool, tennis courts, beach, room service, a/c, TV, laundry service, wheelchair access, NS rooms, children free with parents, complimentary newspapers, senior rates, CC. 10 miles from the St. Petersburg-Clearwater airport. SGL/DBL$55-$130.

Riviera Beach

Area Code 407

Holiday Inn Oceanfront (3700 North Ocean Dr., 33404; 848-3888, Fax 845-9754, 800-HOLIDAY) 223 rooms and suites, restaurant, lounge, entertainment, heated pool, exercise center, beach, in-room refrigerators and coffee makers, no pets, children free with parents, wheelchair access, a/c, TV, NS rooms, fax service, room service, laundry service, 6 meeting roms, meeting facilities for 150, senior rates, CC. 15 miles from the Jupiter Dinner Theater, 8 miles from the Garden Mall. LS SGL/DBL$55-$125; HS SGL/DBL$105-$195.

Motel 6 (3651 West Blue Heron Blvd., 33404; 863-1011, 505-891-6161) 116 rooms, pool, free local calls, children free with parents, NS rooms, wheelchair access, a/c, TV, CC. 4 miles from the Jai Alai fronton, 10 miles from Atlantic beaches. SGL/DBL$35-$44.

Rutledge Resort Motel (3730 Ocean Dr., 33404; 848-6621, Fax 840-1787, 800-348-7964) 60 rooms, restaurant, lounge, outdoor pool, whirlpools, a/c, TV, children free with parents, laundry facilities, no pets, CC. LS SGL/DBL$56-$80; HS SGL/DBL$88-$124.

Sheraton Ocean Inn (3200 North Ocean Dr., 33404; 842-6171, Fax 848-6842, 800-325-3535, 800-221-8090 in Florida) 202 rooms and suites, restaurant, lounge, entertainment, outdoor pool, exercise center, beach, NS rooms, a/c, room service, gift shop, airport courtesy car, in-room refrigerators, TV, children free with parents, wheelchair access, meeting facilities for 50, senior rates, CC. 10 miles from the Palm Beach airport, 7 miles from the dog track and Jai Alai fronton. LS SGL/DBL$80-$90; HS SGL/DBL$100-$110.

Super 8 Motel (4112 West Blue Heron Blvd., 33404; 848-1188, 800-800-8000) 100 rooms and suites, restaurant, outdoor heated pool, children free with parents, free local calls, a/c, TV, in-room refrigerators and microwaves, fax service, NS rooms, wheelchair access, meeting facilities, senior rates, CC. SGL/DBL$50-$85.

Rockledge

Area Code 407

Spitzer's Swiss Motel (3220 South Fiske Blvd., 32955; 631-9445) 19 rooms, free breakfast, lighted tennis courts, pets OK, in-room refrigerators, a/c, TV, NS rooms, children stay free with parents, meeting facilities, CC. SGL/DBL$40-$50.

Ruskin

Area Code 813

Days Inn at Bahia Beach (611 Destin Dr., 33570 ; 645-3291, Fax 645-5283, 800-325-2525) 85 rooms, efficiencies and suites, restaurant, lounge, free breakfast, a/c, TV, wheelchair access, NS rooms, pets OK, children free with parents, beach, laundry facilities, senior rates, meeting facilities, CC. 24 miles from the Tampa airport, 27 miles from the Ringling Museum, 20 miles from Busch Gardens. SGL/DBL$50-$65, STS$110.

St. Augustine & St. Augustine Beach

Area Code 904

Alexander Homestead (14 Sevilla St., 32084; 826-4147) 4 rooms, free breakfast, TV, a/c, children free with parents, private baths, antique furnishings, NS, no pets, CC. SGL/DBL$65-$135.

Bayfront Inn (138 Avenida Menendez, 32084; 824-1682) 39 rooms and efficiencies, outdoor pool, whirlpools, a/c, TV, NS rooms, children free with parents, no pets, CC. SGL/DBL$35-$60.

Best Western Historical Inn (2015 North Ponce de Leon, 32084; 829-90880, Fax 829-6629, 800-528-1234) 39 rooms, free breakfast, outdoor pool, whirlpools, pets OK, kitchenettes, children free with parents, a/c, NS rooms, TV, laundry facilities, wheelchair access, no pets, meeting facilities, senior rates, CC. 6 blocks from the historic district, 5 miles from Atlantic beaches. SGL/DBL$40-$80.

Best Western Ocean Inn (3955 Hwy. A1A, 32084; 471-8010, 800-528-1234) 34 rooms, free breakfast, outdoor pool, children free with parents, a/c, NS rooms, TV, laundry facilities, wheelchair access, pets OK, meeting facilities, senior rates, CC. 6 miles from the historic district, 10 miles from Marineland. SGL/DBL$45-$90.

Casa De La Paz (22 Avenida Menendez, 32084; 829-2915, 800-771-3555) 6 rooms and suites, free breakfast, antique furnishings, a/c, TV, no pets, NS rooms, private baths, senior rates, CC. SGL/DBL$50-$105.

Casa De Solano (21 Aviles St., 32084; 824-3555, 800-771-3555) 4 rooms, free breakfast, NS, no pets, a/c, TV, CC. SGL/DBL$125.

Castle Garden Bed and Breakfast (15 Shenandoah St., 32084; 829-3839) 6 rooms, free breakfast, TV, a/c, local transportation, NS, whirlpools, no pets, senior rates, CC. SGL/DBL$50-$150.

Comfort Inn (3401 A1A South, 32084; 471-1474, 800-228-5150, 800-221-2222) 70 rooms, free breakfast, outdoor pool, whirlpools, in-room refrigerators and microwaves, no pets, a/c, TV, children free with parents, NS rooms, wheelchair access, senior rates, CC. 5 miles from the historic area, 10 miles from Marineland. SGL/DBL$35-$150.

Comfort Inn Historic Area (1111 Ponce de Leon Blvd., 32084; 824-5554, 800-228-5150) 84 rooms, restaurant, free breakfast, outdoor pool, whirlpools, no pets, local transportation, a/c, TV, children free with parents, NS rooms, wheelchair access, senior rates, CC. 1 mile from the Castillo De San Marcos and Flagler College, 3 miles to Atlantic beaches. SGL/DBL$35-$100.

Days Inn Historic (2800 Ponce de Leon Blvd., 32084; 829-6561, Fax 824-0135, 800-325-2525) 124 rooms, restaurant, free breakfast, outdoor pool, in-room refrigerators and microwaves, pets OK, children free with parents, in-room computer hookups, a/c, TV, wheelchair access, NS rooms, laundry facilities, senior rates, CC. A 1/2-mile from Gulf beaches. SGL/DBL$35-$80.

Days Inn (2560 Hwy. 16, 32092; 824-4341, Fax 824-1158, 800-325-2525) 120 rooms, restaurant, free breakfast, outdoor pool, a/c, TV, wheelchair access, NS rooms, pets OK, laundry facilities, children free with parents, senior rates, CC. SGL/DBL$25-$50.

Days Inn (2475 A1A South, 32084; 461-9990, Fax 471-4774, 800-325-2525) 50 rooms and suites, free breakfast, outdoor pool, whirlpools, a/c, TV, wheelchair access, in-room refrigerators, microwaves and coffee makers, children free with parents, NS rooms, no pets, laundry facilities, senior rates, CC. 5 miles from Marineland. SGL/DBL$40-$90.

Econo Lodge (311 Hwy. A1A South, 32084; 471-2330, 800-4-CHOICE) 49 rooms, restaurant, outdoor pool, whirlpools, children free with parents, no pets, NS rooms, wheelchair access, a/c, TV, in-room refrigerators and microwaves, senior rates, CC. 5 miles from the historic district, 12 miles from Atlantic beaches. LS SGL/DBL$30-$54; HS SGL/DBL$60-$100.

Edgewater Inn (2 St. Augustine Blvd., 32084; 825-2697) 19 rooms and efficiencies, outdoor pool, a/c, TV, no pets, NS rooms, CC. SGL/DBL$40-$80.

HoJo Inn (2550 Hwy. 16, 32092; 32085; 829-5686, Fax 826-0489, 800-I-GO-HOJO) 64 rooms, restaurant, free breakfast, outdoor pool, children free with parents, wheelchair access, NS rooms, TV, a/c, laundry facilities, pets OK, senior rates, meeting facilities, CC. 3 blocks from the factory outlet mall, 6 miles from the historic district. SGL/DBL$30-$42.

Holiday Inn (3250 Hwy. A1A South, 32084; 471-2555, Fax 461-8450, 800-HOLIDAY) 151 rooms, restaurant, lounge, outdoor heated pool, children free with parents, wheelchair access, a/c, TV, NS rooms, fax service, room service, pets OK, laundry service, 3 meeting rooms, senior rates, CC. 5 miles from the historic area and Flagler College, 13 miles from Marineland. SGL/DBL$80-$130.

Holiday Inn Downtown (1300 Ponce de Leon Blvd., 32084; 824-3383, Fax 829-0668, 800-HOLIDAY) 122 rooms, restaurant, lounge, outdoor pool, exercise center, children free with parents, wheelchair access, no pets, a/c, TV, NS rooms, fax service, room service, laundry service, meeting facilities for 100, senior rates, CC. 3 miles from Atlantic beaches, 1 mile from Flagler College, 3 blocks from the historic area. SGL/DBL$70-$95.

Holiday Inn Express (2310 Hwy. 16, 32084; 823-8636, Fax 823-8728, 800-HOLIDAY) 52 rooms and suites, free breakfast, outdoor pool, exercise center, children free with parents, wheelchair access, free local calls, a/c, TV, NS rooms, fax service, room service, laundry service, meeting facilities for 30, senior rates, CC. 5 miles from Flagler College, 9 miles from Atlantic beaches. SGL/DBL$46-$70.

Howard Johnson Lodge (137 San Marco Ave., 32084; 824-6181, 800-I-GO-HOJO) 77 rooms and suites, outdoor pool, jacuzzi, local transportation, kitchenettes, children free with parents, wheelchair access, NS rooms, TV, a/c, laundry facilities, no pets, in-room refrigerators, senior rates, meeting facilities, CC. 5 miles from the St. Augustine airport, 5 blocks from the historic district, 1.5 miles from Atlantic beaches. SGL/DBL$40-$90.

Howard Johnson Resort Hotel (2050 Hwy. A1A, St., 32084; 471-2575, 471-1247, 800-752-4037, 800-I-GO-HOJO) 144 rooms, restaurant, lounge, entertainment, outdoor pool, children free with parents, wheelchair access, NS rooms, TV, a/c, laundry facilities, senior rates, meeting facilities for 200, CC. 5 miles from the historic area. SGL/DBL$30-$110.

Kenwood Motel (38 Marine St., 32084; 824-2116) 14 rooms, free breakfast, outdoor pool, antique furnishings, NS no pets, a/c, TV, CC. SGL/DBL$55-$88.

La Fiesta Motor Lodge (3050 Hwy. A1A, 32084; 471-2220, 800-852-6390) 37 rooms, restaurant, outdoor pool, game room, beach, laundry facilities, no pets, NS rooms, a/c, TV, in-room refrigerators, beach, CC. 4.5 miles from the historic district, 15 miles from the St. Augustine airport. SGL/DBL$35-$90.

Ponce De Leon Resort and Convention Center (4000 Hwy. 1, 32085; 824-2821, Fax 829-6108, 800-228-2821) 194 rooms and suites, restaurant, lounge, entertainment, outdoor pool, tennis courts, a/c, TV, American plan available, local transportation, in-room coffee makers, children free with parents, NS rooms, no pets, laundry service, 9 meeting rooms, senior rates, CC. SGL/DBL$75-$95.

Quality Inn (2700 Ponce de Leon, 32084; 824-2883, 800-221-2222, 800-223-4153) 77 rooms and suites, restaurant, outdoor pool, exercise center, whirlpools, no pets, children free with parents, a/c, TV, VCRs, gift shop, wheelchair access, room service, laundry service, NS rooms, meeting facilities, senior rates, CC. SGL/DBL$38-$90.

Quality Inn Interstate (2445 Hwy. 16, 32093; 829-1999, 800-221-2222) 80 rooms and suites, restaurant, outdoor pool, children free with parents, no pets, a/c, TV, wheelchair access, room service, laundry service, NS rooms, meeting facilities, senior rates, CC. 6 miles from the historic area, 9 miles to Atlantic beaches, 40 miles from the Jacksonville airport. SGL/DBL$30-$75.

Ramada Inn (116 San Marco Ave., 32084; 824-4352, Fax 824-2745, 800-2-RAMADA) 100 rooms and suites, restaurant, lounge, entertainment, outdoor pool, whirlpools, pets OK, wheelchair access, NS rooms, free parking, a/c, TV, in-room refrigerators, children free with parents, room service, laundry facilities, meeting facilities, senior rates, CC. In the historic district, 2 miles from the Fountain of Youth. SGL/DBL$60-$130.

Ramada Limited (894 Hwy. A1A, 32084; 471-1440, 800-2-RAMADA) 24 rooms and suites, outdoor pool, jacuzzi, wheelchair access, NS rooms, a/c, TV, children free with parents, room service, in-room refrigerators and microwaves, local transportation, pets OK, laundry facilities, meeting facilities, senior rates, CC. SGL/DBL$60-$130.

Red Carpet Inn (2365 Hwy. 16, 32084; 824-4306, 800-251-1962) 32 rooms, restaurant, lounge, outdoor pool, no pets, children free with parents, TV, a/c, NS rooms, meeting facilities, senior rates, CC. 7 miles from the historic district, 12 miles from Atlantic beaches. SGL/DBL$36-$44.

Red Carpet Inn (3101 Ponce de Leon Blvd., 32084; 829-3461, 800-251-1962) 50 rooms, outdoor pool, children free with parents, no pets, NS rooms, meeting facilities, senior rates, CC. 2 miles from the historic district. SGL/DBL$25-$40.

Rodeway Inn (3552 Ponce de Leon Blvd., 32084; 842-3301, 800-424-4777) 54 rooms, outdoor pool, wheelchair access, no pets, NS rooms, children free with parents, a/c, TV, senior rates, CC. 17 miles from Marineland, 1.5 miles from Castillo de San Marco and the Lightner Museum, 1.5 miles from the Ripley Museum. SGL/DBL$30-$65.

Scottish Inn (2580 Hwy. 16, 32092; 829-5643, 800-251-1962) 48 rooms, outdoor a/c, TV, wheelchair access, pets allowed, NS rooms, children free with parents, free local calls, senior rates, CC. 6 miles from the historic district, 9 miles from Atlantic beaches. SGL/DBL$30-$40.

Scottish Inns (427 Anastasia Blvd., 32084; 824-5055, 800-251-1962) 22 rooms, outdoor a/c, TV, wheelchair access, no pets, fax service, NS rooms, children free with parents, free local calls, senior rates, CC. 5 blocks from the historic district, 1.5 miles from Atlantic beaches, 13 miles from Marineland. SGL/DBL$26-$38.

Scottish Inns (110 San Marco Ave., 32084; 824-2871, 800-251-1962) 26 rooms, outdoor pool, a/c, TV, wheelchair access, pets OK, NS rooms, children free with parents, free local calls, senior rates, CC. SGL/DBL$35-$45.

Saint Francis Inn (279 St. George St. 32085; 824-6068) 11 rooms and suites, free breakfast, NS, a/c, TV, no pets, CC. SGL/DBL$50-$135.

Southern Wind (18 Cordoba St., 32084; 825-3623) 12 rooms, free breakfast, TV, in-room refrigerators and microwaves, no pets, NS, a/c, CC. SGL/DBL$45-$105.

ThriftLodge (2500 North Ponce de Leon Blvd., 32084; 824-1341, Fax 823-9850, 800-525-9055) 31 rooms, outdoor pool, a/c, TV, NS rooms, local transportation, children free with parents, wheelchair access, fax service, senior rates, CC. SGL/DBL$25-$55.

Victorian House Bed and Breakfast (11 Cadiz, 32084; 824-5214) 8 rooms and suites, free breakfast, NS, no pets, antique furnishings, a/c, TV, CC. SGL/DBL$60-$95.

Westcott Guest House (146 Avenida Menendez, 32084; 824-4301) 8 rooms, free breakfast, private baths, antique furnishings, no pets, TV, a/c, CC. SGL/DBL$95-$135.

St. George Island
Area Code 904

Rental & Reservation Services

Alice Collins Realty (65 Gorrie Dr., 32328; 927-2900, 800-423-7418) rental private homes.

Anchor Realty (212 Franklin Blvd., 32328; 800-824-0416) rental condominiums and private homes.

Resort Realty (St. George Island, 32328; 927-2666, 800-332-5196) rental condominiums and private homes.

St. Petersburg
Area Code 813

Rental & Reservation Services

A. Clinton Brooks Realty (5901 Sun Blvd., 33715; 866-7368, Fax 864-4647, 800-551-0161) rental condominiums and apartments.

Best Beach Rentals and Sale (20045 Gulf Blvd., Indian Rocks Beach, 34635; 595-5700, Fax 593-1095, 800-523-2882) rental condominiums, villas and private homes.

B&B Suncoast Accommodations (8690 Gulf Blvd. 33708; 360-1753) rental condominiums and apartments.

Capalbo Realty (4700 34th St. South, St. Petersburg, 33711; 866-2494, 800-237-5960, 800-225-3772 in Florida) rental condominiums.

Check-In Reservation Services (7282 55th Ave. East, Brandenton 34205; 867-7760, 800-237-1033) rental condos and apartments.

Excell Condo Rentals (800-733-4004) rental condominiums and apartments.

Great Miami Reservation Systems (12555 Biscayne Blvd., 33180; 800-821-2183) hotel and condominium reservations.

□□□

Alden Resort Motel (5900 Gulf Blvd., 33706; 360-7081, Fax 360-5957, 800-237-2530, 800-262-3464 in Florida) 143 rooms and efficiencies, outdoor pool, lighted tennis courts, beach, a/c, TV, NS rooms, wheelchair access, children free with parents, no pets, in-room coffee makers, CC. SGL/DBL$120-$159.

Bayboro House On Tampa Bay (1719 Beach Drive Southeast, 33701; 823-4955) 4 rooms and suites, free breakfast, NS, a/c, TV, VCRs, no pets, laundry facilities, CC. SGL/DBL$75-$80.

Bayway Inn (4400 34th St. South, 33711; 866-2471) 52 rooms and efficiencies, outdoor heated pool, no pets, laundry facilities, a/c, TV, children free with parents, CC. SGL/DBL$30-$58.

Best Western Mirage Inn (5005 34th St. North, 33714; 525-1181, 800-528-1234) 177 rooms, restaurant, lounge, entertainment, outdoor heated pool, children free with parents, a/c, NS rooms, TV, laundry facilities, wheelchair access, in-room refrigerators and microwaves, no pets, meeting facilities, senior rates, CC. 5 miles from Sunken Gardens, 7 miles from downtown pier and Florida Suncoast Dome. SGL/DBL$45-$75.

Comfort Inn (1400 34th St. North, 33713; 323-3100, 800-221-2222) 76 rooms, restaurant, free breakfast, outdoor pool, sauna, whirlpools, a/c, TV, children free with parents, NS rooms, no pets, wheelchair access, senior rates, CC. 15 miles from the St. Petersburg-Clearwater airport, 3 miles from Sunken Gardens, 4 miles from the Bayfront Center. SGL/DBL$40-$75.

Days Inn (2595 54th Ave. North, 33714; 522-3191, 800-325-2525) 160 rooms, free breakfast, outdoor pool, in-room refrigerators and microwaves, a/c, TV, wheelchair access, NS rooms, pets OK, children free with parents, laundry facilities, senior rates, CC. 7 miles from the St. Petersburg-Clearwater airport, 10 miles from Gulf beaches, 25 miles from Busch Gardens. SGL/DBL$45-$65.

Days Inn (650 34th St. North, 33713; 321-2958, Fax 327-1625, 800-325-2525) 28 rooms, free breakfast, outdoor pool, airport transportation, a/c, TV, wheelchair access, NS rooms, laundry facilities, children free with parents, senior rates, CC. 7 miles from the St. Petersburg-Clearwater airport, 6 miles from Gulf beaches, 19 miles from the Tampa airport. SGL/DBL$39-$45.

Days Inn and Marina (6800 34th St. South, 33711; 867-1151, Fax 864-4494, 800-325-2525) 157 rooms, restaurant, free breakfast, lounge, outdoor heated pool, lighted tennis courts, in-room refrigerators and coffee makers, gift shop, children free with parents, no pets, a/c, TV, wheelchair access, NS rooms, laundry facilities, senior rates, 4 meeting rooms, meeting facilities for 375, CC. 5 miles from Gulf beaches, 9 miles from the Tyrone Mall, 5 miles from the Florida Suncoast Dome. SGL/DBL$50-$120.

Empress Motel Apartments (1503 North 9th St., 33704; 989-0635) 34 rooms and apartments, outdoor pool, kitchenettes, no pets, a/c, TV, CC. SGL/DBL$30-$50.

Econo Lodge South (3000 34th St. South, 33711; 867-1111, 800-4-CHOICE) 120 rooms and suites, restaurant, lounge, outdoor pool, tennis courts, children free with parents, pets OK, in-room refrigerators, NS rooms, wheelchair access, a/c, TV, senior rates, CC. SGL/DBL$35-$60.

Grant Motel and Apartments (9046 4th St. North, 33702; 576-1369) 30 rooms and 1- and 2-bedroom apartments, outdoor pool, laundry facilities, kitchenettes, no pets, CC. LS SGL/DBL$30-$45; HS SGL/DBL$40-$58.

Hilton and Towers (333 1st St. South, 33701; 894-5000, Fax 823-4797, 800-HILTONS) 333 rooms and suites, restaurant, lounge, entertainment, outdoor heated pool, whirlpools, exercise center, children free with parents, NS rooms, beach, in-room refrigerators and coffee makers, no pets, wheelchair access, room service, laundry facilities, a/c, 12 meeting rooms, TV, meeting facilities for

1,000, senior rates, CC. 22 miles from the Tampa airport, 26 miles from Busch Gardens, 2 miles from Salvador Dali Museum. SGL/DBL$125-$150.

Holiday Inn Downtown (234 3rd Ave., North, 33701; 822-4814, 800-283-7829, 800-HOLIDAY) 71 rooms, restaurant, free breakfast, lounge, outdoor heated pool, exercise center, jacuzzis, no pets, children under 19 free with parents, wheelchair access, a/c, TV, NS rooms, complimentary newspaper, fax service, antique furnishings, room service, laundry service, meeting facilities for 300, senior rates, CC. 2 blocks from the Museum of Fine Arts and Sunken Gardens, 25 miles from the St. Petersburg-Clearwater airport, 10 miles from Gulf beaches. SGL/DBL$56-$75.

Holiday Inn (4601 34th St. South, 33711; 867-3131, 800-HOLIDAY) 134 rooms, restaurant, lounge, outdoor pool, exercise center, children free with parents, wheelchair access, pets OK, a/c, TV, NS rooms, fax service, room service, laundry service, meeting facilities, senior rates, CC. 5 miles from the downtown area, 3 miles from the Thunder Dome, 5 miles from Gulf beaches. SGL/DBL$35-$55.

Howard Johnson Hotel (3600 34th St. South, 33711; 867-6070, Fax 867-6591, 800-I-GO-HOJO) 172 rooms, outdoor heated pool, children stay free with parents, in-room refrigerators, local transportation, a/c, TV, NS rooms, pets OK, senior rates, meeting facilities, CC. 17 miles from the St. Petersburg-Clearwater airport, 30 miles from Busch Gardens. SGL/DBL$50-$75.

La Quinta Inn North (4999 34th St. North, 33714; 527-8421, Fax 527-8851, 800-531-5900) 120 rooms, free breakfast, outdoor heated pool, complimentary newspaper, free local calls, fax service, laundry service, NS rooms, pets OK, wheelchair access, TV, a/c, meeting facilities, senior rates, CC. 6 miles from the St. Petersburg-Clearwater airport, 15 miles from the Tampa airport. SGL/DBL$45-$65.

Kentucky Motel (4246 4th St. North, 33703; 526-7373) 10 rooms, a/c, TV, in-room refrigerators, no pets, CC. SGL/DBL$22-$39.

Mansion House (105 5th Ave. Northeast, 33701; 821-9391, Fax 831-9754) 6 rooms, free breakfast, a/c, no pets, NS, private baths, laundry facilities, CC. SGL/DBL$50-$60.

Ramada Inn (3601 34th St. South, 33711; 867-1377, Fax 864-2546, 800-2-RAMADA) 85 rooms and suites, restaurant, lounge, outdoor pool, wheelchair access, NS rooms, free parking, a/c, TV, children free with parents, local transportation, room service, laundry facilities, meeting facilities, senior rates, CC. 15 miles from the St. Petersburg-Clearwater airport. SGL/DBL$45-$95.

Stouffer Vinoy Resort (501 5th Ave. Northeast, 33701; Fax 822-2785, 894-1000, 800-HOTELS-1) 360 rooms and suites, restaurant, lounge, entertainment, outdoor heated pool, exercise center, lighted tennis courts, airport courtesy car, wheelchair access, NS rooms, no pets, in-room computer hookups, local transportation, complimentary newspaper, TV, a/c, room service, children free with parents, fax service, gift shop, beauty shop, in-room refrigerators, 16 meeting rooms, 6,120 square feet of meeting and exhibition space, senior rates, CC. 20 miles from the Tampa airport. LS SGL/DBL$130-$250; HS SGL/DBL$230-$350.

Valley Forge Motel (6825 Central Ave., 33710; 345-0135) 27 rooms and efficiencies, outdoor pool, a/c, TV, pets OK, in-room refrigerators, NS rooms, CC. SGL/DBL$45-$55.

St. Petersburg Beach

Area Code 813

Best Western Sirate Beach Resort (5390 Gulf Blvd., 33706; 367-2771, Fax 360-6799, 800-528-1234) 155 rooms, restaurant, lounge, entertainment, outdoor pool, beach, children free with parents, a/c, NS rooms, TV, laundry facilities, wheelchair access, water view, in-room computer hookups, no pets, in-room microwaves, meeting facilities, senior rates, CC. 5 miles from shopping mall. SGL/DBL$85-$200.

Colonial Gateway Inn (6300 Gulf Blvd., 33706; 367-2711, Fax 367-7068, 800-237-8918) 200 rooms and suites, restaurant, lounge, entertainment, heated pool, in-room refrigerators, game room, beach, NS rooms, no pets, children free with parents, kitchenettes, senior rates, CC. LS SGL/DBL$65-$95; HS SGL/DBL$90-$115.

Coral Reef Resort (5800 Gulf Blvd., 33706; 360-0821, 800-553-6599) 129 rooms and condominiums, restaurant, lounge, entertainment, outdoor pool, whirlpools, laundry facilities, a/c, TV, in-room refrigerators, no pets, children free with parents, senior rates, CC. SGL/DBL$95-$185.

Days Inn Beach Resort (6200 Gulf Blvd., 33706; 367-1902, Fax 367-4422, 800-325-2525) 102 rooms, restaurant, lounge, entertainment, free breakfast, heated pool, beach, a/c, TV, wheelchair access, children free with parents, NS rooms, VCRs, laundry facilities, no pets, kitchenettes, senior rates, CC. SGL/DBL$85-$150.

Dolphin Beach Resort (4900 Gulf Blvd., 33706; 360-7011, Fax 367-5909, 800-237-8916) 173 rooms and efficiencies, restaurant, outdoor pool, beach, no pets, in-room refrigerators and coffee makers, children free with parents, a/c, TV, laundry facilities, 4 meeting rooms, CC. SGL/DBL$75-$135. SGL/DBL$65-$99; HS SGL/DBL$95-$125.

Don CeSar Resort (3400 Gulf Blvd., 33706; 360-1881, Fax 367-6952, 800-247-9810) 277 rooms and suites, restaurant, lounge, heated pool, beach, whirlpools, lighted tennis courts, NS rooms, sauna, a/c, TV, VCRs, children free with parents, American Plan available, laundry facilities, local transportation, senior rates, 14 meeting rooms, CC. LS SGL/DBL$145-$185; HS SGL/DBL$240-$265.

Hilton Hotel (5250 Gulf Blvd., 33706; 360-1811, 800-HILTONS) 151 rooms and suites, restaurant, lounge, entertainment, outdoor pool, exercise center, children free with parents, NS rooms, wheelchair access, room service, laundry facilities, a/c, TV, in-room refrigerators, 6 meeting rooms, senior rates, CC. 28 miles from Tampa airport, 24 miles from St. Petersburg-Clearwater Museum. SGL/DBL$120-$160, STS$275-$395.

Holiday Inn (5300 Gulf Blvd., 33706; 360-6911, Fax 360-6172, 800-HOLIDAY) 148 rooms, restaurant, lounge, entertainment, outdoor heated pool, exercise center, beach, kitchenettes, no pets, children free with parents, wheelchair access, a/c, TV, kitchenettes, game room, gift shop, NS rooms, fax service, room service, laundry service, meeting facilities for 50, senior rates, CC. 30 miles from the St. Petersburg-Clearwater airport. SGL/DBL$60-$140.

Howard Johnson Lodge (6100 Gulf Blvd., 33706; 360-7041, Fax 360-8941, 800-I-GO-HOJO) 116 rooms and efficiencies, restaurant, lounge, entertainment, outdoor heated pool, beach, no pets, children free with parents, wheelchair access, NS rooms, TV, a/c, laundry facilities, in-room refrigerators and coffee makers, car rental desk, senior rates, meeting facilities, CC. 20 miles from the St. Petersburg-Clearwater airport. LS SGL/DBL$65-$88; HS SGL/DBL$92-$118.

Island's End Resort (1 Pass-a-Grille Way, 33706; 360-5023, Fax 367-7890) 6 rooms and cottages, outdoor pool, beach, laundry facilities, a/c, TV, VCRs, kitchenettes, no pets, CC. SGL/DBL$410W-$605W.

Lamara Motel Apartments (520 73rd Ave., 33706; 360-7521) 16 rooms, outdoor heated pool, laundry facilities, kitchenettes, a/c, TV, no pets, CC. SGL/DBL$40-$80.

Palm Crest Motel (3848 Gulf Blvd., 33706; 360-9327) 18 rooms, outdoor heated pool, laundry facilities, no pets, kitchenettes, beach, a/c, TV, CC. SGL/DBL$40-$75.

Ramada Inn (12000 Golf Blvd., 33706; 360-7051, Fax 367-6641, 800-2-RAMADA) 121 rooms and suites, restaurant, lounge, entertainment, outdoor heated pool, whirlpools, wheelchair access, NS rooms, free parking, a/c, TV, children free with parents, local transportation, kitchenettes, room service, laundry facilities, meeting facilities, senior rates, CC. 28 miles from the Tampa airport. SGL/DBL$70-$140.

Tradewinds At St. Petersburg Beach (5500 Gulf Blvd., 33706; 367-6461, Fax 360-3848, 800-237-0707) 577 rooms and 1- and 2-bedroom suites, restaurant, lounge, entertainment, outdoor pool, tennis courts, whirlpools, saunas, a/c, TV, laundry facilities, local transportation, VCRs, in-room refrigerators, microwaves and coffee makers, NS rooms, gift shop, no pets, children free with parents, beach, 25 meeting rooms, 25,000 square feet of meeting and exhibition space, senior rates, CC. 28 miles from the Tampa airport. LS SGL/DBL$115-$225; HS SGL/DBL$175-$310.

Wander Club Residence (3850 Gulf Blvd., 33706; 363-0001, Fax 363-0600) 70 rooms and condominiums, restaurant, lounge, outdoor heated pool, whirlpools, sauna, laundry facilities, beach, a/c, TV, no pets, kitchenettes, senior rates, CC. SGL/DBL$570W-$1,000W.

Safety Harbor

Area Code 813

Safety Harbor Motel (1106 Main St., 34659; 726-1563) 10 efficiencies, outdoor pool, a/c, TV, children free with parents, CC. SGL/DBL$32-$38.

Safety Harbor Spa and Fitness Center (105 North Bayshore Dr., 34659; 726-1161, Fax 726-4268, 800-237-0155) 212 rooms and suites, restaurant, lounge, entertainment, outdoor pool, tennis courts, sauna, exercise center, a/c, TV, barber and beauty shop, NS rooms, wheelchair access, laundry facilities, boutiques, senior rates, 11 meeting rooms, CC. SGL/DBL$250-$395.

Sanford

Area Code 407

Days Inn (4650 Hwy. 46, 32771; 323-6500, 800-325-2525) 119 rooms, restaurant, outdoor pool, a/c, TV, wheelchair access, children free with parents, pets OK, NS rooms, in-room computer hookups, laundry facilities, senior rates, CC. 40 miles from Walt Disney World, 4 miles from Big Tree Park. SGL/DBL$28-$45.

Holiday Inn Marina (530 North Palmetto Ave., 32771; 323-1910, Fax 322-7076, 800-HOLIDAY) 100 rooms, restaurant, lounge, entertainment, heated pool, exercise center, children free with parents, wheelchair access, a/c, TV, room service, no pets, NS rooms, in-room coffee makers, fax service, room service, laundry service, meeting facilities for 100, senior rates, CC. 1 mile from the Central Florida Zoo, 15 miles from Stetson University. SGL/DBL$50-$75.

Super 8 Motel (4750 Hwy. 46 West, 32771; 323-3445, 800-800-8000) 104 rooms and suites, restaurant, outdoor pool, children free with parents, free local calls, a/c, TV, in-room refrigerators and microwaves, kitchenettes, pets OK, fax service, NS rooms, wheelchair access, meeting facilities, senior rates, CC. SGL/DBL$35-$60.

Sanibel Island

Area Code 813

Rental & Reservation Services

Century 21 AAIM Realty (695 Tarpon Bay Rd., 33957; 472-2546, 800-237-3342) rental condominiums and apartments.

Vacations in Paradise Rentals (800-237-8906) rental condominiums and apartments.

VIP Realty Group (8250 College Pkwy., Fort Myers, 33919; 481-6111, Fax 481-8477, 800-237-7526) rental condos and apartments.

Grande Island Real Estate (1630 Periwinkle Way, 33957; 472-5322, Fax 472-5722, 800-962-3314) rental condos and private homes.

Premier Properties of Pointe Santo de Sanibel (2445 West Gulf Dr., 33957; 472-9100, Fax 472-0487, 800-824-5442, 800-237-6008) rental condominiums.

The Prudential Florida Realty Rental Division (800-237-6285) rental condos, apartments, townhouses and private homes.

Sanibel Accommodations (2427 Periwinkle Way, 33957; 472-3191, Fax 472-4519, 800-237-6004) rental condominiums and apartments.

Sanibel Realty Vacation Properties (1630 Periwinkle Way, 33957; 472-6565, 800-445-1566) rental condominiums and apartments.

The Vacation Shoppe (11595 Kelly Rd., Fort Myers, 33908; 454-1400) rental condominiums, apartments and townhouses.

□□□

Beachview Cottage (3306 West Gulf Dr., 33957; 472-1202, Fax 472-4720) 22 cottages, outdoor pool, kitchenettes, a/c, TV, no pets, CC. LS SGL/DBL$60-$125; HS SGL/DBL$65-$135.

Best Western Inn (3287 West Gulf Dr., 33957; 472-1700, Fax 472-5032, 800-528-1234, 800-645-6559) 45 rooms, free breakfast, heated pool, tennis courts, children free with parents, a/c, NS rooms, TV, laundry facilities, wheelchair access, water view, beach, no pets, in-room refrigerators and microwaves, meeting facilities, senior rates, CC. 2 miles to golf course. SGL/DBL$90-$200.

Blind Pass Condominiums (5117 Seabell Rd., 33957; 472-6981, Fax 472-1489) 38 2- and 3-bedroom apartments, outdoor heated pool, sauna, tennis courts, a/c, TV, in-room refrigerators, microwaves and coffee makers, no pets, laundry facilities, CC. SGL/DBL$550W-$1,500W.

Casa Ybel Resort (2255 West Gulf Dr., 33957; 472-3145, Fax 481-4947, 800-237-8906, 800-237-8906 in Florida) 114 rooms and 2-bedroom condominiums, restaurant, lounge, outdoor heated pool, beach, tennis courts, whirlpools, VCRs, a/c, TV, in-room refrigerators, microwaves and coffee makers, no pets, children free with parents, laundry facilities, CC. SGL/DBL$165-$345.

The Colony Resort (419 East Gulf Dr., 33957; 472-5151, 800-342-1704) 1-bedroom apartments and 1- and 2-bedroom cottages, outdoor pool, no pets, in-room refrigerators, microwaves and coffee makers, laundry facilities, CC. 1BR$82, 2BR$100-$110.

Gallery Motel (541 East Gulf Dr., 33957; 472-1400) 32 rooms, apartments and cottages, outdoor heated pool, beach, kitchenettes, no pets, in-room refrigerators, microwaves and coffee makers, laundry facilities, a/c, TV, CC. SGL/DBL$90-$225.

Island Inn (3111 West Gulf Dr., 33957; 472-1561, Fax 472-0051) 56 rooms and apartments, restaurant, outdoor heated pool, tennis courts, in-room refrigerators and coffee makers, no pets, laundry facilities, Modified American Plan available, CC. LS SGL/DBL$75-$120; HS SGL/DBL$95-$175.

Lighthouse Resort and Club (210 Periwinkle Way, 33957; 472-4161) 1-bedroom apartments, outdoor pool, tennis courts, beach, no pets, a/c, TV, children free with parents, CC. 1BR$495W-$1,200W.

Pelican's Roost Condominiums (605 Donax St., 33957; 472-2996) 21 2-bedroom condominiums, outdoor heated pool, lighted tennis courts, in-room microwaves and coffee makers, a/c, TV, beach, no pets, CC. SGL/DBL$775W-$1,450W.

Ramada Inn (1131 Middle Gulf Dr., 33957; 472-4123, Fax 472-0930, 800-2-RAMADA) 98 rooms and efficiencies, restaurant, lounge, outdoor heated pool, wheelchair access, tennis courts, NS rooms, a/c, TV, children free with parents, beach, in-room refrigerators, microwaves and coffee makers, no pets, local transportation, room service, laundry facilities, meeting facilities, senior rates, CC. SGL/DBL$110-$235.

Sanibel Arms Condominiums (805 East Gulf Dr., 33957; 472-2259) 43 condominiums, outdoor heated pool, beach, no pets, a/c, TV, in-room microwaves and coffee makers, VCRs, laundry facilities, CC. SGL/DBL$465W-$1,155W.

Sanibel Inn (937 Gulf Blvd., 33957; 472-3181, 800-237-1491) 90 rooms and 1-bedroom efficiencies, restaurant, lounge, outdoor pool, a/c, TV, kitchenettes, children free with parents, no pets, laundry facilities, meeting facilities, senior rates, CC. SGL/DBL$139-$149, 1BR$149-$165.

Sanibel Moorings (845 East Gulf Dr., 33957; 472-4119) 108 rooms and 1-, 2-, and 3-bedroom apartments, heated pool, tennis courts, beach, a/c, TV, no pets, in-room microwaves and coffee makers, wheelchair access, laundry facilities, kitchenettes, CC. SGL/DBL$945W-$1,650W.

Sanibel Siesta Condominiums (1246 Fulger St., 33957; 472-4117, 800-548-2743) 56 2-bedroom suites, outdoor heated pool, laundry facilities, kitchenettes, wheelchair access, children free with parents, no pets, beach, CC. SGL/DBL$1,099W-$1,435W.

Shalimar Resort (2823 West Gulf Dr., 33957; 472-1353) 33 rooms and cottages, heated pool, beach, kitchenettes, a/c, TV, no pets, CC. SGL/DBL$546W-$1,015W.

Song Of The Sea (863 Gulf Dr., 33957; 472-2220, 800-237-8906, 800-282-8906 in Florida) 30 rooms and efficiencies, free breakfast, outdoor heated pool, whirlpools, no pets, laundry facilities, in-room microwaves and coffee makers, beach, wheelchair access, children free with parents, a/c, TV. SGL/DBL$135-$290.

Sundial Beach and Tennis Resort (1451 Middle Gulf Dr., 33957; 472-4151, Fax 472-0554, 800-237-4184, 800-282-3405 in Florida) 240 rooms and suites, restaurant, lounge, entertainment, outdoor heated pool, whirlpools, lighted tennis courts, beach, a/c, TV, children free with parents, wheelchair access, NS rooms, no pets, gift shop, senior rates, 10,000 square feet of meeting and exhibition space, 9 meeting rooms, meeting facilities for 300, CC. 20 miles from the Ft. Myers airport. 1BR$250-$358, 2BR$329-$435.

Surfrider Beach Club (555 East Gulf Dr., 33957; 472-2161, 800-282-7097 in Florida) 35 1-bedroom apartments, outdoor pool, tennis courts, beach, no pets, in-room refrigerators, microwaves and coffee makers, laundry facilities, CC. 1BR$595W-$650W.

The West Wind Inn Resort (3345 Gulf Dr., 33957; 472-1541, Fax 472-8134, 800-824-0476, 800-282-2831 in Florida) 104 rooms, restaurant, restaurant, lounge, outdoor pool, tennis courts, in-room refrigerators, children free with parents, no pets, a/c, TV, wheelchair access, NS rooms, CC. SGL/DBL$185-$205.

Santa Rosa Beach

Area Code 904

Rental & Reservation Services

Garrett Realty Services (3723 East Hwy. 30A, 32459; 231-5387, 800-537-5387, 800-238-7262) rental condominiums and hotels.

Rivard of South Walton Rentals (2100 Magnolia St., 32459; 231-4446, 800-423-3215) rental condos, apartments and private homes.

Sandi Nichols Associates (Santa Rosa Beach 32459; 231-1522, 800-648-5833) rental apartments, condominiums and private homes.

□□□

Capistrano Condominiums (Hwy. 30A, 32459; 800-336-Gulf) 2- and 3-bedroom condos, beach, laundry facilities, free with parents, a/c, TV, no pets, wheelchair access, CC. 2BR/3BR$75-$227.

Mistral (Hwy. 30A, 32459, 800-336-Gulf) 24 1- and 2-bedroom condominiums, beach, laundry facilities, children free with parents, no pets, wheelchair access, CC. 1BR/2BR$70-$153.

One Seagrove Place (Santa Rosa Beach 32459; 231-5032, 800-368-9100) 129 2-bedroom apartments, outdoor pool, beach, lighted tennis courts, exercise center, children free with parents, in-room refrigerators, microwaves and coffee makers, no pets, senior rates, CC. 2BR$110-$150.

Red Carpet Inn (8110 North Tamiami Trail, 34243; 355-8861, 800-251-1962) 32 rooms and efficiencies, outdoor pool, children free with parents, pets OK, laundry facilities, TV, a/c, NS rooms, meeting facilities, senior rates, CC. 3 miles from the Jungle Gardens, 7 miles from Gulf beaches. SGL/DBL$25-$49.

St. Armands Inn (700 Ben Franklin Dr., 34236; 388-2161, 800-441-2113) 116 rooms and efficiencies, restaurant, outdoor pool, beach, no pets, children free with parents, NS rooms, CC. SGL/DBL$70, EFF$80.

Sarasota Motor Inn (7251 North Tamiami Trail, 34243; 355-7747, 800-237-2636, 800-282-6827 in Florida) 158 rooms and efficiencies, restaurant, lounge, outdoor pool, no pets, senior rates, CC. LS SGL/DBL$30; HS SGL/DBL$35-$50.

Scottish Inns (4309 North Tamiami Trail, 34243; 355-9326, 800-251-1962) 50 rooms, restaurant, free breakfast, outdoor a/c, TV, wheelchair access, laundry facilities, pets OK, NS rooms, children free with parents, free local calls, senior rates, CC. 3 miles from the downtown area, 1 mile from the Sarasota airport and Ringling Museum, 3 miles from Lido Beach. SGL/DBL$35-$60.

Sleep Inn (900 University Pkwy., 34234; 359-8558, 800-221-2222) 80 rooms, free breakfast, outdoor pool, wheelchair access, NS rooms, children free with parents, no pets, airport transportation, in-room refrigerators and microwaves, airport transportation, in-room computer hookups, senior rates, a/c, TV, meeting facilities, CC. A 1/4-mile from the Sarasota airport, 3 miles from Gulf beaches, 2 miles from the Ringling School of Art. SGL/DBL$50-$90.

ThriftLodge (270 North Tamiami Trail, 34236; 366-0414, Fax 365-7918, 800-525-9055) 28 rooms, outdoor pool, children free with parents, laundry service, a/c, TV, NS rooms, wheelchair access, fax service, CC. 2 miles from Gulf beaches and Ringling Museum. SGL/DBL$25-$70.

Timberwood (7964 Timberwood Circle, 34238; 924-7541, 800-824-5444) 110 rooms and 2-bedroom apartments, outdoor heated pool, lighted tennis courts, whirlpools, children free with parents, a/c, TV, in-room microwaves, no pets, kitchenettes, laundry facilities, meeting facilities, CC. At the Sarasota Square Mall. SGL/DBL$770W.

Wellesley Inn At Sarasota (1803 North Tamiami Trail, 34234; 366-5128, 800-444-8888) 106 rooms and suites, free breakfast, outdoor heated pool, a/c, TV, in-room refrigerators and microwaves, no pets, children free with parents, wheelchair access, NS rooms, airport transportation, fax service, meeting facilities, CC. SGL/DBL$40-$105.

Satellite Beach

Area Code 407

Rental & Reservation Services

Condominium Rentals (1455 Hwy. A1A, Indian Harbour Beach, 32937; 773-9313) rental condominiums and apartments.

□□□

Days Inn (180 Hwy. A1A, 32937; 777-3552, 800-325-2525) 104 rooms, free breakfast, outdoor pool, whirlpools, pets OK, a/c, TV, wheelchair access, NS rooms, water view, children free with parents, laundry facilities, senior rates, CC. 18 miles from the Kennedy Space Center, 1 mile from Patrick Air Force Base, 15 miles from cruise ship terminal. SGL/DBL$40-$70.

Ramada Inn Oceanfront Resort (1035 Hwy. A1A, 32937; 777-7200, Fax 773-4608, 800-2-RAMADA) 108 rooms and suites, restaurant, lounge, entertainment, outdoor heated pool, sauna, lighted tennis courts, local transportation, in-room refrigerators and microwaves, wheelchair access, NS rooms, a/c, TV, children free with parents, room service, laundry facilities, no pets, in-room computer hookups, meeting facilities for 300, senior rates, CC. 10 miles from the Melbourne airport. SGL/DBL$65-$95.

Seaside

Area Code 904

Josephines Bed and Breakfast (101 Seaside Ave., 32459; 231-1940, Fax 561-8596, 800-848-1840) 9 rooms, restaurant, free breakfast, outdoor pool, a/c, TV, meeting facilities, CC. SGL/DBL$120-$195.

Seaside (Seaside 32459; 231-1320, Fax 231-2219) 150 rooms and 1- , 2- , and 3-bedroom cottages, pool, tennis courts, whirlpools, a/c, TV, VCRs, no pets, kitchenettes, CC. SGL/DBL$130-$485.

Sebastian
Area Code 407

Sandrift Motel (14415 Hwy. 1, 32958; 589-4546) 53 rooms and efficiencies, restaurant, lounge, outdoor pool, a/c, TV, in-room coffee makers, no pets, kitchenettes, children free with parents, CC. LS SGL/DBL$30-$40; HS SGL/DBL$40-$50.

Sebring
Area Code 813

Days Inn (1406 Hwy. 27 North, 33870; 382-1148, 800-325-2525) 37 rooms, free breakfast, outdoor pool, kitchenettes, a/c, TV, wheelchair access, NS rooms, no pets, laundry facilities, senior rates, CC. SGL/DBL$40-$85.

Holiday Inn (6535 Hwy. 27 North, 33870; 453-6200, Fax 452-6200, 800-HOLIDAY) 148 rooms, restaurant, lounge, entertainment, outdoor pool, exercise center, sauna, no pets, children free with parents, wheelchair access, a/c, TV, NS rooms, fax service, room service, laundry service, meeting facilities for 400, senior rates, CC. SGL/DBL$55-$85.

HoJo Inn (2919 Hwy. 27 South, 33870; 385-6111, 800-I-GO-HOJO) 42 rooms and efficiencies, restaurant, lounge, outdoor pool, children free with parents, wheelchair access, NS rooms, TV, a/c, fax service, no pets, laundry facilities, senior rates, meeting facilities, CC. SGL/DBL$35-$75.

Inn on the Lakes (3100 Golfview Rd., 33870; 471-9400) 161 rooms and efficiencies, restaurant, lounge, entertainment, pool, gift shop, in-room refrigerators, laundry service, no pets, barber and beauty shop, room service, a/c, TV, children free with parents, meeting facilities, senior rates, CC. SGL/DBL$50-$125, STS$125-$155.

Kenilworth Lodge (836 East Lakeview Dr., 33870; 385-0111) 138 rooms and villas, outdoor pool, no pets, a/c, TV, children free with parents, laundry facilities, CC. SGL/DBL$35-$50, 1BR$40-$66.

Ridge Resort at Sun n' Lake (4101 Sun n' Lake Blvd., 33872; 385-2561, 800-237-2165) 69 1- and 2-bedroom villas, restaurant, outdoor pool, lighted tennis courts, whirlpools, a/c, TV, children free with parents, laundry facilities, no pets, senior rates, 6 meeting rooms, CC. 1BR$375W-$655W, 2BR$525W-$890W.

The Santa Rosa Inn (509 North Ridgewood Dr., 38870; 385-0641) 25 rooms and suites, a/c, TV, children free with parents, no pets, CC. SGL/DBL$49, STS$95.

Sunset Beach Motel (2221 East Lakeview Dr., 33870; 385-6129) 42 rooms, a/c, TV, NS rooms, wheelchair access, children free with parents, meeting facilities, CC. SGL/DBL$30-$65.

Siesta Key
Area Code 813

Best Western Siesta Beach Resort (5311 Ocean Blvd., 34242; 349-3211, Fax 349-7915, 800-528-1234, 800-223-5786) 53 rooms and 1- and 2-bedroom apartments, outdoor heated pool, whirlpools, spa, children free with parents, a/c, NS rooms, TV, laundry facilities, wheelchair access, no pets, kitchenettes, meeting facilities, senior rates, CC. LS SGL/DBL$60-$75; HS SGL/DBL$110-$140.

Captiva Beach Resort (6772 Sara Sea Circle, 34242; 349-4131) 19 rooms and 2-bedroom apartments, outdoor heated pool, no pets, laundry facilities, kitchenettes, CC. LS SGL/DBL$260W-$575W; HS SGL/DBL$500W-$1,175W.

Crescent View Beach Club (6512 Midnight Pass Rd., 34242; 349-2000, 800-344-7171) 27 rooms and apartments, outdoor heated pool, whirlpools, beach, no pets, children free with parents, laundry facilities, a/c, TV, kitchenettes, CC. SGL/DBL$110-$210.

Gulf Terrace Apartments (1105 Point-O-Rocks Rd., 34242; 349-4444) 12 rooms and apartments, outdoor heated pool, laundry facilities, no pets, a/c, TV, kitchenettes, CC. SGL/DBL$60-$130.

Sara Sea Inn Beach Resort (6760 Sara Sea Circle, 34242; 349-3244, Fax 349-4999) 20 rooms, outdoor heated pool, a/c, TV, wheelchair access, NS rooms, children free with parents, no pets, CC. SGL/DBL$69-$129.

Silver Springs
Area Code 904

Days Inn (5001 East Silver Springs Blvd., 32688; 236-2891, 800-325-2525) 56 rooms, restaurant, outdoor pool, a/c, TV, VCRs, pets OK, children free with parents, wheelchair access, NS rooms, laundry facilities, senior rates, CC. A 1/2-mile from Appleton Cultural Museum. SGL/DBL$35-$60.

Econo Lodge (5331 Northeast Silver Springs Blvd., 32688; 236-2383, 800-4-CHOICE) 48 rooms, outdoor pool, whirlpools, in-room refrigerators, children free with parents, no pets, NS rooms, wheelchair access, laundry facilities, a/c, TV, senior rates, CC. 5 miles from the Ocala National Forest, a 1/2-mile from the Appleton Museum, a 1/4-mile from the Silver Springs Theme Park. SGL/DBL$35-$55.

Holiday Inn Motel (5751 East Silver Springs Blvd., 34489; 236-2575, Fax 236-2575, 800-HOLIDAY) 103 rooms, restaurant, lounge, outdoor pool, children free with parents, wheelchair access, in-room refrigerators and microwaves, no pets, VCRs, a/c, TV, NS rooms, fax service, room service, laundry service, meeting facilities for 150, senior rates, CC. 1 block from Silver Springs and Wild Waters, 1 mile from the Appleton Museum. SGL/DBL$45-$60.

Howard Johnson Motor Lodge (5565 East Silver Springs Blvd., 34489; 236-2616, 800-I-GO-HOJO) 40 rooms and apartments, outdoor pool, children free with parents, wheelchair access, NS rooms, TV, a/c, laundry facilities, in-room refrigerators and microwaves, pets OK, senior rates, meeting facilities, CC. 11 miles from the Ocala airport, 6 miles from downtown. SGL/DBL$35-$48.

Scottish Inns (5401 Northeast Silver springs Blvd., 34489; 236-2782, 800-251-1962) 22 rooms, a/c, TV, wheelchair access, NS rooms, children free with parents, free local calls, no pets, senior rates, CC. 2 miles from Silver Springs, 4 miles from Ocala National Forest. SGL/DBL$20-$32.

Spring Side Motel (5440 East Silver Springs Blvd., 34488; 236-2788) 28 rooms and efficiencies, a/c, TV, no pets, in-room refrigerators, CC. SGL/DBL$20-$30.

Stage Stop Inn (5131 Northeast Silver Springs Blvd., 34488; 236-2501, 800-554-8871) 75 rooms, restaurant, outdoor pool, pets OK, children free with parents, NS rooms, laundry facilities, a/c, TV, CC. SGL/DBL$35-$48.

Sun Plaza Motel (5461 East Silver Springs Blvd., 34488; 236-0216) 47 rooms and efficiencies, restaurant, outdoor pool, in-room refrigerators, NS rooms, pets OK, a/c, TV, CC. SGL/DBL$25-$40.

South Bay
Area Code 407

Okeechobee Inn (265 North Hwy. 27, 33493; 996-6517) 120 rooms, a/c, TV, pets OK, children free with parents, CC. SGL/DBL$40-$45.

Starke
Area Code 904

Best Western Motor Inn (1290 North Temple Ave., 32091; 964-6744, 800-528-1234) 51 rooms, free breakfast, outdoor pool, children free with parents, a/c, NS rooms, TV, laundry facilities, wheelchair access, in-room refrigerators, pets OK, meeting facilities, senior rates, CC. 7 miles from the golf course, 11 miles from Camp Blanding Prison. SGL/DBL$40-$48.

Days Inn (1101 North Temple Ave., 32091; 964-7600, 800-325-2525) 100 rooms, restaurant, free breakfast, lounge, outdoor pool, pets OK, in-room refrigerators, a/c, TV, wheelchair access, NS rooms, children free with parents, pets OK, laundry facilities, meeting facilities, senior rates, CC. 1 mile from the downtown area, 12 miles from the Florida State Prison. SGL/DBL$45-$85.

Sleepy Hollow Motel (2317 North Temple Ave., 32091; 964-5006) 13 rooms, outdoor pool, a/c, TV, in-room refrigerators, pets OK, CC. SGL/DBL$25-$28.

Stuart
Area Code 408

Harborfront Bed and Breakfast (407 Atlantic Ave., 34994; 288-7289) 4 rooms and suites, free breakfast, no pets, a/c, TV, no children, CC. DBL$60-$70, STS$70-$90.

Harbour Ridge (13431 Wax Myrtle Trail, 34995; 336-1800, Fax 336-0516) 30 apartments, outdoor heated pool, a/c, TV, children free with parents, in-room refrigerators and microwaves, wheelchair access, laundry facilities, no pets, CC. LS SGL/DBL$130; HS SGL/DBL$195.

Holiday Inn Downtown (1209 South Federal Hwy., 34995; 800-HOLIDAY) 120 rooms, restaurant, lounge, outdoor heated pool, exercise center, sauna, whirlpools, children free with parents, wheelchair access, a/c, TV, NS rooms, beach, local transportation, in-room refrigerators and microwaves, no pets, fax service, room service, laundry service, 3 meeting rooms, meeting facilities for 150, senior rates, CC. 1 mile from the historic district, 4 miles from the Treasure Coast Mall, 3 miles from the Elliott Museum. SGL/DBL$60-$78.

The Homeplace (501 Akron Ave., 34994; 220-9148) 3 rooms, free breakfast, NS, no pets, a/c, TV, SGL/DBL$60-$100.

Howard Johnson Motor Lodge (950 South Federal Hwy., 34994; 287-3171, Fax 220-3594, 800-I-GO-HOJO) 82 rooms, restaurant, free breakfast, lounge, outdoor pool, children free with parents, wheelchair access, NS rooms, TV, a/c, room service, no pets, laundry facilities, senior rates, meeting facilities for 150, CC. 40 miles from the Palm Beach airport, 20 miles from the Jai Alai fronton. SGL/DBL$75-$90.

Indian River Plantation Resort (555 Northeast Ocean Blvd., 34996; 225-3700, Fax 225-0003, 800-444-3389) 306 rooms and suites, restaurant, lounge, entertainment, outdoor heated pool, whirlpools, lighted tennis courts, kitchenettes, beach, room service, a/c, TV, gift shop, laundry facilities, airport transportation, in-room refrigerators and microwaves, children free with parents, no pets, 13 meeting rooms, 15,000 square feet of meeting and exhibition space, meeting facilities for 800, senior rates, CC. 3 miles from the Stuart airport, 45 miles from the Palm Beach airport. LS SGL/DBL$130-$335; HS SGL/DBL$200-$400.

Ramada Inn (1200 South Federal Hwy., 34994; 286-6011, Fax 288-2423, 800-2-RAMADA) 124 rooms and suites, restaurant, lounge, entertainment, outdoor heated pool, wheelchair access, jacuzzi, car rental desk, NS rooms, free parking, a/c, TV, children free with parents, room service, laundry facilities, meeting facilities, senior rates, CC. SGL/DBL$45-$80.

Sugar Loaf Key

Area Code 305

Sugarloaf Lodge (Sugar Loaf Key 33044; 745-3211, Fax 745-3389) 55 rooms and efficiencies, restaurant, lounge, entertainment, outdoor pool, tennis courts, laundry facilities, a/c, TV, NS rooms, children free with parents, no pets, CC. SGL/DBL$85-$100.

Sun City

Area Code 813

Comfort Inn (718 Cypress Village Blvd., 33570; 633-3318, 800-221-2222) 75 rooms and efficiencies, outdoor pool, whirlpools, a/c, TV, children free with parents, NS rooms, wheelchair access, fax, no pets, senior rates, CC. 24 miles from Busch Gardens and Tampa Stadium, 28 miles from the Tampa airport. SGL/DBL$40-$80.

Sun City Center Inn (1335 Rickenbacker Dr., 33571; 634-3331, 800-282-8040 in Florida) 100 rooms, restaurant, lounge, entertainment, outdoor pool, lighted tennis courts, in-room refrigerators, a/c, TV, pets OK, children free with parents, laundry service, meeting facilities, senior rates, CC. SGL/DBL$45-$65.

Sunny Isles

Area Code 305

Beacharbour Ocean Resort (18925 Collins Ave., 33160; 931-8900, 800-643-0807) 235 rooms, restaurant, entertainment, outdoor pool, gift shop, a/c, TV, NS rooms, wheelchair access, children free with parents, no pets, senior rates, CC. SGL/DBL$65-$100.

Monaco Oceanfront Resort (17501 Collins Ave., 33160; 932-2100, Fax 931-5519, 800-227-9006) 113 rooms, restaurant, outdoor pool, exercise center, sauna, in-room refrigerators and microwaves, gift shop, game room, NS rooms, a/c, TV, wheelchair access, no pets, beach, airport transportation. Jan-Jul SGL/DBL$60-$130.

Radisson Pan American Ocean Hotel (17875 Collins Ave., 33160; 932-1100, Fax 935-2769) 146 rooms and suites, restaurant, lounge, outdoor pool, lighted tennis courts, exercise center, game room, gift shop, room service, free newspaper, beauty shop, a/c, TV, NS rooms, wheelchair access, children free with parents, no pets, in-room refrigerators, senior rates, CC. SGL/DBL$85-$190.

Suez Oceanfront Resort (18215 Collins Ave., 33160; 932-0661, Fax 937-0058, 800-432-3661 in Florida) 150 rooms, efficiencies and 2-bedroom suites, restaurant, lounge, outdoor heated pool, lighted tennis courts, beach, a/c, TV, in-room refrigerators, NS rooms, children free with parents, wheelchair access, no pets, senior rates, meeting facilities, CC. SGL/DBL$50-$165.

Sunrise
Area Code 305

Hilton Hotel (3003 North University Dr., 33322; 748-7000, Fax 572-0799, 800-HILTONS) 297 rooms and suites, restaurant, lounge, entertainment, outdoor pool, exercise center, children free with parents, NS rooms, wheelchair access, room service, laundry facilities, in-room refrigerators and microwaves, a/c, TV, 9 meeting rooms, meeting facilities for 860, senior rates, CC. 12 miles from the regional airport and Atlantic beaches, 15 miles from the Convention Center. SGL/DBL$115-$150.

Surfside
Area Code 305

Beekman Towers Apartment Motel (9499 Collins Ave., 33154; 861-4801, Fax 865-5971, 800-237-9367) 120 1- and 2-bedroom apartments, outdoor heated pool, whirlpools, spa, beach, a/c, TV, wheelchair access, children free with parents, no pets, in-room refrigerators, kitchenettes, senior rates, CC. 1BR$120-$150, 2BR$225.

Holiday Inn Palms on the Ocean (9449 Collins Ave., 33154; 865-6644, Fax 861-6569, 800-843-6974, 800-HOLIDAY) 170 rooms, restaurant, lounge, entertainment, indoor heated pool, exercise center, children free with parents, beach, wheelchair access, a/c, TV, no pets, gift shop, local transportation, NS rooms, fax, room service, laundry service, meeting facilities for 200, senior rates, CC. 6 miles from the Convention Center, 15 miles from the Miami airport, 2 blocks from the shopping mall. SGL/DBL$75-$120.

Rodney Ocean Suites (9367 Collins Ave., 33154; 864-2232, Fax 864-32045, 800-327-1412) 99 rooms and suites, restaurant, free breakfast, outdoor pool, a/c, TV, NS rooms, wheelchair access, no pets, children free with parents, in-room refrigerators, senior rates, CC. SGL/DBL$56-$85.

Tallahassee
Area Code 904

American Inn (2726 North Monroe St., 32303; 386-5000) 52 rooms, a/c, TV, VCRs, pets OK, NS rooms, children free with parents, laundry facilities, CC. SGL/DBL$30-$37.

Best Inns of America (2738 Graves Rd., 32303; 562-2378, 800-BEST-INN) 75 rooms, free breakfast, outdoor pool, exercise center, children free with parents, a/c, TV, pets OK, free local calls, NS rooms, wheelchair access, fax service, meeting facilities, CC. 2 miles from the State Capitol, 10 miles from the Tallahassee Airport, 1/2-mile from the shopping mall. SGL/DBL$37-$48.

Best Western Pride Inn (2016 Apalachee Pkwy., 656-6312, Fax 942-4312, 800-528-1234, 800-827-7390) 78 rooms and suites, free breakfast, restaurant, outdoor pool, children free with parents, in-room refrigerators, pets OK, a/c, NS rooms, TV, laundry facilities, wheelchair access, meeting facilities, senior rates, CC. SGL/DBL$45-$60.

Cabot Lodge (1653 Raymond Diehl Rd., 32303; 386-7500, 800-223-1964) 160 rooms and suites, outdoor pool, no pets, a/c, TV, VCR, in-room refrigerators and microwaves, children free with parents, NS, CC. SGL/DBL$60-$70.

Cabot Lodge (2735 North Monroe St., 32303; 386-8880, Fax 386-4254, 800-432-0701 in Florida) 160 rooms, outdoor pool, no pets, laundry facilities, children free with parents, a/c, TV, CC. SGL/DBL$61-$65.

Comfort Inn (2727 Graves Rd., 32303; 562-7200, 800-221-2222) 100 rooms, outdoor pool, whirlpools, a/c, TV, children free with parents, NS rooms, wheelchair access, in-room computer hookups, laundry facilities, no pets, senior rates, CC. 10 miles from the State Capitol, 9 miles from the Tallahassee airport, 4 miles from Lake Jackson. SGL/DBL$45-$70.

Courtyard by Marriott (1018 Apalachee Pkwy., 32301; 222-8822, 800-228-9290, 800-321-2211) 154 rooms and suites, restaurant, lounge, outdoor pool, exercise center, in-room refrigerators, microwaves and coffee makers, a/c, VCRs, complimentary newspaper, children free with parents, kitchenettes, a/c, TV, NS rooms, wheelchair access, meeting facilities, senior rates, CC. SGL/DBL$55-$95.

Days Inn Downtown (722 Apalachee Pkwy., 32301; 877-6121, 800-325-2525) 100 rooms, restaurant, outdoor pool, a/c, TV, wheelchair access, NS rooms, laundry facilities, children free with parents, in-room refrigerators, microwaves and coffee makers, pets OK, senior rates, CC. SGL/DBL$38-$48.

Days Inn (2800 North Monroe St., 32303; 385-0136, 800-325-2525) 115 rooms, free breakfast, outdoor pool, pets OK, a/c, TV, wheelchair access, NS rooms, free local calls, laundry facilities, senior rates, CC. 3 miles from the State Capitol and Florida State University, 5 miles from Maclay Gardens, 3/4 mile from the shopping mall. SGL/DBL$35-$60.

Days Inn University Center (1350 West Tennessee St., 32304; 222-3219, 800-325-2525) 47 rooms, free breakfast, outdoor pool, a/c, TV, wheelchair access, children free with parents, free local calls, in-room coffee makers, NS rooms, no pets, laundry facilities, senior rates, CC. 5 miles from the Tallahassee airport. SGL/DBL$30-$40.

Days Inn South Government Center (3100 Apalachee Pkwy., 32301; 877-6121, 800-325-2525) 180 rooms, free breakfast, outdoor pool, a/c, TV, wheelchair access, NS rooms, in-room refrigerators, children stay free with parents, pets OK, laundry facilities, free local calls, meeting facilities, senior rates, CC. 3 miles from the State Capitol, 4 miles from Florida State University. SGL/DBL$35-$40.

Econo Lodge North (2681 North Monroe St., 32303; 385-6155, 800-553-2666, 800-4-CHOICE) 82 rooms, restaurant, children free with parents, no pets, laundry facilities, NS rooms, wheelchair access, a/c, TV, senior rates, CC. A 1/2-mile from the Tallahassee Mall, 4 miles from Lake Jackson, 3 miles from Florida State University. SGL/DBL$30-$55.

Executive Suite Motor Inn (522 Scotty's Lane, 32301; 386-2121, Fax 386-3632, 800-342-0090) 114 rooms and suites, restaurant, free breakfast, outdoor pool, whirlpools, kitchenettes, a/c, TV, children free with parents, no pets, NS rooms, 5 meeting rooms, senior rates, CC. $35-$45.

Governor's Inn (209 South Adams St., 32301; 681-6855, Fax 222-3105, 800-342-7717 in Florida) 40 rooms and 2-bedroom suites, free breakfast, whirlpools, complimentary newspaper, airport courtesy car, in-room refrigerators, a/c, TV, no pets, laundry facilities, fireplaces, antique furnishings, 2 meeting rooms, senior rates, CC. SGL/DBL$120-$150.

Hampton Inn (3210 North Monroe St., 32303; 562-6735, 800-HAMPTON) 93 rooms, restaurant, free breakfast, outdoor pool, exercise center, children free with parents, NS rooms, wheelchair access, in-room computer hookups, fax service, TV, a/c, VCRs, in-room refrigerators, no pets, free local calls, meeting facilities, senior rates, CC. SGL/DBL$45-$55.

Holiday Inn Northwest (2714 Graves Rd., 32303; 562-2000, Fax 562-8519, 800-HOLIDAY) 179 rooms, restaurant, free breakfast, lounge, outdoor pool, exercise center, children free with parents, wheelchair access, pets OK, a/c, TV, NS rooms, fax service, room service, laundry service, meeting facilities for 150, senior rates, CC. 4 miles from the downtown area, 7 miles from the Tallahassee airport, 5 miles from the Civic Center. SGL/DBL$68-$73.

Holiday Inn Parkway (1302 Apalachee Pkwy., 32301; 877-3141, 800-HOLIDAY) 126 rooms, restaurant, outdoor pool, exercise center, children free with parents, wheelchair access, a/c, TV, NS rooms, fax service, room service, laundry service, meeting facilities for 200, senior rates, CC. 1 mile from the downtown area and Capitol Building, 6 miles from the Tallahassee airport, a 1/4-mile from the Governor Square Mall. SGL/DBL$54-$65.

Holiday Inn University Center (316 West Tennessee St., 32301; 222-8000, Fax 222-8113, 800-HOLIDAY) 174 rooms, restaurant, lounge, outdoor pool, exercise center, children free with parents, wheelchair access, a/c, TV, NS rooms, fax service, room service, laundry service, 8 meeting rooms, senior rates, CC. 4 miles from the Tallahassee airport, 2 miles from the Governors Square Mall, 3 blocks from the downtown area and Capitol Building. SGL/DBL$65-$85.

Howard Johnson (1355 Apalachee Pkwy., 32303; 877-3171, Fax 942-2918, 800-I-GO-HOJO) 150 rooms, restaurant, free breakfast, lounge, entertainment, outdoor pool, children free with parents, wheelchair access, NS rooms, TV, a/c, laundry facilities, airport transportation, no pets, senior rates, meeting facilities, CC. 8 miles from the Tallahassee airport, 2 miles from Florida A&M University, a 1/2-mile from the Governors Mall. SGL/DBL$40-$45.

Killearn Country Club and Inn (100 Tyron Circle, 32308; 893-2186, Fax 668-7637, 800-476-4101) 40 rooms and suites, restaurant, lounge, entertainment, outdoor pool, exercise center, lighted tennis courts, children free with parents, laundry facilities, a/c, TV, in-room refrigerators, no pets, senior rates, meeting facilities, CC. SGL/DBL$55-$85.

Knights Inn (2728 Graves Rd., 32303; 562-4700, 800-843-5644) 48 rooms, outdoor pool, wheelchair access, NS rooms, TV, a/c, in-room refrigerators and microwaves, fax service, VCRs, senior rates, CC. 4 miles from the Tallahassee airport and the State Capitol, 5 miles from Florida State University, 2 miles from the Governors Mall. SGL/DBL$38-$43.

La Quinta Inn North (2905 North Monroe St., 32303; 385-7172, 800-531-5900) 154 rooms, restaurant, free breakfast, lounge, outdoor pool, complimentary newspaper, free local calls, fax service, laundry service, NS rooms, pets OK, wheelchair access, TV, a/c, meeting facilities, senior rates, CC. 11 miles from the Tallahassee airport, 8 miles from Lake Jackson. SGL/DBL$48-$55.

La Quinta Inn South (2850 Apalachee Pkwy., 32301; 878-5099, Fax 878-6665, 800-531-5900) 134 rooms, free breakfast, outdoor heated pool, complimentary newspaper, free local calls, fax service, laundry service, NS rooms, wheelchair access, TV, a/c, meeting facilities, senior rates, CC. SGL/DBL$48-$54.

Master Hosts Inn (1630 North Monroe St., 32303; 224-6183, 800-251-1962) 92 rooms, restaurant, lounge, outdoor pool, no pets, in-room refrigerators, NS rooms, a/c, TV, children under 18 free with parents, senior rates, meeting facilities, CC. 2 miles from the State Capitol, 6 miles from Lake Jackson, 4 miles from Florida A&M University. SGL/DBL$26-$38.

Motel 6 Downtown (1027 Apalachee Pkwy., 32301; 877-6171, 505-891-6161) 100 rooms, outdoor pool, free local calls, children free with parents, NS rooms, wheelchair access, a/c, TV, CC. 2.5 miles from Florida State University, 1 mile from the State Capitol, 4 miles from the Leon County Fairgrounds. SGL/DBL$28-$33.

Motel 6 North (1481 Timberlane Dr., 32308; 893-7587, 505-891-6161) 153 rooms, outdoor pool, free local calls, children free with parents, NS rooms, wheelchair access, a/c, TV, CC. 1 block from the Farmers Market. SGL/DBL$28-$36.

Motel 6 West (2738 North Monroe St., 32312; 386-7878, 505-891-6161) 101 rooms, outdoor pool, free local calls, children free with parents, NS rooms, wheelchair access, a/c, TV, CC. 4 miles from the Florida State University, 1 mile from the Governors Mall, 4 miles from McKay State Park. SGL/DBL$28-$36.

Quality Inn and Suites (20200 Apalachee Pkwy., 32301; 877-4437, 800-221-2222) 100 rooms and suites, outdoor pool, exercise center, whirlpools, in-room refrigerators and microwaves, children free with parents, a/c, TV, wheelchair access, room service, laundry service, NS rooms, no pets, meeting facilities, senior rates, CC. 12 miles from the Tallahassee airport, 2 miles from the State Capitol, 3 miles from Florida A&M. SGL/DBL$55-$75.

Radisson Hotel (415 North Monroe St., 32301; 224-6000, 800-333-3333) 116 rooms and suites, restaurant, lounge, entertainment, outdoor pool, sauna, exercise center, in-room refrigerators, microwaves and coffee makers, children free with parents, VCRs, wheelchair access, NS rooms, TV, a/c, local transportation, no pets, children free with parents, 3 meeting rooms, senior rates, CC. SGL/DBL$85-$110.

Ramada Inn North (2900 North Monroe St., 32303; 224-6000, Fax 422-1025, 800-2-RAMADA, 800-228-9822) 200 rooms and suites, restaurant, lounge, entertainment, outdoor heated pool, wheelchair access, NS rooms, a/c, TV, children free with parents, room service, airport transportation, in-room refrigerators and microwaves, no pets, fax service, car rental desk, laundry facilities, 11 meeting rooms, senior rates, CC. 5 miles from Florida A&M University, 4 miles from the Civic Center, 1 mile from the shopping mall. SGL/DBL$60-$95.

Red Roof Inn (2930 North Monroe St., 32303; 385-7884, 800-843-7663) 109 rooms, NS rooms, fax service, wheelchair access, complimentary newspaper, pets OK, children free with parents, a/c, TV, free local calls, senior rates, CC. 7 miles from the Tallahassee

Regional Medical Center, 10 miles from the Tallahassee airport, 3 miles from Florida State University. SGL/DBL$33-$45.

Seminole Inn (6737 Mahan Dr., 32308; 656-2938) 60 rooms, a/c, TV, pets OK, children free with parents, CC. SGL/DBL$40-$45.

Sheraton Tallahassee (101 South Adams St., 32301; 224-5000, 800-325-3535) 246 rooms and suites, restaurant, lounge, entertainment, pool, exercise center, NS rooms, a/c, room service, TV, children free with parents, wheelchair access, 24-hour room service, pets OK, in-room refrigerators, microwaves and coffee makers, laundry service, airport transportation, fax, 7 meeting rooms, meeting facilities for 500, 5,300 square feet of meeting and exhibition space, senior rates, CC. 8 miles from the Tallahassee airport. SGL/DBL$70-$180.

Shoney's Inn (2801 North Monroe St., 32303; 386-8286, 800-222-2222) 112 rooms, restaurant, free breakfast, heated pool, a/c, TV, in-room refrigerators, no pets, laundry facilities, children free with parents, free newspaper, NS rooms, wheelchair access, fax, meeting facilities, senior rates, CC. SGL/DBL$35-$90.

Sleep Inn (1695 Capital Circle NW, 32302; 575-9753, 800-221-2222) 80 rooms, free breakfast, outdoor pool, wheelchair access, no pets, NS rooms, children free with parents, fax, a/c, TV, VCRs, meeting facilities, senior rates, CC. 4 miles from the Florida Museum of Natural History, 3 miles from Tallahassee airport. SGL/DBL$40-$60.

Super 8 Motel (2702 North Monroe St., 32303; 386-8818, Fax 386-6556, 800-848-8888) 62 rooms and suites, restaurant, children free with parents, free local calls, a/c, TV, in-room refrigerators and microwaves, no pets, fax service, NS rooms, wheelchair access, meeting facilities, senior rates, CC. 30 miles from the University of Florida and State Capitol. SGL/DBL$35-$50.

Tampa

Area Code 813

Rental & Reservation Services

Great Miami Reservation Systems (12555 Biscayne Blvd., 33180; 800-821-2183) hotel and condominium reservations.

□□□

Americana Inns (321 East Fletcher Ave., 33612; 933-4545, Fax 935-4118, 800-766-6546) 100 rooms and suites, outdoor pool, no pets, a/c, TV, kitchenettes, children free with parents, NS rooms, senior rates, CC. SGL/DBL$25-$45.

Amerisuites (10007 Princess Palm Ave., 33619; 622-8557, Fax 620-4866) 55 rooms, free breakfast, outdoor heated pool, children free with parents, pets OK, a/c, TV, in-room refrigerators, microwaves and coffee makers, free local calls, meeting facilities, senior rates, CC. SGL/DBL$60-$105.

Budget Host Motel (3110 West Hillsborough Ave., 33614; 876-8673, Fax 800-626-7064) 36 rooms, restaurant, laundry facilities, NS rooms, wheelchair access, a/c, TV, children free with parents, airport transportation, kitchenettes, no pets, senior rates, CC. 4 miles from Busch Gardens, 1 mile from Tampa Stadium. SGL/DBL$28-$40.

Budget Inn (2001 East Busch Blvd., 33612; 932-3997, Fax 933-7848, 800-527-0605) 26 rooms and suites, free breakfast, outdoor heated pool, jacuzzi, kitchenettes, a/c, TV, children free with parents, in-room refrigerators, no pets, CC. SGL/DBL$30-$46.

Budgetel Inn (4811 Hwy. 301 North, 33610; 626-0885, Fax 623-3321, 800-4-BUDGET) 102 rooms, free breakfast, outdoor pool, children free with parents, a/c, wheelchair access, NS rooms, free local calls, in-room computer hookups, fax service, in-room refrigerators and microwaves, pets OK, VCRs, TV, meeting facilities, CC. 16 miles from the Tampa airport, 8 miles from Busch Gardens, 7 miles from the downtown area. SGL/DBL$39-$46.

Budgetel Inn (602 Faulkenburg Rd., 33619; 684-4007, Fax 681-3042, 800-4-BUDGET) 102 rooms and suites, outdoor pool, children free with parents, a/c, wheelchair access, NS rooms, free local calls, in-room refrigerators, microwaves and coffee makers, in-room computer hookups, fax, VCRs, TV, meeting facilities, CC. 18 miles from the Tampa airport, 4 miles from the Florida State Fairgounds, 6 miles from the downtown area. SGL/DBL$40-$50.

Choice Inn (2523 East Busch Blvd., 33612; 933-6760) 40 rooms, outdoor heated pool, a/c, TV, laundry facilities, children free with parents, NS rooms, no pets, CC. SGL/DBL$30-$45.

Comfort Inn (2106 East Busch Blvd., 33612; 931-3313, 800-221-2222) 50 rooms, outdoor pool, whirlpools, no pets, a/c, TV, kitchenettes, children free with parents, NS rooms, wheelchair access, senior rates, CC. 15 miles from the Tampa airport, 1 mile from Busch Gardens, 2 miles from the Tampa greyhound dog track. SGL/DBL$36-$75.

Courtyard by Marriott (3805 West Cypress, 33607; 874-0555, Fax 870-0685, 800-228-9290, 800-874-0555) 145 rooms and suites, outdoor pool, whirlpools, airport transportation, in-room refrigerators, microwaves and coffee makers, VCRs, complimentary newspaper, children free with parents, kitchenettes, airport courtesy car, a/c, TV, NS rooms, wheelchair access, in-room computer hookups, pets OK, meeting facilities, senior rates, CC. SGL/DBL$50-$110.

Crown Sterling Suites (11310 North 30th St., 33612; 971-7690, Fax 972-5525, 800-433-4600) 129 suites, outdoor heated pool, whirlpools, a/c, TV, NS rooms, in-room refrigerators and microwaves, wheelchair access, in-room computer hookups, laundry facilities, 3 meeting rooms, senior rates, CC. SGL/DBL$75-$110.

Crown Sterling Suites Tampa Airport (4400 West Cypress St., 33607; 873-8675, Fax 879-7196, 800-443-4600) 260 suites, outdoor pool, a/c, TV, in-room refrigerators and microwaves, no pets, NS rooms, laundry facilities, wheelchair access, senior rates, 5 meeting rooms, CC. SGL/DBL$75-$110.

Days Inn (2901 East Busch Blvd., 33612; 933-6471, 800-325-2525) 179 rooms, restaurant, pool, pets OK, a/c, TV, wheelchair access, NS rooms, laundry facilities, senior rates, CC. A 1/2-mile from Busch Gardens, 7 miles from the Tampa airport, 15 miles from Gulf beaches, 1 mile from the University Mall. SGL/DBL$30-$60.

Days Inn Busch Gardens North (701 East Fletcher, 33612; 977-1550, Fax 247-3893, 800-325-2525, 800-433-8033 in Florida) 254 rooms, restaurant, outdoor pool, free breakfast, a/c, TV, wheelchair access, pets OK, NS rooms, children free with parents, laundry facilities, meeting facilities, senior rates, CC. 5 miles from Busch Gardens, 13 miles from the Tampa airport, 2 miles from the University of South Florida. LS SGL/DBL$32-$44; HS SGL/DBL$35-$55.

Days Inn Busch Gardens East (2520 North 50th St., 33619; 247-3300, Fax 977-6556, 800-325-2525, 800-433-8033 in Florida) 200 rooms and suites, restaurant, free breakfast, lounge, entertainment, outdoor pool, Modified American Plan available, pets OK, a/c, TV, wheelchair access, NS rooms, children free with parents, laundry facilities, senior rates, CC. 8 miles from the Tampa airport, 1 mile from the Florida Exposition Park. SGL/DBL$45-$70, STS$75-$135.

Days Inn Fairgrounds (9942 Adamo Dr., 33607; 623-5121, Fax 628-4989, 800-325-2525, 800-835-3297) 100 rooms, free breakfast, outdoor pool, a/c, TV, wheelchair access, no pets, laundry facilities, in-room refrigerators, microwaves and coffee makers, no pets, children free with parents, NS, meeting facilities, senior rates, CC. 14 miles from Busch Gardens, 2 miles from the State Fairgrounds, 4 miles from the Convention Center. SGL/DBL$40-$70.

Days Inn-Hawaiian Village (2522 North Dale Mabry, 33607; 877-6181, Fax 875-6171, 800-325-2525) 283 rooms, a/c, TV, wheelchair access, NS rooms, no pets, laundry facilities, car rental desk, children free with parents, senior rates, CC. 2 miles from the Tampa airport and Convention Center, 10 miles from Busch Gardens, 3 miles from Ybor City. SGL/DBL$30-$70.

Days Inn Rocky Point Island (7627 Courtney Campbell Causeway, 33607; 281-0000, Fax 281-1067, 800-237-2555, 800-325-2525) 147 rooms and suites, restaurant, lounge, entertainment, outdoor pool, a/c, TV, wheelchair access, NS rooms, no pets, laundry facilities, car rental desk, meeting facilities, senior rates, CC. 2 miles from the Tampa airport, 13 miles from Busch Garden, 1 mile from the shopping mall. SGL/DBL$50-$90.

Days Inn (515 East Cass St., 33602; 229-6432, Fax 228-7534, 800-325-2525) 180 rooms, outdoor pool, children free with parents, a/c, TV, wheelchair access, NS rooms, no pets, laundry facilities, senior rates, meeting facilities for 600, CC. 7 miles from the Tampa airport, 9 miles from Busch Gardens, 6 miles from the University of Tampa, 9 blocks from the Convention Center. SGL/DBL$30-$100.

East Lake Inn (6529 East Hillsborough Ave., 33610; 622-8339) 25 rooms, a/c, kitchenettes, TV, in-room refrigerators, no pets, NS rooms, senior rates, CC. SGL/DBL$30-$40.

Econo Lodge (1701 East Busch Blvd., 33612; 933-7681, 800-4-CHOICE) 238 rooms, restaurant, lounge, outdoor pool, children free with parents, pets, OK, NS rooms, laundry facilities, wheelchair access, a/c, TV, meeting facilities, kitchenettes, senior rates, 1 mile from Busch Gardens and the greyhound dog track. CC. SGL/DBL$30-$45.

Econo Lodge (2905 North 50th St., 33619; 621-3541, Fax 626-9108, 800-55-ECONO) 100 rooms, outdoor pool, children free with parents, no pets, laundry facilities, NS rooms, wheelchair access, a/c, TV, meeting facilities for 125, senior rates, CC. 3 miles from downtown Tampa, 2 miles from Ybor City, 4 miles to Busch Gardens. SGL/DBL$30-$45.

Econo Lodge Midtown (1020 South Dale Mabry, 33629; 254-3005, 800-55-ECONO) 74 rooms, outdoor pool, children free with parents, no pets, laundry facilities, NS rooms, wheelchair access, in-room refrigerators and microwaves, a/c, TV, senior rates, CC. 3 miles from Tampa Stadium, 4 miles from Tampa airport. SGL/DBL$30-$44.

Economy Inns of America (6606 East Buffalo Ave., 33619; 623-6667, 800-826-0778, 800-423-3018 in Florida) 128 rooms, free local calls, wheelchair access, a/c, children free with parents, TV, NS rooms, pets OK, senior rates, CC. SGL/DBL$35-$53.

Embassy Suites (555 North Westshore Blvd., 33609; 875-1555, Fax 287-3664, 800-EMBASSY) 221 1- and 2-room suites, restaurant, lounge, free breakfast, lounge, heated pool, whirlpool, exercise center, sauna, room service, laundry service, wheelchair access, complimentary newspaper, pets OK, airport courtesy car, free local calls, in-room computer hookups, NS rooms, gift shop, local transportation, meeting facilities, CC. 2 miles from the Tampa airport, 1 block from the Westshore Mall, 4 miles from the downtown area, 16 miles from Busch Gardens. SGL/DBL$110-$150.

Friendship Inn (2500 East Busch Blvd., 33612; 933-3958, 800-424-4777) 34 rooms, outdoor pool, exercise center, a/c, TV, NS rooms, children free with parents, wheelchair access, senior rates, meeting facilities, CC. 4 blocks from Busch Gardens, 3 miles from the University of South Florida, 6 miles from Ybor City. LS SGL/DBL$22-$38; HS SGL/DBL$28-$44.

Guest Quarters On Tampa Bay (3050 North Rocky Point Drive West, 33607; 888-8800, Fax 888-8743, 800-424-2900) 203 1- and 2-room suites, restaurant, outdoor pool, exercise center, sauna, whirlpools, TV, a/c, in-room refrigerators, local transportation, laundry service, fax service, NS rooms, wheelchair access, airport courtesy car, no pets, children free with parents, 7 meeting rooms, CC. SGL/DBL$100-$140.

Hampton Inn (4817 West Laurel St., 33607; 287-0778, Fax 287-0882, 800-426-7866) 134 rooms, free breakfast, outdoor pool, children free with parents, NS rooms, wheelchair access, in-room computer hookups, pets OK, fax service, TV, a/c, in-room refrigerators, airport transportation, free local calls, meeting facilities, senior rates, CC. 1 mile from the Tampa airport, 5 miles from the downtown area, 12 miles from Busch Gardens, 13 miles from the Florida State Fairgrounds. SGL/DBL$50-$75.

Hilton at Metrocenter (2225 Lois Ave., 33607; 877-6688, Fax 879-3264, 800-HILTONS) 240 rooms and suites, restaurant, lounge, entertainment, outdoor heated pool, exercise center, lighted tennis courts, children free with parents, NS rooms, no pets, gift shop, airport courtesy car, wheelchair access, room service, laundry facilities, a/c, TV, 14 meeting rooms, senior rates, CC. 2 miles from the Tampa airport, 4 miles from the downtown area. SGL/DBL$90-$150.

HoJo Inn (3314 South Dale Mabry, 33629; 837-1059, Fax 831-6930, 800-I-GO-HOJO) 38 rooms and efficiencies, restaurant, free breakfast, lounge, outdoor pool, children free with parents, wheelchair access, NS rooms, TV, a/c, laundry facilities, senior rates, meeting facilities, CC. 5 miles from the Tampa airport, 3 miles from Tampa Stadium, 15 miles from Gulf beaches. SGL/DBL$30-$48.

Holiday Inn Airport (4500 West Cypress St., 33602; 879-4800, Fax 873-0234, 800-HOLIDAY) 500 rooms and suites, restaurant, lounge, entertainment, outdoor heated pool, whirlpools, in-room refrigerators, airport transportation, children free with parents, wheelchair access, a/c, TV, NS rooms, fax service, room service, laundry service, 11 meeting rooms, meeting facilities for 1,500, senior rates, CC. A 1/4-mile from the shopping mall, 1 mile from Tampa Stadium and the Tampa airport. SGL/DBL$70-$125.

Holiday Inn Ashley Plaza Convention Center (111 West Fortune St., 33602; 223-1351, Fax 221-2000, 800-HOLIDAY) 313 rooms and suites, restaurant, lounge, entertainment, outdoor heated pool, exercise center, whirlpools, in-room refrigerators, microwaves and coffee makers, airport transportation, gift shop, children free with parents, wheelchair access, a/c, TV, NS rooms, fax service, room service, laundry service, 10 meeting rooms, senior rates, CC. 5 miles from the Tampa airport, 1 block from the Performing Arts Center, a 1/4-mile from the University of Tampa, 3 miles from the State Fairgrounds. SGL/DBL$70-$96.

Holiday Inn Busch Gardens (2701 East Fowler Ave., 33612; 971-4710, Fax 977-0155, 800-HOLIDAY) 398 rooms and suites, restaurant, lounge, outdoor pool, exercise center, children free with parents, wheelchair access, in-room refrigerators and coffee makers, local transportation, in-room computer hookups, pets OK, a/c, TV, NS rooms, fax service, room service, laundry service, 6 meeting rooms, meeting facilities for 500, senior rates, CC. 1 block from the University of South Florida, 12 miles from the Tampa airport, 8 miles from the downtown area. SGL/DBL$80-$100.

Holiday Inn (10221 Princess Palm Ave., 33610; 623-6363, Fax 621-7224, 800-HOLIDAY, 800-334-6610) 265 rooms, restaurant, lounge, entertainment, outdoor pool, lighted tennis court, whirlpools, exercise center, children free with parents, wheelchair access, a/c, TV, limousine service, NS rooms, fax service, room service, airport transportation, pets OK, in-room refrigerators, laundry service, 19 meeting rooms, meeting facilities for 800, 22,000 square feet of meeting and exhibition space, senior rates, CC. 12 miles from the Tampa airport, 1 mile from the State Fairgrounds, 5 miles from Ybor City, 6 miles from Busch Gardens. SGL/DBL$90-$103.

Holiday Inn State Fair (2708 North 50th St., 33619; 621-2081, Fax 626-4387, 800-HOLIDAY, 800-423-3749) 182 rooms, restaurant, lounge, entertainment, outdoor pool, whirlpools, car rental desk, airport transportation, in-room refrigerators and microwaves, children free with parents, wheelchair access, a/c, TV, VCRs, pets OK, NS rooms, fax service, room service, laundry service, 7 meeting rooms, meeting facilities for 300, senior rates, CC. 1 mile from the Expo Park and State Fairgrounds, 4 miles from Busch Gardens and the downtown area, 2 miles from the factory outlet mall. SGL/DBL$45-$70.

Howard Johnson Lodge (4139 East Busch Blvd., 33617; 988-9191, Fax 988-9195, 800-228-2000, 800-I-GO-HOJO) 99 rooms, restaurant, lounge, entertainment, outdoor pool, children free with parents, wheelchair access, NS rooms, TV, a/c, laundry facilities, senior rates, meeting facilities, CC. 1 block from Busch Gardens, 2 miles from the University of South Florida, 30 miles to Gulf beaches. SGL/DBL$40-$68.

Howard Johnson (720 East Fowler Ave., 33612; 971-5150, 800-I-GO-HOJO) 140 rooms, restaurant, free breakfast, outdoor heated pool, airport transportation, children free with parents, wheelchair access, NS rooms, fax service, TV, a/c, in-room refrigerators and microwaves, pets OK, laundry facilities, senior rates, meeting facilities, CC. 10 miles from the Tampa airport, 6 miles from the downtown area, 2 miles from Bush Gardens, 1 mile from the Sun Dome. SGL/DBL$45-$55.

Howard Johnson Lodge (2055 North Dale Mabry, 33607; 875-8818, Fax 876-4964, 800-I-GO-HOJO) 139 rooms and suites, restaurant, lounge, outdoor heated pool, children free with parents, wheelchair access, NS rooms, TV, a/c, laundry facilities, fax service, senior rates, meeting facilities, CC. 2 miles from the Tampa airport, a 1/4-mile from the shopping mall, 5 miles from MacDill Air Force Base. SGL/DBL$38-$68.

Hyatt Regency Tampa (2 Tampa City Center, 33602; 225-1234, Fax 223-4354, 800-228-9000, 800-233-1234) 518 rooms and 1- and 2-bedroom suites, restaurant, lounge, entertainment, outdoor heated pool, whirlpools, exercise center, no pets, laundry service, in-room refrigerators and coffee makers, VCRs, in-room computer hookups, local transportation, room service, TV, a/c, NS rooms, wheelchair access, 19 meeting rooms, meeting facilities for 1,800, 30,000 square feet of meeting and exhibition space, senior rates, CC. 6 miles from the Tampa airport. SGL/DBL$80-$175.

Hyatt Regency Westshore (6200 Courtney Campbell Causeway, 33607; 874-1234, Fax 286-9864, 800-228-9000, 800-233-1234) 445 rooms and suites, restaurant, lounge, entertainment, indoor and outdoor heated pools, whirlpools, exercise center, lighted tennis courts, gift shop, airport courtesy car, in-room refrigerators, room service, water view, TV, a/c, NS rooms, no pets, children free with parents, in-room computer hookups, wheelchair access, 19 meeting rooms, 20,000 square feet of meeting and exhibition space, 19 meeting rooms, senior rates, CC. SGL/DBL$125-$200.

La Quinta Inn (2904 Melbourne Blvd., 33605; 623-3591, Fax 620-1375, 800-531-5900) 128 rooms, free breakfast, outdoor heated pool, complimentary newspaper, free local calls, fax service, laundry service, NS rooms, wheelchair access, pets OK, TV, a/c, meeting facilities, senior rates, CC. 10 miles from the Tampa airport. SGL/DBL$42-$60.

La Quinta Inn Airport (4730 West Spruce St., 33607; 287-0440, Fax 286-7399, 800-531-5900) 122 rooms, heated pool, complimentary newspaper, free local calls, fax service, laundry service, NS rooms, wheelchair access, TV, a/c, airport transportation, pets OK, children free with parents, meeting facilities, senior rates, CC. 1 mile from the Tampa airport. SGL/DBL$55-$70.

Marriott Hotel Airport (Tampa Airport, 33623; 879-5151, Fax 879-0721, 800-228-9290) 295 rooms and suites, restaurant, lounge, indoor pool, whirlpools, exercise center, in-room refrigerators, a/c, VCRs, in-room refrigerators, gift shop, children free with parents, TV, NS rooms, wheelchair access, in-room computer hookups, no pets, 16 meeting rooms, meeting facilities, senior rates, CC. At the Tampa airport, 1 mile from the shopping mall. SGL/DBL$90-$160.

Marriott Westshore (1001 North Westshore Blvd., 33607; 287-2555, 800-228-9290) 309 rooms and suites, restaurant, lounge, free breakfast, indoor and outdoor heated pools, whirlpools, airport transportation, in-room refrigerators, a/c, VCRs, gift shop, game room, children free with parents, TV, NS rooms, wheelchair access, no pets, 11 meeting rooms, senior rates, CC. 5 miles from the Tampa airport. SGL/DBL$90-$160.

Masters Economy Inn (6010 Hwy. 579, 33584; 621-4681, Fax 623-1061, 800-633-3434) 121 rooms, outdoor pool, pets, NS rooms, laundry facilities, in-room microwaves, a/c, TV, VCRs, senior rates, CC. SGL/DBL$22-$45.

Motel 6 Downtown (333 East Fowler, 33612; 932-4948, 505-891-6161) 150 rooms, outdoor pool, free local calls, children free with parents, NS rooms, wheelchair access, a/c, TV, CC. 4 miles from Busch Gardens, 14 miles from the Tampa airport, 5 miles from the Convention Center. SGL/DBL$31-$36.

Motel 6 Fairgrounds East (6510 North Hwy. 301, 33610; 628-0888, 505-891-6161) 108 rooms, outdoor pool, free local calls, children free with parents, NS rooms, wheelchair access, a/c, TV, CC. 7 miles from Busch Gardens, 13 miles from the Hillsborough State Park, 10 miles from the dog track. SGL/DBL$30-$36.

Omni Tampa Hotel (700 North Westshore Blvd., 33609; 289-8200, Fax 289-9166, 800-843-6664) 278 rooms and suites, free breakfast, restaurant, lounge, entertainment, heated pool, sauna, exercise center, limousine service, laundry service, children free with parents, wheelchair access, NS rooms available, a/c, TV, airport transportation, pets OK, 14 meeting rooms, 13,000 square feet of meeting and exhibition space, meeting facilities for 600, senior rates, CC. 2 miles from the Tampa airport. SGL/DBL$80-$145.

Quality Hotel Airport Plaza (1200 North Westshore Blvd., 33607; 282-3636, 800-221-2222) 240 rooms and suites, restaurant, outdoor pool, exercise center, children free with parents, a/c, TV, wheelchair access, room service, laundry service, no pets, NS rooms, meeting facilities, senior rates, CC. 2 miles from the Tampa airport, 5 miles from the downtown area, 13 miles from the Fairgrounds. SGL/DBL$48-$96.

Quality Hotel Riverside Hotel (200 North Ashley Dr., 33602; 223-2222, Fax 273-0839, 800-AT-TAMPA) 286 rooms, restaurant, outdoor pool, exercise center, sauna, no pets, airport courtesy car, a/c, TV, children free with parents, in-room computer hookups, NS rooms, meeting facilities, senior rates, CC. 6 miles from the Tampa airport, 2 blocks from the Convention Center, 3 miles from the Tampa Cruise Terminal. SGL/DBL$75 -$130.

Quality Inn Busch Gardens (210 East Fowler Ave., 33612; 933-7275, 800-221-2222) 140 rooms and suites, restaurant, lounge, outdoor pool, exercise center, children free with parents, a/c, TV, wheelchair access, room service, laundry service, NS rooms, meeting facilities, senior rates, CC. 25 miles from Tampa Stadium, 10 miles from Tampa Bay Downs and the Tampa airport. SGL/DBL$35-$55.

Quality Suites at USF and Busch Gardens (3001 University Center Dr., 33612; 971-8930, 800-786-7446, 800-221-2222) 150 suites, restaurant, free breakfast, lounge, outdoor heated pool, whirlpools, in-room computer hookups, children free with parents, a/c, TV, wheelchair access, room service, laundry service, in-room refrigerators and coffee makers, NS rooms, meeting facilities, senior rates, CC. 12 blocks from the Sun Dome, 8 blocks from Busch Gardens. SGL/DBL$70-$90.

Radisson Bay Harbor Inn (7700 Courtney Campbell Causeway, 33607; 281-8900, Fax 281-0189, 800-333-3333) 257 rooms and suites, restaurant, lounge, entertainment, outdoor pool, exercise center, lighted tennis courts, whirlpools, no pets, in-room refrigerators, microwaves and coffee makers, barber and beauty shop, VCRs, wheelchair access, airport transportation, NS rooms, TV, a/c, children free with parents, 11 meeting rooms, senior rates, CC. SGL/DBL$95-$130.

Ramada Airport Hotel (5303 West Kennedy Blvd., 33609; 877-0534, Fax 286-2563, 800-228-2828) 250 rooms and suites, outdoor pool, wheelchair access, NS rooms, a/c, TV, children free with parents, room service, laundry facilities, airport transportation, no pets, 14 meeting rooms, senior rates, CC. 10 miles from Tampa Stadium and the Convention Center, 15 miles from MacDill Air Force Base. SGL/DBL$50-$70.

Ramada Inn (400 East Bears Ave., 33613; 961-1000, Fax 961-5704, 800-2-RAMADA) 154 rooms and suites, restaurant, lounge, entertainment, outdoor pool, wheelchair access, NS rooms, free parking, a/c, TV, children free with parents, room service, laundry facilities, pets OK, meeting facilities for 125, senior rates, CC. SGL/DBL$42-$95.

Ramada Resort and Conference Center (820 Busch Blvd., 33612; 933-4011, Fax 932-1784, 800-228-2828) 255 rooms and suites, restaurant, lounge, entertainment, indoor and outdoor heated pool, exercise center, sauna, game room, lighted tennis courts, gift shop, wheelchair access, NS rooms, local transportation, car rental desk, a/c, TV, children free with parents, no pets, room service, laundry facilities, 13 meeting rooms, senior rates, CC. SGL/DBL$65-$115.

Ramada Inn Stadium (4732 North Dale Mabry, 33614; 877-6061, Fax 876-1531, 800-2-RAMADA) 314 rooms and suites, restaurant, lounge, entertainment, outdoor pool, wheelchair access, NS rooms, free parking, local transportation, a/c, TV, children free with parents, room service, laundry facilities, airport transportation, pets OK, meeting facilities for 350, senior rates, CC. SGL/DBL$55-$75.

Red Roof Inn (2307 East Busch Blvd., 33612; 932-0073, Fax 933-5689, 800-843-7663) 110 rooms and suites, outdoor pool, spa, NS rooms, fax service, wheelchair access, complimentary newspaper, children free with parents, a/c, TV, free local calls, senior rates, CC. A 1/2-mile from Busch Gardens, 16 miles from the Tampa airport, 8 miles from the downtown area. SGL/DBL$42.

Red Roof Inn (5001 North Hwy. 301, 33610; 623-5245, Fax 623-5240, 800-843-7663) 109 rooms, restaurant, pets OK, NS rooms, fax service, wheelchair access, complimentary newspaper, children free with parents, a/c, TV, free local calls, senior rates, CC. 12 miles from the Tampa airport, 5 miles from the Port of Tampa, 8 miles from Busch Gardens. SGL/DBL$35-$50.

Residence Inn by Marriott (3075 North Rocky Point Dr., 33607; 281-5677, Fax 281-5677, 800-228-9290, 800-331-3131) 176 suites, free breakfast, outdoor pool, hot tubs, in-room refrigerators, coffee makers and microwaves, laundry facilities, TV, a/c, VCRs, free newspaper, fireplaces, children free with parents, NS rooms, wheelchair access, airport transportation, pets OK, meeting facilities, CC. 2 miles from the Tampa airport, 6 miles from the downtown area, 12 miles from Busch Gardens. SGL/DBL$105-$150.

Scottish Inns (4530 East Columbus Dr., 33605; 621-4661, 800-251-1962) 46 rooms, pets OK, a/c, TV, wheelchair access, NS rooms, children free with parents, free local calls, senior rates, CC. 6 miles from Busch Gardens, 8 miles from Tampa Stadium. SGL/DBL$26-$31.

Scottish Inns (11414 Central Ave., 33612; 933-7831, 800-251-1962) 48 rooms, restaurant, lounge, pets OK, a/c, TV, wheelchair access, NS rooms, children free with parents, free local calls, senior rates, CC. 1 mile from the University of South Florida and Busch Gardens, 15 miles from the Tampa airport. SGL/DBL$20-$35.

Sheraton Grand Hotel (4860 West Kennedy Blvd., 33609; 286-4400, Fax 286-4053, 800-325-3535) 325 rooms and suites, restaurant, lounge, entertainment, outdoor pool, exercise center, airport transportation, gift shop, in-room refrigerators, no pets, 24-hour room service, NS rooms, a/c, TV, children free with parents, gift shop, wheelchair access, 11 meeting rooms, meeting facilities for 750, 12,000 square feet of meeting and exhibition space, senior rates, CC. 3 miles from the Tampa airport, 12 miles from Busch Gardens, 23 miles from Gulf beaches. SGL/DBL$120-$200, STS$250-$550.

Sheraton Tampa East Hotel (7401 East Hillsborough Ave., 33610; 626-0999, Fax 622-7893, 800-325-3535) 276 rooms and suites, restaurant, lounge, entertainment, outdoor pool, exercise center, whirlpools, airport transportation, gift shop, pets OK, NS rooms, a/c, room service, TV, children free with parents, wheelchair access, 10 meeting rooms, meeting facilities for 1,200, 20,000 square feet of meeting and exhibition space, senior rates, CC. 13 miles from the

Tampa airport. 2 miles from the Florida State Fairgrounds. SGL/DBL$105-$125, STS $175-$275.

Shoney's Inn (8602 New Morris Bridge Rd., 33617; 985-8525, Fax 988-3552, 800-222-2222) 122 rooms, restaurant, free breakfast, outdoor pool, a/c, TV, children free with parents, complimentary newspaper, NS rooms, free local calls, wheelchair access, fax service, senior rates, meeting facilities, CC. SGL/DBL$45-$65.

TraveLodge (9202 North 30th St., 33612; 935-7855, Fax 935-7985, 800-578-7878) 146 rooms and suites, restaurant, lounge, free breakfast, outdoor pool, wheelchair access, complimentary newspaper, laundry service, TV, a/c, free local calls, fax service, NS rooms, in-room refrigerators and microwaves, pets OK, children free with parents, meeting facilities for 300, senior rates, CC. 10 miles from Tampa Stadium, 2 miles from the dog track, 12 miles from the Tampa airport and Gulf beaches. SGL/DBL$45-$70.

Tropicana Inn (4528 East Columbus Dr., 33605; 621-4651, 800-522-3462) 117 rooms, restaurant, free breakfast, airport courtesy car, outdoor pool, a/c, TV, NS rooms, wheelchair access, children free with parents, CC. SGL/DBL$38-$50.

Wyndham Harbour Island Hotel (725 South Harbour Island, 33603; 229-5000, 800-822-4200) 300 rooms and suites, restaurant, lounge, entertainment, outdoor heated pool, whirlpool, exercise center, in-room refrigerators and coffee makers, room service, airport courtesy car, a/c, TV, NS rooms, wheelchair access, complimentary newspaper, boutiques, no pets, room service, 10 meeting rooms, 4,800 square feet of meeting and exhibition space, meeting facilities for 240, senior rates, CC. 15 miles from the Tampa airport, 1 block from the Convention Center. SGL/DBL$140-$200, STS$300-$850.

Tarpon Springs

Area Code 813

Days Inn (40050 Hwy. 19 North, 34688; 934-0859, Fax 937-4153, 800-325-2525) 32 rooms and apartments, free breakfast, outdoor pool, pets OK, a/c, TV, wheelchair access, NS rooms, laundry facilities, senior rates, CC. 1 mile from the Innisbrook Golf Course, 3 miles from Howard Park Beach, 11 miles from Tampa Bay Downs, 2 miles from the sponge docks. SGL/DBL$35-$70.

Innisbrook Resort and Golf Club (Hwy. 19, 34688; 456-2000, Fax 942-2000, 800-456-2000) 1,000 rooms and 1- and 2-bedroom condominiums, restaurant, lounge, entertainment, indoor and outdoor heated pools, lighted tennis courts, sauna, whirlpools, exercise facilities, a/c, TV, Modified American Plan available, no pets, game room, children free with parents, beauty shop, gift shop, in-room refrigerators and microwaves, NS rooms, room service, laundry facilities, 38 meeting rooms, CC. LS SGL/DBL$85-$126; HS SGL/DBL$175-$210.

Quality Inn (4486 Suncoast Blvd., 32688; 934-5781, Fax 934-1755, 800-221-2222) 114 rooms and suites, restaurant, outdoor pool, exercise center, whirlpools, sauna, children free with parents, a/c, TV, kitchenettes, wheelchair access, room service, no pets, laundry service, NS rooms, meeting facilities, senior rates, CC. LS SGL/DBL$49-$55; HS SGL/DBL$65-$70.

Quality Inn (38724 Hwy. 19 North, 32688; 934-5781, Fax 934-1755, 800-CLARION) 46 efficiencies and suites, restaurant, outdoor pool, exercise center, sauna, whirlpools, no pets, children free with parents, a/c, TV, wheelchair access, room service, laundry service, NS rooms, meeting facilities, senior rates, CC. A 1/2-mile from Lake Tarpon, 4 miles from the Tarpon Springs sponge docks, 15 miles from the St. Petersburg-Clearwater airport. SGL/DBL$49-$90.

Scottish Inn (110 West Tarpon Ave., 34689; 937-6121, 800-251-1962) 40 rooms, outdoor pool, pets OK, in-room refrigerators, a/c, TV, wheelchair access, NS rooms, children free with parents, free local calls, senior rates, CC. 1 mile from the Tarpon Springs sponge docks, 3 miles from Gulf beaches. SGL/DBL$28-$39.

Spring Bayou Bed and Breakfast (32 West Tarpon Ave., 34689; 938-9333) 2 rooms, free breakfast, NS, no children, no pets. SGL/DBL$60-$95.

Tarpon Shores Inn (710 Hwy. 19 South, 34689; 938-2483, 800-441-7688) 51 rooms, outdoor heated pool, sauna, whirlpools, in-room refrigerators, children free with parents, no pets, a/c, TV, kitchenettes, senior rates, laundry facilities, meeting facilities, CC. LS SGL/DBL$32-$40; HS SGL/DBL$50-$55.

Thieveries

Area Code 904

HoJo Inn (101 West Burleigh Blvd., 32778; 343-4666, 800-I-GO-HOJO) 40 rooms and suites, restaurant, lounge, outdoor pool, children free with parents, wheelchair access, NS rooms, TV, a/c, laundry facilities, senior rates, meeting facilities, CC. SGL/DBL$35-$60.

Inn on the Green (700 East Burleigh Blvd., 32778; 343-6373, Fax 343-7216, 800-938-4653) 92 rooms and efficiencies, outdoor pool, a/c, TV, wheelchair access, NS rooms, children free with parents, no pets, laundry facilities, senior rates, CC. SGL/DBL$50-$95.

Tavernier

Area Code 305

Rental & Reservation Services

Ganim Realty (82205 Overseas Hwy., Islamorada, 33036; 664-4577, 800-741-0541) rental condos, private homes, apartments and townhouses.

□□□

Blue Lagoon Resort (99096 Overseas Hwy., 33037; 451-2908) 12 rooms and cottages, children free with parents, no pets, kitchenettes, a/c, TV, CC. LS SGL/DBL$45-$75; HS SGL/DBL$55-$100.

Conch-On-Inn (103 Caloos St., 33070; 852-9309) 7 rooms and efficiencies, kitchenettes, a/c, TV, children free with parents, CC. SGL/DBL$35.

Divers Cove (Tavernier 33070; 852-5312) 4 rooms and 1- and 2-bedroom efficiencies, kitchenettes, children free with parents, a/c, TV, CC. SGL/DBL$55-$65.

Island Bay Resort (Tavernier 33070; 852-4087, 800-654-KEYS) 8 rooms and efficiencies, outdoor pool, kitchenettes, children free with parents, laundry facilities, no pets, beach, CC. LS SGL/DBL$45-$75; HS SGL/DBL$55-$85.

Keys Motel (90611 Old Hwy., 33070; 852-2351, 800-841-8901) 18 rooms and efficiencies, pool, no pets, a/c, TV, children free with parents, CC. LS SGL/DBL$40-$140; HS SGL/DBL$55-$165.

Ocean Pointe (Tavernier 33070; 853-3000, Fax 853-3007, 800-882-9464) 48 2-bedroom condominiums, outdoor pool, beach, tennis courts, a/c, TV, wheelchair access, children free with parents, in-room refrigerators, microwaves and coffee makers, senior rates, CC. SGL/DBL$130-$170.

Tropic Vista Motel (90701 Overseas Hwy., 33070; 852-8799, 800-537-3253) 26 rooms and efficiencies, jacuzzi, a/c, TV, children free with parents, no pets, CC. SGL/DBL$43-$53.

Tierra Verde
Area Code 813

Tierra Verde Yacht and Tennis Club (200 Madonna Blvd., 33715; 867-8611) 66 1- and 2-bedroom apartments, restaurant, outdoor pool, tennis courts, whirlpools, room service, a/c, TV, wheelchair access, NS rooms, children free with parents, CC. 1BR/2BR$60-$135.

Wander Club (1515 Pinellas Bayway, 33715; 864-4747, Fax 867-9602) 62 rooms and condominiums, outdoor heated pool, sauna, whirlpools, exercise center, lighted tennis courts, a/c, TV, no pets, in-room refrigerators, local transportation, meeting facilities, senior rates, CC. SGL/DBL$450W-$850W.

Titusville
Area Code 407

Best Western Space Shuttle Inn (3455 Cheney Hwy., 32780; 269-9100, Fax 383-4674, 800-528-1234, 800-523-7654) 126 rooms and efficiencies, restaurant, lounge, heated pool, children free with parents, a/c, gift shop, in-room refrigerators and microwaves, NS rooms, TV, laundry facilities, wheelchair access, pets OK, meeting facilities, senior rates, CC. 10 miles to Atlantic beaches, 4 miles from the Astronaut Hall of Fame. SGL/DBL$45-$66.

Days Inn (3480 Garden St., 32796; 269-9310, 800-325-2525) 122 rooms, restaurant, lounge, outdoor pool, pets OK, a/c, TV, wheelchair access, children free with parents, NS rooms, laundry facilities, local transportation, senior rates, CC. 40 miles from the Orlando airport. SGL/DBL$45-$65.

Holiday Inn Kennedy Space Center (4951 South Washington Ave., 32780; 269-2121, Fax 267-4739, 800-HOLIDAY) 117 rooms, restaurant, lounge, outdoor pool, exercise center, children free with parents, wheelchair access, a/c, TV, NS rooms, fax service, room service, laundry service, in-room computer hookups, no pets, in-room refrigerators, meeting facilities for 150, senior rates, CC. 2 miles from the Astronaut Hall of Fame, 5 miles from the downtown area, 15 miles from Cocoa Beach. SGL/DBL$45-$85.

Howard Johnson Lodge (1829 Riverside Dr., 32780; 267-7900, Fax 267-7080, 800-I-GO-HOJO) 104 rooms, restaurant, lounge, outdoor pool, exercise center, children free with parents, wheelchair access, NS rooms, TV, a/c, VCRs, in-room refrigerators, microwaves and coffee makers, no pets, car rental, laundry facilities, senior rates, meeting facilities, CC. SGL/DBL$40-$60; HS SGL/DBL$60-$80.

La Cita Golf and Country Club Resort (777 Country Club Dr., 32780; 383-2582) 37 1- and 2-bedroom apartments, outdoor heated pool, lighted tennis courts, exercise center, whirlpool, a/c, TV, NS rooms, wheelchair access, children free with parents, laundry service, no pets, CC. SGL/DBL$80-$140.

Quality Inn Kennedy Space Center (3755 Cheney Hwy., 32780; 269-4480, Fax 383-0646, 800-221-2222) 142 rooms and suites, restaurant, lounge, outdoor pool, exercise center, children free with parents, a/c, TV, wheelchair access, room service, laundry service, in-room refrigerators, kitchenettes, NS rooms, meeting facilities, senior rates, CC. 2 miles from the regional airport, 3 miles from the Kennedy Space Center, 15 miles from Canaveral National Seashore. SGL/DBL$36-$60.

Ramada Inn (3500 Cheney Hwy., 32780; 269-5510, Fax 296-3796, 800-2-RAMADA) 124 rooms and efficiencies, restaurant, lounge, outdoor pool, lighted tennis courts, whirlpools, in-room refrigerators, no pets, wheelchair access, NS rooms, a/c, TV, children free with parents, room service, laundry facilities, meeting facilities, senior rates, CC. 10 miles from Atlantic beaches, 5 miles from the Kennedy Space Center, 25 miles from Port Canaveral. SGL/DBL$55-$68.

TraveLodge Kennedy Space Center (3810 South Washington Ave., 32780; 267-9111, Fax 267-0750, 800-578-7878) 105 rooms, restaurant, lounge, outdoor pool, free breakfast, outdoor pool, wheelchair access, complimentary newspaper, laundry service, TV, a/c, free local calls, fax service, NS rooms, in-room refrigerators and microwaves, no pets, children free with parents, meeting facilities, senior rates, CC. SGL/DBL$40-$50.

Treasure Island

Area Code 813

Algiers Resort Motel (11600 Gulf Blvd., 33706; 367-3793) 17 rooms and suites, outdoor heated pool, laundry facilities, kitchenettes, a/c, TV, in-room refrigerators and microwaves, no pets, CC. SGL/DBL$45-$95.

Bayside Inn (11365 Gulf Blvd., 33706; 367-1291, Fax 367-1291) 23 rooms, outdoor heated pool, no pets, a/c, TV, laundry facilities, kitchenettes, senior rates, CC. SGL/DBL$35-$80.

Bilmar Beach Resort Hotel (10650 Gulf Blvd., 33706; 360-5531, Fax 360-2362, 800-826-9724) 172 rooms and suites, restaurant, lounge, entertainment, outdoor heated pools, whirlpools, no pets, a/c, TV, room service, kitchenettes, in-room refrigerators and coffee makers, children free with parents, 3 meeting rooms, senior rates, CC. LS SGL/DBL$70-$85; HS SGL/DBL$110-$125.

Buccaneer Resort Motel (10800 Gulf Blvd., 33706; 800-826-2120) 56 rooms, restaurant, lounge, outdoor pool, beach, a/c, TV, NS rooms, wheelchair access, children free with parents, laundry facilities, CC. SGL/DBL$40-$58.

Captain's Quarters Inn (10035 Gulf Blvd., 33706; 360-1659, 800-526-9547) 8 1-bedroom efficiencies, outdoor pool, a/c, TV, kitchenettes, no pets, children free with parents, laundry facilities, senior rates, CC. 1BR$65-$75.

Friendship Inn (11799 Gulf Blvd., 33706; 360-1438, 800-424-4777) 32 rooms, outdoor pool, exercise center, a/c, TV, NS rooms, children free with parents, wheelchair access, senior rates, CC. 17 miles from the St. Petersburg-Clearwater airport, a 1/2-mile from Johns Pass. LS SGL/DBL$38-$50; HS SGL/DBL$60-$85.

Holiday Inn (11908 Gulf Blvd., 33706; 367-2761, 800-HOLIDAY) 117 rooms, restaurant, lounge, entertainment, outdoor heated pool, exercise center, children free with parents, wheelchair access, a/c, TV, beach, gift shop, game room, no pets, NS rooms, fax service, room service, laundry service, meeting facilities, senior rates, CC. 7 miles from the downtown area, 5 miles from the shopping mall. SGL/DBL$80-$150.

Howard Johnson Resort Inn (11125 Gulf Blvd., 33706; 360-6971, Fax 360-9014, 800-I-GO-HOJO) 84 rooms, restaurant, outdoor heated pool, laundry facilities, a/c, TV, children free with parents, in-room refrigerators, game room, NS rooms, no pets, senior rates, CC. LS SGL/DBL$65-$75; HS SGL/DBL$90-$100.

Malyn Motel Apartments (282 107th Ave., 33706; 367-1974, Fax 823-0068) 20 apartments, heated pool, a/c, TV, children free with parents, kitchenettes, CC. SGL/DBL$48-$54.

Nautilus On The Gulf Motel (10084 Gulf Blvd., 33706; 360-6798) 12 1-bedroom apartments, a/c, TV, no pets, NS rooms, beach. LS SGL/DBL$23; HS SGL/DBL$32.

Page Terrace (10500 Gulf Blvd., 33706; 367-1997) 35 rooms and efficiencies, outdoor heated pool, laundry facilities, no pets, a/c, TV, in-room refrigerators, children free with parents, NS rooms, CC. SGL/DBL$35-$95.

Sea Chest (11780 Gulf Blvd., 33706; 360-5501) 21 rooms, outdoor heated pool, no pets, laundry facilities, in-room refrigerators and coffee makers, a/c, TV, CC. SGL/DBL$60-$110.

Thunderbird Beach Resort (10700 Gulf Blvd., 33706; 367-1961, Fax 360-4567, 800-367-BIRD) 64 rooms, restaurant, lounge, entertainment, outdoor heated pool, beach, children free with parents, kitchenettes, a/c, TV, no pets, CC. SGL/DBL$55-$125.

Trails End (11500 Gulf Blvd., 33706; 360-5541) 54 rooms and efficiencies, restaurant, outdoor heated pool, beach, no pets, a/c, TV, in-room refrigerators, NS rooms, CC. SGL/DBL$35-$70.

The Twins Apartment (12520 Gulf Blvd., 33706; 360-7420) 11 rooms and 1- and 2-bedroom apartments, outdoor heated pool, a/c, TV, no pets, laundry facilities, CC. SGL/DBL$230W-$350W.

The Voyager Beach Club (11860 Gulf Blvd., 33706; 360-5520) 44 condominiums, outdoor pool, a/c, TV, no pets, in-room refrigerators, microwaves and coffee makers, children free with parents, laundry facilities, beach, CC. LS SGL/DBL$50-$100; HS SGL/DBL$75-$125.

Venice

Area Code 813

Best Western Sandbar Hotel (811 North Esplanada, 34285; 488-2251, Fax 485-2894, 800-528-1234, 800-822-4853) 44 rooms, restaurant, outdoor heated pool, children free with parents, a/c, NS rooms, TV, laundry facilities, wheelchair access, beach, no pets, meeting facilities, senior rates, CC. 1 mile from the shopping mall, golf course and tennis courts. SGL/DBL$130-$150.

Best Western Resort Inn (455 Hwy. 41 Bypass North, 34292; 485-5411, Fax 484-6193, 800-528-1234) 160 rooms, restaurant, lounge, outdoor heated pool, children free with parents, local transportation, a/c, NS rooms, TV, laundry facilities, wheelchair access, pets OK, meeting facilities for 400, senior rates, CC. LS SGL/DBL$50-$86; HS SGL/DBL$85-$98.

Days Inn (1710 South Tamiami Trail, 34293; 493-4558, 800-325-2525) 73 rooms, restaurant, free breakfast, outdoor pool, kitchenettes, a/c, TV, wheelchair access, NS rooms, no pets, laundry facilities, meeting facilities, senior rates, CC. 2.8 miles from Gulf beaches, 19 miles from the Sarasota airport, 2 miles from the Ringling Museum, 1 block from the Venetian Mall. SGL/DBL$45-$95.

El Patio Hotel (229 West Venice Ave., 34285; 488-7702) 10 rooms and suites, outdoor pool, a/c, children free with parents, NS rooms, no pets. SGL/DBL$28-$44.

Motel 6 (281 Venice Blvd., 33595; 488-7395, 505-891-6161) 103 rooms, outdoor pool, free local calls, children free with parents, NS rooms, wheelchair access, a/c, TV, CC. 16 miles from Mineral Springs, 25 miles from the Ringling Museum and Sarasota airport. SGL/DBL$28-$35.

Vero Beach
Area Code 407

Aquarius Oceanfront Resort (1526 S. Ocean Dr., 32963; 231-5218) 27 rooms and 1- and 2-bedroom apartments, restaurant, outdoor heated pool, laundry facilities, in-room refrigerators, beach, NS rooms, senior rates, CC. SGL/DBL$50-$100, 1BR$95, 2BR$110.

Comfort Inn (950 Hwy. 1, 32960; 569-0900, 800-221-2222) 66 rooms, restaurant, lounge, outdoor pool, local transportation, a/c, TV, no pets, children free with parents, NS rooms, laundry facilities, wheelchair access, senior rates, CC. 3 miles from the regional airport, 13 miles from the Jai Alai fronton, 3 miles from Atlantic beaches. SGL/DBL$40-$85.

Days Inn (8800 20th St., 32966; 562-9991, Fax 562-0716, 800-325-2525) 231 rooms, restaurant, free breakfast, outdoor pool, a/c, TV, wheelchair access, NS rooms, no pets, laundry facilities, in-room refrigerators, children free with parents, senior rates, CC. SGL/DBL$45-$65.

Days Inn (3244 Ocean Dr., 32963; 231-2800, Fax 231-3446, 800-325-2525) 110 rooms, restaurant, lounge, entertainment, outdoor heated pool, in-room refrigerators, microwaves and coffee makers, a/c, TV, wheelchair access, children free with parents, NS rooms, no pets, laundry facilities, meeting facilities, senior rates, CC. 3 miles from the Dodgers Training Camp and Melbourne airport. SGL/DBL$70-$135.

Guest Quarters Suite Hotel (3500 Ocean Dr., 32963; 231-5666, Fax 234-4866, 800-424-2900) 55 1- and 2-room suites, restaurant, lounge, outdoor pool, exercise center, sauna, whirlpools, TV, a/c, local transportation, laundry service, fax, NS rooms, wheelchair access, in-room refrigerators and microwaves, no pets, 2 meeting rooms, CC. LS SGL/DBL$95-$215; HS SGL/DBL$175-$245.

HoJo Inn (1985 90th Ave., 32966; 778-1985, 800-I-GO-HOJO) 68 rooms, restaurant, free breakfast, restaurant, lounge, pets OK, outdoor pool, children free with parents, wheelchair access, NS rooms, fax service, in-room refrigerators, TV, a/c, laundry facilities, senior rates, meeting facilities, CC. 6 miles from the Vero Beach airport, 5 miles from Dodgertown, 12 miles from Atlantic beaches. SGL/DBL$55-$60.

Holiday Inn (8797 20th St., 32966; 567-8321, Fax 569-8558, 800-HOLIDAY) 117 rooms, restaurant, lounge, entertainment, heated pool, exercise center, children free with parents, wheelchair access, airport transportation, game room, a/c, TV, NS rooms, pets OK, fax, room service, laundry service, meeting facilities for 350, senior rates, CC. 3 miles from Dodgertown Stadium, 4 miles from the Vero Beach airport, 8 miles from Atlantic beaches. SGL/DBL$45-$75.

Holiday Inn (3384 Ocean Dr., 32963; 231-2300, Fax 234-8069, 800-HOLIDAY) 104 rooms and efficiencies, restaurant, lounge, outdoor pool, exercise center, beach, children free with parents, wheelchair access, a/c, TV, NS rooms, fax service, room service, laundry service, meeting facilities, senior rates, CC. 1.5 miles from downtown, 4 miles from the Dodger Training Stadium. SGL/DBL$55-$85.

Howard Johnson (1725 Hwy. 1, 32960; 567-5171, Fax 567-5194, 800-525-5420, 800-I-GO-HOJO) 82 rooms, outdoor heated pool, children free with parents, wheelchair access, NS rooms, TV, a/c, laundry facilities, no pets, senior rates, meeting facilities, CC. 2 miles from the Vero Beach airport. SGL/DBL$45-$100.

The Islander Motel (3101 Ocean Dr., 32963; 231-4431) 16 rooms, restaurant, outdoor pool, in-room refrigerators, a/c, TV, kitchenettes, no pets, children free with parents, CC. SGL/DBL$50-$90.

Landmark Motor Lodge (1701 Hwy. 1, 32960; 562-6591) 48 rooms, outdoor pool, pets OK, kitchenettes, children free with parents, NS rooms, a/c, TV, senior rates, CC. SGL/DBL$35-$60.

Riviera Inn (1605 South Ocean Dr., 32963; 234-4112) 35 rooms and efficiencies, restaurant, outdoor heated pool, beach, children free with parents, a/c, TV, no pets, senior rates, CC. SGL/DBL$40-$70.

Surf and Sand Motel (1516 South Ocean Dr., 32963; 231-5700, Fax 231-9386) 25 rooms and efficiencies, restaurant, heated pool, in-room refrigerators, beach, a/c, TV, CC. SGL/DBL$85-$115.

Wabasso

Area Code 407

Pennwood Motor Lodge (Wabasso 32970; 589-3855) 25 rooms and efficiencies, outdoor pool, no pets, in-room refrigerators, children free with parents, a/c, TV, CC. SGL/DBL$30-$52.

Wakulla Springs

Area Code 904

Wakulla Springs Lodge and Conference Center (1 Spring Dr., 32305; 224-5950, Fax 561-7251) 27 rooms, restaurant, a/c, TV, no pets, children free with parents, 6 meeting rooms, CC. SGL/DBL$45-$80.

Weeki Wachee

Area Code 904

Comfort Inn (9373 Cortez Blvd., 34613; 596-9000, 800-221-2222) 65 rooms, outdoor pool, exercise center, no pets, a/c, TV, children free with parents, NS rooms, wheelchair access, senior rates, CC. A 1/4-mile from Weeki Wachee and Buccaneer Bay, 20 miles from Crystal River. SGL/DBL$45-$90.

Holiday Inn (6172 Commercial Way, 34613; 596-2007, Fax 596-0667, 800-HOLIDAY) 122 rooms, restaurant, lounge, outdoor pool, exercise center, pets OK, VCRs, children free with parents, wheelchair access, a/c, TV, NS rooms, fax, room service, laundry service, meeting facilities for 150, senior rates, CC. SGL/DBL$65-$73.

Wesley Chapel

Area Code 813

Saddlebrook Golf and Tennis Resort (100 Saddlebrook Way, 33543; 973-1111, Fax 973-4504, 800-729-8383) 537 rooms, condominiums and suites, restaurant, lounge, entertainment, outdoor heated pool, sauna, whirlpools, lighted tennis courts, game room, no pets, kitchenettes, a/c, TV, airport transportation, in-room refrigerators, 33 meeting facilities, senior rates, CC. LS SGL/DBL$90-$145; HS SGL/DBL$160-$325.

West Palm Beach

Area Code 407

Rental & Reservation Services

Great Miami Reservation Systems (12555 Biscayne Blvd., 33180; 800-821-2183) hotel and condominium reservations.

◻◻◻

Best Western Inn (1800 Palm Beach Lakes Blvd., 33401; 683-6810, Fax 478-2580, 800-528-1234) 198 rooms, outdoor heated pool, children free with parents, a/c, NS rooms, TV, laundry services, wheelchair access, airport transportation, in-room refrigerators and coffee makers, no pets, meeting facilities, senior rates, CC. 1 block from Expos training field, 2 miles from dog track, 1 block from shopping mall. LS SGL/DBL$45-$55; HS SGL/DBL$75-$85.

Comfort Inn (1901 Palm Beach Lakes Blvd., 33409; 689-6100, 800-221-2222) 157 rooms, outdoor pool, a/c, TV, children free with parents, NS rooms, wheelchair access, senior rates, CC. 3 miles from the Palm Beach airport, 1 mile from the golf course, 3 miles from the Worth Ave. shopping area. SGL/DBL$50-$100.

Comfort Inn (5981 Okeechobee Blvd., 33417; 697-3388, Fax 697-2834, 800-221-2222) 113 rooms, outdoor pool, a/c, TV, children free with parents, NS rooms, wheelchair access, in-room refrigerators and microwaves, laundry facilities, no pets, senior rates, CC. 8 miles from the Jai Alai fronton, 15 miles from Lion Country Safari, 4 miles from the Palm Beach airport. SGL/DBL$40-$80.

Courtyard by Marriott (600 Northpoint Pkwy., 33407; 650-9000, Fax 471-0122, 800-331-3131) 149 rooms and suites, restaurant, lounge, free breakfast, outdoor pool, in-room refrigerators, microwaves and coffee makers, VCRs, complimentary newspaper, in-room computer hookups, no pets, children free with parents, kitchenettes, a/c, TV, NS rooms, wheelchair access, meeting facilities, senior rates, CC. LS SGL/DBL$50-$70; HS SGL/DBL$90-$100.

Days Inn (6255 Okeechobee Blvd., 33417; 686-6000, 800-325-2525) 154 rooms and 1-bedroom suites, restaurant, lounge, outdoor heated pool, whirlpools, children free with parents, a/c, TV, VCRs, wheelchair access, NS rooms, laundry facilities, pets OK, senior rates, meeting facilities, CC. 3 miles from the Florida Fairgrounds and Kravis Center, 8 miles from Atlantic beaches, 4 miles from the Expos Training Camp. SGL/DBL$45-$85.

Days Inn Airport (2300 45th St., 33407; 689-0450, Fax 686-7439, 800-325-2525) 234 rooms, restaurant, lounge, free breakfast, outdoor pool, a/c, TV, wheelchair access, NS rooms, no pets, laundry facilities, local transportation, in-room refrigerators, airport transportation, children free with parents, senior rates, CC. 7 miles from Atlantic beaches, a 1/2-mile from the Jai Alai fronton, 5 miles from the Palm Beach airport. LS SGL/DBL$35-$60; HS SGL/DBL$65-$80.

Economy Inns of America (4123 North Lake Blvd., 33407; 626-4918, 800-826-0778) 96 rooms, free breakfast, outdoor heated pool, free local calls, wheelchair access, a/c, children free with parents, TV, NS rooms, airport transportation, pets OK, senior rates, CC. 2 miles from the Jai Alai fronton, 4 miles to Atlantic beaches, 6 miles from the dog track, 8 miles from the Palm Beach Jr. College. SGL/DBL$38-$55.

Hampton Inn Airport (1505 Belvedere Rd., 33406; 471-8700, 800-HAMPTON) 136 rooms, outdoor pool, exercise center, airport transportation, children free with parents, NS rooms, wheelchair access, pets OK, local transportation, in-room computer hookups, fax service, TV, a/c, free local calls, meeting facilities, senior rates, CC. 1 mile from the Palm Beach airport, 7 miles from Atlantic beaches, 2 miles from the downtown area and shopping mall. SGL/DBL$50-$85.

Hibiscus House (501 30th St., 33407; 863-5633) 7 rooms, free breakfast, outdoor pool, no pets, a/c, TV, NS, CC. SGL/DBL$55-$78.

Hilton Hotel (150 Australian Ave., 33406; 684-9400, Fax 689-9421, 800-HILTONS) 247 rooms and suites, restaurant, lounge, entertainment, outdoor heated pool, exercise center, lighted tennis courts, airport transportation, in-room refrigerators, no pets, children free with parents, NS rooms, wheelchair access, room service, laundry facilities, a/c, TV, 12 meeting rooms, senior rates, CC. A 1/2-mile from the Palm Beach airport, 3 miles from Atlantic beaches. LS SGL/DBL$60-$110; HS SGL/DBL$80-$120.

Ho Jo Inn (1901 Okeechobee Blvd., 33409; 683-3222, 800-I-GO-HOJO) 72 rooms, restaurant, lounge, outdoor pool, children free with parents, wheelchair access, in-room refrigerators, NS rooms, TV, a/c, laundry facilities, senior rates, meeting facilities, CC. 2 miles from the Palm Beach airport, 2 miles from Palm Beach Atlantic College, 6 miles from the South Florida Fairgrounds. SGL/DBL$38-$100.

Holiday Inn International Airport and Conference Center (1301 Belevedere Rd., 33405; 659-3880, 800-HOLIDAY) 200 rooms, restaurant, free breakfast, lounge, outdoor heated pool, exercise center, sauna, whirlpools, children free with parents, wheelchair access, a/c, TV, NS rooms, airport transportation, no pets, in-room refrigerators, fax service, room service, laundry service, 9 meeting rooms, senior rates, CC. 1 block from the Palm Beach airport, a 1/2-mile from the downtown area. SGL/DBL$55-$110.

Knights Inn (2200 45th St., 33407; 478-1554, 800-843-5644) 117 rooms and efficiencies, outdoor pool, wheelchair access, NS rooms, TV, a/c, in-room refrigerators and microwaves, fax service, VCRs, laundry facilities, kitchenettes, senior rates, CC. 3 miles from Atlantic beaches, Palm Beach Mall and the Palm Beach airport, 15 miles from Lion Country Safari. SGL/DBL$35-$55.

Omni Hotel West Palm Beach (1601 Belevedere Rd., 33406; 689-6400, Fax 683-7150, 800-THE-OMNI) 220 rooms and suites, restaurant, lounge, entertainment, outdoor pool, sauna, exercise center, lighted tennis courts, airport transportation, kitchenettes, laundry service, NS rooms, wheelchair access, NS rooms available, a/c, TV, 5,000 square feet of meeting and exhibitions space, meeting facilities for 750, CC. 1 block from the Palm Beach airport. SGL/DBL$80-$150.

Palm Beach Polo and Country Club (13198 Forest Hill Blvd., 33414; 798-7000) 105 rooms and 2- and 3-bedroom suites, restaurant, lounge, entertainment, indoor and outdoor heated pools, tennis courts, whirlpools, exercise center, in-room refrigerators and coffee makers, NS rooms, a/c, TV, no pets, laundry service, meeting facilities, CC. SGL/DBL$90-$290.

Parkway Motor Lodge (4710 South Dixie Hwy., 33405; 833-4644, 800-523-8978) 28 rooms and efficiencies, free breakfast, a/c, TV, children free with parents, in-room refrigerators, NS rooms, CC. SGL.DBL$40-$80.

Radisson Suite Inn (1808 Australian Ave., 33409; 689-6888, 800-333-3333) 174 rooms and suites, restaurant, lounge, entertainment, outdoor pool, exercise center, in-room refrigerators, microwaves and coffee makers, airport transportation, laundry service, children free with parents, VCRs, wheelchair access, NS rooms, TV, a/c, pets OK, children free with parents, 6 meeting rooms, senior rates, CC. LS SGL/DBL$80; HS SGL/DBL$110.

Ramada Hotel and Conference Center (630 Clearwater Park Rd., 33401; 833-1234, 800-2-RAMADA) 349 rooms and suites, restaurant, lounge, outdoor pool, lighted tennis courts, whirlpools, airport transportation, wheelchair access, NS rooms, a/c, TV, children free with parents, room service, laundry facilities, in-room refrigerators and microwaves, 12 meeting rooms, meeting facilities for 1,000, senior rates, CC. 1 mile from the Palm Beach airport and Atlantic beaches, 10 miles from the Port of Palm Beach, a 1/4-mile from the downtown area, 3 miles from the Palm Beach airport. SGL/DBL$95-$155.

Wellesley Inn (1910 Palm Beach Lakes Blvd., 33409; 689-8540, Fax 687-8090, 800-444-8888) 106 rooms, restaurant, free breakfast, outdoor heated pool, pets OK, a/c, TV, children free with parents, laundry facilities, NS rooms, senior rates, CC. SGL/DBL$40-$100.

White Springs

Area Code 904

Days Inn (I-75 and Hwy. 136, 32096; 397-2155, 800-325-2525) 26 rooms, free breakfast, a/c, TV, wheelchair access, NS rooms, pets OK, children free with parents, laundry facilities, senior rates, CC. SGL/DBL$30-$35.

Scottish Inns (I-75 and Hwy. 136, 32096; 800-251-1962) 40 rooms, outdoor pool, pets OK, a/c, TV, wheelchair access, NS rooms, children free with parents, free local calls, senior rates, CC. 15 miles from the Florida Sports Hall of Fame, 20 miles from the Lake City airport, 3 miles from the Stephen Foster Memorial. SGL/DBL$25-$35.

Suwanee River Motel (Hwy. 41, 32096; 397-2822) 16 rooms, a/c, TV, pets OK, children free with parents, CC. SGL/DBL$18-$30.

Wildwood

Area Code 904

Days Inn (I-75 and Hwy. 44, 34785; 748-2000, 800-325-2525) 120 rooms, restaurant, free breakfast, outdoor pool, pets OK, a/c, TV, wheelchair access, NS rooms, laundry facilities, senior rates, CC. 16 miles from the Webster Field Market, 15 miles from Hunts Gator Farm. SGL/DBL$45-$53.

Red Carpet Inn (Wildwood 34785; 748-4488, 800-251-1962) 116 rooms, restaurant, outdoor pool, children free with parents, TV, a/c, NS rooms, pets OK, meeting facilities, senior rates, CC. SGL/DBL$19-$28.

Winter Garden

Area Code 407

Best Western Inn (13603 West Colonial Dr., 34787; 654-1188, Fax 654-0140, 800-528-1234) 102 rooms, restaurant, lounge, outdoor heated pool, exercise center, in-room refrigerators and coffee makers, children free with parents, a/c, NS rooms, TV, laundry facilities, wheelchair access, pets OK, meeting facilities, senior rates, CC. SGL/DBL$40-$80.

Winter Haven

Area Code 813

Admirals Inn (5665 Cypress Gardens Blvd., 33880; 324-5950, Fax 324-2376, 800-247-2977) 160 rooms, restaurant, lounge, outdoor pool, a/c, TV, children free with parents, pets OK, laundry facilities, NS rooms, wheelchair access, senior rates, CC. LS SGL/DBL$55-$65.

Budget Host Driftwood Motel (970 Cypress Gardens Blvd., 33880; 294-4229, 800-283-4678) 22 rooms and efficiencies, restaurant, outdoor heated pool, in-room refrigerators, pets OK, laundry facilities, NS rooms, kitchenettes, wheelchair access, a/c, TV, children free with parents, senior rates, CC. SGL/DBL$30-$65.

Cypress Motel (5651 Cypress Gardens Rd., 33884; 324-5867) 21 rooms, outdoor heated pool, in-room refrigerators, a/c, TV, NS rooms, laundry facilities, pets OK, children free with parents, senior rates, CC. SGL/DBL$30-$60.

Days Inn (200 Cypress Gardens Blvd., 33880; 299-1151, Fax 297-8019, 800-325-2525) 105 rooms, restaurant, lounge, free breakfast, outdoor pool, lighted tennis courts, no pets, in-room refrigerators, a/c, TV, wheelchair access, NS rooms, laundry facilities, children free with parents, senior rates, CC. 3 miles from Cypress Gardens, 1 block from the Convention Center. SGL/DBL$38-$80.

Holiday Inn Cypress Gardens (1150 3rd St., 33880; 294-4451, Fax 293-9829, 800-HOLIDAY) 225 rooms and suites, restaurant, lounge, outdoor pool, exercise center, children free with parents, wheelchair access, in-room refrigerators, no pets, a/c, TV, NS rooms, fax service, room service, laundry service, meeting facilities for 250, senior rates, CC. 1 block from the downtown area and the Winter Haven Mall, 1.5 miles from Cypress Gardens, 2 blocks from the Civic Center and Chain O'Lakes Ball Park. SGL/DBL$56-$80.

Howard Johnson (1300 3rd St. Southwest, 33880; 294-7321, Fax 299-1673, 800-I-GO-HOJO) 100 rooms, lounge, entertainment, heated pool, children free with parents, wheelchair access, NS rooms, TV, a/c, kitchenettes, laundry facilities, senior rates, meeting facilities, CC. A 1/2-mile from the downtown area, 45 miles from the Orlando airport. LS SGL/DBL$35-$60; HS SGL/DBL$85-$95.

JD's Southern Oaks Bed and Breakfast (3800 Country Club Rd., 33881; 293-2335) 5 rooms, free breakfast, a/c, TV, no children, no pets, NS, CC. SGL/DBL$65-$115.

Quality Inn Townhouses (975 Cypress Gardens Blvd., 33880; 294-4104, 800-221-2222) 32 rooms and suites, outdoor pool, no pets, in-room refrigerators and coffee makers, children free with parents, a/c, TV, wheelchair access, laundry service, NS rooms, meeting facilities, senior rates, CC. SGL/DBL$45-$66.

Ranch House Motor Inn (1911 Cypress Gardens Blvd., 33880; 294-4104, Fax 324-0537) 55 rooms and 2-bedroom efficiencies, outdoor heated pool, kitchenettes, no pets, a/c, TV, laundry facilities, children free with parents, CC. SGL/DBL$35-$70.

Red Carpet Inn (2000 Cypress Gardens Blvd., 33880; 324-6334, 800-251-1962) 36 rooms and 2-bedroom apartments, outdoor pool, children free with parents, no pets, kitchenettes, TV, a/c, NS rooms, in-room refrigerators, meeting facilities, senior rates, CC. A 1/2-mile from Cypress Gardens, 15 miles from the Bok Tower, 30 miles from Walt Disney World. LS SGL/DBL$26-$32; HS SGL/DBL$50-$65.

Ye Olde English Motel (1901 Cypress Gardens Blvd., 33884; 324-3954, Fax 324-5998) 23 rooms and efficiencies, outdoor heated pool, a/c, TV, laundry facilities, children free with parents, no pets, senior rates, CC. SGL/DBL$30-$70.

Winter Park
Area Code 407

Best Western Mount Vernon Motor Inn (110 South Orlando Ave., 32789; 647-1166, Fax 647-8011, 800-528-1234) 147 rooms, restaurant, lounge, entertainment, outdoor pool, children free with parents, a/c, NS rooms, TV, laundry facilities, wheelchair access, in-room refrigerators, no pets, meeting facilities, senior rates, CC. 4 blocks from shopping mall, 5 miles from Jai Alai fronton and dog track. SGL/DBL$55-$85.

Days Inn (901 North Orlando Ave., 32789; 644-8000, Fax 644-0032, 800-325-2525) 103 rooms, restaurant, free breakfast, outdoor pool, jacuzzi, local transportation, a/c, TV, wheelchair access, NS rooms, in-room refrigerators, children free with parents, no pets, laundry service, senior rates, CC. SGL/DBL$55-$80.

Fairfield Inn by Marriott (951 Wymore Rd., 32789; 539-1955, 800-228-2800) 135 rooms, outdoor heated pool, whirlpools, children free with parents, NS rooms, remote control TV, free cable TV, free local calls, laundry service, a/c, wheelchair access, fax service, meeting facilities, senior rates, CC. 3 miles from Rollins College, 4 miles from the Naval Training Center. SGL/DBL$40-$60.

The Langford Resort Hotel (300 East New England Ave., 32789; 644-3400, Fax 628-1952) 213 rooms and suites, restaurant, lounge, outdoor pool, exercise center, a/c, TV, pets OK, children free with parents, laundry service, wheelchair access, NS rooms, senior rates, meeting facilities, CC. LS SGL/DBL$65-$95; HS SGL/DBL$110-$115.

Park Plaza Hotel (307 Park Ave. South, 32789; 647-1072, Fax 647-4081, 800-228-7220) 27 rooms and 2-room suites, restaurant, a/c,

TV, NS rooms, in-room refrigerators and coffee makers, laundry facilities, wheelchair access, no pets, CC. SGL/DBL$90-$135, STS$160.

Yulee

Area Code 904

Nassau Holiday Motel (53 Hwy. 17, 32097; 225-2397) 31 rooms, restaurant, a/c, TV, wheelchair access, children free with parents, no pets, CC. SGL/DBL$30-$35.

Zephyrhills

Area Code 813

Best Western (5734 Gall Blvd., 34248; 782-5527, Fax 783-7102, 800-528-1234) 52 rooms, outdoor pool, children free with parents, a/c, NS rooms, TV, laundry facilities, wheelchair access, in-room refrigerators, fax service, no pets, senior rates, CC. SGL/DBL$40-$54.